StyleCity
EUROPE

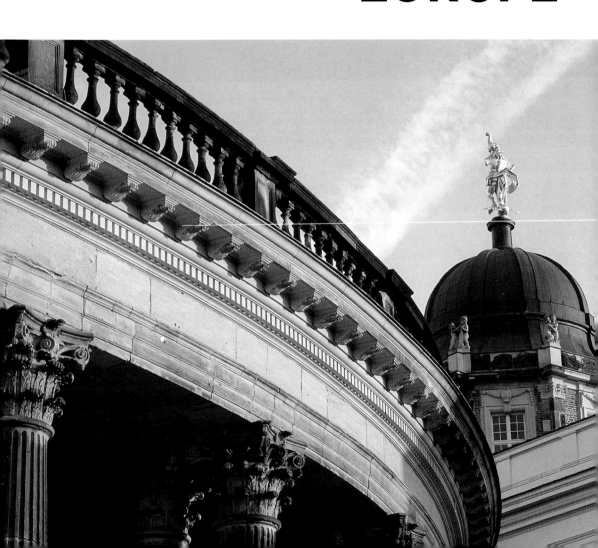

StyleCity

EUROPE

With over 900 color photographs and 14 maps

Thames & Hudson

Contents

Like the diamonds that are famously polished here, Amsterdam has many facets. It is this versatility that is the key to the passion the city evokes in its more than 700,000 inhabitants and over twice that number of annual visitors. Its layers are a reflection of the country for which it is the social and economic – if not political – capital. In the 17th century, its 'Golden Age', Amsterdam was the greatest trading city in the world. And the Netherlands remains a powerful nation – it owns the electronics giant Philips and shares Unilever and Shell with the Brits. Yet you would be forgiven for not being familiar with the origins of these global corporations, as one of the country's other assets is its Calvinist-imbued modesty when it comes to cultural achievements, a virtue recognized by Simon Schama in his 1987 study, *The Embarrassment of Riches*. The Dutch embody the pragmatic, long-term view with regard to socio-economic developments; industrial, even architectural, decisions are all weighted by an awareness that finances peak and trough.

The eye-wateringly high tax rate is the big leveller in the Netherlands, and is why public transport runs so efficiently, why streets are clean, why the city is rich in public art and monuments, and why there is so much social growth and new architecture on the fringes of the suburbs. Only through centuries of rigorous social planning has Amsterdam evolved into the series of neighbourhoods that form it today. Each has its own beguiling characteristics and resident type. The Dutch frequently complain about their excessive population density (the highest in Europe), but the 165 canals that encircle and intersect the city prevent claustrophobia from ever really setting in. The healthy attitude to getting around using, wherever possible, car- and pedestrian-free *fietspads* (cycle paths; there are 400,000 bicycles in Amsterdam alone) is another enterprising method of harmonious existence, rather than compromise, in a very small city.

The socializing behaviour of Amsterdam has been forged by a few crucial personalities whose names form the basis of the creative pages of an Amsterdam *Who's Who*. These stories are mapped by their own tastes and desires and those of their maturing contemporaries, which have evolved from theatrical party-performances in crazy clubs and taking art outside of the white cube to shoving it right back in again and dining in hidden eateries. Through it all, these design adventures are accompanied by a laid-back sense of humour, a tone intrinsic to Amsterdam. The resulting quality shared by all the store-, *horeca*- and gallery owners is the belief in taking a simple idea and having the tenacity to develop it for mass consumption, yet all the while maintaining its existence in the village-like structure of the city. Visitors seeking culture, decadence, glamorous nightlife, or an exploration of liberal socialism will not be disappointed. Amsterdam's ability to satiate desire, however extraordinary, is unsurpassed.

Westerdok

44 Westerpark

Haarlemmerweg

Haarlemmerbuurt
& Westerpark

7

Het Ij

37

Ooster
dok

Jordaan

1, 3, 4, 10,
16, 19, 22,
23, 27, 29,
31, 34, 38,
42, 43, 45

CENTRAAL
STATION

Oosterdok

NIEUWMARKT

Old
West

WATERLOO
PLEIN

Artis
Artis

Natura
Artis
Magistra

41

Horius
Botanicus

Plantage Middenlaan

Rembrandt-
plein

Tuschinski
Theater

Museum
Willet-
Holthuysen

Oost

17

Museum
van Loon

Grachten-
gordel
South

WEESPERPLEIN

Frederiks-
plein

Mauritskade

Van Gogh
Museum

Rijks-
museum

Stedelijk
Museum

Tweede
Weteringplantsoen

Museum
Plein

Museum
District

11, 26,
30, 40

13

Marie
Heineken
plein

14

WIBAUTSTRAAT

Vondelpark

Sarphatipark

5

De Pijp

32

Zuid

C. Troost
plein

Zuid

AMSTEL

Olympic
Stadium

8

6 ↓

sleep

Seven One Seven is undoubtedly about the personal touch. A flight of stairs leads from the imposing grandeur of street-level Prinsengracht to the front door of this 19th-century listed building, where visitors must ring the doorbell and wait to be received before entering. The marble hallway leads into a library well stocked with both magazines and overstuffed furniture grouped around the fireplace. There is no visual clue that this is anything other than a private home. This was the intention of the original owner, Kees van de Valek, in the eighteen months that he occupied and decorated the house before selling it – contents as seen – to its current proprietors, the Oyster Group. Each of the eight rooms (guaranteeing that there are never more than sixteen guests in the hotel at any time) is unique and has been given a name that hints at the inspiration for its style; the 'Picasso' suite has

five windows overlooking the canal and walls that feature the work of the Spanish master. Guests sleep on hand-made antique-style brass beds from Deptich Designs, covered in sheets by Westpoint USA and wrapped in blankets commissioned from Welsh textile designers Melin Tregwynt. All rooms are equipped with Bang & Olufsen DVD and stereo systems, along with a selection of music and movies. This 'extra' is inclusive in the room rate, as is breakfast, which can be taken in the dining room on the ground floor, on the patio, or delivered in a picnic basket to your room. The complimentary courtesy extends to all drinks and food consumed on the premises (within reason) and substantiates the original ambition to create a home away from home.

The Warmoesstraat used to be a seedy backstreet and the Winston a low-budget backpackers' paradise. Times have changed. While the street is still situated on the edge of the red-light district, it has been repaved and cleaned up. And so, in a manner of speaking, has the hotel. Aldert Mantje and Andre Mesman are both artists who have been working in public spaces for the past three decades. Mantje paints and once belonged to the notorious art collective Seymour Likely, who named their performance-art nightclub after this imaginary artist, while Mesman is a visual installation artist. Their work outside of the white cube brought them to the attention of Frans Verlinden, the hotel's owner, who wanted to provide a more structured environment for their work. After extending the Winston in 1995, Verlinden installed the duo as creative directors in 1997. From this position they formed a link between the design colleges and visual artists of the Netherlands and the commercial arena. Every year they run competitions in the art academies, offering winners the opportunity to realize their design in a hotel room. Armed with a small budget (€500–700), the students have styled rooms that explore the idea of space through lighting, minimalism, and an inspiring use of provocative photography; one of their designs took the form of a Cuban monk's cell, complete with robes. Mantje and Mesman also operate with large brands such as Heineken, Smirnoff and Durex, all of whom have sponsored rooms, thereby increasing both the budget and the profile of the designer. Hugo Kaagman is the well-known name behind the Heineken room, which combines a contemporary Dutch brand with traditional Dutch imagery. Most recently, Willum Geerts produced controversial images for the ground-level bar. Mesman emphasizes that all this design is not high art, and that the hotel is low budget. But to stay at the Winston is a unique opportunity to immerse oneself in an energetic, continually evolving contemporary art project.

THE OLD ALMSHOUSE

3 The Dylan

Keizersgracht 384
Rooms from €370

This urban sanctuary originally opened as Blakes in 1999. Recently renamed the Dylan, it has been re-invented by award-winning designers FG Stijl (see The College Hotel; p. 14). The site has a rich history dating back to the 17th century; in 1612 Samuel Coster founded the Duytsche Academie theatre here (donating the profits to orphanages to avoid religious disapproval), and in 1632 architect Jacob van Campen built a stone theatre. Visitors included a Prince of Orange, a King of Poland and a Russian Tsar, and for its centennial celebration Vivaldi himself conducted the orchestra. But in 1772 the complex burned down and the only remaining original structure today is the doorway. The site was sold to a Catholic charity, who subsequently built a bakery to feed the poor; today, that bakery forms the hotel's stylish restaurant. FG Stijl designed the new Barbou bar in white bone, combined with black, gold and white leather, while the Ariana salon, named after the first actress to grace the theatre's stage, boasts porcelain chandeliers. Many of the bedrooms have retained their celebrated grey and raspberry colour schemes, but the designers have tried to respect the site's past by using the blue and green tints popular in the 17th century in the more intimate spaces.

4 **Canal House Hotel**
Keizersgracht 148
Rooms from €170

The Canal House Hotel is just as its name suggests: a hotel in a grand 17th-century Dutch house located in the prestigious canalside Keizersgracht. The owners, Brian and Mary Bennett, had been presiding over the successful micro-hotel Number 31 (p. 135) in Dublin for many years, when they found themselves drinking in the Canal House Hotel bar with its previous proprietors. They were Americans who had undertaken to restore the house when first acquiring it in the 1960s, and had since opened it to the public as a hotel. Brian mentioned over a drink that he wasn't averse to making them an offer, should they ever wish to sell, and the next thing Mary knew she was running a twenty-six-room establishment in the heart of Amsterdam. The original deeds of the house date back to 1640 and many of the patrician features are still apparent, including the narrow corridors with

high ceilings running the length of the house and opening into an elegant drawing room overlooking a lush green garden. This now doubles as a dining room and houses a grand piano, classic fireplace and mirrors; guests are served breakfast here. Luxurious panelling, plasterwork, and more fireplaces and mirrors are found throughout the hotel's unusual layout. Reflective of the lack of space in this city, the Canal House Hotel practically wraps itself around another house, and some of the rooms are reached by climbing up or down little private staircases at the end of slim hallways. The rooms themselves are comfortable and retain the 17th-century theme, with bare beams holding up the roof of the attic floor. The higher the storey, the more cramped the space becomes, but the eccentric asymmetry of the rooms is appealing. The charming ground-floor bar is also seductive.

5 **The College Hotel**
Roelof Hartstraat 1
Rooms from €235

Within months of opening, the College Hotel won both the Prix Villégiature Paris and the *Theme.NL* Hospitality & Style award for its stunning interior design. The 1894 building is a former school, a role still evident in its wide staircases and converted gymnasium, now a trend-setting restaurant under chef Schilo van Coevorden (previously head chef at Blakes). The design throughout pays homage to Holland's rich artisan heritage, and the menu celebrates the Golden Age of Dutch cuisine. In fact, all things Dutch are celebrated, most noticeably by a 1.5-metre-high Delft Blue tulip vase in the onyx and Fendi-leather bar, which has become one of the hottest watering holes in town. There are also seven chandeliers in the public areas (the largest is in the ladies' room and features diamond crystals). In the forty bedrooms, the colour scheme used in the restaurant (moss greens and cream) and bar (orange, lavender and brown) has been toned down to warm browns, and the specially commissioned Italian bed linen was sourced from the same manufacturer who provides Prada with their own sheets and pillow cases. All the furniture, designed by FG Stijl (see The Dylan; p. 12) and hand-crafted in Italy, is unique to the hotel, with the restaurant's tables and chairs featuring silk tassels and individually bronzed screws; techniques and effects which hark back to those of the 17th century. As its name suggests, the hotel is a training ground for students at the Hotel School (who sculpt hand-made chocolates for the rooms and bake fresh croissants for breakfast), and the rates are set lower than average to compensate. Each room is different; room 123, in the former chemistry lab, has a cozy reading nook in the window, perfect for a quiet afternoon.

6 The Lute Suites
Amsteldijk Zuid 54–58
Rooms from €275

After luring foodies to his restaurant in Ouderkerk aan de Amstel, Peter Lute teamed up with another celebrated Dutch innovator, Marcel Wanders of Moooi (see Van Oosterom; p. 284), to create a new attraction in the suburbs. The pair took on a row of seven 18th-century cottages (once part of the estate of a gunpowder factory), with views over the Amstel and converted them into serviced apartments. The result is Lute Suites, a hotel where each suite has its own entrance and each cottage is a separate unit. More than just a place for restaurant diners to lay their heads, Lute Suites marked one of Wanders' first forays into architecture, and Moooi furniture and fittings fill the renovated spaces. Each suite is unique and has a living room, kitchenette and separate bath- and bedrooms. Bisazza tiles and Boffi accessories complete the feeling of contemporary luxury. There is a reception area and two boardrooms, but not the usual lobby or shared public space. Breakfast comes courtesy of the Lute restaurant, the reason behind the location of these Suites. But Lute and Wanders have planned Lute Suites as the first of many such 'Suites' to be spread across Amsterdam, creating a wall-less hotel with stand-alone self-contained apartments that could pop up anywhere.

eat

7 Café-Restaurant Amsterdam
CHILDREN, CHIPS AND CHIC
Watertorenplein 6

Twenty-two floodlights that once lit stellar soccer moments at the Ajax and Olympic stadiums now shine down on the diners at Amsterdam. This former water pumping station built in 1897 was converted into a café-restaurant in 1996 by Liesbeth Mijnlieff, who owned two other restaurants, Mijnlieff and Verkendam. She is no longer involved with Amsterdam, but can be found over on the Eilanden as part of the team behind the Lloyd Hotel. Her visionary flair for egalitarianism inspired a menu that was designed to appeal to all. Expressed as a democratic restaurant, it features dishes that would have something for everyone, whether dining on a budget or an expense account. Considered one of the most beautiful industrial buildings in the country, it still carries clues to its former function, not least in the looming diesel engine next to the bar and the interior's vast size, which has made this a totally child-friendly environment.

8 Vakzuid
SPORTING LIFE
Olympisch Stadion 35

A restaurant in the old Olympic stadium, designed by the sensational architect Paul Linse (whose shark-filled aquarium mesmerizes travellers at Schiphol Airport), and run by two of Amsterdam's best-loved restaurateurs, Philippe and Georgy Bedier de Prairie: all of this is Vakzuid ('section south'). The stadium, designed by De Stijl founding member Jan Wils, hosted the first-ever Olympic games in which women competed in 1928, and athletes still train here today, now overlooked by the diners and dancers of fabulous Vakzuid. Split over four levels, the establishment comprises a terrace, dance area, subterranean cocktail lounge, restaurant and private suite for business meetings or parties. The vivacity of its owners and their vision of a concept club with such unusual dimensions have won them a gold medal (in the entertainment sense) from the affluent, connected crowd that they pull in. It is a haunt of the fashionocracy, who come to be seen or to eat the exquisite Indonesian fusion cuisine by master chefs Andy Tan and Volef Geboers.

9 De Bakkerswinkel
THE BAKER'S SHOP
Warmoesstraat 69

An old tea warehouse has been transformed into a huge lunchroom serving afternoon teas from trolleys and a selection of pies from the on-site kitchen, located in what was once the porter's lodge. De Bakkerswinkel's quiche plate (there are at least two choices daily), so often a nondescript dish elsewhere, here resembles a giant slice of crumbling gâteau perched on a mountain of green lettuce. Cake, from chocolate cheese to carrot, is also served in slabs rather than slivers. The lunchroom is large enough to host several parties simultaneously and has seating for up to fifty in a private room at the back. It is an attractive place to stop for refreshment, and its unassuming façade makes what is hidden within even more of a charming surprise.

10 Pompadour
POMP AND SPLENDOUR
Huidenstraat 12

Bram Ouwehand and Escu Gabriels have been serving their celebrated pastries from this cozily decadent 'tea shoppe' since 1990. They acquired the site as a chocolaterie, which was founded in 1960, and turned it into the renowned establishment it is today with skills that Gabriels developed as chef for Belgian chocolatiers Leonidas. Every year the couple make the pilgrimage to Fauchon in Paris for training and return with new recipes, such as passion-fruit crème with Tahitian vanilla. Their popular wares often sell out early in the day, and Pompadour also makes regular deliveries to the Royal Palace. Although Queen Beatrix herself has not been seen in the tearoom, her sister Princess Irene was for a long time a regular customer.

11 Spring
SUMMER WINTER FALL
Willemsparkweg 177

Ralph Woerde worked as a chef in this restaurant before buying it for himself in 2003. His culinary basis is in 'good fresh products', and he especially loves cooking seafood as he thinks that fish is 'honest and healthy'. The linear design with its vault-like windows overlooking the street is by design firm Concrete (see Supperclub Cruise; p. 19). The view outside is usually obscured by a striking flower sculpture courtesy of florist Menno Kroon (p. 23), who is conveniently located across the street. Woerde thinks the designers' *pièce de résistance* is the toilets, encased in gold fibreglass, which glow with an amber hue. He has another kitchen and private dining room on the first floor, where he offers more exclusive catering and cookery classes.

12 De Kas
FRESH FOOD, FRESH IDEAS
Kamerlingh Onneslaan 3

This former municipal nursery threw open its glass doors in 2001 as organic restaurant De Kas. Owner Gert Jan Hageman managed to retain the building's original girders, and friends and family planted the first 5,000 seedlings. The architectural result is a refreshing excess of space, height and light. His team, like his concept, is strong and original: Walter Abma oversees the produce (herbs and Mediterranean vegetables in the summer and various types of lettuce in the winter) both on-site and at their land on the Purmer Polder, and chef Ronald Kunis was formerly at London's River Café. Hageman himself earned the restaurant Vermeer its first Michelin star as its chef in 1993.

13 Altmann
DRESS UP FOR DINNER
Amsteldijk 25

Arne Altmann opened this classy restaurant and bar after starting off as a concierge at Blakes Hotel, and the influence of his former employer can be detected in the food and service. Chocolate-coloured tables are silhouetted against light walls, and the restaurant is divided into a curving banquette near the bar and the main dining area. Separate to this is a raised level for 'public dining', where sitters have a better view over the buzzing environment. Altmann is located in a listed building, a renovated 19th-century bathhouse (formerly a car park) that Arne and his stylist girlfriend converted into this sleek cocktail bar and restaurant serving global cuisine by another ex-Blakes employee, chef Mohammed Mahroui. The menu changes daily, and can feature tabouleh with grilled vegetables and an aubergine feta mousse, or tuna carpaccio with summer beetroot and ginger-soy dressing.

THE TART OF MY AUNT
14 De Taart van m'n Tante
Ferdinand Bolstraat 10

FOOD FOR THE PEOPLE
15 Café de Jaren
Nieuwe Doelenstraat 20–22

SOUTH AFRIKAANS
16 Pygma-Lion
Nieuwe Spiegelstraat 5a

A humorous name for an amusing cake shop. Siemon de Jong and Noam Offer began making pastries for Amsterdam's grand cafés and colluded with local artists to create provocative and bizarre yet always delightful cakes. This innovative attitude gained them a nationwide reputation, and now the Dutch Royal Family and local celebrities number among their regular clientele. Summer 2003 saw the opening of a B&B above the store: 'Cake Under My Pillow'. The mind boggles, but what better place to savour gâteaux?

One of the city's larger and more unusual cafés, Café de Jaren, with its double-storey interior and simple décor of brown, cream and blue tiling and functional furniture, is a popular choice. In the warmer months, seating spills onto the huge waterfront terrace and first-floor balcony. Both overlook this amphibian traffic-logged stretch of the Amstel. The café's relaxed attitude means that regulars can linger over the papers and enjoy a solitary coffee for hours without having to order more.

The Netherlands and South Africa have borrowed from each other's cultures for centuries, and South African Matthias Kleingeld has continued the practice at Pygma-Lion. His use of exotic ingredients in family recipes could mean embarking on a culinary safari where crocodile, antelope and zebra are served up with more mundane vegetable accompaniments. Brie and coconut ostrich kebabs, zebra *frikhandel* or crocodile steak with wild-fruit chutneys are just a few examples of the combination of cultures to be found.

INDONESIAN SPICE ROUTE

17 Tempo Doeloe

Utrechtsestraat 75

SAIL AWAY

18 Supperclub Cruise

Ruyterkade Pier 14

Tempo Doeloe ('the good old times') presumably refers to those times when Indonesia was a colony outpost and its flavours and recipes were introduced to the Netherlands. This restaurant serves traditional Indonesian cuisine and is presided over by Mr Ghabriel, who has decorated the small yet cozy space with flowers and Indonesian puppet dolls. Tempo Doeloe's homage to the smorgasbord comes in the form of a *rijst tafel* (rice table); anyone not yet versed in the spiciness of Indonesian cuisine should heed the waitress's advice.

The original Supperclub concept proved so popular that IQ Creative, the company behind the scheme, moved the whole experience onto the water. Douwe Werkman and Bert van der Leden spent about €1 million on a 1960 ship once used by the late Queen Juliana to entertain visiting dignitaries. Design firm Concrete (see Spring; p. 17) was commissioned to repeat the winning formula of the landlocked Supperclubs, and created a deck for enjoying cocktails as the ship sails into Amsterdam's harbour, a sultry red and black bar, and a restaurant in which guests dine in a vast square, white-cushioned bed-style lounge. The evening unfolds with a chance to catch the sunset and spectacular views in comfort on the top deck before heading downstairs to the bar to sip Champagne while DJs spin their tunes. You can finally retire to dinner on the lower deck as Supperclub Cruise sets sail from Pier 14 behind Centraal Station.

drink

19 Bar ARC

Reguliersdwarsstraat 44

Bar ARC (Angelique Rob Company) in the heart of Amsterdam's gay scene serves up cocktails and glamour thanks to the Fabulous Shaker Boys (the cocktail company who trained the bar staff) and the interior by Eric Kuster of B. Inc Interior Stuff. Glass, leather and wenge wood provide the backdrop to lights that change colour to mirror the mood of the bar and the weather outside. With the addition of subdued reflective gold lacquer behind the bar and an orange-gold broken laminate skin on the wall, Bar ARC attracts a grown-up crowd who move on when they want to enjoy more than just drinks and the French International cuisine of this very democratic establishment.

MONKEY TROUBLE

20 In 't Aepjen

Zeedijk 1

No. 1 Zeedijk is among the oldest buildings in Amsterdam, and one of only two original wooden structures still standing in the city centre. Zeedijk itself recently underwent a facelift in the form of repaving, but for a long time it was a notoriously sleazy street, wrapping around the east side of the red-light district. The bar started life as a sailors' hostel in 1550, and the innkeeper was generous enough to permit seamen who had gambled or drunk their money away to pay him with the monkeys they had brought back from their travels. The sailors who slept there were immediately identifiable because they were always scratching, having stayed 'in the monkeys', a colloquialism that has filtered into the language; the Dutch now refer to people in trouble as in *de aap gelogeerd* ('stayed in the monkey'). The reason for In 't Aepjen's longevity is partly its rich history, but also its warm and mellow tones as a perfect backdrop for a *beertje* ('little beer').

WHISKY A GO-GO

21 Café de Still

Spuistraat 326

About 350 different types of whisky are a good reason to visit Café de Still. The name is a play on the word 'distillery'; *de still* in Dutch means 'the quiet', and *stillen* 'to quench' – in this case a thirst.

The bar opened in the early 1990s and has changed ownership a few times, but it has always had the love and support of its regulars (who once clubbed together to save the bar when its original owner could no longer run it for health reasons). For those who want to develop their palate, the bar will arrange tasting sessions. There are the famous malts such as Macallen, Glenfiddich and Highland Park (who provided the banquette at the back of the bar), alongside lesser known, rarer flavours from Old Pulteney and Caol Ila, a house favourite distilled on the Scottish island of Islay.

OLD BUT NEW

22 Morlang

Keizersgracht 451

Named after the psychological drama *Morlang*, which was written here by the film's director Tjebbo Penning, this designer bar – and restaurant – is split over two levels. Stone steps lead up to the rococo façade, and the entrance is through a red velvet curtain that arcs over the door and protects customers from blustery weather outside. A linear bar divides the long space and a leather banquette faces the bar wall, lit up by the soft caramel and sugar hues of the spirit-filled bottles. A spiral staircase leads down to the subterranean restaurant, where the all-day menu mixes salads with spicy Indonesian soups. Close to the busy shopping alley of Leidsestraat, Morlang is firmly on the beaten track yet retains an exclusive allure, thanks to the tempered balance of a contemporary watering hole in a grand old Dutch canalside building. Sister venue NL Bar has opened in New York.

DRINKING AND ARCHITECTURE

23 Walem

Keizersgracht 449

The classic geometry of steel lines and dividing panels of glass create the façade of a canal-view building on the grand Keizersgracht that could only be the work of Gerrit Rietveld, and is the public face of what claims to be Amsterdam's first designer bar. Walem has certainly been around for a while, and although the décor and ownership have changed, the façade and the industrial staircase in the centre of the restaurant have not. The effect of the granite and wood interior is softened if you sit in the large terraced garden out back or at

one of the few canalside tables that are placed in the sunshine in warmer months. Located next door to Morlang (see left), the two venues are inevitably busy and customers dart between the two waiting for the best table. Walem has managed to remain the occasional playground of Dutch soap-opera stars and the local glitterati.

DRINKS AWAY!

24 Kapitein Zeppos

Gebed Zonder End 5

Being hidden up a very missable alleyway is a useful way to give drinkers at Kapitein Zeppos the feeling that they are off the beaten track and have discovered an alcoholic underbelly of Amsterdam. And indeed they have, as the average local will also have failed to notice this gem of a bar (named after a famous Belgian television star of the 1960s), despite the fact that it is located at the heart of the city's university complex and is just off Nes, Amsterdam's main promenade for fringe theatre. As such, this place is perfect for a quiet drink, and the bar will make both the solitary drinker or revelling party feel welcome. Having been a cigar factory in its former life, today the space has been divided into an old-school bar complete with Delft tiling on the walls and tables, a foliage-sheltered area outside, and a romantic restaurant. Ideal for the clandestine encounter.

TASTING HOUSE

25 Wynand Fockink

Pijlsteeg 31

This distillery originally opened in 1679 and was taken over by Wynand Fockink in 1730. The name has remained even though the tasting house was bought by Dutch distillers Bols in 1955. Entrance is via a narrow alleyway at the back of the Krasnapolsky Hotel on the Dam Square. The main tasting room looks as if it has not changed since the 17th century; there are no gambling machines or music, or even tables or chairs. There are, however, spitting troughs built into a low wooden bar. Wynand Fockink offers twenty different *jenevers* (including those flavoured with coriander, aniseed or caramel) and fifty old Dutch liquors, all brewed under the house label. They further mix the drinks on-site, resulting in popular favourites such as the berry-flavoured *Boswandeling*.

shop

FLORISTRY FANTASY
26 Menno Kroon
Cornelis Schuytstraat 11

Florist Menno Kroon has seen his work and reputation travel far and wide across the Netherlands. At the crack of dawn he and his team of ten fellow florists travel to the flower auctions at Aalsmeer and Vleuten to buy their daily selections, and four times a year he reinvents the look of his shop, celebrating this with an opening. Recently Kroon commissioned Walther van Ekkendonk to paint parrots on the walls; the florists then created bouquets using only the vibrant colours of the birds. Whatever the season, the decadent abundance of such exotic blooms as Lady's Slipper orchids, protea flowers, ginger, mascari and heliconia is breathtaking.

COUTURE CULTURE
27 Van Ravenstein
Keizersgracht 359

Van Ravenstein is a one-stop shop for Belgian fashion in the Netherlands. Although Dutch herself, Gerda van Ravenstein's affinity for the famous Antwerp Six designers of the 1990s means that most collections are represented. Dries van Noten (p. 41), Ann Demeulemeester (p. 39) and Dirk Bikkembergs are the only remaining designers from the original six; the next generation has arrived in the form of A.F. Vandevorst, Bernhard Willhelm and Véronique Branquinho (p. 41). The style is defined by practical design with functional tailoring, and its local popularity is attributable to its appeal to tall Dutch women who get around on bicycles. The impeccable tailoring based on deconstruction techniques has kept these names at the forefront of international fashion for more than a decade.

CHOCOLATE OPERA
28 Puccini Bomboni
Staalstraat 17

When chocolates outsold the cakes and other candies at her dessert shop, Ans van Soelen narrowed her scope but not her selection. She sells enormous, divine chocolates from a contemporary glass store not far from the Amsterdam opera house (hence the inspiration behind the shop's name), which are made on-site from all natural ingredients. Van Soelen's products are unique in local chocolate culture as she refrains from using sugar, fondant or butter in any of her recipes. She is not afraid to experiment with flavour, however, and lemongrass, thyme, rhubarb, nutmeg, pepper and vanilla with poppy seed have all been infused into her plain, milk and white varieties. Part of the concoction process can be witnessed through a glass façade to the side of the shop, which allows an enticing peek into the delectable world of chocolate couture.

LEATHER DESIGN
29 Hester van Eeghen
Hartenstraat 37 [bags] and 1 [shoes]

The popularity of Hester van Eeghen's bags, wallets, purses and, most recently, shoes has resulted in her supplying over a hundred outlets across Holland, Germany, Switzerland and Japan. Her designs are eye-catching for both their bright colours (she uses vibrant reds and acid limes, as well as the more neutral shades of leather) and their bold shapes, and are frequently featured in museum exhibitions (including the Stedelijk). Van Eeghen's status in the industry now means that she is in a position to help young designers, and she conceives competitions held in academies throughout the Netherlands.

COUTURE AND BOILER SUITS
30 Mart Visser Haute Couture
Paulus Potterstraat 30a

One of the Netherlands' leading couturiers, Mart Visser, celebrated a decade of success in 2003. His by-appointment atelier and salon moved into a former bank designed by Diederik Dam, opposite the Van Gogh Museum (p. 27), and he was honoured with a retrospective exhibition at the Gemeente Museum in The Hague – all this by the age of just thirty-five, no mean feat for a man whose tailoring technique was honed in the atelier of Holland's answer to Yves Saint Laurent (see p. 246), Frans Molenaar, and Anne Klein in New York. Visser prides himself on his couture and dresses the most famous women in the country. His renown has resulted in international expansion, and the 'Bagage', 'Chaussure', 'Belt', 'Bridalwear', 'Prêt à Porter' and beach- and resort-wear ranges will soon be available across Europe.

JUST OUT OF TIME
31 JOOT
Hartenstraat 15

A shared creative instinct, an aversion to dust and a desire to make the act of book-buying an event drove Simon de Jong and Stefan Reiters to set up JOOT. Standing for 'just out of time', the store's distinctive full-metal façade is from the Michel de Klerk school of architecture. They call their 'bookery' the 'first kinky antiquarian bookshop ever', and with its open space, light colours, industrial metallic cases and leaded glass, it is indeed the antithesis of a traditional second-hand store. A strong selection of literature, art and philosophy titles combines with original art from the changing exhibitions mounted in the gallery space.

MIFFY THE RABBIT
32 The Nijntje Shop
Beethovenstraat 71

Nijntje is one of Holland's best-loved children's characters and best-known exports, instantly recognizable under the name Miffy. The Dutch for rabbit is *konijn* and, with the diminutive *tje* added, connotes something 'small and sweet'. This girl bunny was the creation of Dick Bruna, who won the Children's Book Award for *Nijntje in the Tent* in 1966 and is famous for characters that appear in over a hundred picture books. The Nijntje Shop stocks most of his storybooks, along with all the other popular Bruna paraphernalia.

GONE POTTY
33 Pol's Potten
KNSM-Laan 39

This former cocoa-bean warehouse is filled with household accessories and custom-made kitchen units in which to store them. Run by three industrial designers, Pol's Potten is the outlet for the crockery, glassware and cutlery that they bring back from the Far East, mixed with objects found closer to home. Wood and steel shelves divide the area into corridors, and colour, texture and shape are provided via chunky glassware, delicate candelabras, plastic bowls and misshapen lights that cover them. A huge *Verboden te Roeken* ('no smoking') sign is painted across one of the beams, and the look of the shop constantly changes with the turnover of stock and ironic window displays.

The relationship between owners Dick Dankers and Cok de Rooy and furniture and industrial designers has produced a dynamic collection, and their shop stages exhibitions that are often produced in association with other reputable institutions, such as the Mondriaan Foundation. The enthusiasm that greeted these interdisciplinary shows led Dankers to see the potential for providing designers with an unequalled opportunity to present their work. The access to Dutch talent and its success in the international arena led to the formation of the Dutch Individuals Foundation, which Dankers and de Rooy use to assist young designers into the industry. Armed with their achievements and success, they have most recently started an on-site Textile Museum, which provides the only looms in Europe on which to weave original pure linen damask.

In 1880 the Boas brothers' diamond factory was the largest of its kind in the whole of Europe. The three brothers purchased rough stones in London, polished them in Amsterdam, and sold them in Paris. With the German occupation, the Boas family fled the country and never really returned to take up the diamond reins in the same way again. The factory eventually closed in 1944, but was acquired in 1990 by the grandsons of Samuel Gassan, who himself had founded a diamond business in 1945. Architect Ed Veenendaal has recreated the Emerald City as its interior, an aptly imposing and stark environment in which to buy precious stones. Free 90-minute tours are on offer daily, and give visitors the opportunity to witness the diamond polishing and setting process as well as a glimpse into the private world of international diamond dealing.

This cigar shop founded by Pantaleon Gerhard Coenraad Hajenius in 1826 moved to its current humidity-controlled location in 1915. The Art Déco interior is a national monument and features oak-panelled walls and a richly decorated ceiling, as well as the largest cigar library in Europe. It sells the exclusive three lines of Hajenius cigars: the 'Sumatra' selection (lighter, the morning smoke), the 'Grand Finale' range (which blends tobacco from Sumatra, Havana and Brazil as the after-dinner smoke of choice) and the 'HBPR' ('hand-bunched, pressed rolled', specially made to a traditional method in Nicaragua). The shop houses private humidors and couriers supplies to the owners when their personal stock runs low. Courses are held for cigar novices, and the cigars themselves can be enjoyed on-site with a tea or coffee.

A SENSE OF RIGHT
37 Vivian Hann
Haarlemmerdijk 102

THESE BOOTS ARE MADE FOR WALKING
38 Paul Warmer
Leidsestraat 41

DRY DESIGN, HOT IDEAS
39 Droog @ Home
Staalstraat 7b

American-born Vivian Hann combines an assortment of dinnerware, cutlery and glassware from the finest suppliers in the world with hand-made ceramics from local Dutch artists. The shop's small interior is typical of her appreciation for contrasting styles and materials, with a 1967 stainless-steel coffeepot alongside mother-of-pearl spoons and porcelain crockery to emphasize their 'sense of right'. Major brands such as Artoria, Royal Copenhagen, Orrefors, Georg Jensen, Rosenthal and Stelton have captured her imagination and she has found a place to arrange them 'correctly' in the overall look of the store. Two of Hann's personal favourites are the beautiful porcelain cups by Dutch firm JAS/MV and a perfectly balanced stirring spoon by C. Hugo Pott, while designer Margot Nije reveals her wit in the lipstick imprint glazed onto the rim of her inventive ceramic beakers.

Warmer is to boots what Blahník (p. 213) is to the strappy slingback. Fifteen years ago, husband-and-wife team Paul and Renée Warmer narrowed the remit of their clothing line to footwear and have been making shoes that lead seasonal trends ever since. Flat, pointed boots retain the edge of high fashion but are functional, too, combining stretch elastic with soft leather to hold calf shape and mould the boot top right over the knee. Heeled varieties have been made in glittering silver and more recently in neon pink, orange and green. It is not surprising that Benelux stylists look to Warmer for ideas, as the window displays also tell current fashion tales. 'Some of our clients ask what clothes they should buy each season', admits Renée, 'as they know that their fashion choices will be dictated by what they are wearing on their feet. And that will be down to our designs.'

Gijs Bakker and Renny Ramakers founded Droog Design in 1993 with an aim 'to make a contribution to the international debate about design through projects, exhibitions, workshops and publications'. Renowned in the design arena for initiating and developing experimental projects, the company was behind Jurgen Bey's streetscape project in Tokyo and Marcel Wanders' knotted chair. The Droog team nurtures young talent by inviting graduates to assist with commissions received from international firms and institutions, which over the years have included such design studios as Concrete (see Spring and Supperclub Cruise; pp. 17, 19), Blender and Flex in Delft and United Statements of Rotterdam. Their work is witty, clever and practical; here at Droog @ Home you can see it in action as the space doubles as an exhibition gallery and store.

see

CONTEMPORARY ARCHITECTURE
40 Van Gogh Museum
Paulus Potterstraat 7

The main structure of this museum, which houses the world's largest collection of Dutch masters, was designed by Gerrit Rietveld and opened in 1973, having used Rietveld's drawings to complete the building after his death in 1964. A new wing added in 1999 was designed by Kisho Kurokawa, whose repertoire already included museums in Japan and the airport at Kuala Lumpur. His work sits well beside the black lines and geometric shapes that characterize Rietveld's design; the cones, ellipses and squares form a symbiosis between Western rational geometry and Eastern asymmetry.

BOTANICAL GARDEN
41 Hortus Botanicus
Plantage Middenlaan 2a

The city's botanical gardens began life as an apothecary's herb garden. The vegetation population was expanded by the arrival of ships from the Dutch East India Company, laden with newly discovered seed varieties and tropical plants intended for medicinal use at the Hortus Medicus. Fifty years later, in 1682, it put down permanent roots in the Plantage Middenlaan. Some of the original specimens are still growing in the palm greenhouse, which was built in 1912. There are three other greenhouses with temperatures set for alternative climates: tropical, subtropical and desert. The gardens feature Dutch tulips, flesh-eating plants, Victoria Amazonica water lilies and an Agave from the early 19th century, the oldest potted plant in the world. Over 6,000 plant varieties constitute what has become one of the largest botanical collections in existence.

PHOTOGRAPHY
42 Huis Marseille
Keizersgracht 401

This gallery is the pre-eminent photography space in Amsterdam. Located in an equally impressive 17th-century house, Huis Marseille (named after the French merchant who built it) is a photographic foundation that exhibits both Dutch and international work. It was inaugurated as the seat of the Foundation for Photography in 1999 after architect Laurens Vis and architectural firm Benthem Crouwel adapted the building to host such exhibitions as the inaugural show 'Albert Londe/Daan van Golden' and 'Cuba in Marseille', featuring Wim and Donata Wenders' photographs of the Buena Vista Social Club. Huis Marseille also has its own permanent collection of contemporary photography.

ART ON A GLOBAL SCALE
43 Torch
Lauriergracht 94

Both loved and hated for its daring programme, Torch is the Netherlands' premier gallery for contemporary art and is the name that has consistently appeared on the international art fair circuit since its foundation as a podium for young contemporary art. Designed by architect Peter Sas, the space is located in an area renowned for galleries that feature young artists. Torch itself represents Anton Corbijn, Annie Sprinkle, Ellen Kooi and Teun Hocks, and sells the incredible 'wonderpills' (which solve all life's problems) by Dana Wyse. Twenty years of cutting-edge art were celebrated with a commemorative show in 2004.

WESTERN GAS FACTORY
44 Westergasfabriek
Haarlemmerweg 8–10

Just west of the city centre is Amsterdam's foremost multimedia venue. The buildings of the old gas factory were listed as historic monuments and renovation took place around them. The culture park was designed by American landscape artist Kathryn Gustafson and, although the park wasn't completed until 2003, project manager Evert Verhagen opened the buildings in 1992 to host the Drum Rhythm Festival, as well as a continuing party of DJs and live performances. Now that the park has been enhanced by picnic lawns, tennis courts and a huge pond, the project is focusing on the buildings themselves. One is already home to leading theatre company ToneelGroep Amsterdam, which continues to present shows there. The undertaking is an inspirational example of the metamorphosis from a defunct, polluted inner-city space into a cultural hot spot that attracts patronage on an international scale.

ANTIQUE BOUTIQUE
45 Spiegelkwartier
• Eduard Kramer, Nieuwe Spiegelstraat 64
• Dekker Antiquairs, Spiegelgracht 9

For centuries, Amsterdam has counted among the major antiques centres of Europe. The Rokin and surrounding areas have the oldest reputation in this collector arena. But since the construction of the Rijksmuseum at the turn of the 19th century, the Spiegelstraat, which runs down to its architectural entrance from the city centre, has evolved as the 'new' antiques neighbourhood. The antiquarians who set up shop here offer an impressive selection of paintings, ceramics, glass, coins, jewelry, books, furniture and, of course, Delft tiles. The range of knowledge at Eduard Kramer is unsurpassed, and entrance into this family business requires delicate manoeuvring around cabinets and precariously placed ornaments. Dekker Antiquairs' collection of Jacobean twisted glassware belongs in a museum, as do the finds in many of the shops that line this stretch. Unless you are a serious collector, the shops are best enjoyed as lessons in art and history, and chatting to dealers is usually rewarding. With their experience and know-how they could be running the art museums themselves.

SQUAT ART
46 W139
Warmoesstraat 139

When they first squatted in this building in 1979, the collective of artists had little idea that nearly thirty years later they would be commemorating their position as one of Amsterdam's most cutting-edge spaces in a 383-page retrospective volume. Back then, the Warmoesstraat was an undesirable, derelict backstreet, but the artists were pleased to find a usable production house in which to exhibit raw art. After someone fell through the ceiling during one of the infamous rambunctious openings, the staff and volunteers took on caretaking roles and started to restore the space. This restoration has recently shifted up a few gears and W139 are temporarily moving out so that the building can be transformed under the experienced eye of Sjoerd Soeters (who is responsible for much of the architecture on the Eilanden), Vincent Smulders and Bob van Reeth.

ANTWERP

Take one look at the medieval finery depicted in the stained-glass windows of Antwerp's magnificent Gothic cathedral, and you'll realize that this city's affinity for fashion dates back centuries. But it was in the 1980s – the decade of padded shoulders, big belts and even bigger hair – that a loose association of local designers decided to really shake things up. The 'Antwerp Six' – Dirk Bikkembergs, Ann Demeulemeester (p. 39), Walter van Beirendonck (p. 38), Dries van Noten (p. 41), Dirk van Saene and Marina Yee – staged iconoclastic fashion shows and events that made fashionistas around the globe rethink their wardrobes. Antwerp's contemporary fashion industry hasn't looked back since. The knock-on effect into the worlds of hospitality and cuisine has been inevitable, and the city's collection of appealing boutique hotels, restaurants and bars (several in historic buildings) is able to hold its own on the international stage. But don't let the fascination with fashion and image fool you into thinking that Antwerp is an overly precious, fussy and superficial place. Nothing could be further from the truth. As a thriving international port and the world's premier diamond-trading centre, there's a down-to-earth business sense to Belgium's second largest city, home to 450,000 people. Unencumbered by the international power politics and bewildering cultural mish-mash of big brother Brussels, Antwerp is a relaxed, free-spirited city, proudly Flemish but happy to embrace whatever the world brings it.

Antwerp's 'Golden Age' was in the 17th century, when the port was the economic heart of Europe and home to artists such as Peter Paul Rubens (see p. 43) and Anthony van Dyck. It was during this time that the canny city fathers offered a safe haven to Portuguese Jews fleeing persecution; it was these refugees that eventually set up the diamond industry that today accounts for the third largest share of Belgium's GDP. The fruits of this trade and other industries can be seen all over the city, from the temples to 19th-century commerce that line the Meir (Antwerp's equivalent of Oxford Street) to the sturdy brick warehouses of the Eilandje docks. With town and harbour having long since gone their separate ways, Het Eilandje is just one of many districts undergoing regeneration and reinvention. A long-awaited TGV terminus is nearing completion at Centraal Station (p. 43), while the city's new and visually arresting law courts (p. 43), designed by Richard Rogers, rise in a series of steel-coated, shark-like fins above the Het Zuid (p. 43) neighbourhood. As interesting as these and other areas, such as Zurenborg with its beautiful enclave of Belle Époque architecture, are to explore, it is to the city's historic core that most visitors gravitate. Antwerp's Old Town is a rambler's delight, a maze of narrow streets leading into secluded cobblestone squares and courtyards that on warmer days fill up with amiable locals sipping coffee and beer. There couldn't be a more pleasurable way of spending the day.

StyleCity Antwerp

1 De Witte Lelie
2 Slapen Enzo/Charles Rogier XI
3 Restaurant Bernardin
4 Docklands Reinvented
5 Den Artist Brasserie/Hippodroom
6 Maritime Memories
7 Dôme/Dôme sur Mer
8 De Vagant
9 Désiré de Lille
10 L'Entrepot du Congo/Bar Tabac
11 King Kong
12 Walter
13 Huis A Boon
14 Korte Gasthuisstraat
15 Ann Demeulemeester
16 Galalith
17 Lange Gasthuisstraat
18 Nationalestraat
19 Kledingzaak
20 Kammenstraat
21 Onze-Lieve-Vrouwekathedraal
22 Het Zuid
23 Centraal Station
24 ModeNatie
25 Rubenshuis

Approximate scale

1/2 kilometre

1/4 mile

7

sleep

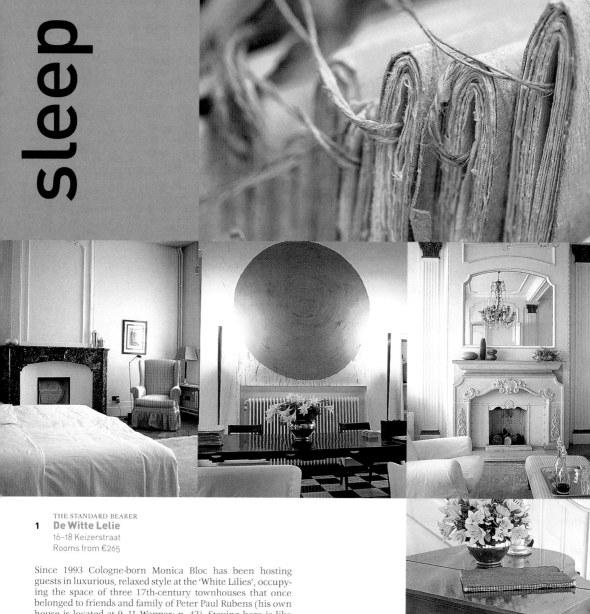

THE STANDARD BEARER
1 **De Witte Lelie**
16–18 Keizerstraat
Rooms from €265

Since 1993 Cologne-born Monica Bloc has been hosting guests in luxurious, relaxed style at the 'White Lilies', occupying the space of three 17th-century townhouses that once belonged to friends and family of Peter Paul Rubens (his own house is located at 9–11 Wapper; p. 43). Staying here is like having been invited to an elegant house party hosted by a well-to-do Antwerp friend. The hotel's ten distinctively individual, light-filled rooms are impeccably presented, each with fresh flowers, chocolates and decanters of port and sherry to hand. Breakfast is served from a huge, well-stocked kitchen and can be enjoyed in the courtyard garden.

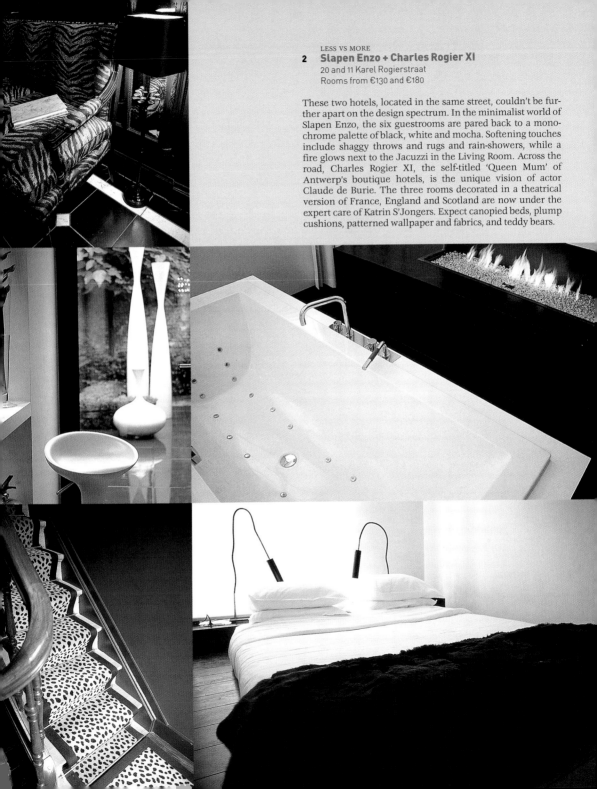

2 Slapen Enzo + Charles Rogier XI

20 and 11 Karel Rogierstraat
Rooms from €130 and €180

These two hotels, located in the same street, couldn't be further apart on the design spectrum. In the minimalist world of Slapen Enzo, the six guestrooms are pared back to a monochrome palette of black, white and mocha. Softening touches include shaggy throws and rugs and rain-showers, while a fire glows next to the Jacuzzi in the Living Room. Across the road, Charles Rogier XI, the self-titled 'Queen Mum' of Antwerp's boutique hotels, is the unique vision of actor Claude de Burie. The three rooms decorated in a theatrical version of France, England and Scotland are now under the expert care of Katrin S'Jongers. Expect canopied beds, plump cushions, patterned wallpaper and fabrics, and teddy bears.

eat

GOURMET FEAST
3   Restaurant Bernardin
17 Sint-Jacobsstraat

Bernard Lescrinier has made dishes such as tartare of Antwerp beef and mullet with shallots the highlight of this classy Franco–Belgian restaurant, in the shadow of St Jacob's church, the final resting place of Peter Paul Rubens. But you would expect nothing less than the finest in technique and presentation from an alumnus of London's Le Gavroche. And it's a pleasure to be able to watch the cooks at work in the open kitchen from the elegantly classy interior, enhanced by colourful modern artworks.

PUMP IT UP
4   Docklands Reinvented
• Het Pomphuis, 7 Siberiastraat
• Lux, 13 Adriaan Brouwerstraat
• Bassin, 1 Tavernierkaai

At the northern extremity of Het Eilandje is a former pump house for a dry dock. The handsome brick building has been restored and transformed into a restaurant and café. Come more for the light-flooded, waterside location and atmosphere redolent of the glory years of Antwerp's seafaring trade than for the Oriental-meets-Pacific-Rim cuisine. The reinvention of the docks can be witnessed closer to the Old Town at either trendy lounge bar and restaurant Lux or the more old-fashioned Bassin in the former lock-keeper's house.

JUST LIKE GRANDMA MADE
5   Den Artist Brasserie + Hippodroom
45 Museumstraat and 10 Leopold de Waelplaats

The unfussy and comforting food your Belgian grandmother used to make (should you have been lucky enough to have one) is what's on the menu here. This attractive Art Déco space, ideal for lunch when museum-hopping in the area, specializes in Belgian favourites such as meat loaf with cherries, Ostend-style fish soup, and duck with roasted apple. If you're looking for something a bit fancier in atmosphere and more daring in cuisine, try the neighbouring Hippodroom, a favourite with the local art set.

The patina is part of the charm at De Kleine Zavel, a former sailors' dorm, and it's not difficult to imagine that the wooden crates hold empty bottles from which sailors might once have drank. Today's diners can partake of dishes such as rice paper rolls, plump with local shrimps, or vegetable salad with candied eel. Its sister establishment, boutique Hotel 't Sandt, stands on the opposite corner, while a block away is Café Beveren, an old-timer's bar complete with antique jukebox, another leftover of the area's maritime past.

The beautiful Belle Époque architecture of Joseph Bascourt can be seen all over Zurenborg, and for a glimpse inside one of his buildings all you have to do is book a meal at Dôme. Chef Julien Burlat works wonders creating dishes that look and taste delicious, and the whole experience is enhanced by top-class service. Across the road is the associated bistro Dôme sur Mer, which specializes in the freshest of seafood. With a fish tank filling one wall and an open, marble-surrounded kitchen, the atmosphere is like a holiday in the city. It's the perfect place to enjoy the fruits of Belgium's seas.

drink

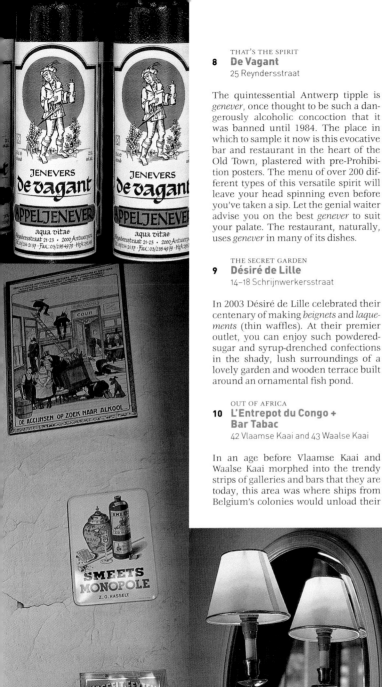

The quintessential Antwerp tipple is *genever*, once thought to be such a dangerously alcoholic concoction that it was banned until 1984. The place in which to sample it now is this evocative bar and restaurant in the heart of the Old Town, plastered with pre-Prohibition posters. The menu of over 200 different types of this versatile spirit will leave your head spinning even before you've taken a sip. Let the genial waiter advise you on the best *genever* to suit your palate. The restaurant, naturally, uses *genever* in many of its dishes.

In 2003 Désiré de Lille celebrated their centenary of making *beignets* and *laquements* (thin waffles). At their premier outlet, you can enjoy such powdered-sugar and syrup-drenched confections in the shady, lush surroundings of a lovely garden and wooden terrace built around an ornamental fish pond.

In an age before Vlaamse Kaai and Waalse Kaai morphed into the trendy strips of galleries and bars that they are today, this area was where ships from Belgium's colonies would unload their booty. On Vlaamse Kaai, L'Entrepot du Congo is an atmospheric bar from those times, although its pared-back interior of simple wooden chairs, wood panelling, high ceilings and black-and-white tiled floor avoids any African connections. On Waalse Kaai, across the broad strip of scrubby grass that acts as a giant car park, is the seemingly unremarkable Bar Tabac. But its anti-style look seems to hit the mark with Antwerp's hipsters, who hang out here drinking beers and grooving to DJ-spun tunes well into the small hours.

Antwerpeans of a certain age remember fondly the underground arts centre King Kong where, it's said, the electronic (and hugely influential) band Joy Division once played in the early 1980s. In 2006, King Kong was reborn as a relaxed café-bar with DJs taking the place of bands. It's the kind of place where there's a mish-mash of interior design, from old school desks to the stylish bar and swinging basket chairs in the open playground area at the rear.

THE ICONCLAST
12 Walter
10 Sint-Antoniusstraat

IF THE GLOVE FITS…
13 Huis A Boon
2–4 Lombardenvest

SWEET THINGS
14 Korte Gasthuisstraat
- Burie, no. 3
- Philip's Biscuits, no. 11
- Goossens, no. 31

Take a former garage, use the shopfront windows for art installations, suspend a giant plastic donut for a sales desk, and construct a wooden chalet in which to display clothes: Walter, named after Walter van Beirendonck, the member of the Antwerp Six who looks most like a Hell's Angel, is certainly the most intriguing of Antwerp's boutiques. Here, van Beirendonck's trademark T-shirts are sold alongside clothes and accessories by kindred fashion spirits Dirk van Saene, Bruno Pieters and Peter Pilotto.

Patsy Sarteel's great-uncle opened this delightful store specializing in made-to-measure gloves back in 1884. Given an Art Déco makeover in 1924, the shop hasn't changed since, right down to the neatly stacked emerald-green boxes in which are stored the many styles and sizes of exquisite gloves, some made with the finest peccary leather or lamb-skin and lined with silk or cashmere. Sarteel herself should be declared a national treasure for her uncanny ability to accurately guess a glove size with just one glance at a customer's hand.

Avoid this pedestrianized street in the city's historic centre if you are on a diet. Within steps of each other you'll find the elegant confectionery shop Burie, which makes chocolates in the shape of cut diamonds; Philip's Biscuits, special-izing in delicious macaroons and butter and ginger biscuits shaped by hand; and Goossens, founded in 1884 and supplier of irresistible baked goods, including sweet raisin rolls, meat pies and cheese puffs.

MODERN ROMANCE

15 Ann Demeulemeester
38 Verlatstraat

The work of Antwerp's reigning queen of fashion has been described as 'modern romance at its best'. Her inspiration has come from many sources, including the Abstract Expressionist painter Jackson Pollock and the Hassidic Jewish community of her adopted home. Clue into her latest vision at the flagship store opposite the Koninklijk Museum voor Schone Kunsten (p. 43), a large, high-ceilinged space in which a pocket garden of ferns can be viewed through windows in the changing rooms.

BUTTONS & JEWELS

16 Galalith
42 Zirkstraat

Galalith is a milk-based plastic that was popular with jewelry designers in the early 20th century before synthetic plastics were developed. It's also the name that Pascale Masselis has given to her shop, tucked away in the Old Town, where you can view her Art Nouveau-inspired jewelry designs. Here you'll also find Antwerp's most impressive collection of buttons – some 10,000 different types – all stored in a handsome 19th-century French wood cabinet that fills up one side of the store.

BOUTIQUE BROWSE

17 Lange Gasthuisstraat
• Verso, no. 11
• Louis, 2 Lombardenstraat
• Flamant, nos 12–14

If for nothing else, visit Verso to admire the stained-glass domed roof over the boutique's collection, which includes such up-and-coming designers as Raf Simons, Dirk Schönberger and Kris van Assche. The front of the store sports a sleek café-bar. Much more intimate is Louis, the boutique in which Ann Demeulemeester (see left) first sold her collection in the 1980s. Flamant, too, is well worth a look for its colourful design and decent value.

When Dries van Noten took over a decaying men's clothing store on the corner of Nationalestraat and Drukkerijstraat to create his 'fashion palace', he kick-started a movement that would turn the once quiet neighbourhood of Sint-Andries into Antwerp's fashion mecca. Today, a visit to the immaculately turned-out hub of van Noten's elegant clothing empire is the essential overture to a shopping spree along Nationalestraat. At no. 24, sisters Violetta and Vera Pepa, part of a new guard of Antwerp designers, offer slinky women's clothes in wool and silk, as well as their own shoes and belts for the full fashion look. Véronique Branquinho's coolly stylish flagship store at no. 73 offers ready-to-wear apparel for both men and women. And down at no. 110, Prêt à Partir showcases the collection of Anita Evenpoel, whose quirky coats and hats show the Japanese influence in their multiple layers and folds.

Wim Neels is the man responsible for the European garment collection of Muji, the popular Japanese 'no-brand brand' that features utilitarian yet stylish goods. His own menswear collection – called Taille (size) and labelled simply with the size of each garment (from 46 to 54) – can be viewed at this neat little corner store. *Taille* in French also means 'cut with precision', which is exactly what these monochrome pieces are. The shop is at the north end of Kloosterstraat, a street lined with antique shops that make for a fascinating browse on the way to Het Zuid.

Despite the recent opening of state-of-the-art music centre AMUZ in the converted Baroque church of St Augustinus, the vibe along Kammenstraat is more punk rock than classical. Go with the rock 'n' roll, khaki, fatigues and denim flow at teen- and dancewear boutique Fish & Chips, a jumble of a place that also hosts music and art shows. The perfect spot for lunch is Soep & Soup, a pleasing, contemporary take on the soup kitchen, while the black-tiled café-bar Berlin is as good a pit stop during the day as it is a chill-out and chat-up spot of an evening.

see

21 Onze-Lieve-Vrouwekathedraal
21 Groenplaats

Rising proudly above Antwerp's cobble-stone centre is the 14th-century Onze-Lieve-Vrouwekathedraal (Cathedral of Our Lady), an operatically grand building. Circumnavigate its Gothic exterior to inspect the richly detailed carved stonework – it looks particularly good at night when floodlit. Then enter the cavernous, ornate interior where pride of place is bestowed on three enormous paintings by Rubens (see below). The tourist office is nearby on the triangular-shaped Grote Markt, a smaller but hardly less ostentatious version of Brussels' Grand Place (p. 127).

ART AND JUSTICE
22 Het Zuid
- Koninklijk Museum voor Schone Kunsten, 2 Leopold de Waelplaats
- MuHKA, 32 Leuvenstraat
- Provinciaal Museum voor Fotografie, 47 Waalse Kaai
- Justitiepaleis, 20 Bolivarplaats

For those short of time, the essential museum in the Het Zuid district is the Koninklijk Museum voor Schone Kunsten (Royal Museum of Fine Arts), which covers Flemish painting from the 14th century to the present day. If your tastes run to more contemporary works, then head to the Museum van Hedendaagse Kunst Antwerpen (MuHKA), a stark, light-flooded space in a former grain silo, or the Provinciaal Museum voor Fotografie, occupying a former warehouse. Spearheading the regeneration of southern Antwerp and adding a dash of modern architectural glamour is the Justitiepaleis (law courts), designed by Richard Rogers.

RAILWAY CATHEDRAL
23 Centraal Station
- Diamantmuseum, 19–23 Koningin Astridplein
- Zoo Antwerpen, 26 Koningin Astridplein
- Designcenter de Winkelhaak, 26 Lange Winkelhaakstraat

A cosmopolitan community buzzes around Louis Delacenserie's iron-and-glass Centraal Station (1905), whose gilded entrance hall makes for a spectacular entrance to the city. The close proximity of the railway was one of the main reasons that Antwerp's four diamond exchanges were built here. For a glimpse into the history of the diamond industry, visit the modern Diamantmuseum on the square fronting the station; if you get the urge to buy a diamond or two for yourself, head to jeweler-lined Vestingstraat. Between the museum and the station lies the zoo, built in 1843 and of note mainly for its architecture (check out the 'Egyptian Temple', home to the elephants and giraffes). The nearby Designcenter, built on the site of former slums, is an exhibition space, workshop, library and showcase for local design.

FASHION HQ
24 ModeNatie
- MoMu, 28 Nationalestraat
- Brasserie National, 32 Nationalestraat
- Copyright Bookshop, 28a Nationalestraat

ModeNatie, the nucleus of Antwerp's fashion industry, occupies the pointed corner of Nationalestraat and Drukkerijstraat, once home to the city's gas corporation. Here you'll find the fashion museum MoMu, as well as the Fashion Academy and the Flanders Fashion Institute. MoMu mounts at least two major exhibitions a year, and even if the items on display aren't to your liking, it's well worth a visit to admire the revamped interior by Marie-José van Hee. In the same building are Copyright Bookshop and über-cool café Brasserie National, designed by Vincent van Duysen.

FAVOURITE SON
25 Rubenshuis + Grand Café Horta
9–11 Wapper and 2 Hopland

Devotees of Antwerp native Peter Paul Rubens should hasten to the place where he lived and worked for over twenty years. When the house was turned into a museum in 1946, its interiors were redecorated according to an inventory drawn up on Rubens' death. The results give a remarkable impression of what it must have been like during his life. Afterwards stop in at the nearby Grand Café Horta, a sinuous structure inspired by the work of Victor Horta. It incorporates salvaged sections of Horta's Maison du Peuple, which was demolished in Brussels in 1964.

Described by Lord Byron as the 'place I preferred on the whole to any I have seen', Athens blurs the line between myth and reality, history and legend, and fires the imagination as no other city in the world. Named for the goddess of wisdom, Athens' past is ever-present in the majestic vision of the Parthenon hovering above the city. The sacred buildings of the Acropolis symbolize Greece's Golden Age, an extraordinary flourishing of art, philosophy and government that 2,500 years later continues to inspire. For first-time visitors these ancient sites are a must, yet few people know the beauty of Athens' modern face. This is a city of opposites, of antiquity and modernity, and calm amidst the chaos. Ask any Athenian what he is doing and the answer is likely to be *treho* ('running'); ask him out for coffee or an impromptu *ouzo* and suddenly he has all the time in the world. There is much more to this city than ancient temples, and each year visitors outnumbering the country's entire population converge upon it, each with his own expectations.

Goethe claimed that 'of all peoples, Greeks have dreamt the dream of life best'. Today modern-day bon viveurs pursue the good life in Athens with enthusiasm, from simple pleasures to more cosmopolitan pursuits. After a cold winter Athenians like to spend as much time as possible outdoors, in streetside cafés, seaside clubs, or restaurant-bars for dining al fresco and dancing under the stars. Year-round sunshine has led to a thriving outdoor culture, in which lingering for hours over coffee is not so much a luxury as a way of life. The city also boasts an indefatigable nightlife. Athenians rarely dine before 10 p.m., venturing out to clubs only after midnight. With venues that feature everything from *rembetika* to *bouzoukia*, plus a calendar full of religious holidays and public festivals, 'everything in moderation' is a phrase that does not apply after dark in Athens. For the gastronome, dining options range from traditional tavernas to the new wave of modern restaurants offering contemporary interpretations of classic Greek dishes alongside new trends in Mediterranean cuisine. The past ten to twenty years have also seen the establishment of numerous state-of-the-art wineries, resulting in the development of a new, world-class Athenian viniculture.

Withstanding countless invasions, both ancient and modern, Athens has risen from the ashes. The city is like a great poem or novel to which one returns with nostalgia, longing to experience it again as if for the first time. From Kifissia to Piraeus, residents and visitors alike continue to dis-cover Athens anew, a continually changing, perplexing and enchanting place bathed in a light that elevates even its most undistinguished features. To submit to her charms is to join in a conspiracy for pleasure, inventing your own Athens as you go off the beaten track, embarking on a journey sure to inspire what poet Odysseus Elytis, winner of the 1979 Nobel Prize for Literature, described as a 'love story with godlike dimensions'.

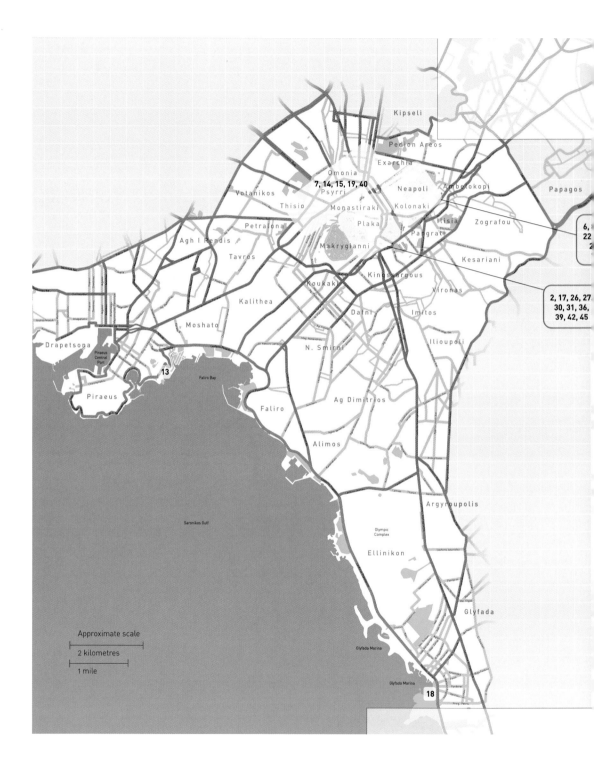

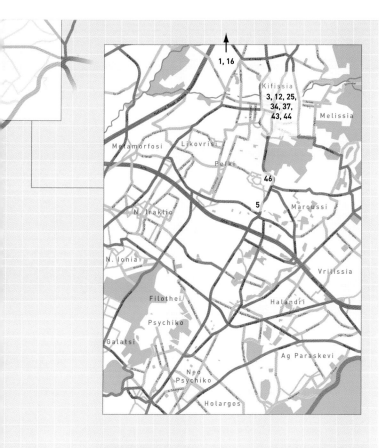

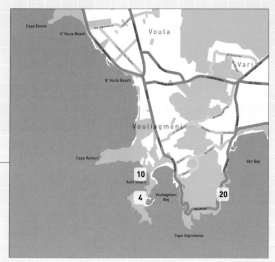

StyleCity Athens

sleep

1 Life Gallery Athens
103 Thiseos
Rooms from €250

Located in the residential area of Ekali, an hour from the city centre and fifteen minutes from Kifissia's commercial district, the intimate Life Gallery Athens creates a welcome respite amongst the cedars and pine trees. Architects Klein/Haller and Vassilis Rodatos created this minimalist sanctuary with subtle earth tones, natural textures and an airy spaciousness that give this small luxury hotel the feeling of a secluded retreat. The thirty rooms include three suites, three art studios and twenty-four open-plan deluxe rooms, all of which have ample seating areas, verandas with uninterrupted views, and sensual lighting. The living space incorporates cleverly designed bathrooms stocked with Korres products, and extends to encompass a functional work space. Works by such contemporary Greek artists as Takis, Kessanlis, Lappas and Gyparakis adorn the walls, while drinks and music flow in the Pisco Sour bar. All of the furniture has been created by top international designers, including Gervasoni, Molteni and Interni. In the summer, the expansive bar spills out into the pool area, where diners can enjoy drinks and dinner al fresco in a cool, relaxing atmosphere, complete with comfortable wicker chairs at poolside restaurant Avenue 103. Overlooking the pool is a wonderful library where you can submerge yourself in both the cozy armchairs and in the collection of books devoted to Greek literature, art and history. Also at Life Gallery Athens is the obligatory spa, with every indulgent feature you could ask for, including a meditation room filled with flickering tea lights. It seems almost sacrilegious to mention the conference centre in a place so disposed to relaxation, but the facilities make for the ideal setting in which to combine business with pleasure.

Built in 1842 as a private residence, this legendary landmark is a hotel of unrivalled opulence and is steeped in the city's history. Having recently undergone a lavish renovation project costing over €70 million, the hotel has been restored to its former glory, and the hand-carved architectural details, glittering gold-leaf meander motif and elegant ionic columns evoke its original 19th-century grandeur. Centrally located on Syntagma Square, the Hotel Grand Bretagne has seen the world's most famous personalities walk through its doors. The 321 rooms and suites combine opulence with sophisticated technology, a happy marriage most clearly seen in the Royal and Presidential suites, both of which surpass all previous notions of luxury. A private steam room, gym, fireplace, dining room, and even a wine cellar are among the amenities of these indulgent suites. Some of the standard rooms have small balconies and are not as spacious, but boast the same luxurious décor and mod cons. Wander into the winter garden with its lofty stained-glass ceiling, palm trees, and winged bronze statues for a suitably decadent atmosphere in which to have brunch or a very British afternoon tea, or quaff a cocktail in the Alexander Bar, named for the hand-made 18th-century tapestry depicting Alexander the Great on one of his exploits. Here you can pair a cognac or vintage port with a cigar from the walk-in humidor. Diners can opt for one (or more) of four venues: the brasserie-style GB Corner with its Mediterranean cuisine, a favourite haunt of ministers and high-profile businessmen; the roof garden, offering similar fare along with breathtaking views of the Parthenon; the exclusive dining space in the Churchill Room (named after the man himself who stayed here on several occasions); or a monastery table in the Cellar, amidst the 2,600 bottles that make up the hotel's wine collection.

3 Semiramis Hotel
48 Harilaou Trikoupi
Rooms from €220

When Dakis Joannou commissioned Karim Rashid to create Greece's first 'design' hotel, the inevitable result was something unique and dynamic. Located in the quiet northern suburb of Kifissia, the hotel strives to create an ultra-modern oasis informed by cool and contemporary design. Rashid's innovative design for the forty-two rooms combines functionality with a style characterized by organic shapes, undulating lines and vibrant colours, and lends a neo-Pop aesthetic and feeling of tranquillity and cool comfort. The five poolside bungalows overlook a perpetually flowing waterfall, while the penthouse suites, enclosed by sliding-glass windows, command wonderful views from verandas as large as the rooms themselves of the Penteli mountains and the bustling city centre beyond. Special care has been taken with the lighting throughout the hotel, which changes imperceptibly from one hue to another. Works from Joannou's collection by well-known artists, including Jeff Koons, Tim Noble, Spencer Tunick, Christopher Wool, Claire Woods and Vanessa Beecroft, provide the finishing flourishes. For guests who cannot tear themselves away from the Semiramis experience, the restaurant-bar offers Mediterranean dishes with a twist.

LUXURIOUS RESORT

4 Astir Palace Resort
40 Apollonos
Rooms from €250

Located on a private peninsula dubbed the 'Athenian Riviera', this palatial resort is only a 25-kilometre journey out of the city. The rambling property, covered with pine trees and commanding magnificent views over the Saronic Gulf, is skirted by sandy beaches, all of which contribute to the feeling of being far away from it all, while being only thirty minutes from downtown Athens, the airport and Cape Sounio. The site contains three complexes (Arion, Nafsika and Aphrodite), each possessing its own distinct character. The recently refurbished Arion offers a more classical aesthetic, while Nafsika is preferred by those with minimalist tastes; both won awards for their revolutionary designs courtesy of Voutsinas, Vourekas, Giorgiadis & Decavalas. The Aphrodite complex, built in the 1980s, is a quieter family affair. Other pleasures include taking a swim off one of the hotel's three private beaches or a dip in the pool, or choosing between the seven restaurants on the property, including the beachside Taverna 37, the casual Kimata, the Sao Restaurant with its Polynesian menu, the upmarket Club House, and the ground-floor Gourmet Grill Room, serving Mediterranean cuisine in this spectacular island setting.

eat

5 THE BEST OF CRETE
Krisa Gi
23 Agiou Konstantinou

You will find all the traditional fare at this Cretan restaurant, from hand-made phyllo pies stuffed with wild greens and herbs, soft goat's cheese or onions, to the classic rusk bread topped with diced tomatoes, *anthotyro* cheese and capers, and doused with olive oil. The *apaki* (smoked pork sautéed in a mélange of herbs) is extraordinary, as is the rabbit baked in a yogurt sauce. Accompany your meal with one of the excellent Cretan wines on offer, such as *Xerolithia* made from Vilana grapes, or try the local spirit, *raki*.

6 MEZE MECCA
To Ouzadiko
25–29 Karneadou

Located in the Lemos Shopping Centre, right in the heart of bustling Kolonaki, To Ouzadiko has no sign outside. But locals know just where to go for some of the best *meze* in town, and flock here day and night for the delicious small dishes traditionally accompanied by a glass of *ouzo* or *tsipouro*. Owner Stella Perdika makes deciding what to order a pleasant dilemma; popular specialties include roast suckling pig, butterfly-grilled sardines, and croquettes, some made from courgettes, chickpeas and tomatoes.

7 LEFT AND RIGHT
Aristera Dexia
140 Pireos and 3 Andronikou

A dramatic glass walkway showcasing the wine cellar divides this cavernous space, and gives the restaurant its directional name: 'left' and 'right'. Controversial designer Kyrios Cryton created a simple yet conceptually divisive interior, well suited to the inventive modern cuisine of Santorini native Chrysanthos Karamolegos. Co-owner Dimitris Litinas is behind the wine cellar, which has been named the best in an Athenian restaurant for five years running and boasts over 2,000 labels, eighty of which are Greek.

The signature dish at this newest addition to the Kolonaki culinary scene is octopus slow-cooked in Vinsanto and honey over crispy potatoes. Other dishes include risotto with scallops, langoustines and spinach, and vegetarian linguine with artichoke hearts and Parmesan. Desserts are creative renditions of classics like *moustalevria* made from grapes scented with mastic, or the chocolate *kormos* made with chestnuts. Papadakis also offers a selection of after-dinner spirits from grappa and cognac to *tsipouro* for the perfect finish.

Acknowledged as one of Athens' finest restaurants, Spondi is a must for any serious foodie. The romantic lighting, barrel-vaulted ceilings and works of art all create an intimate atmosphere in which to appreciate the dishes to come. From the moment the amuse bouche arrives (potato soup with spinach mousse, drizzled with truffle oil), you know that you are in for something special. Try fennel-encrusted scallops with anise, pigeon filet with mushrooms served over crisp potatoes, or sweetbreads with truffles and chestnuts.

Ithaki's location overlooking Vouliagmeni Bay and the Astir Palace Resort (p. 51) provides a glamorous backdrop for a memorable meal. Although there are poultry and beef options, Ithaki is all about seafood: lobster-stuffed sole, langoustines in cognac sauce, marinated *gavros* (pilchards) with avocado mousse. There are fish of all shapes and sizes, from *barbounia* (red mullet) to *rofos* (sea bass), which can be grilled, fried or baked, or prepared the local way – plain, with only olive oil and lemon.

11 48 The Restaurant

48 Armatolon and Klefton

One of the most visually exciting and highly acclaimed restaurants in Athens is 48 The Restaurant, located near the Panathinaikos football stadium and the US Embassy. Retaining much of its former warehouse-industrial design, the interior has been transformed by ISV Architects into a modern, minimalist space. Arnold Chan (of Isometrix)'s geometric lighting niches illuminate the space with ever-changing hues of pink, green, yellow and blue. Outside, a wall of water flowing under the glass floor creates a dramatic atmosphere for summer dining. Cypriot chef Christoforos Peskias, who formerly ran Balthazar (p. 57), offers the very best of modern Greek cuisine, with menus that change daily according to the availability of local ingredients. Leave the choice of wine to sommelier Yiannis Kaimenakis, who will suggest the perfect accompaniment from the outstanding wine list of over 500 labels.

MASTELLO AND WINE

12 Gefsis Me Onomasia Proelefsis

317 Kifissias

When Alexandros Zoumboulis decided to convert his family's elegant mansion into a temple to food and wine for like-minded connoisseurs, he began by sourcing ingredients from the furthest reaches of Greece. The name of the restaurant means 'flavours of designated origin', and affirms Zoumboulis's commitment to seeking out the very best regional purveyors. Foodies will appreciate the resulting gastronomic experience of authentic Greek cuisine with a twist. The restaurant is also alleged to have the best selection of cheese in the city, offering aged *graviera* from Crete, *mastello* from Chios, and *ladotiri* from Lesvos. Be sure to take advantage of a wine list that features predominantly Greek wines from the Vinifera wine shop next door. Owned by Zoumboulis's brother Panos, it carries a comprehensive selection of vintages from all over the country. The familial collaboration of Gefsis Me Onomasia Proelefsis and Vinifera celebrates the two brothers' love of good food and great wine, which, like all good things, begs to be shared.

NAUTICAL NOSH

13 Jimmy & the Fish

46 Alexandrou Koumoundourou

Mikrolimano in Piraeus is one of the Mediterranean's most charming and picturesque harbours, and is lined with small fishing boats and charming restaurants. Bypass the wily sharks attempting to seduce the uninformed into their touristy tavernas, and head directly for diamond-in-the-rough Jimmy & the Fish. Famous for its lobster-spaghetti-for-two served in the skillet, shrimp flambéed in *ouzo*, and octopus slow-cooked in red wine, the restaurant's long-standing reputation is based on its consistent quality and the freshness of its seafood. The service is impeccable, leaving you free to soak in the atmosphere and watch the sailboats, their multi-coloured flags fluttering in the wind, gliding in and out of the harbour with the island of Aegina visible in the distance. Inside, the wood-panelled décor, accented with nautical antiques, creates a cozy atmosphere in winter, while in summer the seaside deck allows diners the sensation of having set sail for distant shores.

1920S ART DÉCO

14 Ideal

46 Panepistimiou

Return to La Belle Époque at Ideal, one of the oldest restaurants in Athens. A complete renovation in 1990 restored it to the splendour of its heyday in 1922, when it first opened its doors. Designs inspired by the sensuous opulence of the Art Déco period can be seen in the light fixtures, stained-glass ceilings and floral motifs on the walls. Everywhere you look, it is possible to appreciate the efforts that have gone into indulging the senses. The cuisine is classic Greek fare with some of the best *keftedakia* (meatballs) you are ever likely to encounter, made with *ouzo* and cumin, or try the braised lamb shank in a white wine sauce with oregano and feta. Ideal's central location just off Omonia Square makes it a popular meeting place for those nostalgic for ages past.

MICHELIN STAR
15 Varoulko
80 Pireos

With distinctive flair, Lefteris Lazarou, considered by many to be the best chef in Athens, has changed the face of contemporary Greek cuisine at his seafood-only restaurant, Varoulko. The first Greek restaurant to receive a Michelin star, Varoulko has left the backstreets of Piraeus and is now located in Keramikos, the city's revitalized former industrial centre. In the summer when the roof is opened for al fresco dining, tables command magnificent views of the Parthenon. Let the chef surprise you with his tasting menu of unexpected combinations, including black-ink cuttlefish soup with crab and grouper cheeks, a sublime braid of garfish filet in a sauce of Corinthian grapes, and monkfish liver in honey, bay leaf and caramelized raisin vinegar. Dining at Varoulko is a superb culinary experience, best accompanied by a bottle (or two) from the comprehensive wine list featuring regional varieties.

THE TOAST OF RHODES
16 Ta Kioupia
2 Olympionikon and Dexamenis, Politia Square

Ta Kioupia first opened its doors on Rhodes in 1980, serving recipes based upon the traditional cuisine of the island. This Athenian location in Kifissia followed in 1996, and today the restaurant is run by second-generation owner Vangelis Koumbiadis. For the total experience, the tasting menu is a must. Diners can help themselves from the procession of communal platters, or be served by staff offering samples of some thirty different flavours. Savour this gastronomic journey in what feels like a medieval wine cellar, while taking in the views of the city beyond. Menus change with the seasons, but certain dishes remain year round, including *trahana* soup made from rooster and bulgur wheat, and warm aubergine and pine-nut salad assembled at the table. Lamb baked in vine leaves is also a favourite, as are dishes slow-cooked in wood-burning ovens and clay pots (*kioupia*), from which the restaurant takes its name. For dessert, try the famous home-made *kadaifi* ice cream, or *mouhalebi*, a pomegranate-flavoured rice pudding.

drink

ABYSSINIAN NIGHTS
17 Café Avyssinia
7 Kinetou, Avyssinia Square

Wedged in among the antiques dealers in Monastiraki's Avyssinia Square, Café Avyssinia still serves Greek coffee prepared the traditional way in a *hovoli*, baked in hot sand in a copper *briki*. But the word 'café' is deceiving, as Athenians come here for more than coffee; also on offer is national drink *ouzo* and *meze* influenced by owner Ketty Koufonicola's native Thessaloniki (her *taramosalata* is arguably the best in Athens). On weekend afternoons tables are placed outside in the square where Greek ballads are sung to the accompaniment of an accordion.

DANCE BY THE SEASIDE
18 Balux
58 Leof Posidinos

Open to the sea and stars, this popular dance venue attracts a youthful crowd from April to October. It features a swimming pool around which revellers dance to R&B, house, techno, and the occasional 1980s remix spun by guest DJs, who create a high-energy atmosphere that keeps the party going throughout the night. The minimalist décor of this sprawling space incorporates beds enclosed in columns of curtains, while the cocktail bar offers some 200 mixed drinks. By day, the club operates as a private poolside café-bar. Beach bunnies can order a light meal, indulge in a bit of volleyball, or just admire the beautiful people of Athens.

GLAMOROUS BOUZOUKIA
19 Athens Arena
166 Pireos

Sculptor Costas Varotsos turned his hand to architecture and produced this *bouzoukia* nightclub, one of the most glamorous destinations in town. With a total capacity of 4,000, the club uses undulating glass booths to discreetly section off the teeming masses into private parties without interrupting the fluidity of the space. The exterior of the building is designed to resemble a star-lit sky, a poetic allusion to the stars within. Athens Arena is part of larger project Pantheon, an enormous complex that will include other nightclubs, cinemas and restaurants. There will even be a helipad for jet-setters who just wish to drop in for the show.

ISLAND ADVENTURE
20 Island
27th km Leof Athinon-Souniou

Built over different levels, strewn with giant pillows, and decorated with low tables overlooking the sea, this sophisticated destination doesn't disappoint. Billowing curtains ruffle in the gentle night breeze and candles flicker in romantic luxury as bronzed beauties and their statuesque beaux sip cocktails while listening to chill-out house music to the sound of waves gently lapping the shore. Those requiring more than liquid refreshment will find a restaurant offering snacks and Mediterranean cuisine. The ubiquitous Byzantine chapel found on most Greek islands is not absent from this 'island' either, making it a popular site for weddings. This is one place where you are destined to fall in love.

RUM WITH A VIEW
21 Galaxy Bar
Athens Hilton, 46 Vassilissis Sofias

Perched atop the Athens Hilton and overlooking the city below, Galaxy Bar appears to hover at the end of the universe. Plush suede armchairs and black floors embedded with sparkly mirrors add to the glamorous and contemporary atmosphere, as do the pleated paper sculptures by the artist Pavlos. Cocktail aficionados will appreciate the selection of occasionally unusual spirits, from Louis XIII cognac to Zacapa rum, accompanied by caviar, sushi, or a fine cigar from the humidor.

SPEAKEASY SOUL
22 Half Note Jazz Club
17 Trivonianou

Half Note is the city's top jazz club, but also features R&B, funk, and world music from Brazil to Senegal. Located next to First Cemetery in Athens' greenest neighbourhood, the club's atmosphere is reminiscent of the underground bars of the speakeasy era, with soulful serenades echoing across a crowded, smoky setting. While the décor of Half Note is traditional wood and stone, with photographs of the great and good who have graced its stage, the acoustics and lighting are ultra-modern. Open from October to May, with live music nightly, Half Note is always popular and reservations are a must.

IN THE FRAME
23 Frame
1 Dinokratous, Plateia Dexameni

Around the corner from the St George Lycabettus hotel is its casual bar-restaurant, Frame. In cold weather, Athenians come to this retro 1970s space with its funky furniture and psychedelic paintings for food and drink. In the summertime, the action moves across the road to the canopy-covered garden. The wooden deck, enormous chandelier and colourful sofas and pillows, together with the DJ spinning tunes, create a party vibe that is somewhere between revelling and relaxing.

THE BEAUTIFUL PEOPLE
24 Balthazar
27 Veranzerou

This bar-restaurant, a veritable oasis in the Ambelokipi district, seems worlds away from the hustle and bustle of the city. Built in 1902 as the home of wealthy industrialist Alexander Pirris, Balthazar harmoniously blends history with discreet modern touches to create a sophisticated yet relaxed setting. The romantic mansion is abandoned in summer in favour of its inner courtyard, with intimate sofas tucked away among the palm trees and lit by colourful lanterns. Visitors to Balthazar can lounge while sipping Champagne cocktails or glasses of wine from the Peloponnesus, while those in the mood for more hearty fare can sample the deliciously creative Mediterranean menu of chef Yiorgos Tsiaktsiras.

MEDITERRANEAN MENU
25 Prytaneion
37 Kolokotroni, Kefalari Square

In the middle of leafy Kefalari Square, the artsy atmosphere of Prytaneion is hip enough to draw all age groups for coffee and drinks. If you come for a meal, bring an appetite large enough to accommodate the enormous portions of over a hundred Mediterranean-inspired dishes. This lively restaurant is the perfect place in which to escape the summer heat under misting ceiling fans, or to retreat to from the winter cold, surrounded by works by contemporary Greek artists like Bernadaki, Pavlos, Moralis and Gaitis. The service is friendly and attentive without being obtrusive, and the setting is trendy and laid back. Open all day, year round.

shop

This charming shop is part of the Ilias Lalaounis Jewelry Museum, which offers a glimpse into the history of jewelry-making through the designs of master goldsmith Ilias Lalaounis. Located on the site of his father's workshop, the collection comprises over 4,000 pieces of jewelry and miniature sculptures, some of which are reminiscent of the Minoan, Mycenaean and Byzantine eras, while others are inspired by nature, including a 'DNA' series with its molecular motifs and the 'Motion-in-Space' range with its diamond-studded planets. On the ground floor, visitors can experience the methods and materials of the goldsmith up close with a look into his studio, but beware of the gift shop – you may want one of everything.

You will find books on everything from archaeology and philosophy to dictionaries and cookbooks at Eleftheroudakis, Athens' most comprehensive bookstore. Indulge in a serendipitous browse over the seven floors of English- and Greek-language publications, or pick up something for your travels – perhaps the obligatory phrase book to get you in and out of trouble. And what of all the gifts and souvenirs you must take back (if you go back)? At Eleftheroudakis you will find all of these, and more. The top floor also has a very good café sporting a tastefully minimalist décor that serves coffee and snacks. A must for all bibliophiles.

If you happen to be wandering through Kolonaki and notice a crowd longingly eyeing up a window display, you can be sure that the store in question is Kalogirou, Athens' premier shoe emporium. With two locations only a few minutes' walk from each other off Kolonaki Square, window shoppers are easily seduced inside by the covetable labels, from Prada to Ferragamo, Church's to Tod's, to Kalogirou's own line. The shop's location inside a 19th-century neoclassical mansion covers four floors: the ground floor is devoted to handbags and accessories; the first floor to women's dress shoes; and the second to casual sports shoes. A separate entrance leads the men to their own floor for classic styles from brogues to loafers, as well as accessories and travel items. The quality and selection ensure that for many locals 'Kalogirou' is synonymous with 'shoes'.

Lina Fanourakis, one of Athens' most celebrated jewelers, continues the over 140-year-old family tradition of creating by hand exceptional, and highly original, works of art. Drawing inspiration from numerous sources, even nature's humblest creatures are transformed into superbly crafted objets d'art in 18- and 22-karat gold. In one collection of exquisite brooches, shapes are based on such unusual motifs as sea urchins, dragonflies and beetles, while another series, inspired by the Greek countryside, evokes the transient beauty of spring and features poppies in white gold encrusted with rose-cut diamonds. Intricate gold bracelets and rings woven to resemble the pleated and folded fabric of ancient statuary are reminiscent of Mycenean techniques. From lavish and bold to intricate and delicate, there is no homogeneity to Fanourakis's style, but rather an eclectic and enchantingly eccentric approach to design.

The traditional art of making clothes by hand may be slowly dying out with today's frenetic pace and consumer appetites for fleeting fashions, but there are always exceptions to the rule. One of those bucking the trend is Apostolis Hadzilias, who has been hand-tailoring suits with an artist's attention to detail since 1949. Apprenticed at the age of thirteen, Hadzilias has since become a master of his trade, and uses only the finest materials imported from all over Europe. With painstaking precision and exacting standards, he creates suits with an extraordinary fit that you will never tire of wearing.

31 Martinos
BYZANTINE TREASURE
50 Pandrossou

32 Kombologadiko
NO-WORRIES BEADS
9 Amerikis

33 Planet Earth
HATS OFF
7 Ploutarchou

In Monastiraki, famous for its bustling flea markets and antiques dealers, you will find the incomparable Martinos, housed over four floors of what was once the family home. Third-generation Eleni Martinos oversees this treasure trove of Cycladic vases, Roman marble statuary and 17th- and 19th-century Byzantine icons. Many of these items are not allowed to leave the country, but alternative temptations are to be found among the pistols and ornate daggers, repoussé gunpowder boxes in silver, traditional coin necklaces and elaborate Byzantine gold earrings with drops of emeralds, rubies and pearls. Martinos also specializes in Greek and Ottoman embroideries and regional costumes, and 19th-century portraits jostle for space with works by more modern artists, including Lytras, Parthenis and Tsarouchis.

Not to be confused with a rosary, the Greek *komboloy* exists purely for pleasure and contemplation. Although many theories exist regarding its origin, one thing is certain – if you are in the market for one you are sure to find something to suit your taste among the hundreds on display at Kombologadiko. *Komboloys* can be made from a variety of materials, including semi-precious stones, bone, horn, glass and coral, as well as the traditional amber. The size and number of beads also varies, but it is generally agreed that they should be strung on a silk cord, rather than a chain. The friendly staff of Kombologadiko can also customize anything you wish on the premises, where you will find *komboloys* ranging in price from €10 to €10,000. It is worth a stop, if just for the visual delight.

Those with a penchant for original and unusual millinery will be utterly taken with Katerina Karoussos's boutique. Her evocative and extravagant designs are realized in straw, felt, or something on the more exotic side, and shoppers never fail to be charmed by her hand-sewn creations. Suitable for any occasion, there are a myriad of styles to suit any taste and personality. Wide-brimmed hats trimmed with ribbons, lacey turbans and roguish berets are reminiscent of days past, but all bear Planet Earth's trademark contemporary twist, whether a slightly turned-up back or a whimsical asymmetry. Karoussos also makes gloves, bags, belts and shawls in her cozy workshop, where a pleasant afternoon can be whiled away trying on hats to suit your every desire.

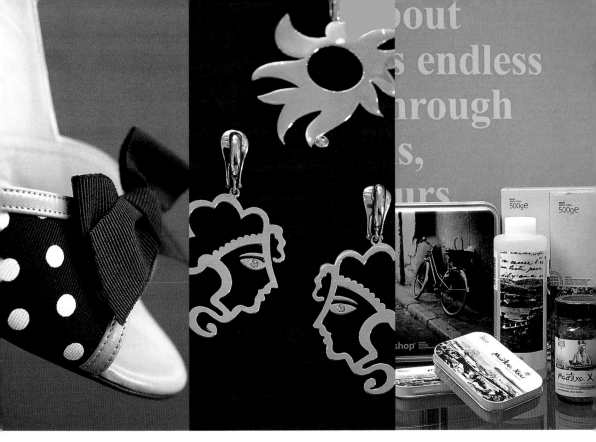

SHOES FOR THE STYLISH
34 Old Athens
1–3 Argiropoulou and Levidou

Vassilis Zoulias has long been known in the world of sartorial chic for wearing many different professional hats, including as fashion editor of Greece's premier women's magazine, *Gineka*, director for some of the country's top designers, and consultant to many more on the international stage. In 2003 he launched a line of shoes and handbags that captivate both the romantically inclined and more independent personalities. Zoulias's style exudes the aristocratic elegance of a bygone era, with enough tailoring to bring it bang up to date. His graceful lines are imbued with a contemporary flair for the unexpected, mixing a variety of fabrics with patterns from sassy tartan and polka dots to sumptuous suede and snakeskin.

POM-POMS AND EVIL EYES
35 Liana Vourakis
42 Pindarou

While Liana Vourakis's designs draw on tradition, they are anything but traditional. Working with such familiar Greek motifs as the national flag, the traditional pom-pom shoes of the *Evzones*, the evil eye, garlic and pomegranates, Vourakis uses a range of materials and colours to transform these themes into decorative household objects, jewelry and good-luck charms with a sophisticated style that is all her own. Although her inspiration draws from traditional sources such as Minoan frescos and 19th-century embroideries, her works take on surprisingly novel forms, from silver butterfly crowns to Limoges ashtrays. Her imitators are numerous, but there is only one Liana Vourakis, whose feel-good lifestyle shop is full of eminently covetable objects.

FROM THE MASTIC TREE
36 Mastiha Shop
6 Panepistimiou and Kriezotou

This unique shop features products made from *mastiha*, the resin from the bark of the mastic tree, which only grows on the Aegean island of Chios, despite efforts to cultivate it elsewhere. Mastiha Shop, near Syntagma Square, offers a range of products based on the resin's culinary, medicinal, therapeutic and cosmetic properties. A line of mastic-flavoured food and drink includes the aperitif *mastiha* (made with honey), *soumada* liqueur (made from almonds), *kaimaki* ice cream, and desserts and biscuits, both savoury and sweet. Health products that purport to prevent and treat such ailments as stomach ulcers, diabetes, and even cancer are available, as are aromatic soaps and face and body creams produced in collaboration with Greek cosmetic company Korres.

see

ENVIRONMENTALLY AWARE
37 Gaia Centre
100 Othonos

The Gaia Centre, the Goulandris Museum of Natural History's (p. 64) new centre for environmental research and education, opened in 2001. Unlike most museums that frown on touching the displays, the centre encourages visitors, particularly children, to interact with the exhibits in order to better understand the problems (and possible solutions) involved in environmental issues. The exhibition begins with displays concerning the Earth's systems and how they function, moving on to an exploration of how humans have utilized its natural resources and suggesting more environmentally friendly ways of doing so. Unique to the museum is the 'Geosphere', with a screen almost two storeys high upon which digital images of the planet are projected, accompanied by music. Images of mankind's achievements are shown, alongside those of war and pollution. This review of history ends by emphasizing the pressing need to modify human behaviour to create a more harmonious relationship between man and nature.

HISTORY LESSON
38 Benaki Museum
1 Koumbari and Vassilissis Sofias

Housed in a neoclassical mansion across from the National Gardens (p. 64), the museum was founded by art collector Antoni Benaki in 1931. Exhibits are organized chronologically, from prehistoric and ancient Greece through to the Roman era and medieval Byzantium. Other floors offer political and cultural glimpses into the country's history, from the fall of Constantinople in 1453 to the formation of the Greek state after the War of Independence (1832). On display are textiles, costumes, weaponry, and two period rooms reconstructed from an Ottoman mansion in northern Greece. After swotting up on your Greek history, venture upstairs to the roof garden for a bite to eat at the first-rate café-restaurant. An ideal place for taking a break from museum-hopping (the Goulandris Museum of Cycladic Art is only a five-minute walk away; p. 64), the café offers a small selection of traditional favourites, including *lahanodolmades avgolemono* (cabbage rolls stuffed with mince and rice, in an egg and lemon sauce). On Thursday evenings when the museum is open until midnight and admission is free, the café offers a special buffet supper.

ANCIENT AMPHITHEATRE
39 Odeon of Herodes Atticus
Dionisou Areopagitou

Herodes Atticus, benefactor and friend of the emperor Hadrian, built the amphitheatre that bears his name on the south slope of the Acropolis in memory of his wife, Aspasia Annia Regilla, in 161 AD. Restored in the 1950s, the theatre is used today for entertainment organized by the annual Athens Festival, and its tiers of Roman arches provide a spectacular backdrop for productions held by opera and ballet companies, orchestras and theatre troupes from around the world. Maria Callas and Luciano Pavarotti (and Sting) are among the singers who have graced the moonlit stage of the 5,000-seat Odeon (also known as the Herodion). Performances take place every evening in the summer.

SEEING RED
40 Athinais
34–36 Kastorias

This converted silk factory in the run-down neighbourhood of Votanikos has been transformed into a multipurpose complex that hosts conferences and art exhibitions, both ancient and modern. It also features a theatre, concert hall and open-air cinema showing film classics. Hungry? The excellent restaurant Red is located here, too, as well as the more casual brasserie Votanikos and Boiler Bar. Originally designed by Thomas Gazetas in the 1920s, the recent renovation, completed in 2000, was overseen by husband-and-wife team Nassos Kokkineas and Marilena Mamidakis. The 6,500-square-metre building's exposed stone, glass and steel elements have been retained to preserve its original industrial style, and to provide an impressive forum for culture, business and entertainment under one roof.

40 Goulandris Museum of Cycladic Art

4 Neofytou Douka

This museum's collection of Cycladic art, spanning the period from 5000 to 2000 BC and donated by Nikoloas and Ekaterini Goulandris, is one of the most comprehensive of its kind in the world. Designed by Ioannis Vikelas, the minimalist marble building is well suited to the aesthetic of the collection, which features the familiar marble figurines whose exquisite simplicity inspired the work of Modigliani. A glass corridor joins it to the 19th-century Stathatos Mansion, designed by Ernst Ziller, which hosts the venue's temporary exhibitions and is one of the best examples of neoclassical architecture in Athens. The museum also has a café and gift shop carrying books, educational games, and items inspired by Cycladic art.

A WALK IN THE PARK

41 National Gardens

Irodou Attikou

Behind the Parliament Building lie the 40 lushly verdant acres of the National Gardens, within which countless unexpected pleasures await discovery. Created at the behest of Queen Amalia in the 1830s, it is one of the most peaceful and enchanting places in the city for a quiet stroll. Winding paths lead past benches with languid lovers, towering palm trees, duck ponds, a small botanical museum, Roman mosaics, a tiny zoo, and statues of such illustrious figures as the philhellene Lord Byron and Greece's national poet, Dionysios Solomos. The gardens' focal point is the impressive Zappeion Exhibition Hall, with its graceful façade framed by Corinthian columns. The building was designed by Danish architect Theophilus Jansen in 1888 with an endowment from the Zappas cousins, whose statues may be seen on either side of the entrance. Aegli, the city's first open-air cinema, is located next door.

ART ENTERPRISE

42 Mihalarias Art

260 Kifissias and Diligianni

The well-known art restorer and dealer Stavros Mihalarias opened his newest gallery in a restored neoclassical building just off Kifissias Avenue, which has been transformed into a multifaceted art space that spans three levels and is hung with museum-quality works for discerning art lovers to admire or acquire. The ground floor hosts exhibitions of contemporary Greek and international artists, while the first floor is reserved for the gallery's permanent collection of painting and sculpture from the late 19th and early 20th centuries, Byzantine icons (some dating from the 16th century), antiquities, and other objets d'art. Those interested in larger works can take a stroll through the sculpture garden outside. For less expensive items, visit the retail space in the basement for limited-edition etchings and miniature sculptures.

STUFFED ANIMALS

43 Goulandris Museum of Natural History

13 Levidou

It is an extraordinary pleasure to linger among the lions and tigers and bears (oh my!) at the Goulandris Museum of Natural History, and see the wide-eyed wonder on children's faces as they roam among the creatures on display. In addition to promoting the preservation, exhibition and study of plants, animals and minerals, the museum, founded in the 1960s by Angelos and Niki Goulandris, also strives to raise public awareness about the environment and the perils it faces. Today the museum's specimens, from all over Greece, number in the hundreds of thousands, and the botanical collection is especially impressive, with over 200,000 species, 145 of of which have been discovered by the museum's own researchers. This remarkable collection is housed in an elegant villa, along with the Anemones coffee shop and a gift shop that sells Hermès scarves and porcelain plates designed by Niki Goulandris, along with the usual museum publications.

PLUMS AND PISTACHIOS

45 Aristokratikon

9 Karagiorgi Servias

Aristokratikon, the city's finest confiserie, has been producing hand-made chocolates and sweets since 1928. Ever faithful to his secret family recipes, George Bitsopoulos has expanded the range over the years to include over 120 temptingly delicious goodies made with nuts or flavoured with fruit, liqueur and cream. In a workshop at the base of Mt Lycabettus, a small team use Greek products such as hand-picked plums from Skopelos, pistachios from Aegina, chestnuts from Pelion, and sour cherries from Tripoli to create sweets that are shipped fresh each day to Aristokratikon's two locations. This sweetshop is a chocoholic's dream, but be sure not to miss the sublime (and addictive) pistachio sticks.

PUPPET SHOW

46 Spathario Museum of Shadow Theatre

Vassilissis Sofias and D. Ralli,
Kastalias Square

This unique museum pays tribute to the history and art of the folk tradition of shadow-puppet theatre. Founded by one of the genre's greatest performers, Eugenios Spatharis, the collection of puppets (made by Spatharis himself) takes the visitor on a journey through the magical world of the popular hero Karagiozis, who has delighted generations of Greeks since he first arrived from the East (where he was known as Karagöz) in the late 19th century. An eternal underdog whose wily ways get him in and out of mischief, Karagiozis, along with a colourful cast of characters drawn from Greek history and mythology, 'reflects the soul and spirit of the people'.

BARCELONA

Barcelona boasts a unique heritage of cultural achievement, political and military independence and artistic refinement. It is a regional rather than national or international capital city like Paris or London, and yet its smaller size seems to crystalize its many attributes into a brilliant urban gem: compact, accessible, coastal, with historic quarters, as well as substantial renovated sections that are tourist-friendly without being blandly commercialized. Much of its newfound popularity has been gained with the high-profile projects completed for the Summer Olympics of 1992. The Olympic stadium and Santiago Calatrava's poetic telecommunications tower exclaiming rather than marring the hillside landscape in Montjuïc were just the beginning. The cleaning up of beaches, the building of the Olympic Village and Port (to designs by Bohigas, Martorell and Mackay) and rehabilitation of Port Vell with the new aquarium, IMAX theatre and connecting walkways, bridges and clusters of restaurants reclaimed and revealed a stunning shoreline for public enjoyment. The programme of improvements continues and brings with it a new artistic and cultural flowering.

Despite the developments around the waterfront, visitors are drawn to the Cuitat Vella, the 'old city' that encompasses the area around the Catedral and the rest of the Barri Gòtic, the Ribera, Barceloneta and the Raval, each with its distinctive feel. The Barri Gòtic is a medieval quarter of narrow passages, studded wood doors, massive low arches and grand stone palaces. The Ribera, too, exudes Gothic enchantment and has the city's first designed street, Carrer de Montcada. The Ribera, once a run-down quarter near the harbour, is today home to the crackling nightlife of El Born. The area known as the Raval, which was for centuries beyond the pale, was claimed first by the monasteries and then by the overflowing population. For generations it was a gritty haven for outsiders; now, it is evolving into an edgy artistic quarter.

From the tiny streets of the Cuitat Vella to the wide Eixample and beyond, it is evident that the city's aesthetic achievement is a serious pursuit. So much so, in fact, that the Royal Institute of British Architects named all of Barcelona worthy of the annual Royal Gold Medal in 1999. Meanwhile, contemporary designers of furniture and fashion have achieved international renown but are the tip of the iceberg in a place where new talent is on show everywhere, from small galleries and showrooms/shops/ateliers to clubwear designers with global followings. New and fantastically designed bars have emerged to cater to the design-conscious youth, and local chefs are challenging the culinary giants of the past to put Catalan cuisine firmly on the gastronomic destination map. This small creative centre, which counts Picasso and Miró (see p. 88) among its best-known cultural exports and which has stood for centuries of independence, exudes a spirit of optimism, modernity and innovation that shines from the depths of the Barri Gòtic to the heights of Tibidabo.

Bonanova

Sant
Gervasi
de Casoles

1, 7, 25

11

15

31

Approximate scale

1 kilometre

1/2 mile

Eixample

5, 10, 14, 22,
28, 36, 37,
40, 41, 49, 50

l'Esquerra
de l'Eixample

54

Sant
Antoni

El
Raval

6, 9, 12, 13,
20, 23, 24,
34, 42, 52

3, 4, 8
18, 26,
33, 38,
46, 47
La
Ribe

16, 32, 48

Catedral

2, 19, 21, 30,
35, 43, 45

Barri
Gòtic

Montjuïc

Barcelo

StyleCity Barcelona

MIAMI CHIC

1 Gran Hotel la Florida

Carretera da Vallvidrera al Tibidabo, 83–89

Rooms from €360

Hotels are relatively good in the city, especially after the industry boom of the last couple of years, but with its stunning views and an eye toward ostentatious comfort, the Gran Hotel la Florida is a gem. This is one of Barcelona's newest hotels, as well as one of its oldest. Gran Hotel la Florida, perched 300 metres above the city in the Tibidabo hills (but only fifteen minutes away from the city centre) is a listed 'Noucentista' building, dating from 1925 and designed by architect Ramón Raventós, the creative mind behind Poble Espanyol (1929). A recent (and impressive) facelift has rescued the original façade, and the hotel has become a haven for those craving a little exclusivity. The fifty-two rooms and twenty-two suites offer spectacular views of the city, the mountains and the valley, and are decorated in pure Art Nouveau style. Each room is fully equipped with all the usual mod cons one would expect from a five-star hotel, and the suites have their own gardens and Jacuzzis on the outdoor terrace. The hotel's restaurant, L'Orangerie, headed up by chef Daniel Bausá, serves a fusion of Catalan and Spanish flavours, including sautéed sea scallops with cucumber sponge and 'gazpacho sauce', and lobster carpaccio with tomato-bread sherbet in a vinaigrette of Arbequina olives, while the Miramar bar offers the ideal setting for a drink overlooking the city. This whimsical hotel seems destined to become one of the hottest destinations in town, adding to its impressive list of services a beauty centre, hairdresser, spa offering Ice treatments, hydrotherapy and a nightclub. Ernest Hemingway, Rock Hudson and Jimmy Stewart are among the past visitors who have experienced the grandeur and luxury of the Gran Hotel la Florida.

2 Hotel Neri
Carrer de Sant Sever, 5
Rooms from €170

Hotel Neri is housed in a tasteful conversion of a petite 18th-century palace into this modern and cozy guesthouse. The hotel couldn't be better situated, resting at the quiet end of a very busy area in the Gothic quarter, near the cathedral and a stone's throw from the city's hot spots and tourist attractions. The eclectic atmosphere and contrasting sensual décor, with its attempts to marry the original austere features of the building with up-to-the-minute stylish details, will delight your senses as soon as you enter the lobby. The fanciful combination of colours on the different floors sets a calming atmosphere, complemented by the fresh scent of acacia and lavender lingering in the air. Some of the twenty-two rooms still have their original 18th-century paintings on the ceilings and furnishings, and the rustic and chunky furniture contrasts with the plasma TVs and Internet facilities. In the lounge are guides to Barcelona and Catalonia and novels by local authors, as well as magazines on travel and design; a private room that seats ten is available for working breakfasts and meetings. Up on the roof, the terrace is a confined deck space with a shower and a few hammocks in which to sunbathe or watch the sunset while enjoying an early drink. The elegant Neri Restaurant, overlooking the Plaça Sant Felip Neri, offers a Mediterranean-cum-Arab cuisine prepared by chef Jordi Ruiz, who has done time at the world-famous El Bulli. There are three different *menú degustacións*, based on the principles of freshness and tradition with a twist in the presentation and treatment. Highly recommended.

3 **Park Hotel**
Avinguda Marquès de l'Argentera, 11
Rooms from €150

Straddling the boundary between the Ribera and Barceloneta, and with the port just a short walk away, the Park Hotel exhibits the air of a seaside resort. The glass block and turquoise tile on the curving corner façade sound the first note of 1950s modern, but there is plenty to follow, including the squared spiral stair, perforated balcony partitions, and the wonderfully retro bar itself. The hotel was originally designed by architect Antoni de Moragas i Gallisá, and it was something of a design statement in its heyday. Like many Barcelona gems, it had a period of neglect but has been undergoing steady refurbishment. While some elements might lack the polish they once had, the design is so genuine and of a piece that it scarcely matters. Abac, the celebrated restaurant downstairs, serves as the hotel breakfast buffet until noon; afterwards the formal restaurant takes over, so be sure to book if you intend to have dinner or lunch there. Rooms retain their 1950s design elements but have been updated with dark wood, brown fabrics and white linen, and those with terraces overlook the Plaça de Palau. Guests here are well placed for sampling the high-end delights of Passadis del Pep (p. 79) and the more traditional Can Solé and Restaurant 7 Portes.

4 Hotel Banys Orientals
Carrer de l'Argentería, 37
Rooms from €100

Although one of Barcelona's newest hotels, it would be difficult to find one better placed for exploring the streets of the old city, or with more stylish facilities. Just around the corner from the historic Carrer de Montcada and metres from the magical Santa Maria del Mar (p. 90), the Hotel Banys Orientals is one of Barcelona's most design-conscious hotels yet at the same time manages to maintain some of the most reasonable tariffs. This kind of hotel would be a treat in any city, but here it really does put you in the heart of things. The public areas and forty-four rooms are all decorated in sleek, minimal style warmed up with dark wood, a few antiques and artworks and some notable design objects, including contemporary four-poster beds and Lucite chairs by Philippe Starck. These are offset by gauzy curtains and crisp white bedlinen. There are no suites, but eleven rooms have small balconies overlooking the narrow, medieval streets. The modern character reflects the confluence of art and design in nearby El Born, but it is much more than a superficial makeover. Such an updated sense of design in such a prime location packed with some of the best eating and shopping Barcelona has to offer sounds too good to be true but, luckily for us, now it isn't.

5 **Hotel Omm**
Carrer del Rosselló, 265
Rooms from €115

This acclaimed hotel venture of the ubiquitous Grupo Tragaluz is the result of the collaboration between architect Juli Capella and interior designers Sandra Tarruella and Isabel López, and is already a very popular choice with tourists and business travellers. Its central location near the shops in Passeig de Gràcia and sense of urban luxury keep up a steady stream of guests and returning devotees, and earned Hotel Omm the top gong for best hotel (seventy-five rooms and under) at the 2005 Travel & Leisure Design Awards in New York. The stylish design is reflected in the modern lobby and cocktail bar, which attracts both guests and locals, and in the contrast between the dark passageways and light and airy rooms (there are fifty-nine in total, spread over six floors), each of which is perfectly equipped with everything a traveller would require, including Internet connections and soundsystems. A key space of the hotel, apart from the magnificent restaurant (Moo and Moo Vida), is the roof terrace, with its swimming pool for post-breakfast dips and sweeping views across the city to Gaudí's Casa Milà and out to sea. Located in the hotel's basement, new hot spot on the Barcelona nightlife scene, the Ommsession club, hosts diverse musical acts and DJ sets Thursday to Saturday until 3:30 a.m.

COZY AS A CAMPER

6 **Casa Camper**
Carrer d'Elisabets, 11
Rooms from €190

The rapid rise of small and cozy hotels in Barcelona reflects the city's booming economy and embracing of a more luxurious lifestyle. One such hotel, Casa Camper, is owned by the company behind the sneakers of the same name, a fact that is reflected in the hotel's design philosophy of functionality and comfort over luxury. Strategically located in the multi-cultural neighbourhood of El Raval (and only steps away from the Museu d'Art Contemporani de Barcelona), Casa Camper sits in a 19th-century building that has been converted into a homey twenty-five-room (and one-suite) hotel, designed by Fernando Amat (the man behind contemporary design store Vinçon) and Jordi Tió. Rather ingeniously, each 'room' is actually two rooms, a bedroom and a lounge, situated across the corridor from one another. The bedrooms are tucked away at the back, away from the street, to ensure maximum comfort and a restful stay. The hotel also provides a 24-hour self-service buffet near the lobby, encouraging guests to make themselves at home and to share the dining area with fellow residents. For a more substantial meal, the groovily unusual FoodBall (p. 77) – another Camper venture – is located next door. For relaxation and contemplation, there is a terrace overlooking the characteristic rooftops of the neighbourhood, and a 'vertical garden' consisting of 117 aspidistras stacked neatly one on top of the other. Oozing simplicity and style, the hotel promotes a healthily slow-paced (and non-smoking) experience for its guests. Casa Camper employs a strict guests-only policy, however, so entrance is not permitted to anyone who's not staying at the hotel. Not even for a cup of herbal tea.

eat

LA VENTA

7 La Venta
Plaça del Doctor Andreu

Sitting prettily on the hillside next to the terminus of the city's last remaining tramline, La Venta is neither the anachronism nor the tourist haunt you might expect. The menu is varied, including standbys like *butifarra* (Catalan sausage), fried squid, grilled monkfish (*rape*), hake (*merluza*) and other fish, as well as the less traditional *lasaña de salmón ah mado* (lasagne with smoked salmon) and hearty game and beef, all prepared to a high standard. Take the Tramvia Blau from Plaça John F. Kennedy; from here you might want to continue uphill on the funicular to take in the view of the city from Tibidabo before returning for a memorable lunch or dinner.

CASUAL CAVA AND TAPAS

8 El Xampanyet
Carrer de Montcada, 22

As the name suggests, this is a place known for its Cava, but just as sparkling wine in Spain does not promote the same degree of pretension as it does in various other countries, neither do the bars that sell the stuff. The colourful tiles, stacked casks hung with novelty bottle-openers, well-worn interior and selection of counter-kept tapas (including anchovies – *anxoves* – with a famously secret sauce) bespeak the informal, comfortable atmosphere for which this family-run operation is well known and well loved. The drinks themselves are just about the best antidotes to anything, including the crowds meandering the Carrer de Montcada.

CLANDESTINELY DELICIOUS

9 Romesco
Carrer de Sant Pau, 28

Step into this popular neighbourhood favourite and don't let the aesthetics – or lack of them – diminish your appetite. Just follow your nose and choose from whatever is listed on the board of daily offerings. Robust and well-seasoned traditional food is the order of the day at Romesco, a secret spot located minutes from the Ramblas. The restaurant might be unusual and basic, but it is a Barcelona experience not to be missed.

INDULGE YOUR SENSES

10 Cinc Sentits
Carrer d'Aribau, 58

Located at the upper end of the Eixample district, this new restaurant has already found its place on the Barcelona dining scene. The secret of success at Cinc Sentits (meaning 'five senses' in Catalan) is superlative attention to detail (and to the diner), combined with an eclectic range of culinary delights. Attentive waiters ask for any possible allergies when taking orders, and the 'surprise' menu is unfailingly wonderful. Less adventurous types can choose from La Carta, or 'light menu', at €22 a head. At nighttime the mood changes and the restaurant becomes a mellow environment in which to enjoy a delightful meal.

LEADING EDGE

11 El Racó d'en Freixa
Carrer de Sant Elíes, 22

Producing his inventive dishes with determined style and grace, Ramón Freixa is becoming one of Barcelona's top chefs. Freixa took over the kitchen in 1997, and by 2001 was named the best national chef by Spain's *Guia Gourmetour*. The menu can be traditional or full of surprises: a starter of cocoa pastry filled with mushrooms, vegetables and chestnuts, with bacon ice cream; a variety of fish baked in aromatic Thai broth; and, to finish, coconut cannelloni with caramel yoghurt, aniseed flan and coconut, corn and curry ice cream. The décor is not quite as adventurous, but who's looking at the walls when there is so much art on the plate?

BALLS OF FUN

12 FoodBall
Carrer d'Elisabets, 9

Located next door to Casa Camper (p. 75), this addition to the organic food scene is hard to miss. With its large windows, unusual tables and abundant Camper logos, FoodBall has a magnetic appeal for both the young and the young at heart. Items on the menu are shaped into 'balls' made from healthy ingredients, and served to you whilst sitting on concrete steps. The experience is rather like eating a snack in a *plaça* or on the stoop of a house and may not be your idea of culinary paradise, but it is definitely worth a try.

13 Casa Leopoldo
FINE OLD-FASHIONED
Carrer Sant Rafael, 24

This legendary favourite has been attracting the crowds since 1929 and is full of old-fashioned Spanish charm, from the authentic *azulejos* (decorative tiles) and wood furniture to the bull-fighting photos on the walls. The menu is robust Catalan fare, with lots of grilled fish, stewed beef and home-made pastries. A particularly interesting specialty of scrambled eggs with prawns and garlic seems to be on everyone's top ten. The homey atmosphere belies a serious approach to cuisine, to which the bill will attest.

14 Fernández
TAPAS AND TEA
Passeig del Gràcia, 116

Art and design play as much of a role at Fernández as does the food itself. The menu features classic Spanish dishes, including crystallized cod with potatoes stuffed with truffle or served in a leek soup, and rice with lobster or squid, and familiar flavours are livened up with magical dressings and spices to surprise the palates of hungry diners. Fernández also offers an extensive variety of exotic teas selected by Sans & Sans Colonial and Mariage Frères. Don't miss the intimate ten-seat dining room available for private occasions.

15 Botafumeíro
HILLSIDE SEAFOOD
Carrer Gran de Gràcia, 81

Large and luxurious Botafumeíro casts its gaze oceanwards with a clear nautical theme and a seafood-based menu showcasing its Galician heritage. You'll find men in suits smoking cigars, couples and groups sipping Champagne, and everyone enjoying platterfuls of oysters, shrimp, clams, squid and mussels, not to mention the baked sea bass, sole in butter with tiny shrimp and grilled hake. This is a formal and pricey establishment that has seen the likes of Bill Clinton and King Juan Carlos of Spain at its tables.

16 Quimet i Quimet
CATALAN SUSHI
Carrer del Poeta Cabanyes, 25

Tapas bar Quimet has a bit of a struggle to keep up with the numbers who crowd in to eat standing up, often without even gaining purchase on counter space. They specialize in cold platters of smoked or cured meats and fish, and yoghurt or tomato, mussel and caviar *tostadas*, as well as marinated fish, beans, olives and chilies, many of which can be purchased in tins from behind the counter. Wash it all down with a cool glass of Cava, which will probably have to be passed over to you by the very friendly regular clientele.

17 Comerç 24
INDUSTRIAL FUSION
Carrer del Comerç, 24

One of the bold new design statements in El Born, Comerç 24 takes its cooking seriously, too. Chef Carlos Abellán produces a 'festival' menu that rivals some of the most innovative cooking in Catalonia today, and has made his own contribution to the trend led by Ferran Adrià (of El Bulli) for small, innovative courses with dishes like asparagus in whipped grapefruit purée and sausage-stuffed squid. Desserts mix sweet and savoury in a nod to the latest revival of traditional Catalan favourites.

18 Passadís del Pep
CHEF KNOWS BEST
Plaça de Palau, 2

Down an anonymous passage off the Plaça de Palau is one of those places that intimidate tourists with their own peculiar way of doing things, namely that they don't hand out menus but start serving up portions of wonderful fare along with glasses of Cava almost as soon as someone takes a seat. Diners are offered a preliminary *pica-pica* plate of ham, mussels and oysters and then a fish or seafood course that depends upon what's fresh that day. A pricey but incomparable way to sample Barcelona dining.

drink

19 Granja Dulcinea
Carrer de Petritxol, 2

One of the most popular 'milk bars' in the area, Dulcinea sits demurely on a picturesque little street off of the Plaça del Pi. A colourful painting of the café at the entrance suggests its charms. The interior is decidedly old-fashioned, but the clientele is a mix of generations. Lining one wall is a mountain mural and behind the bar are picturesque bottles of *Cacaolat*, a chocolate milk drink first introduced in Spain in the 1930s and little changed since then. Settle in and combat the afternoon's low blood sugar in true Barcelona style with a thick hot chocolate and something sweet and doughy to go with it.

CAKES AND ART
20 Escribà
Rambla de les Flors, 83

People are drawn in first by the glittering Modernista façade with its violet and green mosaic, Art Nouveau stained glass and swirling decorative motifs. 'We don't only make cakes, we create illusions' is the motto of this pastrymaking dynasty that has held locals in a sugar-induced thrall since Mateu Serra i Capell opened his bakery on the Gran Via in 1906. Today, Christian Escribà presides over the family empire. His legendary reputation as a pastry chef has led him to open his own 'showroom', which clients can visit in order to choose the perfect tart, cake or pastry for special occasions. (Phone for an appointment if you're intrigued.) This historic building on the Ramblas, with interiors to match the fantastical façade, also has a tearoom where lesser mortals can enjoy a cup of coffee, chocolate or tea and some of Escribà's more accessible confectionery thrills. They also sell their own brand of chocolate and Cava. You can also savour the Escribà pastry experience at their beachfront seafood restaurant, Xiringuito Escribà.

COOL FOR CATS
21 Els Quatre Gats
Carrer de Montsió, 3 bis

Located in the Casa Martí designed by Modernista architect Josep Puig i Cadafalch, Els Quatre Gats would be a landmark without its storied past, but the combination of both has made it one of Barcelona's most famous restaurants. Opened in 1897 by Pere Romeu, who modelled it after Le Chat Noir in Paris, Els Quatre Gats was immediately patronized by some of the most important artists of the period, including Ramón Casas, who helped finance it, and Picasso, who held one of his early exhibitions here and allowed Romeu to use one of his designs for the menu cover. The place closed because of debts in 1903, and suffered a less than dignified existence until the late 1970s. In 1989 the building was restored and the restaurant began to retrieve some of its former bohemian glory. Today it overflows with character, artistic ambience and a good deal of bonhomie.

COCKTAILS WITH GAUDÍ
22 La Pedrera at Night
Passeig de Gràcia, 92

Should you be visiting Barcelona in the summer months, you will discover that many places have extended hours and special terrace openings. One of the exceptional outdoor drinking experiences to be had in the city is on top of Gaudí's recently reopened Casa Milà. The fanciful ventilation shafts, the irregular up-and-down pathways and eccentric little archways that make Gaudí's rooftop space a surreal wonderland become an incredibly atmospheric backdrop for cocktails on weekend evenings. Drinkers can sit and admire the architecture, gaze out toward the Sagrada Familia or down over the grand axis of Passeig de Gràcia and Carrer de Provença, or wave to fellow barflies on the roof terrace of the Hotel Condes de Barcelona. But do be warned that the steps can be hazardous after too many cocktails.

DRINKS SINCE 1860
23 Casa Almirall
Carrer de Joaquín Costa, 33

The signage is a little patchy, but the Art Nouveau interior is still pretty much intact, complete with sweeping woodwork carved with vegetal and floral motifs, and goddess torchères. The street was until recently considered seedy, but since the installation of MACBA (Museu d'Art Contemporani de Barcelona) brought a surge of creative energy to this part of the Raval, the bar, opened in 1860, is finding a new generation of clients. But like many old Barcelona spots, Casa Almirall has always had a dedicated following and its appeal is a genuinely well-worn though inspired atmosphere.

DANCE HALL DAYS
24 La Paloma
Carrer del Tigre, 27

A giant-sized yellow frontage with red shutters and a large dove made of fairy lights is the sign for this early 1900s dance hall, which retains its baroque ornament as well as its devotees. From 6 to 9.30 in the evenings Thursday to Saturday it's all ballroom, with a live orchestra playing classic dance numbers for the middle-aged and older crowd. Then it closes its polite doors and re-opens as a DJ club. On Thursdays it's presided over by DJ-duo the Dope brothers (De Lippo and Professor Angel Dust), who play funk, house and Afro-Latino. A dance-hall experience for all generations and tastes.

ABOVE THE FRAY
25 La Balsa
Carrer Infanta Isabel, 4

This wonderfully remote and secluded bower of a restaurant, on a steep hillside in a quiet residential street of Bonanova, was the creation of Oscar Tusquets and Lluís Clotet and won a prestigious design prize in 1979. The entrance is almost hidden in the vegetation, but a little gravel drive leads to an iron gate with an ant motif and next to it a small wall plaque bearing the name. Inside the courtyard, stairs lead up to the main restaurant level, a conservatory space filled with plants inside and an outdoor terrace also surrounded in greenery. The setting alone is worth a trip, but the menu holds up as well. Described as 'international cuisine', the food is happily Spanish- and Catalan-based. Starters include *escudella de pagès* (peasant stew) and *crema de berros con huevo poche* (watercress soup with poached egg). *Croquetas des pescado y gambas con salsa estragón* (fish and shrimp croquettes in tarragon sauce), a stew of blood sausage (*morcilla*), *chorizo* and garbanzo beans or hake (*merluza*) in cuttlefish sauce are stars among the meat and fish dishes, which are joined by daily specials.

26 La Vinya del Senyor
Plaça de Santa Maria, 5

With an angled view of Santa Maria del Mar (p. 90), La Vinya del Senyor is a tiny, pleasant wine bar with relaxed attitude under the management of Ramón Parellada (of the nearby Senyor Parellada). Tucked away across the Plaça de Santa Maria, it's not an obvious tourist haunt, but is near enough to the centre to duck into for a taste of something special during a walk around the old city. A good and varied selection of around 300 native and imported wines, including Cava and Jerez, is served at the counter or at tables upstairs or down or on the ample outdoor terrace.

PARTY CENTRAL
27 Passeig del Born
- Pitín Bar, no. 34
- Plastic Bar, no. 19
- Borneo, Carrer del Rec, 49
- Gimlet, Carrer del Rec, 24

Opposite the bright and modern Sandwich & Friends on the corner of Antic St Joan is Pitín Bar, a well-established resident on this newly trendy block. This is definitely a nighttime prospect, a small glassed-in corner space with shiny surfaces that fills up quickly and is usually packed after 11 or 12 at night. It has been around in some form since 1957, and despite the trendy feel still sells its specialty, *pitin*, a tea prepared in the same way as cappuccino with steamed milk instead of the poured stuff. A little way along the Passeig del Born, on your right you will notice the orange glow emanating from the tunnel-shaped space before you see the sign for the Plastic Bar. Retro yellow-green patterns and hanging silver stars and baubles reminiscent of Sputnik lamps are set off by the underlit orange (plastic) bar that makes everybody's drinks look like space juice but is still weirdly attractive. You'll no doubt be drawn into one or two of the many other haunts on this drinker's paradise of a street, but you'll want to explore the nearby Carrer del Rec, at the northern end of Passeig del Born, as well. The large-scale construction sites don't look very inviting, but this is the general state of things in an area that continues to up and come, and around the worksites the profusion of shops and bars continues unabated. Two of the more worthwhile drinking spots are Borneo, suffused with a groovy, world music vibe and friendly staff – sometimes you can't tell who's who as it all seems so relaxed. Gimlet, the original cocktail bar on the scene, pays homage to the classic New York bar of the 1940s, which must have something to do with the suit-clad barman, the well-dressed clients, and the jazz classics simmering over the hum of conversation. It's a seductive narrow wood-panelled space, and the bar itself is a substantial piece of warm, cherry-coloured wood, something you can lean against with confidence. They do serve gimlets, shaken, not stirred, and pretty much on the mark.

MODERN WINE AND TAPAS
28 Cata 1.81
Carrer de València, 181

They advertise 'vins, *platillos* and whisky', but the clean, modern interior suggests that this is no ordinary tapas and wine bar. It is in fact a new haven for oenophiles with mini gastronomic surprises. There are more than 250 wines on offer by the bottle, with an emphasis on Spanish varieties, and a list of twenty-five by the glass that changes every fifteen days. The small portions of contemporary Catalan cuisine are produced by chef Terésa Olivella, who also creates mini-hamburgers that have become, rather incongruously, a Cata 1.81 trademark. Space is very limited, so be there early.

FRESH AND FRIENDLY
29 Tèxtil Café
Museu de Tèxtil i Indumentària,
Carrer de Montcada, 12

The little café in the restored courtyard of the Palau dels Marquesos de Lliió, home to the Museu Tèxtil, is a modern little place serving coffee and tea and sandwiches, as well as café-menu meals and wine for lunch and dinner. The stone vaults of the ground floor and cobbled courtyard are offset with glass and works of art. The place manages to catch the energetic atmosphere of the popular area for visitors without being the least bit bland or common.

30 Bar Bodega Teo
Carrer d'Ataulf, 18

A *bodega* that dates from 1951, Bar Bodega Teo has benefited from a recent facelift that has freshened the décor and modernized the bar fixtures. But the old-fashioned vibe exemplified by the traditional wine list is still in the air. The interior features brick walls and stylish furniture that bring a cozy and welcoming feel to this tiny space. Bar Bodega Teo is located in a hard-to-find street, but the varieties of wine waiting for you at the end of your search are worth the hunt. Selections of tapas are available to accompany your glass, as are fresh juices for the less alcoholically inclined. Those of an arty disposition can view exhibitions presented monthly by El Corredor del Arte.

CLEAN, WELL-LIGHTED PLACE
31 Cafè Salambó
Carrer de Torrijos, 51

Towards the end of the day, the children go home and the promenading types meander from the Carrer d'Asturies and down the Torrijos, which is lined with interesting shops and cafés, of which café-bar Salambó has to be one of the most appealing in the Gràcia area. The ground floor is an inviting space with scrolled iroko wood benches attracting those who come to read and those who come to sip and talk. Upstairs are more tables and another bar serving good snacks, tapas, wine and hot drinks.

MEMBERS-ONLY WAREHOUSE
32 Mau Mau
Carrer Fontrodona, 33

Become a member of this converted warehouse-turned-lounge-club by asking at the door. Enter through the metal doors that lead to a spacious basement bathed in warm red tones, creating a relaxed subterranean environment in which to spend the evening. The dedicated team behind the venue have a soft spot for funk, hip hop and beats, and their in-house DJs share residency with the Apolo Club, one of the big names of Barcelona's nightlife, located only a few blocks away in the Carrer Nou de la Rambla. Mau Mau is also a good place to finish off the weekend as they often show films, shorts and video art on Sunday afternoons.

shop

FASHION ON THE EDGE
33 Lobby
Carrer de la Ribera, 5

Lobby is Barcelona's response to such achingly trendy places as Colette (p. 241) in Paris, but the difference is that you won't have to suffer long queues or outrageous prices, and the staff and laid-back atmosphere are congenially welcoming. Two large floors conceived by industrial designer Toni Pallejá carry the latest in design, fashion, accessories, books and specialty foods, and all sorts of other objects that make perfect gifts for those who love exclusivity with a little eccentricity.

THE CUTTING EDGE
34 Comité
Carrer del Notariat, 8

Comité presents the designs of up-and-coming talent in a collection of unique and original pieces that are produced and sold on the premises. The imaginative styles of each of the designers who share this shop and atelier (Julia Pelletier, Cecilia Sörensen, Roope Alho, Lucia Blanco, Pia Kahila and Ladies & Gentlemen) add a personal approach to the local fashion circuit, also evident in the accessory range. Set in an intimate environment, decorated with cozy vintage furniture, this shop promotes the fun side of fashion. Comité also has a corner dedicated to books, comics, artwork and music (Ideal Label), and often organizes cultural events.

STREET FASHION
35 Carrer d'Avinyó
- [Z]INK, no. 14
- Sita Murt, no. 18
- So_Da, no. 24

One of the brothels formerly on this street was supposedly the setting for Picasso's *Les Demoiselles d'Avignon*. Now Carrer d'Avinyó is better known for girls (and boys) of a slightly more style-conscious persuasion. [Z]INK is full of vintage Levis and Adidas trainers, but the overall flavour of the selection is pure Barcelona. Sita Murt is a truly avant-garde space made to look like an ancient cave, with giant tubular lighting puncturing the stony surfaces and carrying designs by Esteve, Cultura, Antik Batik, Save the Queen and Pianura, as well as its own label. A particularly Barcelona hybrid creation is So_Da, which during the day is a selec-

tive boutique featuring mostly clothes by international streetwear designers – Miss Sixty, Boxfresh, Pauric Sweeney, Yohji Yamamoto – all displayed in roll-away cabinets. In the evening, the cabinets are moved aside to give access to the bar in the back, and the whole place is bathed in a seductive red glow. These are a few of Avinyó's temptations, so leave yourself plenty of time to sample.

AVANT-GARDE DESIGN OUTLET
36 Hipòtesi
Rambla de Catalunya, 105

Designed in 1997 by Pilar Vila, the cool, ordered space somewhat anonymously in the far reaches of the Eixample shows off some of Barcelona's most talented new designers in jewelry, textiles, ceramics and other artisanal crafts. The minimal, concrete interior is a calm backdrop for the highest-quality one-off and limited-edition pieces by Spanish and international designers as well. An intimate and accessible forum, Hipòtesi is known for leading the way in new design and regularly hosts exhibitions of work by makers from around the world.

WE SHOULD ALL HAVE THEM
37 Bad Habits
Carrer de València, 261

Mireya Ruiz, one of the city's most acclaimed designers, started out selling second-hand clothes (many of which she found in markets in Amsterdam and London) in the Plaça del Sol, but soon began adding her own touches. Now she carries her own original creations, which have garnered her appreciation in the fashion press and the confidence of other Spanish designers whose clothing she also sells in her ultra-modern shop. Her collection features experiments with texture and form, from edgy street designs to close-fitting, sexy ensembles in a mixture of natural and new fabrics.

OENOPHILE'S DELIGHT
38 Vila Viniteca
Carrer dels Agullers, 7

This is a serious wine lover's paradise. With over 3,000 wines and liqueurs, including some fantastic unexported discoveries from the Catalan region, Vila Viniteca is where many city-dwellers (including some of the better restaurants) go to source bottles of

quality. The staff are very knowledgeable and helpful, and some of them can explain the Spanish regions and varieties in English. Of particular note among the walls and cellars of stock, especially for visitors, are wines from the tiny, emerging Catalonian region Priorat, which produces very high-quality reds. Try a bottle of Les Terrasses for a start.

ROASTED DELIGHTS
39 E&A Gispert
Carrer dels Sombrerers, 23

From the quaint wood-fronted shop to the wooden barrels full of roasted nuts and coffee, E&A Gispert is a delight for the senses. What began in 1851 as a small family business, started by Josep Gispert with his sons Enric and Alfons, today continues the tradition of roasting and drying fruits, nuts and coffee on the premises in what is reputedly the only Roman-style log oven still in use in Europe. In addition, the store has expanded the range of natural products from around Spain, including chocolate, honey, olive oil, fruit and vegetable preserves, and regional sweets such as the popular *Alicante*, which resembles almonds in nougat. Awarded the Coq d'Or by Les Gourmands Associés of France in 1999, E&A Gispert really is a unique Barcelona delicacy.

EXOTIC CHOCOLATES
40 Cacao Sampaka
Carrer del Consell de Cent, 292

From a cream-topped *suizo* to a chocolate dessert that features savoury seasonings, chocolate is a gastronomic staple in Barcelona. Cacao Sampaka offers a journey through the history and culture of chocolate around the world. And lest this prove too abstract for the munching public, the store made itself welcome with the inauguration of a new springtime tradition: on 21 March they bring out a chocolate egg weighing 400 kilos and invite members of the public to help hack it into bite-sized bits. But this is only a prelude to what is inside: chocolates in flavours you would never have imagined or dreamed of enjoying, along with truffles, liqueur-filled chocolates, biscuits and solid bars in a variety of densities. The beautifully spare shop interior designed by Antoni Arola features a café in the back where you can sample chocolate drinks and gourmet pastries.

FASHION FAVOURITE
41 Antonio Miró
Carrer del Consell de Cent, 349

An established name in the Spanish fashion world, Miró opened the store Groc in 1968 to sell his own designs. Now Groc sells an array of Spanish and international designers, while Miró has his own outlets, including Miró Jeans. He has licensed designs under Muxart shoes and designed the national team uniforms for the 1992 Barcelona Olympics, as well as the interiors for the minimal Hotel Miró. His clothes are sold worldwide, but this shop designed with Pilar Líbano houses the full range of his new collections.

BOOKS AND JAZZ
42 La Central
Carrer d'Elisabets, 6

Find hours of entertainment in this spacious and quiet bookshop – probably the best in town – in the heart of El Raval. Leaf through the wide selection of humanities, art, design and music publications to your heart's content, and if you can't find what you're after, staff here will be happy to search it out or order it for you. Shoppers can have a seat in the coffee bar and enjoy a snack in the intellectual surroundings. La Central also has a good selection of contemporary jazz and classical music CDs located near the bar.

HERBS OF LIFE
43 Herboristeria del Rei
Carrer del Vidre, 1

A little boutique just off of Plaça Reial, Herboristeria del Rei opened in 1823 and gained the patronage of Isabella II. The old-fashioned corner premises continue to stock a cornucopia of medicinal plants, spices and teas, as well as varieties of honey. The interior is remarkably quaint, although the fountain and little bath, once used – according to legend – for leeches, might provoke a shiver. Look out for packets of saffron tucked into decorative glass jars, which make ideal gifts.

MUSIC AND PASSION

44 Iguapop Gallery & Shop
Carrer del Comerç, 15

RENEWED RETRO

45 Gotham
Carrer de Cervantes, 7

CATALAN PRIDE

46 Orígens 99.9%
Carrer de la Vidrieria, 6–8

If you want to know what's happening in town, pay a visit to this art factory in El Born, backed by national music label Iguapop. The mission of this open-plan space is to bring the latest urban brands to Barcelona and to develop innovative projects that would bridge the gap between art, fashion and music. The shop features exclusive and hard-to-find pieces by Kim Jones, Adidas (p. 109), Sessun and SealKay, along with artist Jordi Labanda's first clothing venture. The venue also occasionally hosts music events.

Gotham, one of Barcelona's top spots for modern design, is a favourite with stylists, film directors and collectors. Concentrating on furnishings and lighting from the 1930s, '50s, '60s and '70s, they carry mostly reproductions of classic designs. Among the most popular items are pieces of 1950s Spanish cabinetry, which they spruce up with vibrant colours. Perhaps because they specialize in reproductions, there is a lighthearted and slightly whimsical air here, a pleasant contrast to the often overly serious world of collecting.

This is a 99.9 per cent Catalonian space (the 0.1 per cent refers to the usual beverage brands), a tapas restaurant and delicatessen selling regional goods, crusading to promote Catalan cuisine. While waiting to be seated, browse through the selection of fine cheeses, olive oils and anchovies for sale, or taste a glass of the local Cava. Once at your table tuck into a selection of vegetarian delights served as either tapas or main courses. But be warned that the restaurant is only open for lunch.

see

The architects behind the Scottish Parliament building, Enric Miralles and Benedetta Tagliabue, provided the creative vision behind this reinterpretation of the 19th-century Mercat de Santa Caterina. The building, with its spectacular roof of over 320,000 brightly coloured tiles, has created a focal point for the much-needed urban regeneration of the Ciutat Vella neighbourhood. Sadly, Miralles died in 2000 before the complex was completed; his many fans wait to see if his spirit will live on in this long-running project.

Bounded by the Jardins de la Ribal on one side and the Teatre Grec on the other, Fundació Joan Miró is also close to the funicular station that brings you up the mountain the easy way. A native of Barcelona, Miró developed the idea of a foundation to receive his works, and those of other artists, with architect Josep Lluís Sert. Sert created the striking white building in 1975, using a highly modern design for exhibitions with plenty of clean white space and natural light. An extension was added by Jaume Freixa in 1986.

Casa Batlló, designed by Antoni Gaudí with Josep Jujol and completed in 1907, demonstrates Gaudí's unique contribution to the Modernista movement. Actually a remodel of an existing building (1877) for a distinguished textile producing family, Gaudí has given free reign to the organic forms that would later distinguish Casa Milà. The Batlló's protruding bays, coloured mosaics and stained-glass windows add elements of sheer fantasy, adamantly defying the gravity, uniformity and dullness of the urban landscape.

50 Fundació Antoni Tàpies
Carrer d'Aragó, 255

Catalan painter Antoni Tàpies was initially attracted to the surrealism of the
Dau al Set group, but later branched out
to make a name for himself with his
abstract forms in paint and mixed
media. His foundation is housed in an
1885 Modernista structure originally
designed by Domènech i Montaner for
a publishing company, its brick and
iron enlivened with Moorish decoration and Tàpies's own *Núvol i Cadira*
metal sculpture. The loft-like space was
remodelled by Lluís Domènech Girbau
and Roser Amadó in 1989.

51 Parc Güell
Carrer d'Olot

Declared a world heritage site in 1984,
the Parc Güell (1900–14) was Gaudi's
most ambitious project, after the
Sagrada Familia. It remains the largest
in terms of area, covering a 20-hectare
site and encompassing gatehouses,
fountains, arcaded and elevated walkways, planters and terraces. The grandest feature is the neoclassical hypostyle
hall, which is at the top of a grand staircase watched over by a giant colourful
salamander. Gaudi intended the hall for
use as a shelter for local market stall-
holders. Everywhere the curving sur-

faces are clad in vibrant mosaics made
from ceramic *trencadis* (jigsaw pieces),
and symbols from Catalan history are
woven throughout. Gaudi's patron,
Eusebi Güell, had envisioned the park
as an English-style, green space that
would be used by the residents of an
élite housing development he planned
to build. Part of the enduring appeal
lies in the fact that the architect
insisted on working with the existing,
undulating landscape, so the elements
rise up on hillsides and are overlooked
at different levels. The houses were
never built, but the park in all its ideal-
ism remains a wondrous product of creative genius given free, subsidized rein.

52 Mercat de la Boqueria Sant Josep

La Rambla, 85–89
• La Maseria de la Boqueria, La Rambla, 91
• Pinotxo, La Boqueria, 66

There has been a market here for centuries. As the city grew the market stayed roughly where it had always been, but a scheme was enacted to create a structure in the grounds of the old convent of the Carmelites of Sant Josep. So the ramshackle collection of stalls was organized in a porticoed square (1836–40), which was never completely finished but covered over in 1860. Today it is still the best place to buy fresh produce in Barcelona. It's crowded and noisy but clean, well organized and bountiful, with rows of stalls filled with all manner of goods. Though you may not need many provisions for a short stay in the city, have a stroll through La Boqueria anyway and choose some Catalan treats for a picnic or country outing: fruits and vegetables, meats, cheeses, baked goods, wine. La Maseria de la Boqueria at the very back of the market specializes in cured and smoked meats; elsewhere, you'll find dried fruits and sweets stands, even a chemist's, and a few tapas bars in case you need to fortify yourself for more shopping. Of these, Pinotxo is the best bet with fine food that includes a house specialty of oysters with Cava. It's open from 6 a.m., so you can have a snack before setting out on the day's adventure.

53 Església Santa Maria del Mar

Plaça de Santa Maria, 1

Despite the absence of a multitude of spires and fretwork, Santa Maria del Mar bespeaks grandeur as if the vaulted space has opened up to the world beyond. It's a fortunate oddity of church architecture that it can amplify space even while enclosing it. Completed in 1383, the church, with its hulking columns supporting ribbon-like ribbed vaulting, is a prime example of Catalan Gothic. The fact that its Baroque decoration was largely destroyed during the Civil War little diminishes the impact of its soaring interior, lit by stained-glass windows, or the sense of awe.

54 Pavelló Barcelona

Avinguda del Marquès de Comillas

Probably one of the most influential buildings of the 20th century, Mies van der Rohe's pavilion designed for the Barcelona Exhibition of 1929 was a harbinger of the Modern movement, with its pristine intersecting planes and focus on materials and surfaces over ornament. Rectangles of glass and marble articulate space without enclosing it, much as the roof projects well beyond the walls so that the whole concept of house building is exploded, or, rather, elegantly reformed. Reflecting pools continue the play of geometry and surfaces in an eloquent justification of 'less is more'.

St JOSEP
LA BOQUERIA

BERLIN

Among the great European capitals, Berlin stands apart in its embodiment of an exhilarating, inspiring and often chaotic Central European history and culture. It is a city of extremes, in which, over the past two centuries, arts, culture and world politics have merged as a unique urban construct. Its erratic development through phases of accelerated intellectual and cultural growth, alternating with plateaus of consolidating creativity, is crucial to the metropolis's socio-political shaping and provides a bridge of understanding over the German–Slav divide.

Once a tranquil medieval 'double' city consisting of Berlin and Cölln, Berlin became the seat of the powerful Hohenzollern family in the 15th century and later the capital of Prussia, a kingdom with a legendary royal lineage leading to Frederick the Great. Occupied by Napoleon's army from 1806 to 1808, the city became the capital of the German Reich in 1871, played host to Germany's development into an industrialized and militarized country under Bismarck, experienced the First World War, lived the 'Golden 1920s', endured the financial crash in the Weimar Republic, witnessed the rise and defeat of the Nazis and the destruction of an entire nation in 1945, was cleaved in two in 1961, and finally reunified when the infamous Wall came down in 1989 and the German government was restored. Today the city is one of the most exciting places in Europe, a global player and a cultural force to be reckoned with.

Through centuries of resisting new orders and regimes, Berlin has reacted with a subversive and often harsh irony, establishing a *Weltanschauung* that teeters between ideology and pragmatism. Nowhere else in Europe can such contradictory intellectual, cultural and political tensions be felt and experienced so vividly or have given rise to such a rich variety of urban life, generated not just by the affairs of state but by the assimilation of countless artistic enterprises and scientific discoveries. The political changes of 1989 led to an enormous enterprise: the physical and social reunification of more than 3.5 million people, divided by a wall but united by a complex and tumultuous history. New urban areas, such as Potsdamer Platz or the government district, are reminders of Berlin's unceasing commitment to rehabilitating itself and to healing the wounds of repeated incursions and depredations. Visitors experience a genuinely fresh urban perspective, made tangible in ambitious architectural projects that rival those of other great cities. Yet Berlin's essential beauty lies in its secluded ambience, palpable, perhaps, in its desire to preserve a slower, more intellectual lifestyle. The condition of a more secluded European metropolis away from the mainstream tourists', politicians' and financiers' tracks has in turn given birth to new attitudes towards design, architecture and lifestyle that permeate the many layers – some more apparent than others – of this unforgettable city.

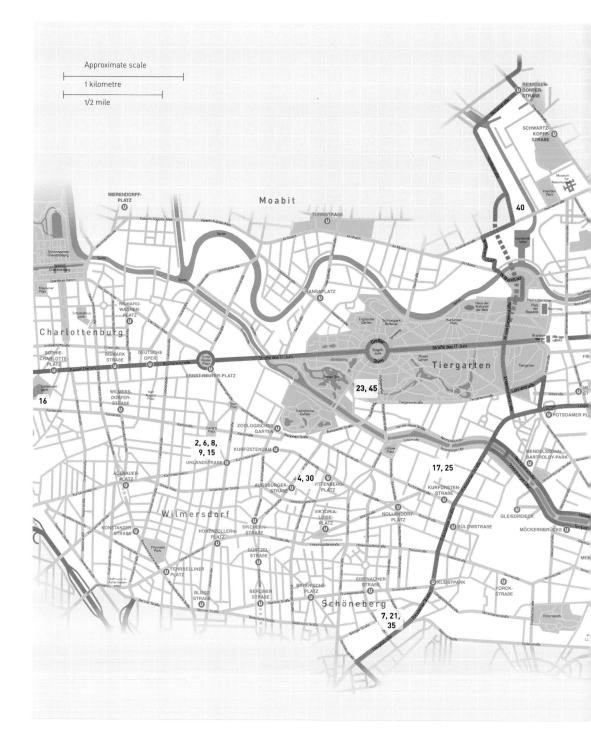

StyleCity Berlin

sleep

1 **Hotel Adlon Kempinski**
Unter den Linden 77
Rooms from €370

Hotel Adlon's story is the stuff of legend. At its inauguration in 1907, Kaiser Wilhelm II decreed that no guest should be allowed to enter the hotel before him and paid a handsome annual retainer of DM150,000 to secure his needs there. The place soon became the unofficial guesthouse for diplomats and a pied-à-terre for the local aristocracy. Its services – hot running water, gas, electricity and a refrigeration system – marked it as the ultimate in luxury at the time and attracted other famous guests, including Albert Einstein, Charlie Chaplin and Greta Garbo, who whispered 'I want to be alone' while filming *Grand Hotel*, which was based on the Hotel Adlon. In 1921 founder Lorenz Adlon's son Louis took over the management, and in time the hotel became known as Berlin's 'Little Switzerland' due to its ability to maintain a neutral international ambience despite the political climate.

Even Hitler once dined there. It was used as a hospital during the Second World War, during which it went untouched until 1945 when an internal fire razed all but one wing to the ground. With the Adlon representing capitalist decadence at its most extreme, the Communist regime converted it into a hostel for apprentices. When the Wall fell in 1989, rebuilding was a sign of optimistic times, and in 1997 the reborn hotel was declared open by Federal President Roman Herzog. So famous is the hotel that books have paid tribute to it, as well as a film, *The Heyday of Hotel Adlon*, directed by Percy Adlon (he also directed *Baghdad Café*). Both George Bushes and the Dalai Lama have been guests of the hotel, which boasts 336 rooms, two restaurants, a spa, two winter gardens, conference facilities and two presidential suites.

Open since 2004, Q! is the brainchild of Wolfgang Loock, who commissioned Berlin- and Los Angeles-based architects Graft to design a building that explored space and the formulaic use of structure in an innovative and practical way. The result is a high-design interior whose multifaceted surfaces help redefine the hotel room; walls are curved to double as pieces of furniture and baths and beds are inherently part of each room's architecture. Thomas Willemeit, Lars Krückeberg and Wolfram Putz, who had collaborated with Brad Pitt on a studio and guesthouse for the actor, wanted to create a sense of curvaceous comfort in the cocoon-like rooms. The colours of Q! suit Berlin; warm tones of red cover the walls and floors of the bar area and are exotically complemented by imitation ostrich leather and balanced by slate and dark wood. Loock took the concept of the private member's bar, so popular in London and New York, and reproduced it in Q!'s own watering hole. He imported Ben Reed, an ex-manager of London's successfully select Met Bar (part of the Metropolitan Hotel) to concoct the drinks list. Food is available, and a rotation of DJs provide the aural backdrop. Underneath the rooms and party central is a subterranean wellness centre. The Sandraum's unique selling point is hot sand floors with a room temperature permanently set to body temperature, which promises to boost the immune system of those who spend time there. Add the Japanese washing zone, which doubles as hammam, and Q! pushes the limits of the design hotel to new boundaries.

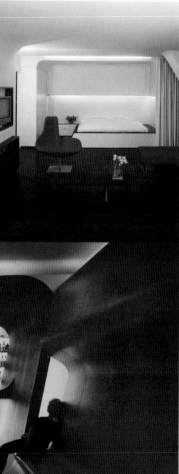

3 **Dorint am Gendarmenmarkt**
Charlottenstraße 50–52
Rooms from €240

The challenge for Harald Klein and Bert Haller, the duo from Mönchengladbach behind the Dorint's high-concept look, was to create a contemporary 'design hotel' on what must be Berlin's most stunning baroque square. The cobbled Gendarmenmarkt is the site of two cathedrals, the Französischer Dom (home to the Huguenot Museum) and the Deutscher Dom, both built by Carl von Gontard for Frederick II during the 1780s as copies of Santa Maria in Montesanto and Santa Maria dei Miracoli in Rome. The views from the guestroom windows onto the square are magnificent. Klein and Haller experimented with lighting effects to create an ambience that would feel cool and inviting, while respecting the rich architectural environs. The Delphinium conference room, for example, is illuminated with glowing floor tiles and sleek chandeliers, creating a futuristic aesthetic. All ninety-two rooms and suites have sliding-glass walls, which allow for adjustment of space and light in the marble-floored bathrooms. The top two floors house a quirky gym and a wellness spa on a decked balcony. The effects of sauna, steam room and plunge pool are enhanced by a relaxation area that boasts reclining chairs, each equipped with a personal stereo.

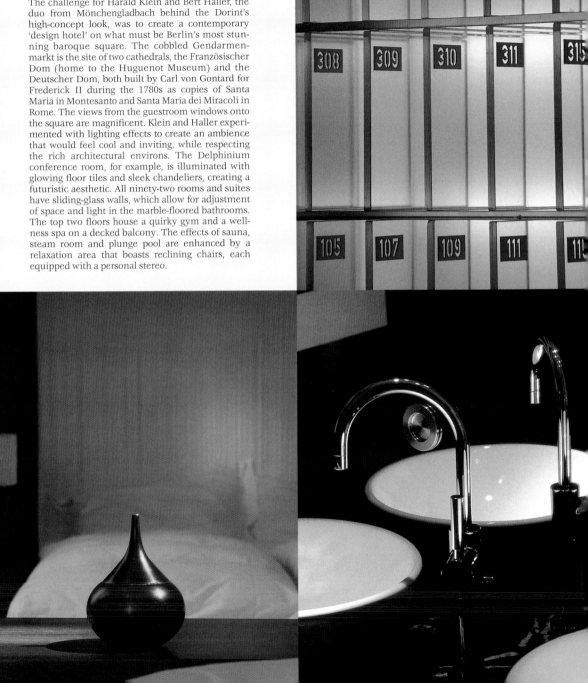

4 Hotel Brandenburger Hof
Eislebener Straße 14
Rooms from €250

A grand façade conceals both the building's former life as an apartment block and the intimate hotel within. Located on a quiet residential street, Hotel Brandenburger Hof was transformed in 1991 into one of the most discreet hotels in the city. Owner Daniela Sauter employed her brother, architect Peter Sauter, to revamp the flats into an eighty-two-room hotel with a formal restaurant, piano bar, library and wellness spa. Together with architect Kenji Tsuchiya, Sauter achieved a sophisticated fusion of modern European design enhanced by traditional Eastern colours and style. One of the hotel's unexpected delights, the Zen-inspired *Wintergarten*, is also the breakfast room and offers an irresistible *Birchermuesli*. Michelin-starred Die Quadriga is now the domain of Bobby Bräuer, who serves classic French cuisine to guests seated on chairs based on a 1904 Frank Lloyd Wright design. In fact, design classics are littered throughout the hotel: Le Corbusier and Mies van der Rohe chairs, Wilhelm Wagenfeld lamps, and limited-edition prints by Ernst Fuchs, Bruno Bruni and Claude Gaveau. Hotel Brandenburger Hof offers a feeling of cultural harmony that is at once peaceful and invigorating.

eat

LUBITSCH

Tagesmenü/10.-

Rosenkohlcremasuppe

Geschmorte Sponfarkel-
haus mit Blaukraut
und Salzkartoffel

5 Café Adler
Friedrichstraße 206

Angelike Böhm opened Café Adler in 1988, and for a year or so the oldest building in Kreuzberg sat overlooking Checkpoint Charlie and the Berlin Wall. The building's history, however, dates back to the 17th century, when it was a pharmacy called the Adler ('eagle'). The interiors have not been altered, and one of the rooms, with its original floors, ceiling and wallpaper, benefits from being maintained as a non-smoking space (smokers are asked to use the front room). In 2002, two of Böhm's employees, Nicola Brosch and Silke Meister, assumed ownership, but little else has changed. Café Adler is well known for its cakes, soups and hearty German cuisine, which includes *geröstete Maultaschen* (an omelette filled with meat-and-spinach ravioli).

OOH-LA-LA
6 Paris Bar
Kantstraße 152

Every capital city has a restaurant to which celebrities flock when they are in town. Since it opened in the 1960s, Paris Bar has been just such a venue for Berlin. Because of its non-stop popularity, owner Michel Würthle opened bistro-style sister eatery Le Bar du Paris Bar next door, where it is possible to get a table without booking weeks in advance. At Paris Bar, German actor Otto Sander has an engraved plaque on the bar at the spot where he regularly sits. Art by regulars crowds every wall, and artists such as Christo, who once wrapped the entire Reichstag in fabric, animate the space itself. The menu is, not surprisingly, French bistro and includes terrific steaks and soups. But it is the action in the restaurant rather than on the plate that makes Paris Bar the place it is.

MORE THAN A BIRD
7 Storch
Wartburgstraße 54

Volker Hauptvogel's career is as colourful as his Alsatian restaurant. A typesetter by trade, he owned the infamous Pinguin-Club until 1988. Having grown tired of the loud music, peanuts and cocktail sausages, he filled his time with music, typesetting and writing, but missed the bustle of catering. When the lease of a corner sauna went unrenewed because of excessive on-site flesh-trading, Hauptvogel leapt at the chance to open his first proper restaurant. Decorated with enamel signs from old beer brands, it has a homey feel further enhanced by the *Bier vom Fass* (beer on tap) and friend Andre Dock's house wine. The central dish is tarte flambé (or onion tart), an Alsatian brand of pizza that uses crème fraîche instead of tomato sauce for the topping. Hauptvogel's own favourites come garnished with garlic, rocket or a typically Berlin preparation called *Eisbein*, which means 'pig leg'.

HOMAGE TO AUSTRIA
8 Ottenthal
Kantstraße 153

Proprietor Arthur Schneller's hope was to create a tiny part of Austria in the heart of Berlin, and with this delightful eatery, complete with an altar to Mozart and parts of an old church clock that once chimed in Schneller's native town of Ottenthal, he has succeeded. The town is known for its vineyards, and Schneller's restaurant doubles as a wine shop selling Austrian vintages, with an astounding 250 wines from the country's sixteen wine regions. Typical dishes include *Debreziner* (smoked sausage) goulash with dumplings roasted in butter, and a ragoût of Austrian chamois with Brussels sprouts, bread dumplings and cranberries. And, of course, there is always the veal escalope, more commonly known as *Wiener Schnitzel*.

STAR IN THE ASCENDANT
9 Lubitsch
Bleibtreustraße 47

A Berlin institution owned by chef Florian Maria Schymczyk and art dealer Volker Diehl, Lubitsch was established in 1994. Schymczyk was already known to the upper echelons of German society as he worked in the kitchens of the Berlin Golf and Country Club during the height of its pre-Wall popularity. Now he cooks his native dishes with an 'international touch' (think calves' liver with roasted onion and apple slices and creamed potato purée) both privately and in this, his first restaurant, named after the German film director who lived in the street before moving to Hollywood in 1943. One appreciative regular is former Chancellor Gerhard Schröder, who has hired Schymczyk for dinner parties of fifteen to twenty people at his home. Other famous fans include Prince Charles (Schymczyk cooked for him once when the Prince was in Berlin) and the late photographer Helmut Newton. Artwork by Diehl, who also has a gallery in Mitte, adorn the walls of Lubitsch.

BREAD AND ROSES
10 Brot und Rosen
Am Friedrichshain 6

Peter Klanns' reputation for serving Italian food has spread by word of mouth. Gerhard Schröder has been for dinner, as has British Prime Minister Tony Blair. In a city awash with Italian restaurants, Klanns's unique selling point is that he does it all himself, sourcing the freshest produce from suppliers he trusts and making his own organic oils. The interior is unfussy and stark white with touches of Prussian grandeur in the form of cornicing and ornaments, which contrast with the modern photographic prints. The restaurant benefits from a view over the pleasant Friedrichshain Park, which offers post-prandial refuge from the fashionable set spilling out of Brot und Rosen onto its terrace in warmer months.

BRIGHT YOUNG THING
11 Facil
Potsdamer Straße 3, 5th floor

At twenty-six, Michael Kempf was the youngest chef in Germany to be awarded a Michelin star, and is a culinary architect in a setting worthy of his skills. Facil is the in-house restaurant of the Lauber & Wöhr-designed Mandala Hotel, although it stands alone as a glass house surrounded by an evergreen terrace. In a room with honey-hued stone floors and filled with Donghia-upholstered chairs, Kempf offers a four-course menu with cheese or dessert or, for the gourmet, seven courses, alongside the changing à la carte menu. Foie gras with truffles, pine nut and apple coriander confit is one specialty, while marinated scallops with melon and mint make a lighter starter. Main courses, such as 'variation of veal in two courses' or 'two variations of venison with cherries and celery' will delight even the most demanding palates.

The generic German word for all sparkling vintages, *Sekt*, originates from this classic restaurant. Actor Ludwig Devrient was here for dinner one night after performing in a Shakespeare play at the *Schauspielhaus* (theatre) and demanded that the waiter bring him 'sack', a Shakespearean colloquialism for sherry. Not understanding and being more familiar with Devrient's penchant for sparkling wine, the waiter brought a glass of his usual tipple. A few hours (and glasses) later, the word 'sack' was being mispronounced as *Sekt* and the word entered the culinary lexicon. The restaurant itself has a colourful history; during the Roaring Twenties, Lutter & Wegner was the watering hole of choice for Josephine Baker and Marlene Dietrich. Today it is the ultra-fashionable establishment of Josef Laggner and a 'must' dining experience, with (of course) *Sekt* and German cuisine served in rooms built to look like libraries for spirits and wine.

The reimagined Reichstag (Parliament building) is a proud and shining symbol of German unity. When it was first built by Paul Wallot in the 1890s, he could not have foreseen the 100 years of turbulent history that would follow, culminating in the destruction of its fine cupola after the Second World War. A century later, British architect Norman Foster was asked to restore the building for the reunified government. His revolutionary design took the form of an all-glass cupola that swirls with visitors ascending its height to enjoy city-wide views and peer down into the politicians' central debating chamber. Though the cupola has become one of Berlin's main tourist attractions, fewer people know about rooftop restaurant Dachgarten, which has the double draw of gourmet cuisine and obligatory reservations that allow diners to jump the queue waiting to get to the roof. Lunch is the best time, as the cuisine is perhaps less inspired than the architecture, and the breathtaking views come at a price.

Recognizable from the fronts of corner shops throughout Italy, the name of Piero de Vitis's second Berlin restaurant is an ironic reference to the habits of reporters (the offices of daily newspaper *Tageszeitung* inhabit the building's upper floors). The restaurant's reputation is based on simple, fresh Italian cuisine, a theme that runs to Osteria No 1 and Malatesta, de Vitis's other eateries. Architect Max Dudler designed the interior, which is stylish and relaxed, thanks to the 6-metre-high ceilings and covered terrace with lemon trees. The café has been an inspiration, and de Vitis knows his art and artists; Wilmer Koenig created a photomontage showing the restaurant when it is empty, and British artist Rachel Whiteread is a friend. He cares about every detail, even sourcing a coffee called Andreatrinci from a small coffee-manufacturing family, who for ten years were the private coffee providers for Benetton.

The name of this charming restaurant is spread about its two rooms in illuminated letters. Not that diners are likely to forget, as there is a quirky dish called '10,000 Leagues Under the Sea', named for the book that made the author Jules Verne famous. Red and ivory walls ensure a feeling of *Gemütlichkeit*, and the little Spanish oak tables squeezed into the space are always full. The portions are huge, hearty and healthy. Buffet lunches are available daily, but the à la carte menu provides substantial dishes with eye-catching names. 'Endless Dream' is linguini with perch and kohlrabi in a herb sauce, whereas 'The Big Apple' is steak marinated in Calvados with apple and marjoram potatoes.

16 Engelbecken
Witzlebenstraße 31

Situated beside the Lietzensee, Engelbecken boasts that rare quality in an
urban restaurant in which customers
feel as though they are in the country,
especially in summertime, when tables
are dragged out onto the street corner
to overlook the azure calm of this
inner-city lake. The German–Austrian
cuisine heightens the illusion of being
in the south, and Engelbecken is justly
proud of its *Braten* and *Schnitzel*. The
name 'Engelbecken' refers to its former
location near its namesake river in
Kreuzberg, where it was a successful
institution eatery. Indoors, a marvel-
lously simple décor of stark white walls
with a green linoleum floor and dark
brown tables and chairs give the traditional menu a modern contrast. After
dinner, lakeside strolls are the perfect
digestif.

HOUSE OF CARDS
17 Café Einstein
Kurfürstenstraße 58

Until its incarnation as Café Einstein,
this stately house on a quiet, tree-lined
street had a wild history. Originally
built as a private residence in 1876, it
became the home of silent-movie
actress Henny Porten, who was later
blacklisted by the Nazis when she married a Jew. In the 1920s, in a mirrored
room behind the library, the salons
became home to an illegal casino
where all Berlin gambled. The Nazis
shut down this illicit activity, but the
house was the only building on the
street that was not razed to the ground
by the Allies' bombs. After Porten's
death in 1955, the descendants of owners of the original Café Einstein,
located on Unter den Linden during
the 1920s, bought the house and ran it
as a café until 1978. Today Elisabeth
Andraschko and her husband own this
Berlin institution and paean to the
Viennese café, with the mouthwatering smell of *Apfelstrudel* among the
many experiences that await visitors.
A classic.

drink

MY NAME IS HELMUT
18 Newton Bar
Charlottenstraße 56

Both the location overlooking the Gendarmenmarkt and the cool interior scream success for this decadently opulent cocktail bar, opened by Lutter & Wegner (p. 102) in 1999. The décor is sophisticated, and the mirrors, lacquered walls, marble flooring and huge prints by fashion photographer Helmut Newton lend an air of 1980s nostalgia. On the first floor, a cigar club and smoking room can be booked for private functions. The cocktail list is impressive, particularly recommended are the Martinis and the whisky selection.

CHEESE TREES
19 Würgeengel
Dresdener Straße 122

This tastefully decorated bar takes its name from Luis Buñuel's cult film *El Angel Exterminador* and is one of the area's nightlife highlights. Crowded, smoky and noisy on any given evening, the interior combines red velvet furniture with a beautiful stucco ceiling and gilt-edged mirrors. Students, artists and barflies mix in this combustible atmosphere. Many choose to follow a drink here with a visit to the adjacent Gorgonzola Club, heading to the restaurant via a tiny 'secret' passageway – useful when the bar spills over.

IN A CITY GARDEN
20 Pratergarten + Hecht Club
Kastanienallee 7–9

Berlin's oldest beer garden is famous for celebrating the German love of conversation and outdoor drinking. Regularly closed down by the police in the pre-1989 era, it reopened in 1996 and its two barn-like *Bierhalle* are now stuffed with beer-swilling locals, even in winter. In summer, lucky guests are entertained by musicians and occasionally street cabaret artists. Located behind an open-air stage in the garden is Hecht Club, a semi-secret cocktail bar. Inside, the décor is a fantastical recreation of a film set 'à la James Bond'.

PARK LIFE

23 Café am Neuen See

Lichtensteinallee 2

In the heart of the Tiergarten, over-looking the Neuen See on one side and the Zoologischer Garten on the other, is Berlin's largest beer garden. Arriving on foot, by bicycle or on one of the boats that can be hired on the lake, guests can take one of the 1,500 seats to enjoy the largely unlandscaped natural surroundings. The park feels rather wild and woody in places – in a Caspar David Friedrich kind of way – which is perhaps why it is somewhat deserted in the winter. The park was once the hunting ground of Prussian royalty, who released animals into it and chased them for sport (hence *Tier-garten*, or 'animal garden').

DR ZHIVAGO

24 Pasternak

Knaackstraße 22–24

Before the Second World War, Berlin was home to a large Russian Jewish community, which included Boris Pasternak, author of *Dr Zhivago*. The restaurant was named in his honour by another Russian Jew, Ilja Kaplan, who moved to Berlin in 1990. Kaplan now has four Russian-themed eateries in the city, including Potemkin, Gorki Park and Bar Gagarin. Situated next door to a synagogue, this restaurant was a pass-port office before being remodelled to resemble the writer's living room in the 1930s, an entirely fitting backdrop to traditional *borscht* and *pelmini*. Kaplan is most proud of his mossberry vodka, made from a Siberian fruit berry and infused into pure potato vodka.

BEER BARREL

21 Felsenkeller

Akazienstraße 2

In 1993, Günter During and Michaela Friedrichs took over an establishment that has been in existence since 1920. There have been only five owners since it opened, a continuity that ensures Felsenkeller's charm, rein-forced by the period shipping para-phernalia, enamelled posters on the walls that bear slogans like 'Hamburg-Amerika Line' and 'Cunard Line Vertre-tung Hier USA & Canada', and an old cigarette display cabinet that houses original packets (not for sale) of Player's Navy Cut cigarettes.

VIENNESE MODERNE

22 Café Schönbrunn

Am Friedrichshain 8

Drawing inspiration from the Viennese café culture, owners Hille Saw and Matthias Petsche chose the name of the city's famous castle for their eatery when it opened in 2000. Niki Winkel-mayer is the architect behind its hip interior, but it is the 1960s space-age pavilion, set amid the leafy greenery of Friedrichshain Park, that sets it apart. Dishes tend toward the more tradi-tional; *Wiener Schnitzel* with potato salad and gherkins on the side is an ever-popular order.

ALL FOR ONE AND ONE FOR ALL

25 Kumpelnest 3000

Lützowstraße 23

This bar is the great equalizer. Ladies and gentlemen, guys and dolls, tramps and pimps, all are present and accounted for in the lively mix that fre-quents Kumpelnest 3000 from about 1 a.m. onward on any day of the week (anyone arriving earlier will find the place empty). Kumpelnest is the last alcoholic port of call at the end of a long night of revelry, so expect to meet any-one and everyone. The crazy broken-glass mosaic on the walls and dusty overstuffed sofas mirror the incongru-ous assortment that is the clientele.

shop

26 Trippen
Rosenthaler Straße 40/41

Michael Oehler and Angela Spieth were frustrated shoe designers who joined forces to create an original approach to footwear. *Trippen* is an old Germanic word for the protective wooden shoes worn over less durable silky varieties during the Middle Ages, and suited the duo perfectly as the company has become internationally synonymous with wooden-soled footwear since its foundation in 1994. When demand for the Trippen shoe took off, Oehler and Spieth patented their sole and natural shape. Today they depend on a network of small, family-run companies to manufacture their product. The décor of the stores is plain and functional to keep the focus firmly on the shoes.

MILLINER EXTRAORDINAIRE
27 Fiona Bennett
Große Hamburger Straße 25

She could hardly have a more English name, but Miss Bennett is definitely a Berliner. Born to a British father and a German mother, she has lived in the city since she was six, and now is one of Berlin's foremost hat designers. A love of performance art meant her early collections were often in novel formats that brought both attention and a loyal clientele. Together with friend Elisabeth Prantner, Bennett held between thirty and forty shows a year, once hiring a ghost train in which the audience rode in past performers wearing Bennett's hats and Prantner's clothes. The shop is a lilac and mint-green space that displays such treasures as her elegant 'stingray' hat, which is crafted from 4,000 tiny feathers that appear to move when they catch the light.

IN AND OUT
28 Breathe
Rochstraße 17

After a decade working for the Lancaster Group, Gregor Vidzer was ready to open his own cosmetics boutique. Together with design firm RoomSafari, Vidzer and Sven Eric Moos created a beauty haven that delights first the eye, then the nose and finally the soul. The owners encourage customers to experiment with pigment palettes, creams or perfume bottles, and the high-ceilinged space enhances the experience. Seagrass matting covers the floor, the white walls are light, and the space smells freshly masculine. Although there is makeup by Bloom and skincare by Julisis, it is obvious that the boys' real passion is perfume; Breathe offers a custom-made variety by Swedish 'fragrance artist' Sissel Tolaas, who concocts an individual scent for each of its patrons.

HOT HATS
29 Hut Up
Oranienburger Straße 32

Famous for its vivacious pinks and effervescent oranges, Hut Up's colour range spans over 125 shades and all are used in Christine Birkle's felt creations. Although *Hut* means 'hat', Birkle has not limited her design talents to headgear; silk, organza and muslin are also woven together with merino wool to make seamless garments. So popular is her original style that Birkle's work is now sold in Japan, the UK, France, Italy and the United States. Nor does she limit herself to women's wear. It was her baby collection that caught the attention of buyers from Donna Karan, Hermès and Dries van Noten (p. 41); Karan now sells Birkle's egg-warmers (brightly coloured felt affairs that could pass as elf's hats) in her New York home store. Hut Up also features felt cushions, glass and hot-water-bottle covers, plush teddy bears and a delightful one-piece baby snuggle-crib, available in blue or powder-puff pink.

ORGIASTIC FOOD FEST
30 KaDeWe
Tauentzienstraße 21–24

International shopaholics may already know that this *Kaufhaus des Westens* is the largest department store in mainland Europe. Built by entrepreneur Adolf Jandorf in 1907, its seven floors are crammed with the latest labels and beauty creams. The crowning glory is the Food Hall on the sixth floor, where every counter is accompanied by a food bar. With a Bols cocktail bar, Champagne bars, oyster and salad bars, a crêperie, *Wurst* houses, a patisserie and chocolaterie, and live fish swimming in tanks awaiting their fate, this is consumption at its most indulgent. Whatever your tastebuds desire, they cannot fail to be rewarded at KaDeWe.

URBAN DIMENSION
31 Pro QM
Almstadtstraße 48

Having recently moved from their former location in a butcher's shop, Pro QM has become one of the city's most important centres for architectural discussion, supported by an outstanding library of books on architecture, planning, politics, design and art theory. Pro QM's focus is urbanism ('pro qm' means 'per square metre'), specifically the idea that a city is not just a built-up area but a space of culture, ideas and development. The venue has become more of a hobby for the three owners, who continue to have an influence on Berlin's dynamic urban evolution through their private practice.

HUNTING FASHION
32 Little Red Riding Hood
Quartier 206/1, Friedrichstraße 71

New Berlin designers have a hip outlet in the city centre thanks to Little Red Riding Hood. The notion of selling underrepresented talent under one roof was immediately celebrated by the local designers who were invited to be part of this carnival of fashion. Located in the basement level of Berlin's über-fashion-conscious Quartier 206 complex (a glamorous mall that is home to Prada, Gucci, Commes des Garçons and Jil Sander, among many others), 'LRRH' is where shoppers can find cutting-edge creations close to home. The energy of the store space is dynamic and features exhibitions of the fashion and aural work on sale.

THE PERFECT NOSE
33 Noesa
Behrenstraße 29

With its futuristic showroom, Noesa has a skincare vision that attempts to change beauty myths. They want people to have soulful skin and to this end have prepared quite a package. With a range of well over thirty products in sleek containers, Noesa's guarantee is for fair prices and content. Using self-styled 'Danadem' and 'Alchemetics' (a plant-based skincare to effect relaxing or invigorating results in the user), director Gerd Gerker blends seven essential oils to create three bases for the products – 'Nobility', 'Momentum' and 'Integral' – which are unique in style, branding and content.

NADA NOUGHT
34 Nix
Oranienburger Straße 32

35 Chocolaterie Estrellas
CHOCOLATE FACTORY
Akazienstraße 21

ÜBER FASHION ICON
36 Claudia Skoda
Alte Schönhauser Straße 35

A play on the German word *nichts* (nothing), this store carries Barbara Gebhardt's collection of clothes that are smart, wearable, durable and functional, a simple ethic that has established her as one of Berlin's most respected designers. Using mostly natural tones (there is an occasional nod to printed fabrics; Nordic reindeer for a winter collection, for example) and stretchy, comfortable cotton-Lycra textiles, Gebhardt makes suits, skirts, trousers and jackets for men, women and children. The detail is playful, but on closer inspection you will find evidence of her true tailoring skills, a tuck here, a cut there, that make the piece. Her imagination is most evident in her accessory range: fleece-wool hats with ear flaps so long they morph into scarves, and fingerless gloves that rise above the elbow and become sleeves.

After training at chocolate company Most, Esther Kurtz set up her own factory and gave it a Spanish name in deference to the language of the countries that are home to the world's cocoa plantations. Kurtz uses traditional methods to develop her own recipes, and sources cocoa from a Venezuelan plantation that produces a mild flavour, allowing her to keep the cocoa concentration high and still be appealing to children. Cocoa blocks and almond paste come from Lübeck, famous for both these delicacies and nougat. To these ingredients, Kurtz adds spices, chilli and German molasses, which is rich in iron but contains no sugar (it was the lifeblood of Berlin after the Second World War). Kurtz also stocks *Berlinoise*, a paste made from hazelnuts, chocolate and cream, as well as items by her favourite chocolatiers, many of whom are now friends.

Claudia Skoda has been around; her move from Ku'damm to Mitte in 2002 was the most visible signal that this sector of Berlin was the place to be for fashionistas, style setters, designers, artists and photographers. But Skoda is now in her sixties, and her story started in 1970s Kreuzberg. For years her legendary knitwear took her to New York, where she had a store on Thompson Street and clothed David Bowie and Tina Turner. Skoda's immediately identifiable knitwear draws attention to the body's curves without revealing too much skin, and as such her work is enigmatically erotic. Her classic lines were defined by multicoloured knitwear, but the recent repertoire embraces angora, viscose, linen, alpaca, mohair and spandex. One piece is a shimmeringly metallic dress that hangs so heavily, the wearer must walk with careful elegance.

Given the freezing economic climate in Berlin at the time, it was with great optimism that Jörg Wichmann and Theresa Meirer opened their space selling fashion, jewelry, art, furniture and product design in 2003. They began by recruiting over sixty local designers (the number keeps growing) and were stunned by how much talent they discovered. 'The notion of selling underrepresented work under one roof was immediately celebrated by everyone we approached,' Wichman says. Going from strength to strength, Berlinomat is now an outlet for the couple's own fashion and jeanswear label, Hotinaf. Wichmann and Meirer share the 280-square-metre space with BetonWare's concrete furniture, Dreigold's jewelry and Extratapete's wallpaper, to name only a few, along with an organic café, all of which add up to a total shopping experience.

DIM ('The Imaginary Factory') began as an experiment by designers Oliver Vogt and Hermann Weizenegger, and was originally directed by Peter Bergmann. Their mission to create unconventional brooms and brushes with and for Berlin's visually impaired has proved astonishingly successful and is celebrated at design shows and exhibitions as far afield as London, Milan, New York and Tokyo. Recent designs from Tim Parsons, Alex Kufus, MotorBerlin and Max Wolf, among others, have included prototypes whose manufacture has raised the profile and the self-esteem of the people who work there. Adhering to the ethos that new products should serve old functions, the quirky designs (wicker coat-hangers and bread baskets that incorporate coffee cups) are well made, clever and timeless.

This sneaker success story began with one man, Adi (Adolf) Dassler, who built a tiny shoe factory into a global sporting-goods brand. He made his first pair of shoes in his mother's washroom in 1920, opened the first factory with brother Rudolf in 1924, and shod the feet of the German national team at the Berlin Olympics in 1936. When the brothers fell out in 1948, Rudolf formed the rival Puma label and Adi founded Adidas, registering the familiar 'three stripes' logo in 1949. The label diversified in the 1960s and '70s to encompass accessories, tracksuits and sporting equipment. After Dassler's death, his son Horst continued the family tradition, but by 1990 Adidas was no longer a family-run enterprise. The legend lives on through the personalities it sponsors and, most recently, its new concept stores. The Berlin branch is one of only two in Germany.

see

ART STATION
40 Hamburger Bahnhof
Invalidenstraße 50–51

Dan Flavin's neon installation hints at the transformation undergone by this former railway station to become the Hamburg Museum for the Present. Opening in its current guise in 1997, its permanent collection is formed by the Erich Marx bequest, which includes works by Andy Warhol, Joseph Beuys, Cy Twombly, Robert Rauschenberg, Sol LeWitt and Bruce Nauman. Recent exhibitions on the upper levels have featured the work of sculptor Ron Mueck and photographer Dayanita Singh, along with an Australian group show, 'The Down Side Up'. The Bahnhof consistently attracts renowned curators and artists, making it Berlin's destination contemporary gallery.

THE SECRET ART GARDEN
41 Sammlung Hoffmann
Sophienstraße 21

A glow of hot red, nauseous yellow or icy blue is the visual siren that lures visitors off the street into this den of contemporary art. Erika and Rolf Hoffmann bought the property after the Wall fell in 1989 to house their extensive art collection, and typifying the gentrification of the Scheunenviertel, they restored the courtyard and lined the entrance ceilings with neon lights to create different mood areas. The Hoffmans also live here and open their art-filled home to the public for appointment-only tours on Saturdays. This unconventional 'gallery' boasts a floor installation by Pipilotti Rist and pieces by Felix Gonzales-Torres, Nan Goldin and Douglas Gordon.

CONTEMPORARY ART
42 Kunst-Werke Berlin
Auguststraße 69

In 1990, four art enthusiasts converted this former margarine factory into a space for artistic explorations. From the start, interdisciplinary projects were a vital element in the gallery's programming, and the shows held here helped build the reputation of artistic director Klaus Biesenbach, who is also chief curator at New York's Museum of Modern Art offshoot space, PS1. Kunst-Werke has become one of the most important spaces for contemporary art in the world, with over 2,000 square metres of gallery space and an artist-in-residence programme that sponsored designer Hedi Slimane for two years, while he produced his photo diary of Berlin. The courtyard also houses work by Dan Graham, Carsten Höller and Pedro Reyes, as well as a steel and glass cube that doubles as the Café Bravo.

DEMOLITION DERBY
43 Tacheles
Oranienburger Straße 54–56a

Even given Berlin's constant construction flux, Tacheles is a shocking structure. You cannot help but be captivated by the dereliction of the 1908 shopping arcade, made even more intriguing by the fact that it has been in this state since it was bombed during the Second World War. Plans to remove it were thwarted in 1990 by squatters, and since then it has been occupied by artists' studios and impromptu party organizers. There are restaurants, bars and even a cinema at ground level. Some last, some don't, but Tacheles lives on. Plans to restore the building to its former glory remain on hold, thanks to city-wide budgetary constraints.

AXIS OF EVIL
44 Topographie des Terrors
Niederkirchnerstraße 8

The excavated Topographie des Terrors was once the site of a cluster of buildings that were at the centre of the Nazi regime, including no 8 Prinz-Albrecht Straße, which was the Gestapo headquarters, and the Prinz Albrecht Palais, where the SS leadership was based, making this area the government district of the Third Reich and the location from which the horrors of the Holocaust were masterminded. Reconstruction of buildings to house the documentation centre, plus a stretch of Berlin Wall that is also standing here, has recently been completed.

A WALK IN THE PARK
45 Tiergarten
Straße des 17 Juni 1

Berlin's green heart spreads out over 255 hectares and borders many of the city's neighbourhoods. The Tiergarten was the hunting ground of the Prussian aristocracy and became the largest of the city parks in 1818, when landscape architect Peter Joseph Lenné designed the layout in typically English style. Former thoroughfares still traverse the park; five main roads converge at the Großer Stern (big star) roundabout, which is crowned at the centre by the Siegessäule (victory column), only one of numerous historical sites within the park's borders, including the Schloß Bellevue, home of the president, and the Haus der Kulturen der Welt, the former Hall of Congress and now a permanent exhibition site. Far from being a prim urban park, the Tiergarten comprises wild woods and scattered meadows where families congregate for summer picnics and barbeques.

ANOTHER BRICK IN THE WALL
46 Mauerpark
Eberswalder Straße and Gleimstraße

Meaning 'Wall Park' and occupying a long, slim rectangular area on the western side of one of the few remaining stretches of the Berlin Wall, Mauerpark is the green escape for Prenzlauer Berg. The park's main path is not much more than a dirt track frequented by walkers with very large dogs, but the Wall itself sits atop a steep bank with benches at its base, affording views over industrial Berlin's housing blocks, some overshadowed by the optimistic floating bauble that is the Fernsehturm (television tower). During winter the park is barren, a stark backdrop from which to contemplate the culture once created by the city-divider, but in the summer the park becomes an impromptu 'bring-your-own' beer garden.

MULTIFUNCTIONAL PAST & PRESENT
47 Pfefferberg
Fehrbelliner Straße 92

With its façade resembling an ancient ruin, the old Pfefferberg brewery may seem from afar to date back to Roman times, but the first brick was laid in 1841 and it was not completed until the late 19th century. It housed tenants as varied as Hoffmann-Schokolade and the Germania Brotfabrik, and was used as a forced labour site and air raid shelter during the Second World War, and later still as a bus depot. Pfefferberg is currently in the hands of a trust that is renovating it. Masterminded by architect Bernard Khoury, the renovation project will include a hotel, offices, bars and restaurants, as well as an exhibition space, which featured the work of American artist Frank Stella for its inauguration show.

BRUSSELS

A century ago, it would have been a very brave gambler who staked his money on Brussels – rather than London, Paris or New York – becoming the epicentre of the world's largest and most affluent trading block. But at the dawn of the 21st century, this happy position is the one that the capital of Belgium, Flanders and the European Union (a market of 450 million people) finds itself in. It is not an uncommon aspiration among Bruxellois weary of the old Flemish–French dichotomy to be a mongrel, or *zenneke* as Flemish slang would have it. It's hardly surprising that a multicultural spirit has taken root, with scores of nationalities rubbing shoulders in this compact city and so many languages that you would think you're in a modern-day Tower of Babel. The impact on everything from architecture to fashion and food is profound and adds to the unique atmosphere of a city juggling its own long history and culture with colonial and modern influences from Africa and across Europe.

Brussels grew from the marshy banks of the River Senne, long since covered over, and first blossomed as a trading centre during the Middle Ages. Its ancient pedigree can be explored in the narrow, twisting streets of the Lower Town, centred around the aptly named Grand Place (p. 127). It's here, as you happen on sides of buildings incongruously yet gaily painted with 10-metre-tall cartoon characters, that you begin to get an inkling of the fun and unexpectedly wacky nature of Brussels, a city that gave the world not only Tintin, but also the sensual designs of Art Nouveau. Made up of a patchwork of nineteen different communities, the Brussels vibe changes as frequently as the street signs that flip back and forth between French and Flemish. Modern architecture has not been the city's forte, and it is easy to bypass the garishly modern and largely charmless EU quarter, but even on the shortest trip don't miss the opportunity to head north to Heysel and take in the panoramic view of the city from inside the city's silvery icon of 1950s style, the Atomium (p. 128).

The posh end of Brussels, location of palaces and impressive art collections, is the Upper Town, where you'll find the swankiest of luxury boutiques as well as the antique and bric-à-brac shops of the sophisticated Sablon and the more rough-edged Marolles. Brussels is also beginning to mount a decent challenge to Antwerp as the nation's fashion hub; set aside a healthy block of time for exploring the emporiums on and around the rue Antoine Dansaert (p. 123), the city's answer to Paris's rue du Faubourg St Honoré. The icing on the cake is Brussels' refined dining scene, offering everything from the freshest seafood, served in the most elegant of surroundings, to piping hot waffles. The world-class quality and diversity of locally made chocolates and beer are worth the trip alone. Brussels really is the place in which to get a taste of the good life.

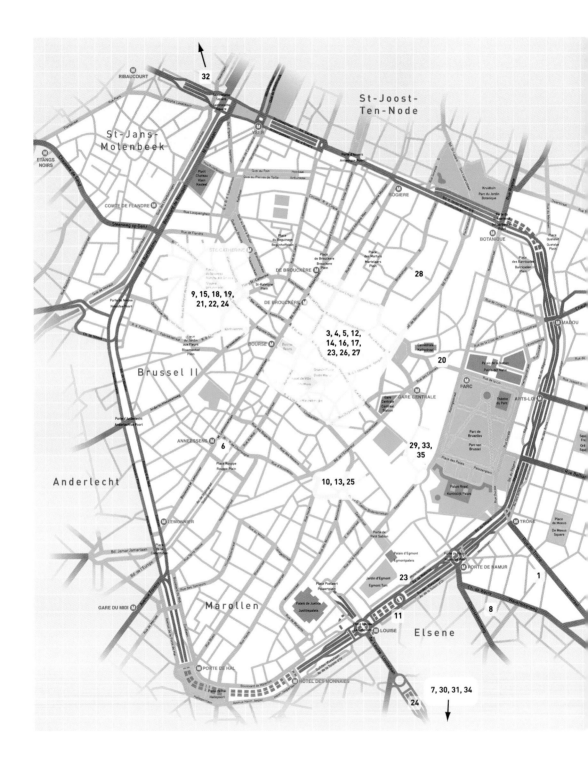

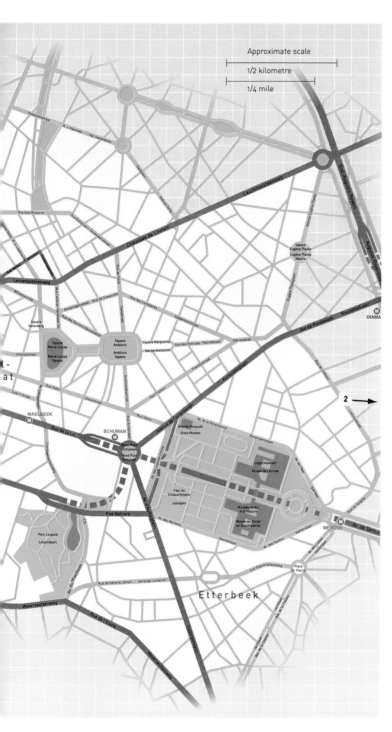

StyleCity Brussels

sleep

1 THE ARTIST'S HOME
Chambres en Ville
19 rue de Londres
Rooms from €90

Tucked away in the Upper Town, these are not just any old hotel rooms. The life of an artist, colonial Africa, the Middle East and the 18th-century Swedish style of Gustavian are the themes that Philippe Guilmin applies to the four guestrooms in his charming B&B, housed in a 19th-century mirror factory. African masks, *kubu* cloths, claw-foot baths and mattresses like giant marshmallows are among the props, along with Guilmin's own paintings. In the dining room, Guilmin serves a lovely breakfast that includes home-made jams around a communal table with a view out to the courtyard.

2 Monty
101 boulevard Brand Whitlock
Rooms from €150

Connoisseurs of modern design will have a field day at the Monty ticking off the various lamps, chairs, tables and other pieces of furniture by the likes of Ron Arad, Charles and Ray Eames, and Philippe Starck. Owner Vivian Vogels has gathered together this collection in a 1930s townhouse, repainted in striking shades of grey and lipstick red, in the heart of the EU quarter. You won't miss the place, as there is a statue of a red cow outside. Business visitors will appreciate the free Internet access and Wi-Fi at this fun and contemporary eighteen-room property.

ROOM COLLECTION
3 Royal Windsor Hotel Grand Place
5 rue Duquesnoy
Rooms from €450

In 2004, the Royal Windsor Hotel Grand Place hit on the idea of inviting top local fashion designers to redecorate the bedrooms and living areas (but, sadly, not the bathrooms) of several of their suites. Twelve designers, including most recently Xavier Delcour and Christina Wijnants, have taken up the challenge. The impressive results range from the stark minimalism of Jean-Paul Knott's white cube room with a leather bed covering from Delvaux (p. 124), to the sinuous curves of the combination desk-bench and bare floorboards of Marina Yee's vision. More comfortable and colourful are the makeovers of Nicolas Woit (p. 123) and Gerald Watelet.

eat

MOULES
ESCARGOTS DE BOURGOGNE

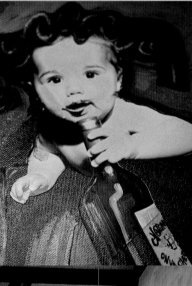

LECH... ZING ANN
RUEGHEL G.SIMENON C.MEUNIER J.BORD...
L BURY PERE DAMIEN AXELLE RED A.VES...
J.ENSOR S.APPELMANS I.BERGHMANS A...
P.DELVAUX E.MERCKX T.BOUTSEN K.CL...
RT MERCATOR J.HENIN J.ICKX BEJART F...
HERGE M.GILLAIN J.NEUHAUS O.STRELLI...
CKRENT J.LIZENE LIO ADAMO LARA FAB...
NS E.DUQUENNE DRIES VAN NOTEN V.VAN...
G.CORBIAU P.HANKAR H.VAN DE VELDE...
CMEESTER M.DE GHELDERODE DUPA M.C...
J.VAN HAMME B.POELVOORDE PANAMAR...
A.VAN DYCK J.VAN EYCK R.DEVOS O.S...
ERGS MORRIS CLOVIS F.SCHUITEN TOO...
DARDENNE H.CLAUS J.HARPMAN A.NO...
HAERS R.WOUTERS T.VANRYSSELBER...
J.C.VANDAMME JOHNNY HA...
RTRAND JACO VAN DORMAEL JAN BUC...
NNE MOHAMMED MOURHIT STEPHA...
UX STEVE HOUBEN HAROUN TAZIEFF SO...
ANY GASTON ROELANTS FRED DE BURGRA...
S ULLA WERBROUCK LUCIEN VAN IMPE JOH...
HERINE ROBERT VAN DE WALLE RAYMOND C...
EEMAN YOLANDE MOREAU MAURICE MAET...
ENS CHRISTIAN DE DUVE ALBERT CLAUDE...

PINTO'S PALACE
4 Belga Queen
32 rue du Fossé-aux-Loups

The former Crédit du Nord Bank, with its vaulted stained-glass ceiling held aloft by marble pillars, is the grand palate on which Antoine Pinto has created Belga Queen. You sense that the Belgian–Portuguese designer had a lot of fun, from the giant egg-shaped lights that change colours to the infamous now-you-see-me-now-you-don't toilet doors. The high-class Belgian fare is made from premium local ingredients; even the wines are from Belgian producers. If you're just in the mood for a snack or a drink, the oyster bar at the entrance is renowned for its shellfish.

FISHERMAN'S CATCH
5 Restaurant Vincent
8–10 rue de Dominicains

Restaurants sit cheek-by-jowl in the narrow lanes of the rue des Bouchers area. It's a lively scene, but most venues serve indifferent food at tourist-inflated prices. One exception is Restaurant Vincent, a brasserie of 1905 pedigree where shuffling waiters in white jackets with gold-braided epaulettes prepare steak tartare from scratch, including the mayonnaise, before your very eyes. It's all very traditional and, admirably for this mercantile area, they won't serve mussels out of season. Most remarkable of all is the tiled interior, which depicts fishermen battling against the elements among more placid rural landscapes.

JUST LIKE HOME
6 Comme Chez Soi
23 place Rouppe

Unless you live in a townhouse with a dazzling Art Nouveau interior designed by Victor Horta (see Musée Horta; p. 127), it's unlikely that Comme Chez Soi will be anything like your home. Nor will the haute cuisine on offer – dishes such as jellied salmon with thyme and lemongrass, or lobster with black truffles – be something that you're used to knocking up in your own kitchen. It's the exemplary service and hospitality of this petite accolade-laden restaurant that really sets the relaxing tone. Book well ahead, or try for a mid-week lunch spot.

AT THE IROMONGERS
7 La Quincaillerie
45 rue du Page

Amid the Art Nouveau architectural splendours of the Ixelles area is this former ironmongers, creatively transformed into a trendy brasserie. Raised metal gangways and a huge antique clock lend an air of a stage set to the place, complemented by the buzzy crowd alert to the possibility that some celebrity could come in to dine at any moment. The highly competent menu includes such possibilities as confit of rabbit leg with garlic and spices, herring and green bean salad, and vanilla macaroon with strawberries.

WINDING DOWN IN THE UPPER TOWN
8 Saint-Boniface
- Belgo Belge, 20 rue de la Paix
- Aux Vieux Bruxelles, 35 rue Saint-Boniface
- Comptoir Florian, 17 rue Saint-Boniface
- L'Ultime Atome, 14 rue Saint-Boniface

When the movers and shakers of the EU are done for the day, the most likely location at which they'll gather to graze is the lively Upper Town area of Saint-Boniface. Within the turreted shadow of St Boniface church lies a hugely appealing collection of relaxed restaurants and brasseries. Belgo Belge, with appliqué babies floating on the walls and ceilings, has a quirky design and serves simple yet accomplished renditions of traditional Belgian dishes; their hamburgers and *moules et frites* come highly recommended. If you're looking for something more traditional, Aux Vieux Bruxelles, in business since 1882, offers exactly what it says on the tin, right down to the red-checked tablecloths and wood-panelled interior. For afternoon tea, it's hard to beat Comptoir Florian, a delightful tea shop offering scores of fine blends and quotes on the art of tea-making from the likes of Proust and Agatha Christie. From breakfast to the midnight hour, L'Ultime Atome is the bustling nucleus of the area, with chairs spilling out of its doors and around its corner spot. Settle in and work your way through the impressively long beer menu.

THROUGH THE BAMBOO GROVE
9 La Manufacture
12 rue Notre Dame du Sommeil

Hidden behind a housing complex in the former tannery workshops of Delvaux (p. 124) is this elegant restaurant. Lush bamboo fills the courtyard, while indoors the design palate consists of browns and blacks and a hard-edged industrial ambience. The cooking is ambitious and can be sampled either à la carte or in the three course 'Wink' or seven-course 'Discovery' menus. Dishes can include fois gras paté with Corinthian grapes, lacquered knuckle of ham with maple syrup, or larded cod with Parma ham.

MAROLLES MAGIC
10 Les Marolles
- L'Idiot du Village, 19 rue Notre-Seigneur
- Marolles Flea Market, place du Jeu de Balle

The one-time working-class area of Les Marolles is a fascinating place in which to soak up an atmosphere that's a million miles away from the classy Sablon. Get up early to snag the gold amidst the dross at the daily flea market in the place du Jeu de Balle, then head to L'Idiot du Village to celebrate. The eclectic décor of this cozy bistro is charming, but it's the beautifully presented and delicious cooking of chef Alain Gascoin that is the highlight. Mackerel tartare with wasabi on a disc of beetroot and a refreshing sweet soup of white peaches with strawberries are the standouts on a menu that changes with the seasons.

IT'S IN THE EYES
11 Cospaia
1 Capitaine Crespel

Overlooking the traffic on boulevard de Waterloo, this restaurant and bar occupies a stunning set of contemporary spaces created by the Dutch interior designer Marcel Wolterinck. Dine amidst a glade of silver wire-work trees in a black room, or under the enigmatic gaze of huge portrait photographs hung in a creamy, high-ceilinged baroque space. Alternatively, hang out on the roomy terrace, by the bar sipping a cocktail, or hide away in the ultra-intimate private dining room, Le Boudoir. The menu runs the gamut from poached egg with white asparagus to lobster fricassee with puy lentils.

drink

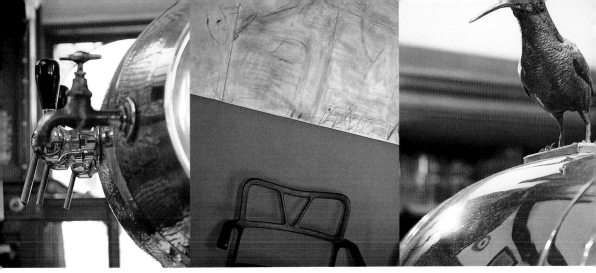

TRADITIONAL TAVERNS
12 À la Bécasse + L'Image de Nostre Dame

11 rue de Tabora and 8 rue du Marché aux Herbes

The clue to finding À la Bécasse is to look in the pavement for the brass inlay of a woodcock (*bécasse*) and then head down the unlikely cobbled alley. The traditional wood-panelled tavern at the end is a cozy, convivial place in which to sample draught Lambic, a naturally fermented beer with no added yeast, served in grey and blue ceramic jugs. Snacks include light meals and local cheeses. The formula is repeated at the nearby (and equally well-hidden) sister establishment L'Image de Nostre Dame, a rustic bar with many dark, dusty corners.

ROYAL APPROVAL
13 Wittamer

6 place du Grand Sablon

For all its ritzy associations, the cobbled Grand Sablon would be so much more appealing if it wasn't used as a car park. But the unappealing clutter of automobiles does not deter from the popularity of the area's cafés, with their terraces perpetually bustling with customers. The best time to visit is the weekend when an antique market blossoms beside Notre-Dame au Sablon. For a prime view, settle into a wicker chair at Wittamer, confectioners to the Belgian court. A family-run business since 1910, there are sections for chocolates, pastries and ice creams – pretty much all irresistible.

BOURSE BEAUTY
14 Le Cirio

18–20 rue de la Bourse

Although its most famous drink is the 'half-en-half' (equal parts of sparkling and still wine), there are no half-measures in the glitzy Belle Époque interior of Le Cirio. What was once an ornate deli catering to the stockbrokers of the neighbouring Bourse is now one of Brussels' most atmospheric bars. A variety of drinking vessels, marionettes and other curios are displayed in illuminated glass cases, and the jolly waistcoated waiters could have come from Central Casting.

CHECKMATE IN ST-GÉRY
15 Le Greenwich

7 rue des Chartreux
- Zebra, 33 place Saint-Géry
- Le Roi des Belges, 35–37 rue Jules van Praet

Little seems to have changed at Le Greenwich since it was built in 1914; chess and card players still battle it out here each day as Magritte is said to have done. The interior (and famously the basement toilets), have all resisted the passage of time. Not so the nearby Halles de Saint-Géry, a covered dairy hall reimagined as a café-bar and exhibition space. This happening venue sports a collection of buzzing bistros and bars, many part of the Fred Nicolay (see p. 123) empire. In summer, there is a mock beach and deck chairs in front of rough-and-ready Zebra, while at Le Roi de Belges the slick retro design celebrates the 1958 Expo.

NO SPITTING IMAGE
16 Toone

21 petite rue des Bouchers

Eight generations of the Géal family have pulled the strings at the Toone, a puppet theatre sequestered away in the heart of the Lower Town. The cast of marionettes (some 1,300 of them) range from cavaliers in pantaloons and thigh-high leather boots to George W. Bush, and star in an incredible range of comedy and drama shows, some with a satirical edge. Even if there is no show, the theatre bar is well worth dropping by for its serene ambience and excellent choice of beers. It is one of a handful of places in the city where you can try Cantillon Gueze, a dry, bitter brew that's a mix of young and old Lambic beer.

OLD BELGIAN CURIOSITY SHOP
17 Goupil le Fol

22 rue de la Violette

Squeeze past the giant plaster-cast bust of some ancient dame in the narrow doorway to enter this multi-roomed and many levelled bar, plastered with questionable art and a ragbag of other wacky paraphernalia. The eccentric owner has added squishy sofas and secluded corners, all of which conspire to lull you into spending a lazy evening sampling the house specialty, fruit wine. A jukebox provides the soundtrack of Belgian pop classics and *chanson* standards by the likes of Edith Piaf, Jacques Brel and Léo Ferré.

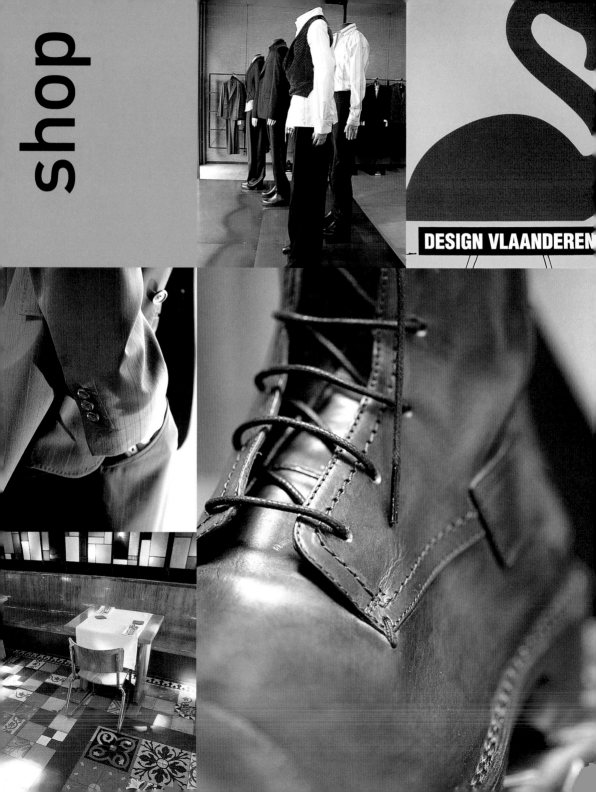

shop

DESIGN VLAANDEREN

Saint-Géry's central spine is rue Antoine Dansaert, a showcase for the city's fashion scene. To see who's worth your shopping while, drop by the information centre Modo Bruxelles, where the helpful staff provide brochures, maps and plenty of advice. Nearby is the Brussels outlet of Martin Margiela, who was replaced by Marina Yee in the official line-up of the Antwerp Six. Then hit the street, starting at the southern Bourse end with legendary jazz and piano bar L'Archiduc. A few doors down at nos 22–26 is Fred Nicolay's Bonsoir Clara, a sunny vegetarian bistro. Cross the road to check out the hand-cast silver-and-gold baubles by self-taught jewelry designer Christa Reniers, then cross back again to team your newly acquired accessories with the romantic designs of Annemie Verbeke at no. 64. Boutique pioneer Stijl at no. 74 is still going strong after over twenty years; stop here and check out what Dries van Noten and Ann Demeulemeesters are up to now. At the back of Nicolas Woit's shop you may catch the designer at work, cutting and stitching his limited-edition dresses with their hint of 1950s chic. A slight detour from the main drag will take you to Jean Paul Knott, who worked for Yves Saint Laurent (see p. 246) and Louis Féraud before launching his own collection.

THE DYNAMIC DUO
19 Shampoo & Conditioner
16 rue des Chartreux

Not a hairdressing salon but the up-and-coming atelier and showroom of young fashion partners Aude de Wolf and Vanessa Vukicevic. You'll find the girls, sporting the same haircut, creating their chic, off-beat dresses at the shop's rear. The idea behind their fashions, inspired by dark fairy tales, are that you can dress them up or dress them down for both day and night.

TALENT SHOWCASE
20 Design Flanders
19 Kanselarijstraat

Ceramics, textiles, jewelry, glass, furniture and graphics are among the many areas of local design fostered and promoted by Design Flanders. Their gallery near the Cathédrale des Sts Michel and Gudule is the place for discovering new talents and innovative products. The exhibitions, which can include works by established and overseas designers, change six times a year. Come here to see textiles and interior designs by Chris Mestdagh, hats by Nicole Baert, wool scarves by Stefanie van Nieuwenhove and jewelry by Audi Pauwels and Kitty Spaenjers.

ROYAL MILLINER

21 Christophe Coppens
2 rue Léon Lepage and 23 place du
Nouveau Marché aux Grains [atelier]

There's certainly a touch of the
dramatic to the hats and scarves of
Christophe Coppens, a legacy of the
talented designer's training at the Brussels Theatre Conservatory. To view the
colourful and imaginative collection of
this milliner to the Belgian royal family, head to his boutique on the corner
of rue Léon Lepage and rue Antoine
Dansaert. Then saunter across to the
far side of nearby place du Nouveau
Marché aux Grains to view the hat-
making process in action at Coppens'
atelier and art gallery in a former
banana warehouse.

OUTSIDE THE BOX

22 Y-Dress?
102 rue Antoine Dansaert

Need to get married in a hurry or make
an instant transformation from fashion
frog into couture princess? No problem! Just pop into Y-Dress? in fashion
favourite rue Antoine Dansaert (p. 123)
and pick up frocks wittily labelled
'Emergency Wedding' or 'Instant
Princess', both with pop-up crinolines.
These and other fun, versatile designs,
such as XS ('extra small') Luggage for
'spontaneous overnights' and T-shirts
that morph into trousers, can be found
at this outlet for the creations of Polish-
born, Brussels-trained designer Alek-
sandra Paszkowska.

IN THE BAG

23 Delvaux
27 boulevard de Waterloo and
31 Gallerie de la Reine

Founded in 1829 by Charles Delvaux,
this luxury leather goods business
makes its bags, belts and other accessories entirely by hand. The process of
crafting one of the trademark handbags, such as the best-selling 'Brilliant'
model designed for the 1958 Expo, can
take up to thirteen hours. Only the
highest-quality calf, lamb, ostrich and
crocodile skins are used. Delvaux's flagship store is a handsome three-storey
townhouse overlooking the boulevard
de Waterloo, but they also have a Lower
Town outlet in Gallerie de la Reine, part
of the elegant covered shopping arcade
Galeries Saint-Hubert, which dates
from 1847.

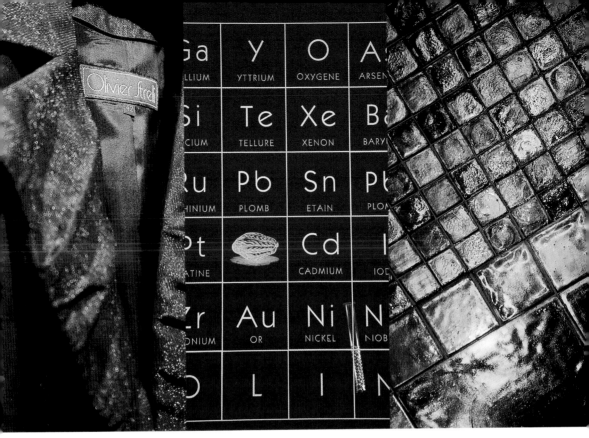

Before the 'Antwerp Six', Martin Margiela (p. 123) and other local designers, there was Olivier Strelli. Born in the Belgian Congo, he gained a passion for textiles and colour from his father, who ran a printing factory. Strelli's garments have been worn by royalty, the Rolling Stones, and even the flight stewardesses of the national airline. Undoubtedly the leading light of Belgian fashion, Strelli's main showcase is in the prestigious avenue Louise, but you can also find his collection at a boutique in rue Antoine Dansaert.

The chic, impeccably packaged and sublimely delicious chocolate creations of Pierre Marcolini have fast become a gold standard for the Belgian confection industry, a remarkable achievement for a company that only began in 1995. Marcolini himself puts his success down to two principles: a respect for the products and a liberated approach to the method of using them. You'll find the highest quality porcelain beans from Mexico used in limited-edition chocolate squares and flavourings such as lemongrass, star anise and Tahitian vanilla. At this flagship store there are also amazing cakes, luscious ice creams, marshmallow and jellies.

Behind an unassuming façade, Agnès Emery has created an extraordinary showroom for her collection of hand-crafted tiles, fabrics, paints, wrought-iron furniture and housewares. Emery has searched for the best crafts from Morocco, India and other such exotic, far-flung places to decorate her magnificent townhouse, with its grand staircase and salons with peeling, plaster mouldings, which hides behind the shopfront of two combined houses. Marvel at the different colours and textures, soak up Emery's romantic vision, and start planning your own interior makeover.

see

GATHERING OF THE GUILDS
27 Grand Place
- 't Kelderke, no. 15
- Dandoy, 31 rue au Beurre

To call the Grand Place a town square is like saying Igauzu Falls is a waterfall – technically correct, but conveying nothing of the immense spectacle and grandeur of the place. It was from 1695 onwards that the Grand Place adopted its busy, baroque look, as dictated by the city's mercantile guilds whose former guildhalls border the cobblestone square. The centrepiece is the Hôtel de Ville (town hall), a magnificent palace completed in 1448, where today you'll find the tourist office. There's so much to take in that you shouldn't feel bad at joining the gawping crowds on the terraces of one of the many cafés and restaurants that line the square's edge. Local recommendations point to 't Kelderke as the best both in terms of hearty Belgian food and prices that are reasonable despite the location. On rue au Beurre, a street leading into the Grand Place, you'll also find Dandoy, an ancient and atmospheric confectionery shop that's another worthy station on the Brussels tourist trail.

COMIC CREATIONS
28 Centre Belge de la Bande Dessinée
20 rue des Sables

Among the more charming surprises of central Brussels are the many buildings decorated with giant paintings of famous comic characters. In the homeland of Tintin, Lucky Luke and the Smurfs, comic strips (*bande dessinée*) are hugely popular, averaging sales of 11 million copies a year. The museum devoted to Belgian comic creations is the place to head to for gaining a true appreciation of this witty and imaginative art form. There's a special section devoted to Hergé's characters, and the whole place benefits from being located in a gorgeous former department store designed by Victor Horta (see right) in 1905.

THE ART OF MUSIC
29 Musée des Instruments de Musique
2 rue Montagne-de-la-Cour

Housed in the Old England Stores (a fabulous iron and glass building designed by Paul Saintenoy in 1898), this museum's collection of musical instruments – everything from accordions to zithers – is one of the finest in the world. The gizmo that enables you to hear many of the instruments in the exhibition isn't 100 per cent reliable, but it's a sure thing that you'll be amazed and delighted by the range and artistry of what's on display, including beautifully detailed pianos, bagpipes and Chinese temple bells. The pleasant rooftop café also provides a wonderful bird's-eye view of the city.

NOUVEAU'S GRAND MASTER
30 Musée Horta
25 rue Américaine

Victor Horta, one of Art Nouveau architecture's founding fathers, built this house for himself between 1898 and 1901. Light floods down from the skylight window at the top of the sensually curved stairwell that leads you up through the building, past sitting rooms with glimpses of the verdant garden outside, and bedrooms leading onto a glassed-in winter garden. Pull back a cupboard to find an ingenious foldaway toilet, note the corresponding design of doorknobs, banisters and the armrests of couches, and marvel at the intense attention to detail and craftsmanship brought to every aspect of this house. You'll never think of interior design in quite the same way again.

FULL STEAM AHEAD!
31 Flagey
place Sainte-Croix
- Café Belga, place Eugène Flagey Plein
- Marie, 40 rue Alphonse de Witte

Seen from across the Ixelles ponds, it's obvious why the nickname of the old Institut National de Radiodiffusion is *le paquebot*, or 'steamship'. Rising in Art Déco-style tiers to a crow's nest-crowned turret, this iconic building, which incorporated several concert halls, was running to seed in the early 1990s before being revamped into the vibrant arts centre it is today. Retitled Flagey, here you'll find a repertory cinema, a clutch of various sized studios for music performances, and Café Belga, a slacker heaven of zinc and chrome created by bar-meister Fred Nicolay (see p. 123). Food of a more serious nature is served just up the road by Lilian Devaux at the cozy, Michelin-starred Marie.

Take an iron crystal molecule, magnify it 165 billion times and build a copy entirely from steel. Engineer André Waterkeyn's iconic structure is currently looking as good, if not better, than it did when first unveiled for the 1958 Expo, thanks to a multi-million Euro facelift. After admiring its surreal mirror-ball surface, head inside to view its retro interior, zigzagging your way up escalators and stairs in the 23-metrelong tubes that link the spheres to the panoramic café-bar. Contrast nostalgic photographs from its Expo heyday with a striking set of new images commissioned from Marie-Françoise Plissart during the renovation.

Victor Horta (see p. 127) was outraged that his vision for a palace of fine arts was compromised when city bureaucrats insisted that shops take up the main façade. Even so, much of the great architect's vision remained intact, and following a long period of restoration and renovation, this multi-purpose arts centre – including several exhibition halls, a world-class concert hall, restaurant, café and bookshop – is looking grand once more. The 'Bozar', as it's now snappily known, offers an impressive year-round programme of performing and visual arts, so it's well worth checking out what's on.

The sublimely beautiful home of banker and patron of the arts David van Buuren and his wife Alice dates from 1928. It's a monument to Art Déco style and houses an outstanding collection of paintings and furnishings, many pieces commissioned especially for the home. The art is eclectic and includes works spanning from Pieter Bruegel the Elder to Rik Wouters. Don't leave without also taking a turn through the 1.5 hectares of gardens, including a maze of yew trees, a plantation of roses and the romantic 'Garden of the Heart'.

As its name indicates, there are several museums here in the one complex, linked by a central entrance hall. The Museum of Ancient Art houses an enormous collection of paintings, sculptures and drawings from the 15th to the 18th centuries, while the Museum of Modern Art picks up the art baton from the 19th century and carries it to the present day, and includes the Antoine Wiertz and Constantin Meunier Museums, devoted to the work of two key figures in Belgian art. A new series of galleries devoted to René Magritte is scheduled to open in 2007. Take a breather between sections in the on-site café.

Dublin, immortalized in song by The Pogues as the quintessential 'Dirty Ol'Town' in 1985, has cleaned up its act in a big way since the new millennium struck. If Shane MacGowan were to go and meet his love by the Gasworks wall today, he would find it unrecognizable as it has been converted into luxury penthouse flats – such is the new Dublin. With this shiny new prosperity and economic success has come great change. Some say for the worse, as the city's cheeky charm and gritty character has been diluted by a more confident and cosmopolitan outlook. But on the upside, the city has never pulsed with possibility the way it does today, with new cafés and bars springing up on every street corner and thousands of new faces infusing the capital with a multi-ethnic energy and diversity.

The trick with Dublin, as with so many cities, is to know where to hit and where to miss on the map. It is essentially small, compact and easy to navigate on foot, which is a bonus as the public transport system still has a long way to go (although the new LUAS tram service has been a great addition to the city). St Stephen's Green and Grafton Street have always been the visitor's main focal points in Dublin, but really it is the tributaries off the main thoroughfare that reveal the city's true charms. Wander west of Grafton Street to explore the cobbled streets of Castle Market and Drury Street, lined with one-off boutiques, restaurants, shoe shops and antique jewelry dealers, then follow the less beaten track on up to the Liberties to discover veritable old Dublin, complete with cobbled streets and horse-drawn hawkers. Visit Christ Church, the magnificent cathedral founded in 600 AD by Strongbow, the first conqueror of Ireland, and St Patrick's cathedral around the corner, where sardonic writer Jonathan Swift is buried. Neighbouring Francis Street, bustling with antique shops, art galleries and eclectic finds, is a must for a browse.

Down the hill to the quays, visitors will notice perhaps the biggest change in the city as the River Liffey reclaims her place as the regal Anna Livia Plurabelle (as she was personified in Joyce's *Finnegans Wake*). With the addition of wooden boardwalks, floral hanging baskets, a Liffey Voyage tour boat (p. 149) and the new Dublin City Moorings, the river has come into her own, set off by the gleaming new Docklands development on the north bank, which boasts the Financial Centre, smart apartment complexes and a selection of restaurants and bars by the water. Over the landmark Ha'penny Bridge lies Temple Bar, once the city's coolest quarter, but now, alas, more sweaty pub than cultural hub. Apart from a few attractions such as the Irish Film Institute and the Food Market (p. 149), Temple Bar is largely to be avoided. Instead, wander up to Cow's Lane, a new street that is an avant-garde fashion hub with its unique boutiques and furniture finds. But despite all this chat of 'new', there's still stacks of old Dublin to delve into, with 'old man' pubs, quiet Georgian squares and leafy St Stephen's Green still as beguiling as ever. Slainte!

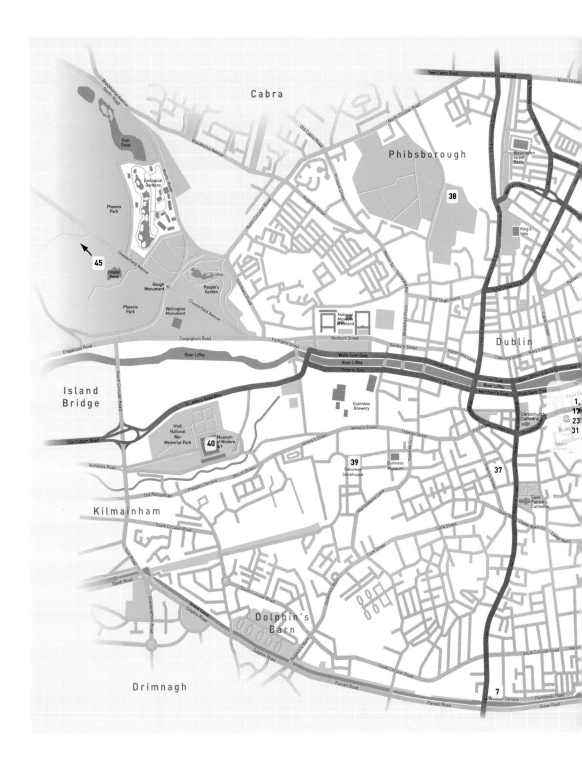

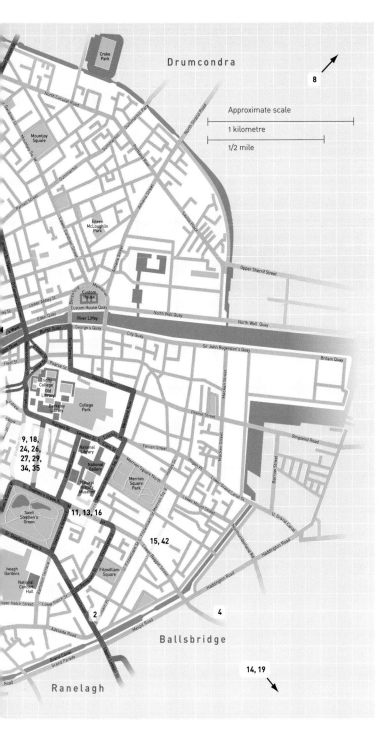

StyleCity Dublin

sleep

U 2 CAN STAY HERE

1   The Clarence
6–8 Wellington Quay
Rooms from €340

U2's rock 'n' roll bolthole by the river (it's owned by Bono and The Edge) is as popular with locals as it is with visitors, mostly due to the hotel's Octagon Bar, which serves up the famous 'Clarence Cosmo'. Paintings by Bono's old school-mate, Virgin Prunes vocalist Guggi (Derek Rowan), are a trademark of the hotel, as is the clerical colour scheme of crimson, royal blue, amethyst, chocolate and gold. In its previous life the building belonged to the Catholic church and operated as a guesthouse for visiting clergy, hence the ecclesiastical theme. In the bedrooms, Shaker-style furniture reinforces the pared-down elegance of the place. Egyptian cotton sheets, king-sized beds, monogrammed slippers and all mod-cons add more than a touch of luxury to your stay.

Once the home of Irish architect Sam Stephenson, 31 Leeson Close is now a stylish and original B&B that is the rarest of things, a genuinely quiet hideaway in the heart of the city. The two houses, one fine Georgian building and the more modest coach house, have been converted by present owners Noel and Deirdre Comer into twenty bedrooms. The en-suite rooms throughout the two houses vary from grand four-poster affairs to cozy single-bed nooks. One highlight of the place has to be the sunken conversation pit in the coach house, along with the mirrored bar/reception area. Its location is also ideal, just five minutes from Grafton Street and the centre of Dublin city life.

3 **Grafton House**

26–27 South Great Georges Street
Rooms from €100

From the team who created Bewley's (p. 144), Eden (p. 139) and the neighbouring Odessa Club (p. 145) comes Grafton House, providing designer duvets to the travel- and club-weary to sink into after partying the night away in the aforementioned establishments. Located on South Great Georges Street in the heart of clubland, Grafton House is ideally situated for those of a nocturnal nature. The hotel offers singles, doubles, a triple and a six-person penthouse, all smartly kitted out in warm, modern tones and fabrics. What makes Grafton House stand out above the rest? The keen room rates, with doubles from €100 per night, including breakfast.

4 Pembroke Townhouse
90 Pembroke Road
Rooms from €120

Pembroke Townhouse, housed in an 18th-century building in Dublin's leafy Ballsbridge area, is a true find in the bustling city. While only a ten-minute stroll from the centre of town, this intimate hotel/guesthouse still retains the charm of a rural retreat. The Pembroke offers its guests a finely tuned blend of comfort, hospitality, convenience and personal attention, and particularly prides itself on the variety and quality of its breakfasts, ranging from omelettes to the full Irish, French toast to lamb's liver with sautéed onions and bacon. There is no restaurant in the hotel, but Pembroke Road and the adjoining Baggot Street offer some of the best dining options in the city, including L'Ecrivain (p. 140) and Langkawi, the highly rated Malaysian restaurant a few doors up. Add to this the stylishly decorated rooms, mod cons and free parking, all starting from just €120 per night.

eat

5 Fallon & Byrne
11-17 Exchequer Street

As Dublin's first proper food hall, Fallon & Byrne set out from the beginning to showcase the best of Irish produce. Come here to stock up on Hicks sausages, Hederman's smoked fish, Irish farmhouse cheeses, salads, cured meats, home-made hummus, olives and other deli essentials. Downstairs, the wine bar serves a stellar selection of wines by the glass complemented by small plates of mouthwatering morsels from the food hall above. The top-floor brasserie, complete with burgundy booths and a zinc bar, offers warm salads, juicy steaks and plenty of hearty fare, such as fish pie en croûte served with creamy mash and roast breast of chicken on the bone with foie gras, cep mushrooms and fondant potatoes.

ROCK UP TO THE TROC

6 Trocadero Restaurant
3 St Andrew Street

Atmosphere, atmosphere, atmosphere is what Trocadero is all about. If it's a bit of renowned Irish *craic* you're after, then 'The Troc' is where to find it. The theatrically decadent mood is set by red velvet booths, tasselled curtains, glittering mirrors and walls adorned with black-and-white head shots of the theatre's great and the good. The free-flowing wine and the mood set by hosts Robert Doggett and Jade are what draw diners back time and again. On your way downstairs to the loo keep your eye out for the shot of Doggett with Brenda Fricker and her Oscar! The Troc is jammed from 6 p.m. to 3 a.m., so be sure to book early and bring a gang.

CANALSIDE FRENCH CUISINE

7 Locks
1 Windsor Terrace

Something of a Dublin dining institution, Locks has been drawing the city's discerning gourmands through its doors to its enviable canalside location for over twenty-five years. The restaurant is decorated in a warm and elegant style with soft lighting, open fires and a soothing atmosphere. There's a timelessness about the ambience that is extremely comforting. Head chef Alan Kinsella is making his mark with his Irish-French cuisine and tempting diners with the likes of loin of rabbit with chorizo mousse, rillette and spring roll, served with a fig compôte and rosemary jus. Desserts are equally sophisticated and the patrician wine list favours France, Bordeaux in particular. Locks has a unique charm, in summer the doors open onto the canal and in winter there are few places cozier or more inviting.

SOLE TO SOLE

8 Aqua
1 West Pier

Howth and Dalkey are Dublin's two main seaside enclaves, just thirty minutes from the city centre. Unlike Dalkey, Howth life is very much focused on its harbour and marina, with the Howth Yacht Club taking centre stage. Here on the marina, in a fine old stone building overlooking the sea, is Aqua, which serves up fresh fish and carnivorous fare in a smart, contemporary setting. Pan-fried sole, crispy calamari and seafood chowder are among the highlights, along with more meaty offerings such as duck confit with wilted pak choy and raspberry-and-mango dressing. Floor-to-ceiling glass make the most of the sea view, while the open kitchen and busy staff create a buzz about the place.

PEOPLE PLEASER

9 Peploe's
16 St Stephen's Green

Peploe's wine bar and restaurant is an easy favourite among Dublin diners, combining as it does excellent food with a buzzy, convivial ambience. Located in the basement of a fine Georgian building on St Stephen's Green, Peploe's is in the heart of it all. The bar area is inviting with its impressive marble bar, grand piano and extensive wine list that includes a dozen vintages of Champagne and about thirty wines by the glass, while the restaurant is comfortably fitted out with padded banquettes and generous tables. The food is unfussy with the emphasis on great flavours and strong ingredients, including the likes of foie gras terrine with brioche, risotto aux cèpes with wilted rocket and Parmesan, and loin of free-range pork gratinated with Roquefort, pear, leeks and a Calvados sauce. After coffee, retire back to the bar for a nightcap and more people-watching.

FARM FRESH

10 Eden
Meeting House Square

Temple Bar, once the city's much-hyped hip quarter, has suffered in recent years, becoming a stag- and hen-party hub. But Eden still leads the gastro-pack in terms of culinary creativity, offering up organic-whenever-possible dishes under the guidance of head chef Eleanor Walsh. The menu is simple but satisfying with an Irish flavour, with plenty of fresh fish, farmhouse cheese and Irish pork and beef. Desserts are a highlight, with home-made sorbet and ice cream and confectionary creations. In the summer, Eden's terrace overlooking Meeting House Square is a prime people-watching spot, sought out by Dubliners and visitors alike.

CARNIVOROUS FARE FROM CLARE

11 Ely Wine Bar
22 Ely Place

Run by husband-and-wife team Eric and Michelle Robson, Ely Wine Bar has earned a reputation in the city as one of the best places for vino and victuals. Signature dishes include a heartwarming Irish Stew, hearty cod fishcakes and one of the best hamburgers in town. All the beef, pork and lamb served is organic and comes from the family farm in Co Clare. The Robsons recently opened a sister bar in Custom House Quay (CHQ), a magnificent glass building by the River Liffey in Dublin's newly gentrified Docklands.

IRISH CHARCUTERIE

12 Chapter One
18/19 Parnell Square

In the 19th century, Parnell Square was undoubtedly the most sought-after address in Dublin. But today this end of town is decidedly less fashionable than its southside counterparts. Despite this, Chapter One, situated on the square, has proved the 'location, location' nay-sayers wrong and has earned a reputation as one of the best restaurants in town. Owned and run by head chef Ross Lewis and maître d' Martin Corbett, it is renowned for its stellar cooking, sparkling personality and smart setting. Lewis is an ardent campaigner for Irish artisan food and highlights it wherever possible in his menus. His Irish charcuterie trolley is not to be missed.

BANGERS AND MASH
13 Bang Café
11 Merrion Row

Bang Café, run by twin brothers Simon and Christian Stokes, takes its name from their fashionista mother Pia Bang and is popular for its contemporary Irish menu and fun, easygoing atmosphere, set off by smart décor, a sleek bar area and professional, friendly staff. Needless to say, the café's bangers and mash is the signature dish. All ingredients are carefully sourced and Irish where possible; suppliers listed on the menu include M&K Meats, fishmonger T. Mulloy, sausage-makers Hicks of Dun Laoghaire, and Gold Riverfarm for organic vegetables.

SOMETHING FISHY
14 Cavistons Food Emporium
58/59 Glasthule Road

Cavistons is run by the ebullient Caviston brothers, Peter and Stephen, whose family have been in the fish business for generations. Having started as a humble fishmongers, they expanded the business to include an upmarket deli and lunchtime fish restaurant. The menu is imaginative and full of wild and wacky piscatorial creations. Expect to be tempted by the likes of pan-fried crab and sweet corn cakes, red pepper mayonnaise, seared scallops, saffron and basil sauce and chargrilled swordfish steak with mango, melon and chilli chutney. The daily specials always offer something surprising.

EAT WITH RELISH
15 L'Ecrivain
109a Lower Baggot Street

While many Michelin-starred establishments are so stuffy you feel afraid to sneeze in the place, this is not the case at L'Ecrivain. Here, the atmosphere is lively and convivial with a piano bar downstairs and generously spaced, opulent dining upstairs. Derry Clarke's food is little short of legendary; set your taste buds tingling with his kataifi-wrapped Dublin Bay prawns with cucumber relish, lemon mayonnaise and chilli jam, followed by soy and honey glazed belly of pork confit, onion mash, glazed apricot and apple and cider froth, with an assiette of peach to finish you off. L'Ecrivain delivers all of the flair but none of the fuss of other Michelin-starred venues.

STARRY NIGHTS
16 Restaurant Patrick Guilbauds
Merrion Hotel, 21 Upper Merrion Street

For almost two decades, Patrick Guilbauds has been the standard bearer for fine French food in Dublin. His two-Michelin-star restaurant has changed locations over the years (and is now ensconced in the deluxe Merrion Hotel), but the quality has never faltered. The restaurant is considered by many to be the best in Ireland, and has won countless awards to this effect. The menu climbs the zenith of haute cuisine and offers the likes of ravioli made with Clogherhead lobster coated in a coconut-scented lobster cream and served with home-made free-range egg pasta, toasted almonds and curry flavoured olive oil, accompanied by some of the best wines ever to grace a cellar. The Merrion Hotel itself also boasts one of the finest 20th-century Irish art collections in the country, so arrive early to take it all in.

drink

PINTS, PLEASE

17 The Long Hall
51 South Great Georges Street

Housed in a listed building, this time-honoured pub has remained largely unchanged since the 19th century. The ornate, slightly kitsch interior, complete with replica muskets and broken clocks, has witnessed countless plans hatched and relationships dispatched over the decades. You will find no sour apple Martinis or Grey Goose vodka served here, just plenty of pints and perhaps a gin and bitter lemon at a push. The Long Hall is the place to come for cracking conversation and proper pints in a real Dublin setting.

TRADITIONAL WATERING HOLE
18 Kehoe's
9 South Anne Street

An oldie but a goodie – Kehoe's is a perennial favourite with Dubliners, and for good reason. It has managed to maintain its quirky, low-key pub character amid lots of newer, glossier competition. Famous for its traditional snug and walled-in atmosphere, Kehoe's is the ideal spot to hide away and lose an afternoon. The previous owner, John Kehoe, lived upstairs until his death and now his (largely unchanged) sitting room houses the quirky upstairs bar. For a cozy night in when you are out on the town, it's got to be Kehoe's.

SPOT OF THE BLACK STUFF
19 Finnegans
2 Sorrento Road

You can't beat Finnegans for a Sunday afternoon pint. This warm and friendly pub in Dalkey is just a short stroll from the sea, so first things first – work up a thirst by taking a stroll through the pretty-as-a-picture village before heading up the hill to the clifftop Vico Road to take in sweeping views of the bay. If the weather is fine, you might even be tempted to take a dip at White Rock beach. Then settle back into Finnegans for a spirit-warming pint of the black stuff; you might even spot local residents Bono, Maeve Binchy or Enya at the bar doing the same.

SUGAR AND SPICE
20 Avoca Café
11–13 Suffolk Street

Avoca began life as a textile business in Co Wicklow back in 1723. In 1979 the Pratt family opened a small shop selling rugs and blankets in Kilmacanogue, with a small café out the back. Twenty-eight years on and three stores later, the Avoca name is synonymous with homeware and colourful clothing, and the Avoca Café boasts two cookbooks and countless awards for their uncomplicated and delicious food. Using only the best Irish ingredients, from Hederman's smoked mussels to Gubbeen bacon and Hicks sausages, they make dishes such as smoked fish platters, organic bacon paninis and bangers and mash something special. But it's their baked goods that steal the show.

NOT SO GRUELLING
21 Gruel
68a Dame Street

As the name suggests, there is nothing light and fluffy about this small café. Instead, Gruel is famous for its signature 'Roast in a Roll', a great hunk of roasted meat in a chunky roll, served with lashings of relish. It's a modern and original take on the Irish carvery lunch and only the seriously hungry need apply. Steaming bowls of soup made with grilled red pepper, spiced prawn or rustic vegetables including butter beans, aubergine and chunks of carrot are also popular, as are the hearty salads. Gruel's interior is also worth a mention; flying in the face of tradition, they were doing 'shabby chic' long before the term was invented.

LOCAL BREWERY
22 The Porterhouse Brewing Company
16–18 Parliament Street

Serious stout fans will enjoy the Porterhouse – a pub that brews its own in Temple Bar. Exclusive to the Porterhouse are three stouts, three ales and three lagers. Top tipples include the Temple Bräu pilsner lager (made with the finest German Hallertau hops and premium Irish malted barley) and Porterhouse Red (a red ale with a traditional hops flavour and underlying caramel characters). A must-visit for budding beer connoisseurs.

SWEET AND SAVOURY
23 Queen of Tarts
4 Cork Hill, Dame Street

This tiny bakery-café near Dublin Castle is one of the city's hidden gems. Originally founded by two pastry chefs, the Queen of Tarts serves some of the finest pastries around. Savouries include pastries filled with chicken, tomato and courgette or spinach, as well as ricotta and mushroom, while among the sweets are traditional favourites like Victoria sponge, raspberry cheesecake, apple and blackberry crumble and lemon meringue pie. The Queen of Tarts is open for breakfast and lunch seven days a week.

DOWNSTAIRS FOR PIZZA
24 Bewley's
78/79 Grafton Street

Bewley's has been a famous landmark on Grafton Street since the early 1900s, renowned as a scribbler's den back to Joyce's and Yeats' day. Recently the landmark eatery was taken over by the trendy Sherland Entertainment Group, who have modernized it by adding new fish restaurant Mackerel upstairs and their signature Café Bar Deli pizza and pasta restaurant downstairs. But the historic interior remains largely intact, with the magnificent Harry Clarke stained-glass windows and mosaic-tiled floor still taking pride of place.

JAZZ AND TAPAS
25 The Globe Bar & Café
11 South Great Georges Street

Another funky offering from the Sherland Entertainment team, the Globe has been drawing Dublin's hip crowd for over ten years. During the day, the cozy space with its red brick walls and dark wood furnishings offers coffee, snacks and free Wi-Fi. As evening falls, Spanish-style tapas are on the menu before the place takes off for the night with lively beats by resident DJs. At midnight the back doors to adjoining late-night club Ri-Ra open and the two venues become one. Visit on Sunday for live jazz and mid-week for free gigs.

Ron Blacks was originally the name of the smallest pub in Dublin (which could cope with a capacity of about thirty punters at a push). When it closed, the license was bought out and the new Ron Blacks opened around the corner, with more than a touch of irony in the name as it is now one of the largest pubs in the capital. The design is slick and the space is sprawling, offering nooks and crannies for a clandestine date and stacks of open space for those who like to see and be seen.

One of Dublin's most well-known pubs, Davy Byrne's has been around for over a hundred years and was immortalized in Joyce's *Ulysses* as the place where Leopold Bloom dropped in for a pint. Today the pub is as popular with locals as it is with visiting Joyce junkies, pulling a busy crowd for one of the great pub lunches in the city. Daily specials include pheasant, game and oysters in season, and smoked salmon and fresh seafood all year round. On the wall are murals of a Joycean Dublin by Liam Proud and Cecil French Salkeld.

Owned and run by Jay Bourke and Eoin Foyle of the ubiquitous Sherland Entertainment Group, this private members' bar is the hottest after-hours destination in the capital, and boasts a restaurant, two bars and a roof terrace heated for smokers' comfort. Come for food, cocktails, chess, fireside chats and groovy tunes late into the night, as well as summer BBQs, winter film nights and wine tastings. Odessa Club offers an overseas membership rate of just €120, well worth opting for if you are a regular visitor to the city.

shop

29 Dolls
32 Westbury Mall, Clarendon Street

Petria Lenehan spent several years in London as a buyer for hip store Hub before returning home to Dublin to set up her own boutique Dolls. Now she stocks a tightly edited collection of labels that includes Karen Walker, Future Classics, Swear, Buddhahood, Peter Jensen, Bi la li, Zakee Shariff and cult Australian labels Metallicus and Body, along with jewelry from Tatty Devine. Petria, who could grace a magazine cover herself, has her own line, too (also called Dolls), a series of limited-edition pieces that use softly printed cotton and antique lace and trimmings with intricate detailing and unusual shapes.

VINTAGE HEAVEN
30 Jenny Vander
50 Drury Street

Vintage shop and Dublin institution Jenny Vander began life in the city's Georges Street Arcade some twenty-five years ago, but current owner Gail Kinsella has taken it to new heights, moving it to its roomier location just a stone's throw away on Drury Street. Easily Dublin's best vintage store, the fashion savvy will find a collection of designer pieces from the 1920s, '30s, '40s and '50s sourced from all over the world. Finds include beautiful antique lace blouses and nightdresses, hand-beaded Victorian jackets, an array of bags and shoes and a good collection of costume jewelry.

GIRLIE TREASURES
31 Costume
10 Castle Market

Costume has been kitting out Dublin's 'It' girls for years. Its appeal is broad, stocking a range of labels by Alice Temperley, Isabel Morant, Anna Sui, Jonathan Saunders and Barbara Bui, as well as accessories by Helen James and bags by Brontibay, Jerome Dreyfuss and MO851. Mothers and daughters will both find treasures here, and it is a favourite with brides. Family-owned and run by Billie Tucker and her two daughters, Tracy and Anne, the designs of yet another daughter, Leigh, are the shop's best sellers; look out for her label Leighlee.

FOR LABEL LOVERS
32 Smock
Unit 5, 20–22 Essex Street West

Thirty-somethings Susan O'Connell and Karen Crawford set up Smock five years ago to offer Dubliners-in-the-know a more avant-garde take on fashion, with edgy tailoring and directional footwear. Keen to bring the deconstructed look to Ireland, they stock a carefully sourced collection of exclusive labels, including a good selection of Belgian designers such as Véronique Branquinho (p. 41), Martin Margiela (p. 123) and Bernhard Willhelm, and other international labels including Mayle, Costume National and Tsumori Chisato.

STYLE COUNCIL
33 Tulle
28 Market Arcade,
South Great Georges Street

Boutique owner Laura Hickey insists that she is not fashion-led, preferring to buy what she likes and what she thinks will flatter her clients. It's an approach that works. Since Tulle opened in Georges Street Arcade it has become a magnet for the hip and stylish looking for quirkier alternatives to more mainstream designs. Look out for wonderful dresses by Leona Edmiston that will take you from the office to the opera, the sophisticated but affordable By Marlene Birger collection, Missoni, Betsey Johnson and J Brand jeans.

PINK CHIC AT CHICA
34 Chica Day + Chica Night
25 and 3–4 Westbury Mall,
Clarendon Street

It doesn't get much more girlie than Chica (both day and night versions), with its pink walls, gold antique mirrors, jewelry cabinets, chandeliers and heart-shaped rails. Sisters Josette, Mena and Mary-Kate Ryan have a colourful, not to mention tongue-in-cheek, approach to fashion, and their two stores, both located in Dublin's chic Westbury Mall, are packed with party frocks, costume jewelry, clutch bags, embellished scarves, bejeweled flip-flops and other downright outrageous offerings. Labels include Acne Jeans, Glory, Actar Actar, Hide & Seek, Watashi-Wa and Zuca.

FASHION MOTHERSHIP
35 Brown Thomas
88–95 Grafton Street

First opening in 1849, Ireland's answer to London's Selfridges has gone from strength to strength in recent years with the opening of a Vera Wang bridal salon and the new Shoe Rooms and Designer Rooms. Expect big names such as Alexander McQueen, Jean Paul Gaultier, Balenciaga, Burberry, Chloé and Missoni, more affordable labels such as Theory and Nicole Farhi, quirkier pieces from the likes of Antik Bachik, and home-grown talent such as young Irish designer Joanne Hynes. The men's department stocks – among others – Hugo Boss, Gant, Prada, Etro, Dolce & Gabbana and Paul Smith. And after a spot of shopping, there is also a nail bar, restaurant and café.

BOOKSTORE ON THE LIFFEY
36 The Winding Stair
40 Lower Ormond Quay

Dublin's much-loved bookshop and café in the Northside overlooking the River Liffey recently reopened to great acclaim. Still selling a good selection of second-hand books on the ground floor of its three-storey premises (connected by the eponymous 18th-century staircase), the Winding Stair's top level has the vibe of a laid-back private library, with comfy sofas and a thoughtful menu that showcases the best of Irish produce with simple but delicious traditional dishes, perfectly seasoned and executed with skill. Of course, the views over the Liffey and the piping-hot coffee make it well worth a detour.

CUTTING-EDGE ART
37 Cross Gallery
59 Francis Street

Located in Francis Street, home to the capital's cluster of antique shops, the Cross Gallery has earned a reputation as a good hunting ground for hot new talent, and its openings draw an eclectic crowd of investors, art lovers and artists. Owner Nicholas Gore-Grimes has been fostering the talents of some of Ireland's most exciting new artists for years, but his atmospheric gallery is also home to the work of such established and highly esteemed artists as John Boyd, Bridget Flannery, Simon English and Jack Donovan.

see

A ROSE BLOOMS IN DUBLIN
38 National Botanic Gardens
Glasnevin

Created in the late 18th century for the study of plant species, it was here that David Moore first discovered potato blight in 1845 and predicted its devastating impact. Today, the 48-acre setting boasts beautiful rose gardens, intricately designed floral carpets, cedar woods, peony borders and hawthorn glens, all criss-crossed by a web of pretty paths and walkways. Of particular interest are the glasshouses, built by the great Dublin ironmaster Richard Turner and filled with flora from around the world.

FOR THOSE WHO WAIT
39 Guinness Storehouse
St James's Gate

The smell of fermented barley has hung over St James's Gate since 1759 when the Guinness brewery first produced its famously turf-dark stout. Today, the scent of barley still hangs heavily as you walk through the Guinness Storehouse, once a storage spot for the brew and now a high-tech museum. Interactive exhibits bring the fermenting process to life and allow a bit of taste-testing. Afterwards, head to the Gravity Bar on the roof to pick up your free pint of the black stuff and savour the panoramic sweep of the city below.

CONTEMPORARY ART SCENE
40 Irish Museum of Modern Art
Military Road, Kilmainham

Nestling in the city's old Kilmainham Barracks, the location of the Irish Museum of Modern Art makes a striking aesthetic statement in its own right. Its exhibition programme regularly juxtaposes the work of leading figures with that of the younger generation to create a debate about the nature and function of art. Exhibited artists have included Martin Puryear, Sophie Calle and Vik Muniz, alongside the more local talents of Louis le Brocquy and Barry Flanagan. There is also a good café in the grounds for refuelling.

Ireland, known as the land of saints and scholars, is famed for her literary heroes, both living and dead: Joyce, Shaw, Yeats, Kavanagh, Heaney, and more. With this in mind, literary lovers will want to make the pilgrimage to the Dublin Writers Museum, located in a beautiful Georgian house at the top of O'Connell Street. From the quirky to the quintessential, the museum showcases the mock Book of Quells, revolutionary plays of the early Abbey theatre, original scripts and draft texts chronicling the life of tormented young author James Joyce, and varied work by 20th-century Irish poets and writers.

Every Saturday, Temple Bar's Meeting House Square comes alive with the sights and smells of the pick of Irish produce as it hosts the city's main farmers' market. Whet your appetite on oysters chucked straight from the shell, Ed Hicks' famous sausages (served up as mouthwatering hot dogs), Frank Hederman's smoked fish, Silke Croppe's award-winning sheep's milk cheese, and Soul Bakery's fresh focaccias and sourdough loaves, not to mention the rows of fabulously fresh organic produce, Spanish stalls, waffle stands and fresh juice and coffee vendors. Come hungry and leave happy.

Farmleigh, located in the heart of the city's lush Phoenix Park, is one of the finest houses in the city. Formerly the home of the Guinness family, the house was purchased by the state in 1999 and restored as a unique 'guesthouse' for visiting government dignitaries. With its Connemara marble pillars, Waterford crystal chandeliers, San Domingo mahogany staircase and priceless artworks, Farmleigh is an architectural gem. Make sure to visit the Nobel Room with its 'living landscape' window in place of a painting above the fireplace. Throughout the summer months, the house hosts a number of cultural events.

The River Liffey was the focal point for the city's traffic and trade in centuries gone by and now enjoys prominence once again. The recent development of the Docklands has brought with it a bustling new district with restaurants, shops, cafés and slick apartment blocks springing up by the water. To make the most of the city's waterside sights, hop on the Liffey Voyage boat which cruises the length and breadth of the river and offers a guided tour along the way, and pay close attention to the views of the undersides of Dublin's historic bridges.

No 29 Lower Fitzwilliam Street is one of many historic houses that line Merrion Square. But this particular five-storey Georgian gem has been painstakingly restored and opened as a museum to showcase the domestic life of the well-to-do family that lived within its walls between 1790 and 1820. Architectural details are the highlights, as conservationists have restored and reproduced the ceiling mouldings, wallpaper, fireplaces and window fittings with striking results.

ISTANBUL

Truly a bit of Turkish delight on a moonlit night, few can fail to fall under the spell of Istanbul's glorious location and breathtakingly beautiful buildings. Confusingly possessing three different names at various times over the centuries (the first being Byzantium), Istanbul has the unique distinction of straddling two continents, Asia and Europe, without being defined by either. The picture-postcard Bosphorus (Boğaziçi) separates the suburbs on the Asian shore from the city centre on the European side, itself further divided by the Golden Horn (Haliç). Geography and history have dictated the evolution of Istanbul's singular and complex character; East meets West here, and the Islamic past mingles with the modern Europe of today. With bygone eras piled in archaeological layers one on top of the other, history oozes from the city's every pore. On the surface, designer shops and trendy cafés appear and vanish at the speed of light; underneath, another world of architectural splendour remains timeless. But in the face of such contrasts, and despite recent decades of ambitious and unsympathetic city planning, Istanbul manages to hang on to its very real charm.

One of several Greek colonies clustered around the shores of the Bosphorus and the Sea of Marmara, Byzantium was already up and running by the middle of the 7th century BC, and was more than a thousand years old by the time Constantine the Great established the city (renamed Constantinople) as the capital of the Eastern Roman Empire in AD 330. After a failed insurrection two hundred years later, the emperor Justinian set out to recreate a grander and more imposing city than ever before. The jewel in his municipal crown was the newly built Hagia Sophia (dedicated in 537), which still stands as Istanbul's most distinctive monument. When the Byzantine Empire collapsed in 1453, Sultan Mehmet II (Mehmet the Conqueror), with the help of a devoted army, created the distinctively Ottoman city that underpins much of modern Istanbul. The modern-day skyline over the Golden Horn, dominated by domes and minarets, is the fruit of this 15th-century vision.

In the the city's oldest quarter, Sultanahmet, the Muslim presence is unmistakable, and within walking distance its Christian Byzantine past can be found in the two urban neighbourhoods of Fener and Balat. The old port neighbourhood of Karaköy, located across the Golden Horn, has been an important trade centre since the days of the Ottoman Empire, its pedestrian thoroughfare İstiklal Caddesi cutting a swathe northwards through the bohemian district of Beyoğlu, a large area that incorporates several neighbourhoods, including trendy Cihangir and Çukurcuma. Snaking north from Beyoğlu and the Sea of Marmara to join the Black Sea, the Bosphorus is famed for both its strategic naval importance and its jaw-droppingly picturesque atmosphere. Despite the continuing problems of pollution and a lack of green spaces, this metropolis of two continents, seven hills and twenty million people remains a city of contrasts and surprises that never fails to fascinate.

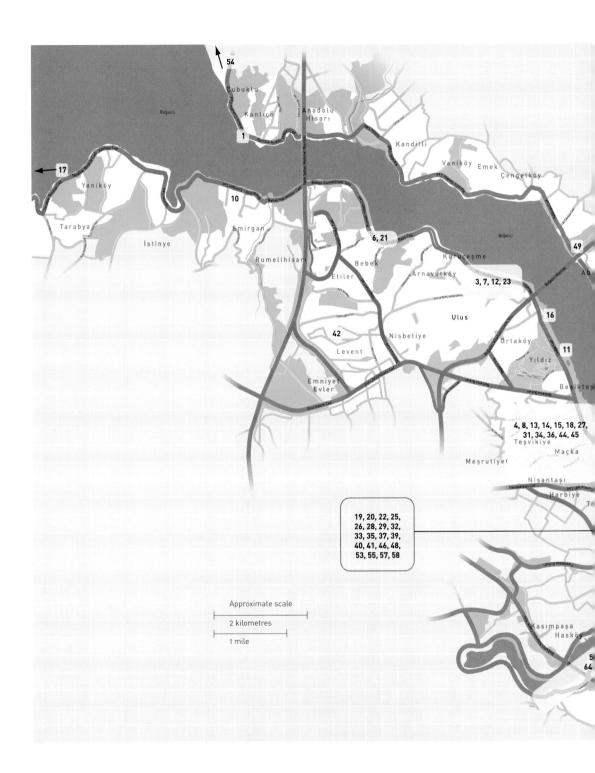

54

Çubuklu

Boğaziçi

Kanlıca

1

Anadolu
Hisarı

Kandilli

17

Yeniköy

Vaniköy Emek

Çengelköy

10

Tarabya

Emirgan

İstinye

6, 21

Boğaziçi

49

Rumelihisarı

Bebek

Kuruçeşme

Etiler

Arnavutköy

3, 7, 12, 23

Ab

16

42

Ulus

Nisbetiye

Ortaköy

11

Levent

Yıldız

Emniyet
Evler

Beşiktaş

4, 8, 13, 14, 15, 18, 27,
31, 34, 36, 44, 45
Teşvikiye

Maçka

Meşrutiyet

Nişantaşı

Harbiye

Ta

19, 20, 22, 25,
26, 28, 29, 32,
33, 35, 37, 39,
40, 41, 46, 48,
53, 55, 57, 58

Approximate scale

2 kilometres

1 mile

Kasımpaşa

Hasköy

5
64

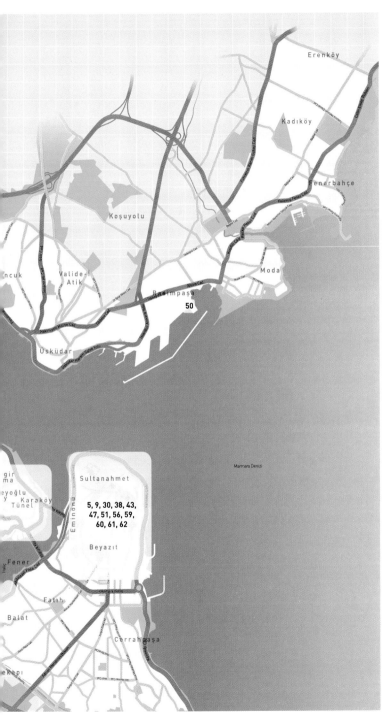

StyleCity Istanbul

sleep

QUALITY TRANQUILITY

1 **A'jia**
Kanlıca-Çubuklu Caddesi 27
Rooms from €250

With dramatic views of the Bosphorus from the tranquil shores of Kanlıca, A'jia (the Japanese word for Asia) is a unique and elegant sixteen-room hotel that takes care that each guest without exception receives the VIP treatment. The original building was once the home of the Ottoman governor Ahmet Rasim Paşa, and until 1970 had been used as a school. Revamped by architect Reşit Soley and managed by the ubiquitous Istanbul Doors Group, the new-look A'jia has injected fresh life into the Asian side of the city. The sophisticated interior, dominated by modern furniture, contemporary art and an all-white colour scheme, is a perfect contrast to the historic exterior. Each room is equipped with a king-sized bed (with equally large and invitingly fluffy goosedown pillows), air conditioning, a personal safe and wireless Internet access. Even the bathrooms provide luxuries for weary guests, and include a robe and slippers. Five of the ten double rooms have a private balcony, three of the six suites have mezzanine floors, and almost all of the rooms, both double and deluxe, look directly onto the Bosphorus. The hotel is accessible by sea, but valet parking is also available for less adventurous travellers. The minimal sophistication employed by Soley for the interior is extended to the superb restaurant, which offers Mediterranean cuisine prepared by award-winning Turkish chef, Mustafa Baylan. During the summer months, the banqueting facilities on the terrace can seat up to 300 diners, or host up to 600 cocktail party guests, to the background accompaniment of music and the engines of passing fishing boats.

Once through the door of this charming hotel, guests feel as if they are stepping (on creaky wooden floors) into the past. Formed by joining four adjacent 19th-century Greek villas, Hotel Daphnis, a self-described 108-year-old rum house, is a special class of hotel. Located in Fener, near Sultanahmet and across the Golden Horn from Karaköy and Beyoğlu, one side overlooks the water, while the other opens onto the historic İncebel Sokak, opposite the Greek Orthodox Patriarchate. A few doors down in the same street as the hotel is the little church of legends, Panaghia Mouchliotissa. Architect and owner Defne Yanger has renovated the hotel's sixteen rooms (three suites and thirteen double-rooms), while retaining the building's former appearance, preserving the hand-painted decorative figures (*kalemişler*) on the walls and the high wooden doors. The old gramophone in the lobby adds more nostalgia to the atmosphere, as do the stained-glass windows, marble sinks and old water pumps. In the basement, Café Daphnis can seat seventy-five diners (forty inside and thirty-five in the flower-filled garden), and offers Greek cuisine accompanied by Mürefte wine. For breakfast, the Full Turkish (*kashar* cheese, olives, tomatoes, cucumbers, ham, honey and coffee) is available, and later diners can enjoy various pasta dishes, along with the more traditional Turkish favourites, *börek* (with eggplant and breadcrumbs) and *Tekirdağ* meatballs.

3 Les Ottomans

Muallim Naci Caddesi 168
Rooms from €1,200

This historic *yali* (summerhouse) in Kuruçeşme with its spectacular waterside location has been converted into the only feng-shui certified luxury hotel in the world. Formerly belonging to Muhsinzade Mehmet Paşa in the 1790s, owner Ahu Kerimoğlu Aysal states that when she found the house, she tried to imagine and re-create how Muhsinzade would entertain his own guests in his home. The beautiful design of Les Ottomans has the unmistakable stamp of interior designer Zeynep Fadıllıoğlu. The eleven suites are distinctively decorated – most are over two storeys with views over the Bosphorus, and all have dining rooms and two bathrooms. The hotel has two restaurants and a signature spa, and its eastern philosophy is felt everywhere. The ground was blessed by feng-shui master Yap Cheng Hai before the project started, and he consulted the staff at every step. There is also a small museum containing objects belonging to several generations of the Muhsinzade family. This is without doubt the place in Istanbul in which to experience the manners, customs and warmth of the Ottomans, both past and present.

4 The Sofa Hotel
Teşvikiye Caddesi 123
Rooms from €170

Named for the traditional Turkish sofas that can be found in each of the hotel's luxurious eighty-two rooms, the Sofa Hotel is located in the chic shopping and gourmet district of Nişantaşı. Designed by Turkish architect Sinan Kafadar, the Sofa Hotel caters to today's individual and corporate travellers with a touch of classic Nişantaşı character. The hotel's restaurant Tuus (p. 161) serves an eclectic 'New Mediterranean' menu in a beautifully designed setting, while Café Sofa offers international meals throughout the day and cocktails into the evening. The top-notch health centre, where patrons can find everything they need for detox and wellness, is under the management of well-known specialist Taylan Kümeli. On the ground floor is the peaceful bookstore Patika, while on the penthouse level is the recently opened art space Art 8, which exhibits the works of both local and international contemporary artists. Here at the Sofa Hotel, guests can enjoy a comfortable stay, safe in the knowledge that every desire has been anticipated and provided for.

eat

THE FISHER KING
5 Balıkçı Sabahattin
Seyit Hasan Kuyu Sokak 50

Of the hundreds of fish restaurants in Istanbul, one of the best, Balıkçı Sabahattin, is located not on the sea but in a three-storey wooden house in Sultanahmet. Owner Sabahattin Korkmaz's passion for freshness doesn't stop with fish, as Aegean herbs and olive oil from the Mudanya region are shipped in daily. Dining in the garden, perhaps on *lakerda* (salted tuna) or *çiroz* (dried mackerel), or at one of the streetside tables underneath fishing nets and coloured bulbs, is an unforgettable experience. Reservations are essential.

COMFORT FOOD
6 Mangerie
Cevdet Paşa Caddesi 69

Mangerie is one of the many recently opened cafés in Bebek that are injecting fresh life into the neighbourhood. Although tucked away on the third floor of an apartment building, it is always crowded with Istanbul's hip and stylish set. On warmer days, a veranda provides a more relaxed eating environment, and guests lounging on the sunbeds will find their eggs Benedict brought to them on a tea tray. Chef Elif Yalın Topkaya is also the host of a weekly cookery programme and a former partner of the House Café.

FANTASY FOOD
7 Ulus 29
Ahmet Adnan Saygun Caddesi

With its hilltop location within Ulus Parkı overlooking the Bosphorus, Ulus 29's setting couldn't be more beautiful. The food is a mixture of French, Italian and Turkish cuisines; among the classic dishes on offer are *kebap* with yoghurt and the ever-popular *fındık lahmacun* (mini-meat pizzas). If you have not yet tired of the Ulus experience after your meal, you can dance the night away at next-door Club 29, where, with its velvet-upholstered daybeds and multitude of cushions, the Arabian Nights fantasy continues until dawn.

DINE IN THE MUSEUM
10 Müze De Changa
Sakip Sabancı Caddesi 22

Eight years of experience in providing delicious meals in a unique atmosphere has been brought to this new restaurant located in the Sakıp Sabancı Müzesi, a historic villa, marked by a bronze horse at the entrance, which has been turned into a museum to showcase the Sabancı's collection of Turkish manuscripts, porcelain and paintings. Again under the consultancy and supervision of renowned Kiwi chef Peter Gordon, the kitchen represents one of the best examples of fusion cooking in Istanbul. A light menu is offered during the day for visitors to the museum, and in the evening the venue turns into an elegant restaurant with an amazing terrace overlooking the Bosphorus. The award-winning design firm Autoban (p. 166) is the team behind the décor.

UNFORGETTABLE DELICACY
11 Erguvan
Radisson SAS Bosphorus Hotel,
Çırağan Caddesi 46

Erguvan is the latest restaurant opened by chef Mehmet Gürs in the Radisson SAS Bosphorus Hotel. Wtih a stunning décor in which Ottoman design meets modern Turkish architecture, diners enjoy the freshest seafood along with an excellent selection of *meze*. During winter, the restaurant serves guests in the elegant, white dining room, while in the summer the action moves out to the terrace for the splendid views. Erguvan is fast becoming the best spot in town for both moonlit dinners *à deux* or less romantic business meetings.

LOCAL CANTEEN
8 Kantin
Akkavak Sokak 16/2

AT THE BAZAAR
9 Pandeli
Mısır Çarşısı 1

Regarded as one of the best chefs in the city, former stylist Şemsa Denizsel's talent in the kitchen is evidenced by the number of customers flocking to her tables. House specialties like *çıtır* (a thin, pizza-like dish) are served in a minimal setting of leather banquettes and wood tables, with more tables at the rear with a garden view. The menu is posted on a blackboard, and Denizsel will gladly explain the choices to hungry diners. Recently she joined forces with archaeologist Sinan Aşkın to open Mimkemal 19, also in Nişantaşı.

At the entrance to Mısır Çarşısı, guests venturing down the steps to the left will find themselves at Pandeli, one of the oldest restaurants in Istanbul. If the aqua-tiled restaurant is not entertaining the likes of Mikhail Gorbachev or Juan Carlos II of Spain, you may be lucky enough to find a table by the small windows overlooking the Golden Horn. Highlights of the menu are sea bass in paper, leg of lamb with vegetables, aubergine pie, and the 'Pandeli Sweet', a medley of several Turkish desserts. Sadly, Pandeli is open only for lunch.

12 Sunset Grill & Bar
Yol Sokak 1

Due to its lushly romantic setting, this restaurant has earned something of a reputation as a favourite location for proposals, and the management often receives requests to hide rings in the pudding. Sunset Grill & Bar began life eleven years ago as a Californian-fusion restaurant, but over time has adopted an international approach and widened its menu. A member of the James Beard Foundation (the only restaurant in Turkey to be so honoured), Sunset is also famous for possessing a vast wine cellar. The garden outside supplies both the kitchen and the bar. In such perfect surroundings, no one would dream of saying 'no.'

LOFTY ASPIRATIONS
13 Loft
Lütfi Kırdar Kongre Sarayı

A chic restaurant housed within a convention centre does not seem like a marriage made in heaven, but since the day it opened its doors in 2002 Loft has claimed the most sought-after tables in the city. A branch of the Borsa restaurant group (see Boğaziçi Borsa; right), Loft serves up international and traditional Turkish dishes with a modern twist. Owner Ümit Özkanca is a graduate of the French Culinary Institute in New York, and the décor of his restaurant, designed by Nazlı Gönensay, has a Manhattan flavour with its large bar at the centre and leather banquettes for those who prefer to distance themselves from the maddeningly noisy crowd.

FIT FOR A SULTAN
14 Hünkar
Mim Kemal Öke Caddesi 21

First opened in 1950, Hünkar has been serving classic Ottoman cuisine ever since. Its fame and popularity ensured that it quickly outgrew its original location in the conservative district of Fatih, and the restaurant moved twice before landing in its present spot in Nişantaşı. In a nod to the restaurant's past, owner and chef Feridun Ürgümü has incorporated street signs from the earlier locations into the modern décor. For those who don't read Turkish, dishes on the menu are visible at the counter in front of the kitchen.

Favourites include *Hünkar Beÿendi* (stuffed aubergine), lamb with quince, and, for diners with a sweet tooth, the deliciously toothsome *irmik helvası* (semolina saffron with pistachio helva).

DINE IN STYLE
15 Boğaziçi Borsa Restaurant
Lütfi Kırdar Kongre Sarayı

It all started in 1927 with a small à la carte restaurant in Bahçekapı, which subsequently expanded into a family-run chain serving traditional Turkish dishes. Such was the popularity of the restaurants that they were more than a match for the onslaught of American fast-food chains opening throughout the city. The latest incarnation, Boğaziçi Borsa, opened in 1996 and retained the traditional focus on home-grown fare. Located along with its sister restaurant Loft (see left) within the less than aesthetically pleasing Istanbul Convention & Exhibition Centre, the restaurant's modern décor, generous seating capacity (it can seat over 500) and excellent service, along with a seriously good wine list, make Boğaziçi Borsa the venue of choice for Istanbul's smart set. *Hurmalı incir tatlısı*, a dessert made with figs and dates, is a highlight of the menu, so make sure to leave space for a full portion.

HOT SPOT IN THE CITY
16 Feriye Lokantası
Çırağan Caddesi 40

Today part of the Kabataş Cultural Complex (which also houses a cinema and exhibition hall), Feriye Lokantası, an Ottoman restaurant offering seasonal menus and organic ingredients, is located within a 19th-century building near the glamorous Çırağan Palace Hotel. Behind this elegant venue is celebrity chef Vedat Başaran, who has also served as head chef for a recent NATO conference while turning out authentic Ottoman recipes. Summer is the best time of the year to enjoy Feriye's charms. Every beachside restaurant worth its sea salt boasts of the stunning views, but those waiting to be savoured at Feriye Lokantası when the tables are brought out onto the promenade terrace are truly something else. After sating your appetite, honey and olive oil are also available at the restaurant for purchase.

17 Kıyı
Kefeliköy Caddesi 126

The concentration of fish restaurants per square metre in Tarabya, a district once the summer resort of the aristocracy, is nothing short of staggering. Kıyı, which opened in the 1960s, is probably the most famous – and celebrity-studded – of them all, not only in Tarabya but throughout the city. 'Same address, same patronage', maintains co-owner Yorgi Sabuncu, when asked about the key to Kıyı's success. 'We are constantly renewing ourselves while doing our best to keep the same old spirit.' This warm and welcoming vibe is perpetuated by the friendly staff and peaceful décor. The walls are covered with timber panelling and a large collection of photographs and paintings by Turkish artists such as Ara Güler and Bedri Baykam. Together with seasonal fish and *meze*, the menu also includes traditional favourites such as *barbunya pilaki* (a cold dish made with dried kidney beans and olive oil) and *arnavut ciğeri* (fried liver). For dinner, reservations are a must.

FASHIONABLE DINING
18 Tuus
Teşvikiye Caddesi 123

Architect-turned-restaurateur Mustafa Toner fulfilled his dream by opening Tuus, located in the Sofa Hotel (p. 157). Together with partners Sahir Erozan, who has been in the luxury hotel business for years, and Cihat Bağcı, who found the location, they have created an elegant restaurant that has become popular with Istanbulians. Artwork on the walls, chosen by art gallery Mac Art, lends a sophisticated ambience. Perfection oozes from every pore of this restaurant, from the cocktails to the menu. Tuus is truly one of the best restaurants in Turkey.

drink

19 Patisserie Markiz
İstiklal Caddesi 360

After an absence of twenty-three years, Patisserie Markiz reopened its doors in the Passage Orientale in Beyoğlu (then called Pera) in 2003. Opened in 1940 and named after Parisian chocolates Marquise de Sevigne, Markiz was popular with Pera's smart set until the premises were sold in 1980. Today, Patisserie Markiz – originally designed by Alexandre Vallaury, the architect of Pera Palas (see Orient Bar; p. 165) – is back to its former Art Nouveau glory, complete with faience panels designed by J.A. Arnoux. The mid-19th-century arcade in which it is housed is somewhat less sympathetically restored. Favourite bakery treats from Markiz include chestnut cake, *baklava* and *macara*.

SCENE TO BE SEEN
20 NuPera + NuTeras
Meşrutiyet Caddesi 149

Prior to the arrival of NuPera in 2001, Istanbul's nightlife was based in Etiler and it never entered the heads of party girls and boys to come to Beyoğlu to dance the night away. Today the clubs and bars are all clustered in Beyoğlu, and NuPera, housed in a 200-year-old building, is simply the best of the lot. On the ground floor is restaurant Lokanta, and next to it is the bar/lounge area, heaving with a stylish crowd during the week and with everybody else at weekends. The downstairs club is open four days a week, while the rooftop NuTeras is only open during the summer months, but well worth a return visit for the mesmerizing views of the Golden Horn.

NEIGHBOURHOOD BAR
21 Lucca
Cevdet Paşa Caddesi 51/b

The pressing need for a café-bar in the neighbourhood, together with its philosophy of catering to the global need for comfort food, guaranteed the overwhelming success of Lucca. Open eighteen hours a day, Lucca is a great place for a full breakfast while reading the newspaper or a quick latte on the way home. At night, the bar buzzes with thirty-somethings and loud music. The venue was formerly home to Bebek Lokal (a popular meeting place in the 1960s), and the original ceiling decorations have been carefully restored. Try to stop by on 'Cleaning Day', a sort of car-boot sale held on the the last Saturday of every month.

FEAST YOUR EYES
22 Leb-i Derya
Kumbaracı Yokuşu 115/7

Istanbul is full of surprises, and visitors often come across the most panoramic views in unexpected places. Walk down Kumbaracı Yokuşu, a steep road full of old apartment buildings, and enter no. 115. The lift will take you to the sixth floor, and a staircase leads you to the seventh and your destination, the delightful restaurant Leb-i Derya. If you can tear your eyes from the view, take a seat at the bar or at one of the wooden tables. The menu offers a dazzling array of cocktails, including *Yasak Elma* ('forbidden apple'), a mix of Martini Bianco, Absolut, Cointreau, lemon and apple juice, and *Masal* ('fairy tale'), a best-seller despite no longer appearing on the menu. Also offering a full menu of contemporary dishes (try *kıtırlı biftek*, slices of beef in tomato sauce with spicy croutons), Leb-i Derya is a place to return to again and again.

FALL IN LOVE
23 Aşşk Café
Muallim Naci Caddesi 64/b

Confident that diners will fall in love with both the perfect location and the food, this seaside café takes its name from a slightly punctuated version of the Turkish word for 'love'. The menu is based on a healthy, organic cuisine, with the result that the café is populated by fitness fanatics on their way to a workout at next door's Planet Health Club. Sunday brunch in the cobbled garden or on the seaside deck is a wonderful way to spend a sunny day, and the 'Aşşk Toast' (cheese, herbs and tomato tucked between slices of Russian bread) is delicious. A large selection of coffee and freshly squeezed juice is also on offer.

COFFEE BREAK
24 Pierre Loti Café
Gümüşsuyu Balmumcu Sokak 1

Pierre Loti was a French romantic novelist who chose Turkey as his second home. After stumbling upon this traditional coffee house on the outskirts of Eyüp in the late 19th century, Loti became a frequent visitor, and the café has been known by his name ever since. Today, the Pierre Loti Café is a modest establishment offering nothing more than Turkish coffee warmed over charcoal, tea served in tulip-shaped glasses, a spot of *nargile* and a few snacks. The interior is decorated in the traditional coffee-house style, with couches, copper tables and low wooden stools. The small glass cabinet next to the entrance displays original editions of Loti's books, and the tiny kitchen is covered with İznik tiles glistening with steam from the boiling coffee pots. Recently, the addition of a souvenir shop has made Pierre Loti a little touristy, but there is no better setting in which to taste authentic Turkish coffee.

COMFORT ZONE
25 Cezayir
Hayriye Caddesi 16

This café-bar-restaurant is located in an old building that once served as a school for children of the Italian Workers' Association. During the summer, be sure to head downstairs for al fresco dining in the garden. In the café section, guests sink into comfortable leather sofas to read the newspapers with their coffee and desserts, while the bar has some tables for dining.

FEEL FRESH
26 Cuppa
Yeni Yuva Sokak 26

Located in lively Cihangir, this lovely café offers smoothies and juices for every ailment, from hangovers to headaches, or for those who just want a detox. Wheatgrass shots are made from grass grown by the owners on-site. The cozy café offers delicious meals as well. With wireless Internet connection and a relaxing atmosphere, Cuppa becomes a 'home office' for the many who linger here throughout the day. Very recently opened, it has achieved great success and recognition in Istanbul in a short time; two new branches have opened at Kanyon (p. 168).

ALWAYS IN VOGUE

27 Vogue

Süleyman Seba Caddesi

Vogue, located in the penthouse suite of a thirteen-storey building and possessing stunning views over the Bosphorus, is undeniably the city's most popular restaurant-bar. Vogue is best enjoyed in the summer, when the weather is warm and the cocktails are at their most refreshing when served on the surrounding terrace. But whatever the season, Vogue is always thronging with jet-setters, thanks to its global cuisine and cocktail bar, which offers a vast menu divided into classics, frozen favourites and the exotic. Vogue's famed wine list carries around 200 international vintages, as well as domestic varieties. Sipping a Mojito on the terrace at sunset, with music provided by DJs in the background, sets the scene for a perfect summer evening in Istanbul.

A LEGEND IN HIS OWN RESTAURANT

28 Yakup 2

Asmalı Mescit Sokak 35–37

It isn't the food or the décor that make Yakup 2 special, but rather the owner himself, Yakup Arslan, who attracts the crowds to this *meyhane* every night of the week. (His method of getting customers to leave their tables at closing time is particularly memorable.) Nearby Refik is run by Arslan's uncle, who brought his nephew from Rize to to the Asmalımescit area to work as his apprentice. After years of training, Arslan took over his uncle's business in 1974. Eight years later, when the popularity of his restaurant outgrew its original premises, Arslan moved the renamed Yakup 2 to its present location. Yakup 2's popularity with regulars is legendary; German musician Detlef Glanert composed a concerto in its honour, and aspiring poets, after enough glasses of *rakı*, write devotional odes on their napkins.

VIEWS FROM ABOVE

29 360 İstanbul

İstiklal Caddesi 309/32

Probably the most hotly anticipated new venue of the last few years, 360 İstanbul's stunning location and celebrity owners ensured that it made the headlines even before it opened. Occupying a rooftop location atop the historic Mısır Apartmanı, 360 İstanbul offers mesmerizing 360° views of sea and city. The building is adjacent to the beautiful church of St Antoine, whose bell tower serves as a perfect backdrop to the restaurant. The ultra-modern interior is black and white, with two enormous circular sofas (one red and one green) designed by Derin to break the monotony. The large bar at the centre offers such cocktails as house specialty '360' (Smirnoff Citrus, Archers, passion fruit and apple juice) and 'Beyoğlu Orgasm' (Baileys, Amaretto and Kahlua). For the adventurous, 'Eau de Haliç' is a lethal mixture of *rakı* and melon liqueur.

BOZA FOR SALE!

30 **Vefa Bozacısı**
Katip Çelebi Caddesi 104/1

Boza, a thick fermented millet drink revered for its nourishing properties, is the oldest known Turkish beverage and is best enjoyed on chilly winter nights. Traditionally *boza* was purchased from street vendors, who carried their wares in large metal jugs through the city. Today these mobile *boza* sellers are a rarity, but Vefa Bozacısı, founded by Hacı Salih Bey in 1876, still operates in its nostalgic premises. The well-preserved shop, now synonymous with the drink, is today run by Bey's great-great-grandsons, who have added balsamic vinegar and pomegranate juice to the repertoire. *Boza* is still a favourite drink among locals, and is popular with adventurous tourists. Though widely available in bottles at supermarkets, the ritual of drinking *boza* freshly poured into a glass from a large jug at Vefa is a true Istanbul experience.

DANCING ON THE CEILING

31 **Buz Teşvikiye**
Abdi İpekçi Caddesi 42/2

When it first opened on the second floor of an office building, Buz, with its stylish décor and superb cocktails, instantly became a hot spot for Istanbul's nighttime revellers. Prices are a bit steep, but the local bohos are always willing to embrace the eccentric, and Buz Teşvikiye provides eccentricity in spades. After moving to new premises in 2002, owners Lal Dedeoğlu and Ender Sanal decided to bring some of the old interior with them. The result is a new look on the ground, including Polaroids of regulars crowding the walls, and the old look adorning the ceiling. So, while sipping your Buz Martini (with thyme and cubed lemon) or frozen tangerine Tequila, if you notice a table or chair hanging upside-down above your head, it doesn't mean that you've had a few too many. It's all just part of the crazy décor at Buz Teşvikiye.

SPIES LIKE US

32 **Orient Bar**
Pera Palas Hotel, Meşrutiyet Caddesi 98–100

You don't have to be a guest at the hotel to enjoy the nostalgic and mysterious atmosphere of Pera Palas. The legendary Orient Bar, located in the lobby of the hotel, whisks diners back to a time of intrigue and elegance. The turn-of-the-century interior is lavishly decorated and includes a huge oriental carpet, topped with comfy velvet-upholstered chairs. Once frequented by local intellectuals, as well as more infamous characters (Mata Hari and Kim Philby have both raised a glass or two here), the tearoom has become a magnet for tourists eager to absorb any atmosphere the spies might have left behind. Despite the sky-high prices, the romantic mood and intriguing history make Orient Bar a must.

shop

Having designed interiors for restaurants and bars all over Istanbul (see Müze de Changa; p. 159), architect Seyhan Özdemir and interior designer Sefer Çaÿlar set up Autoban in 2003. Located in their second-floor studio in Galata overlooking the Golden Horn, Autoban specializes in furniture and lighting design, with an emphasis on natural materials and local production techniques. The duo have recently caught the eye of the international press, and in 2005 were nominated by design magazine *Wallpaper** as Young Designer of the Year.

Shopping emporium Derishow is a must for all dedicated followers of contemporary fashion. Husband-and-wife team Fatoş and Sancar Ahunbay founded Derishow in 1984 to trade their own line of clothing. First working solely with leather (*deri*), the duo soon added other materials to the range and Derishow became the first internationally renowned textile brand to come out of Turkey. A home collection, Mimarca, was launched in 1998. Derishow also offers limited-edition bridal-wear designs. A coffee bar on the ground floor provides welcome respite for weary shoppers and brides-to-be.

With its lack of signage, visitors often miss this treasure trove of Turkish antiques. Owner Erkal Aksoy converted the four-storey house into a showroom for *kilims*, paintings, ceramics, manuscripts, and other decorative objects. Aksoy was one of the pioneers of the changing face of Çukurcuma, and it is thanks to him that the once derelict street is now home to the city's best art galleries and design shops. The charmingly gracious Aksoy welcomes shoppers with home-made cherry liqueur and butter cookies. To experience his hospitality, be sure to arrange an appointment before ringing the bell.

HEAD OF THE GLASS
36 Paşabahçe
Teşvikiye Caddesi 117

HATS & HANDBAGS
37 Mine Kerse
Faikpaşa Yokuşu 1/a

TAKEAWAY HAMMAM
38 Abdulla + Hamam
Halıcılar Çarşısı Caddesi 53

Paşabahçe (also the name of the region in which the factory was founded) is one of the leading glass manufacturers in the world. Founded in 1935, the company's products have been snapped up by such global brands as Conran and Costa Boda. A number of Paşabahçe lifestyle stores have opened nationwide and carry contemporary housewares along with reinterpretations of Anatolian and Ottoman forms, brought to life using ancient glass-blowing techniques. Among these collections are replicas of the world-famous Beykoz glassware and hand-crafted glass decorated with archaeological motifs.

A former assistant to fashion designer Ümit Ünal (p. 168), Mine Kerse set up her eponymous atelier and shop in 2004. Inside the relaxed atmosphere of her showroom, she presents a limited collection of beautifully crafted hats and handbags made from felt and leather, and unusual materials such as machine straps. Kerse works at the studio above the shop, reached by a steel ladder from the ground-floor showroom. A shoe collection of one-off designs is also on the way.

For a little piece of hammam pleasure in the comfort of your own home, visit Abdulla and Hamam, two shops facing one another on Halıcılar Çarşısı Caddesi, in the Grand Bazaar. Owner Metin Tosun, the man behind Fes Café, opened Abdulla and Hamam in 2001. Traditional crafts, including olive oil soaps, luxury towels, mohair blankets, sheepskin covers and *pestemals* (thin, fringed bath towels), are sourced from all over Anatolia. Beaded curtains have recently been added to the repertoire, and visitors can chat with Mr Tosun while he is busily beading them.

TREASURES FROM YESTERYEAR

39 Pied de Poule
Faikpaşa Yokuşu 19/1

A visit to this corner shop in the heart of Çukurcuma is like having a good old rummage in your grandmother's wardrobe. On display are clothes dating from the 1930s, hats, gloves and leather handbags with wooden straps, as well as vintage decorative items, ranging from porcelain to French armchairs. Every item in the shop can be purchased or hired out. Owner Şelale Gültekin started collecting historic clothes from family members as a hobby, and as the collection outgrew her own wardrobe, the hobby turned into a profitable business. Gültekin also makes delicately embroidered cushions, which are among the store's most covetable items. The black-and-white photographs of Gültekin adorning the walls were taken by Nuri Bilge Ceylan, the well-known Turkish director.

URBAN GEAR

40 Bis Wear
Hayriye Sokak 20/3

The owners of Bis Wear, two sisters, started designing hats while they were still students. Following the success of these hats, they abandoned prospective engineering careers and opened their first store within one of Beyoğlu's historic arcades, selling export surplus along with their own designs. With its unusual fabrics and simple but stylish forms, Bis Wear quickly gained a dedicated clientele, who also snapped up the matching shoes, handbags and belts. In 2003, Bis Wear moved to its present location. The small shop within the arcade is still open, but for the real thing, take the ride to Hayriye Sokak.

MUSIC BOUTIQUE

41 Lale Plak
Galip Dede Caddesi 1

Fifty years ago, brothers İbrahim and Yusuf Atala set up their music shop in Tünel Meydanı. Today run by Hakan Atala (the son of one of the founders), the shop still has a long list of regulars, searching out hard-to-find records. Lale Plak's stock focuses on jazz, ethnic and classical music, and its shelves are organized by type, country of origin, period and instrument. Atala knows his customers and musical tastes so well that he keeps track of CDs bought and opportunities missed (to be rectified at a later visit). Refreshingly, the well-informed staff is cheerfully generous with both knowledge and assistance.

CANYON OF SHOPS

42 Kanyon
Büyükdere Caddesi 185

The most distinctive shopping mall in Turkey, Kanyon is also one of the biggest construction projects ever undertaken in Europe and combines office and retail space with residential apartments in one destination. The architecture, a collaboration between Tabanlıoğlu Architects and urban-planning firm Jerde, is a work of art, and the open-air, curved mall gives the impression of shopping along boutique-laden streets, lined with the world's top luxury fashion, electronic and entertainment brands (many making their first appearance in Turkey), rather than in an enclosed mall. Kanyon is set to become the premier fashion destination not only for Istanbul, but for the entire Southern Europe region.

ON THE SOFA

43 Sofa Art & Antiques
NuruOsmaniye Caddesi 85

Established in 1976, this unique space has become a notable name on Istanbul's cultural scene. Sofa Art & Antiques is a little jewel waiting to be discovered; here you will find gold and silver jewelry, glass, engravings, miniatures and calligraphy, tiles, ceramics, mosaics, paintings, textiles, embroidery and needlework. Owner Kaşif Gündoğdu is on a mission to bring the traditional Turkish arts to visitors and Istanbulians alike.

TIMELESS FASHION

44 Gönül Paksoy
Atiye Sokak 1/3 and 6/a

The multi-talented Gönül Paksoy designs everything from clothes to jewelry to shoes, and even dolls made of fabric. In true modern multi-tasking style, she is also a renowned culinary artist. Her two boutiques, both located in Atiye Sokak, have been beloved of visitors and natives alike for the past fifteen years. Possessing a PhD in the use of plants as a source of natural dyes, she experiments with the textures and colours of antique fabrics and creates one-off dresses, shawls and kaftans, as well as handbags. As a designer who is uninterested in current fashion trends, the look of her collections do not radically change from season to season, but remain classically beautiful and eminently desirable. Her jewelry creations inspired by archaeological artefacts are as unique as her fashion designs.

BEDAZZLED

45 Zeynep Erol
Atiye Sokak 8/3

Jewelry designer Zeynep Erol claims to be inspired by her emotions, and her efforts in interpreting her feelings have resulted in a collection of earrings, necklaces, rings and bracelets that combine gold and silver with precious and semi-precious stones in geometric forms. After studying metal techniques at the Grand Bazaar, Erol, a former ballet dancer, set up her atelier-gallery-retail space in 1994. Since then, the minimal setting of her showroom has been frequented by a dedicated stream of customers, who stop to admire the items of jewelry showcased on large wooden blocks and in glass cases projecting from the chalk-white walls. Erol's collections can also be viewed at Aaron Faber in New York and the Electrum Gallery in London.

AVANT-GARDE FASHION

46 Ümit Ünal
Ensiz Sokak 3

A designer with an avant-garde edge, Ümit Ünal began designing fashion collections in the early 1990s and has subsequently won many awards, including the 1997 Fashion Festival International Designer award. His interpretations of different walks of life, such as the 'Himalaya' (2001), 'Fallen Angels' (2004) and 'La Russie' (2005) collections, have gained him a sound reputation in the fashion industry. Housed in a 19th-century building that also hosts the biannual Tünel Festival, his atelier-cum-showroom is worth a visit. With old wooden doors collected from Aegean villages, it forms the perfect backdrop to his delicate creations.

see

HISTORIC BATH & BAR
47 Cağaloğlu Hamamı
Kazım İsmail Gürkan Caddesi 34

Hammams were used as communal baths in ancient times, and after many centuries they remain a social institution. Located in Istanbul's historic district, Cağaloğlu Hamamı was a gift to the city from Sultan Mahmut I and has been in operation since 1741, thus making it Turkey's oldest company. Historic personages, including Edward VII and Florence Nightingale, and celebrities have all been here for a little indulgent pampering. With your *pestemal* and *takunya* (wooden clogs), head to the Old Marble Bar (Cağaloğlu is the only hammam that serves alcohol). Almost as popular as the hammam itself, the bar is a favourite with locals.

WHIRLING DERVISHES
48 Galata Mevlevihanesi
Galip Dede Caddesi 15

Galata Mevlevihanesi attracts hordes of tourists every weekend afternoon at 3 p.m. to see the dervishes whirling away with their headdresses and white skirts (symbolizing the ego's tombstone and shroud). Built in 1491, the original *tekke* (dervish lodge) burned down in 1765, and the present building is a replica. The graveyard with its ornate tombstones contains the remains of the *şeyh* (leader) of the Mevlevihane, Galip Dede, and İbrahim Mütefferika, the founder of the first Arabic-Ottoman printing press in the 18th century.

A ROYAL SUMMER HOUSE
49 Beylerbeyi Sarayı
Abdullahağa Caddesi

Of all the residences of the Ottoman sultans, only Beylerbeyi Sarayı gives the impression of having once been lived in. Designed by Sarkis Balyan for Sultan Abdülaziz, Beylerbeyi was primarily used as a summer house and to accommodate foreign heads of state, including Empress Eugénie of France. The façade (sporting carved garlands of fig and quince) of this architectural gem is in the Ottoman neoclassical style. Inside are six halls and twenty-six chambers, including the Inlaid Pearl Room which contains a chair carved by Abdülaziz himself. Terraced gardens on the sloping hillside behind the palace are connected to the main building by a tunnel which now acts as a sales desk.

READY FOR DEPARTURE
50 Haydarpaşa Tren İstasyonu
İstasyon Caddesi

Overlooking Kadıköy Bay, the Haydarpaşa train station breathes a little old-world glamour into this excessively developed area. A present to the sultan and people of Istanbul from Kaiser Wilhelm II, it was built by two of his compatriots, Otto Ritter and Helmut Cuno, in 1906. The building's sandstone façade leads into an interior festooned with trailing garlands and lit by stained-glass windows. Despite the station's somewhat sad subsequent history – soldiers boarded trains here for the front during the First World War – its opulent beauty is certainly testament to Kaiser Wilhelm's spectacular taste in presents.

MAGNIFICENT MOSQUE
51 Süleymaniye Camii
Prof. Sıddık Sami Onar Caddesi

Le Corbusier described Mimar Sinan as one of only two architects 'who understood the concept of space', and when inside the magical Süleymaniye Camii it is difficult to disagree. Built in honour of Süleyman the Magnificent and completed in 1557, the mosque dominates the skyline, its four minarets indicating that Süleyman was the fourth Ottoman sovereign since the conquest. Enter through the northwest door into the courtyard and, after visiting the tombs of Süleyman and Roxelana, have a peek at the breathtaking views.

CHURCH OF STEEL
52 Bulgar Kilisesi (Sveti Stefan)
Mürsel Paşa Caddesi 87

Just a few blocks away from the Greek Orthodox Patriarchate stands one of Istanbul's most remarkable churches. This neo-Gothic church dedicated to St Stephen of the Bulgars dates from 1871, and was made entirely from iron, cast in Vienna and shipped across the Black Sea. The local story is that the Bulgarian Orthodox community, seized by nationalistic fervour, wanted to leave the Greek Orthodox Patriarchate and build its own church. Sultan Abdülaziz, not overly enamoured with the idea, agreed on the seemingly impossible condition that construction be finished in one month. Had Abdülaziz heard of the term 'prefabricated', the outcome might have been very different.

UP ON THE ROOF
53 Rooftop Churches
- Aya Andrea, Mumhane Caddesi 103
- Aya Panteleymon, Hoca Tahsin Sokak 19
- Aya İlya, Karanlık Fırın Sokak 6/a

Just across the road from İstridye Balık Lokantası is a five-storey architectural beauty used by the Russians prior to World War I as a base on their way to Jerusalem. What makes the building even more special is the rooftop Aya Andrea chapel, a small Russian Orthodox church whose green cupola can just be seen from street level. Two other rooftop churches (Aya Panteleymon and Aya İlya) are also in the area. Aya Andrea is only open to the public on Sundays, but Aya Panteleymon and Aya İlya can be visited on any day, with permission from the caretakers of the apartment buildings.

A SHRINE ON THE HILL
54 Yuşa Tepesi
Yuşa Tepesi Yolu

Located on the highest hill of the Asian side, the site of this enormous mausoleum (12 metres in length) has been revered as a holy place since ancient times. The grave is traditionally believed to be that of the prophet Yuşa, who, according to the Old Testament, was the apprentice of Moses. Faithful flocking to the site today present votive offerings in the hopes of purifying their souls. Pilgrims and visitors alike can revel in the mesmerizing views from the hill, and can satisfy their hunger pangs in nearby Anadolu Kavağı, famed for its many seafood restaurants.

ART OF THE EMPIRE
55 Pera Müzesi
Meşrutiyet Caddesi 141

This museum is housed in one of the most beautiful and historical buildings, designed in 1893 by Achille Manoussos, in Istanbul. The permanent collection is located on the first and second floors and presents a visual panorama of the last two centuries of the Ottoman Empire, comprising Kütahya tiles and ceramics, as well as more than 300 paintings by European artists inspired by the Empire. The upper floors are dedicated to multi-purpose spaces devoted to the work of young Turkish talents. There is a pleasant café and an art shop on the ground floor.

HISTORY OF ART

56 Türk ve İslam Eserleri Müzesi
Atmeydanı Sokağı 46

Initially located within Süleymaniye Camii's *külliye*, the Museum of Turkish and Islamic Art moved to its present location in the İbrahim Paşa palace in 1983. One of the most impressive examples of 16th-century Ottoman architecture, the palace was a gift from Süleyman to his chief advisor İbrahim Paşa, and is the only civilian palace in Istanbul to have survived into the present day. The museum has a collection of more than 40,000 works of art, including the largest rug collection in the world. Of particular interest is the Etnografya Müzesi, a natural history section with exhibits devoted to Turkey's historic peoples, including the Yürüks, a nomadic tribe of Anatolia.

MUSEUM WITH A VIEW

57 İstanbul Modern
Meclis-i Mebusan Caddesi

An old warehouse on the Karaköy pier is now home to the city's first contemporary art museum, backed by the Eczacıbaşı Group who provided both the initial investment and the core collection. The museum covers two floors connected by a glass and steel staircase, an installation designed by Monica Bonvicini for the 2003 Istanbul Biennial. The entrance foyer houses an auditorium, a photography and video art gallery, and a new media centre. A sculpture garden is planned to adorn the entrance in the near future. The museum also houses a shop and a chic and stylish café.

GOT WINGS?

58 Galata Kulesi
Galata Kulesi Sokak

Built by Genoese colonists in the 14th century and rising 60 metres above the Golden Horn, Galata Tower is the city's most prominent landmark. In 1638, Hezarfen Ahmed Çelebi strapped on a pair of artificial wings and glided his way from the top of the tower to the Asian shore, thus making him the first man in history to fly and the tower very famous indeed. Although the upper floors house a very touristy restaurant and nightclub, it is worth venturing up the 307 steps for the panoramic views of the Golden Horn, Sultanahmet and the Bosphorus.

A PLACE TO PAUSE IN TIME

59 İstanbul Arkeoloji Müzeleri
Osman Hamdi Bey Yokuşu

The Istanbul Archaeology Museum's main building, designed by Alexander Vallaury (who took his inspiration from the Alexander Sarcophagus, exhibited inside), is one of the best examples of neoclassical architecture in the city. Behind it is the Museum of the Ancient Orient, containing pre-Islamic objects from the Arabian Peninsula. In the museum's courtyard, the *Çinili Köşk* (Tiled Pavilion), dating to 1472, is one of the oldest examples of civilian Ottoman architecture and showcases the museum's collection of Seljukian and Ottoman tiles, while the beautiful garden, with its historic graveyard, is worth a visit.

HISTORIC STREET, NEW HOSPITALITY

60 Soğukçeşme Sokak
- Ayasofya Pansiyonları
- Konuk Evi
- Sarnıç Restaurant

Sandwiched between Hagia Sophia and Topkapı Sarayı, Soğukçeşme Sokak was an aging cobbled street in the shadows of the great mosque. Years of restoration have swept away the crumbling mansions, and now a row of nine wooden houses operates as a pensione offering Ottoman-style hospitality to its guests. Konuk Evi ('guest house'), on the opposite side of the street, has a beautiful garden in which to sit on sunny summer days. A 1,600-year-old Roman cistern has been converted into the elegant Sarnıç Restaurant, illuminated by candlelit chandeliers.

16TH-CENTURY SPA

61 Çemberlitaş Hamamı
Vezirhanı Caddesi 8

This hammam, in continual use since 1584, is an architectural treasure and remains a focal point for photographers and filmmakers today. The architect installed a floor heating system by inserting pipes into the marble blocks, allowing steam to travel through them and warm the platform. Unfortunately, the system, as well as the women's bath facility, was damaged during a less than successful renovation in 1972. Thankfully the present owner, Ruşen Baltacı, is determined to transform the hammam into a modern spa without damaging its historical integrity.

TRUE BLUE GOLD

62 Kalsedon Maden İşletmeleri
Ayasofya Caferiye Sokak 2

Chalcedony, a blue semi-precious stone that has been in use since 800 BC, is believed to have metabolic and psychological properties. The largest reserve of the stone, often referred to as 'blue gold', is located in Eskişehir, in Central Anatolia. Sırrı and Birsen Gerçin, a husband-and-wife team, are the owners of the mine and of this elegant store-gallery located in the shadow of Hagia Sophia. The 500-year-old building, once home to Fatih the Conqueror's teacher (Sırrı Gerçin is a descendant of the same teacher), now showcases jewelry and decorative accessories made from chalcedony.

DUNGEONS BUT NO DRAGONS

63 Anemas Zindanları
Dervişzade Caddesi

The Anemas dungeons, located behind the Ivaz Efendi mosque and part of the ruined Blachernae Palace, have long been a favourite film location of the Turkish movie industry, doubtless inspired by their grisly past. Two late Byzantine emperors met their untimely ends here, and several more were unwilling guests. Formed by fourteen cells with two basement floors underneath, the prison is named after an Arabic-Byzantine soldier imprisoned here after unwisely rebelling against the emperor Alexios. With its unusual architecture, and despite its somewhat murky atmosphere, the dungeons are well worth a visit – so long as you remember your flashlight.

ELECTRIC SCENE

64 Santral İstanbul
Kazım Karabekir Caddesi 1

Following London's famous example (Tate Modern; p. 220), Istanbul's own Silahtarağa Electricity Power House has been converted into a hip destination. The project aims to preserve the city's first electrical power plant, built in 1911, and convert it into a cultural and educational centre, complete with museums devoted to energy and contemporary art, an international residence programme, a library and information centre, concert halls, a café-restaurant, recreation areas, and an open-air theatre that can seat 7,000.

LISBON

Through all the twists and turns of its tumultuous history, there has clearly been a higher power keeping a watchful eye over Lisbon. From the southern, undeveloped bank of the River Targus, an iconic statue of Christ the Redeemer stands, arm outstretched, protecting and welcoming all to the city built— like Rome — on seven hills. The Romans themselves were in residence for over 400 years, followed a little later by the Moors, until Lisbon became the capital of powerful, mercantile Portugal. The city remains littered with the rich remnants of these golden centuries of world exploration, colonization and Catholicism. Its current look owes much to the reconstruction following the 1755 earthquake, so cataclysmic an event that locals still talk about it as if it happened within living memory. It's not so long since Lisbon emerged from the dark years of the 20th-century dictator, António Salazar; it was during this joyless era that the mournful folk music known as *fado* became synonymous with the city. Today *fado* is so ingrained in Lisbon's soul that you haven't really experienced the city until spending an evening being romanced by a passionate voice accompanied by the insistent strumming of a twelve-sting *guitarra*.

The melancholy and uniquely Portuguese emotion of *saudade* (best summed up as a feeling of loss) is commonly said to hang in Lisbon's air like a delicate perfume hinting at the grandeur of days long past. But dive into the nightly street party that swings in the Bairro Alto (p.186) or battle with the crowds scrambling for delicious custard tarts in Belém (p.193), and you'll think Lisbon anything but a sad place. Check out the fashion scenes of Chiado and Baixa, the confident, contemporary style of its best boutique hotels and restaurants, or the modern architecture out at Parque das Nações, and you'll realize that this is also a city that can stand shoulder to shoulder with fellow European trendsetters. The 1988 blaze that engulfed the dense historic streets of Chiado and preparations a decade later for Expo 1998 foisted a construction boom on Lisbon that is only now beginning to abate. But much of Lisbon's historic fabric remains intact. Wander the narrow, cobbled streets of Alfama beneath the ramparts of the Castelo de São Jorge (p.193) and look out across the Targus over terracotta rooftops, and it can feel as if you've slipped back several centuries.

Lisbon's undulating geography forces a slower pace, the uphill climbs being rewarded by lovely panoramic views across a city, as one *fado* lyric puts it, 'of a thousand windows'. An early evening stroll along pedestrianized Rua Augusta from the regal Arco Triunfal to the broad Rossio Square, the crossroads of downtown Lisbon, is a must. The patterns of the tiles decorating the buildings and the dove-grey and charcoal cobblestones on the pavements and squares here are more visual clues to Lisbon's singular style. Savour it all, as the locals do, with an espresso or glass of wine in hand, relaxing at a pavement café.

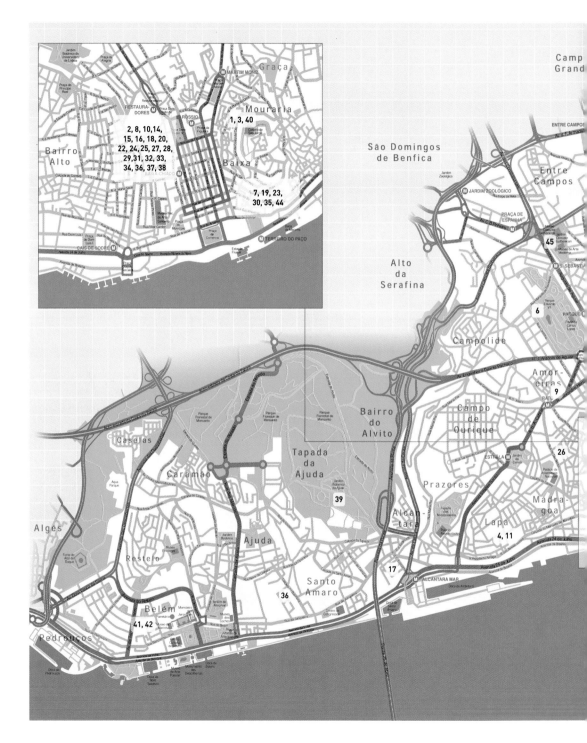

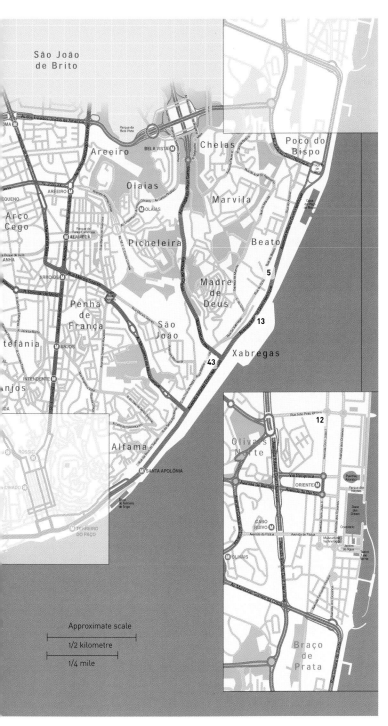

sleep

ROOMS WITH A VIEW
1 Solar dos Mouros
Rua do Milagre de Santo António, 6
Rooms from €136

French artist Luis Lemos is the man behind this appealing boutique hotel, with its grandstand position on way up to the Castelo de São Jorge (p. 193). The views over the River Targus from several of Solar dos Mouros's twelve spacious rooms are breathtaking; others that look out towards the castle aren't too bad either. The eclectic, colourful décor is also striking, and includes contemporary works of art (some by Lemos himself) and African artefacts. Round-the-clock room service is supplied, as is an in-house laundry service. Rooms also come with stereo systems, televisions and air conditioning.

BIRD OF PARADISE

2 **Bairro Alto Hotel**
Praça Luís de Camões, 8
Rooms from €230

Calm prevails in the Bairro Alto's well-designed rooms, decorated in a palette of warm terracotta, cool blue or mellow lemon, each with a different small wall painting of birds by Virgínia Mota. Service is impeccable from staff stylishly attired in uniforms designed by Alexandra Moura. With panoramic views from both its rooftop bar and the chic Restaurante Flores, it takes a great effort to venture outside to the bustling bar district (see Bairro Alto; p. 186) after which the hotel is named.

KITCHEN PALACE
3 Solar do Castelo
Rua das Cozinhas, 2
Rooms from €234

Built where the old kitchens of the Alcaçova Palace once stood, Solar do Castelo abuts the Castelo de São Jorge's (p. 193) stone walls and retains several features of the original 18th-century structure. Some of the compact, comfortable and stylish rooms have castle views, others overlook the central cobbled courtyard with its bubbling water cistern, wooden outdoor furniture and potted plants. Enjoy a glass of port from the honour bar while relaxing in a lush, chocolate-leather upholstered sofa in the spacious lounge.

THE WRITERS' HOUSE
4   York House
Rua das Janelas Verdes, 32
Rooms from €230

Writers such as Marguerite Duras, John le Carré and Graham Greene have all stayed at York House. Climb the stairs from the street and enter the vine-covered courtyard shaded by palms, a hammock swinging in a dark, cool corner, and you can immediately see the appeal of this haven of peace in a former convent. The deluxe rooms, each distinctly decorated – several with contemporary-styled four-poster beds – are the ones to request.

eat

HOUSE OF COD
5 A Casa do Bacalhau
Rua do Grilo, 54

Bacalhau – dried, salted cod – is a staple of Portuguese cuisine and is on the menus at a myriad of different places. This is the only Lisbon restaurant, however, that has truly made it their own. Based in an otherwise unremarkable area midway between Santa Apolónia and Parque das Nações, the restaurant is a pleasing contemporary place in a brick-vaulted room. The menu lists no fewer than twenty-five different salted cod dishes, from a carpaccio with green olives and *pataniscas* (fish cakes) to cannelloni and *bacalhua 'a bras'*, a classic recipe created with fried potatoes, onion and scrambled egg.

VIEW FROM THE HILL
6 Restaurante Eleven
Rua Marquês de Fronteira,
Jardim Amália Rodrigues

Eleven's position at the head of Parque Eduardo VII provides uninterrupted views towards the River Targus. Competing for your attention is the strikingly designed interior of this hip restaurant, the project of eleven friends (hence the name). There's a gold heart sculpture by Joana Vasconcelos, arty abstract photographs by Jorge Cruz, and the inventive Mediterranean-inspired cuisine of Joachim Koerper. Expect dishes such as avocado and crab cannelloni, fois gras terrine with fig mousse, and veal jarrete cooked for sixteen hours.

GASTRONOMY SHOWCASE
7 Terreiro do Paço
Praça do Comércio

At Terreiro do Paço, named after the central square that the restaurant faces, top-class Portuguese cuisine is what's on offer, both at the casual space beside the colonnaded arcade or upstairs in the formal restaurant. The four- or five-course tasting menus are splendid and include delicious dishes like carpaccio of fresh and smoked tuna with black plum jam, and caramelized duck breast and leg in vinegar with pear emulsion. Sample some excellent local wines, too, more of which you can taste next door in ViniPortugal, where you'll learn there's far more to the local viticulture than the production of port.

FOOD WITH ATTITUDE
8 Pap' Açorda
Rua da Atalaia, 57–59

The hearty, simple nature of Portuguese cuisine is exemplified by *açorda*, a porridge-like stew made with stale bread and typically flavoured with prawns and fresh coriander. Pap' Açorda, a trendier-than-thou restaurant in the thick of the Bairro Alto (p. 186), has given the dish a contemporary makeover and made *açorda* a hit with celebrities who flock to this buzzy, appealing space decorated with a trio of decadent chandeliers, a long bar and dusty pink walls. Reservations are recommended, as is a thick skin against the Filipe Faisca-dressed waiters who specialize in service with a snarl.

THE OLD TIMER
9 Casa da Comida
Travessa das Amoreiras

For a quarter of a century, Casa da Comida has been the place in which to enjoy fine renditions of Portuguese cuisine using the best ingredients. The setting is very traditional, with an old gentleman's club-style bar in which to read the menu and sip an aperitif and a lovely courtyard shaded by a soaring date palm and fringed by bougainvillea. A white cockatoo occasionally squawks from her cage in the corner. Service is impeccable and the selection of classic dishes includes a rich seafood soup, succulent roast kid and prawns and port-marinated pheasant.

THE GOLDEN AGE
10 Tavares
Rua da Misericórdia, 35

There has been a restaurant on this spot since 1784, although Tavares's fame dates from 1861 when it was given the grand gilt-mirror and chandelier makeover that remains its trademark. Reopened in 2004 following a splendid restoration, it's now possible to dine here on fancy renditions of Portuguese cuisine – such as *bacalhau* with cumin vinaigrette and vegetable caviar – just as Cary Grant, James Joyce, Catherine Deneuve and superstar *fadista* Amália Rodrigues did in the past. For a more modest taste of the opulent Tavares style, visit the tearoom upstairs.

DINING WITH THE MARIONETTES
11 Convento das Bernardas
- A Travessa, no. 12
- Museu da Marioneta, Rua da Esperança, 146

After the Convento das Bernardas closed in 1834, the building has had a variety of guises, including a school and apartment complex. Some fortunate families still live here, whose local restaurant, A Travessa, is one of Lisbon's best. The appealing menu includes dishes made with rabbit, venison, veal, octopus, monkfish and, of course, cod – all served with home-made bread and local wines. In the same building is the Puppet Museum, which displays marionettes, theatre sets and equipment from around the world.

ORGANIC GOES TRENDY
12 Origens Bio
Alameda dos Oceanos

The standout dining experience in Parque das Nações is this café/shop specializing in organic food. Much care has gone into the stylish interior design, with its striking feature wall of angular wood blocks. The specialty here is organic beef, but there are plenty of other options for vegetarians including a wonderful salad of peppery leaves with sautéed shrimp and diced mango, or a sautéed vegetable *açorda* with tomato emulsion. The shop also stocks organic wines from across Europe.

WHERE THE BOATS COME IN
13 Avenida Infante D. Henrique
- Bica do Sapato, Armazém B
- Delidelux, Armazém B
- Lux Frágil, Armazém A

A whiff of trans-Atlantic glamour lingers at the dockside location of Bica do Sapato ('toe of the shoe'). Make sure you're wearing your best Gucci loafers to join the movers and shakers who gather here particularly for lunch, when only the café is open. In the evenings you can dine on the same modern Portuguese classics in the groovy 1960s-inspired restaurant, with its mix of furniture by Mies van der Rohe and Eero Saarinen, while upstairs is an intimate sushi bar. A more relaxed space in which to enjoy a light meal is Delidelux, whose weekend brunch menu is highly appealing, while nearby Lux Frágil is Lisbon's most fashionable dance club.

drink

SWEET PICK-ME-UP

14 A Ginjinha

Largo de São Domingos, 8

There are several hole-in-the-wall dispensaries for *ginjinha* (a sickly sweet combination of brandy, cherries, sugar and cinnamon), but this is the one that attracts the crowds keen to partake in a quintessential Lisbon drinking experience. The portrait of the slightly annoyed looking man (the first person to sell the potent beverage in the city) looks down as you stand in the street and sip from plastic shot glasses.

A TASTE OF PORT

15 Solar do Vinho do Porto

Rua de São Pedro de Alcântara, 45

There are over 200 different types of port – including vintage, late bottled vintage, *colheita* (tawny) and white – to sample at this institute for Portugal's most famous after-dinner drink. Set in the tapestry-hung ground floor of the São Pedro de Alcântara palace and with soft leather chairs, this is more of an upscale lounge than a bar. Cut the sweetness of the drink with a plate of *barrancos* (thin slices of smoked pork sausage) and local cheeses such as *São Jorge* and *Evora*.

MOORISH DELIGHT

16 Casa do Alentejo

Rua das Portas de Santo Antão, 58

Climb the stairs to this Alentejan cultural centre and restaurant, and it's like stepping into another world. The Moorish fantasy courtyard and staircase is a sight to behold. Wander through the Sala Dr Victor Santos, a crumbling ballroom with brown peeling paint and mammoth chandeliers, to a bar that is a cool, secretive hideaway from the bustle of the city.

17 Alcântara Café + Espaço Lisboa

THE BIGGER THE BETTER

Rua Maria Luisa Holstein, 15 and
Rua da Cozinha Económica, 16

At the stroke of eight, the metal door of
a former warehouse is pushed back to
reveal this ritzy venue designed by
António Pinto, where statues and velvet drapes contrast with the industrial
iron girders, pillars and fans. Daily
Portuguese specials supplement the
brasserie-style menu, but it's really
the buzzing atmosphere that's the main
attraction. Across the road is another
of Pinto's restaurants, Espaço Lisboa, a
fantasy version of traditional Lisbon.

18 Cervejaria Trindade

BAR FOR ALL SEASONS

Rua Nova da Trindade, 20

This brewery has been serving its
own beers in the former canteen of the
Trinos monks for over 150 years. The
building, whose main room is decorated with historic *azulejos* (tiles)
painted with figures representing the
seasons and elements, was declared
a protected part of Lisbon's cultural
heritage in 1986. Artist Maria Keil decorated another room with her mosaic-
style *azulejos* in a more abstract style –
you can see other examples of her work
in several of Lisbon's metro stations.

19 Clube de Fado

THE MUSIC OF FATE

Rua de São João da Praça, 94

Like most of Lisbon's high-profile *fado*
venues, Clube de Fado, owned by gui-
tarist Mário Pacheco, is aimed at the
tourist crowd. But don't be put off, as
you're just as likely to find locals here as
visitors at this classy operation. Candlelit and with a high vaulted stone ceiling, it's an evocative setting for the
strumming guitars and passionate
singing that punctuate the evening in
fifteen-minute sets.

DANCING IN THE STREETS
20 Bairro Alto
- Mahjong, Rua da Atalaia, 3–5
- Portas Largas, Rua da Atalaia, 103–105
- Agência 117, Rua do Norte, 117
- Sneakers Delight, Rua do Norte, 30–32
- Happy Days, Rua do Norte, 60

It's a fiesta every night in the Bairro Alto's dense grid of streets. Crowds spill out of the pocket-sized bars and restaurants along Rua do Norte and Rua da Atalaia onto the narrow, cobblestone streets – dancing, mingling and clutching beers. In such an atmosphere, it hardly matters which bar you drop by, but a couple worth aiming for are Mahjong, with its quirky lampshades of fake bok choi leaves, and the gay-friendly Portas Largas. For late-night shopping there are plenty of boutiques to explore, including Agência 117, and for footwear Sneakers Delight and the retro Happy Days.

PALACE OF PASTRIES
21 Avenida da República
- Pasterleria Versailles, no. 15a
- Galeto, no. 14

Taking after its French namesake, Pasteleria Versailles is perhaps the most genteel of Lisbon's cafés, complete with chandeliers, gilt-edged mirrors and a display case of pastries as long as a tennis court. Waiters in emerald waistcoats move through the tables dispensing *bicas* (espressos) and *pastel de nata*. Cross the road and zip forward to the 1960s at Galeto, an all-American diner decorated in dark, moody style that feels so much more Lisbon than Las Vegas.

BEFORE THE REVOLUTION
22 Café A Brasileira
Rua Garrett, 120

Perpetually busy, whether it's breakfast or close to midnight, this century-old café once had a doorman and a dress code for patrons – only artists, including Lisbon's celebrated poet Fernando Pessoa, were exempt. Pessoa's life-sized sculpture sits outside, oblivious to the throng of tourists. Inside, admire the gilded mirror and dark wood interior, topped off with classic works of early 20th-century Portuguese art; it oozes with pre-revolutionary ambience.

PESSOA WAS HERE
23 Café Martinho da Arcada
Praça do Comércio, 3

Café A Brasileira (see left) was not the only watering hole that Fernando Pessoa frequented. His favourite is said to be this café and restaurant that faces onto the Praça do Comércio and dates back to 1782. Sitting in the shady arcade, sipping on a beer or *bica* and watching the trams rattle around the square is a leisurely way to pass the time. This old-fashioned, atmospheric restaurant is a good place to try such traditional dishes as *bacalhau* or steak with coffee sauce.

EVERYTHING BUT THE KITCHEN SINK
24 Pavilhão Chines
Rua Dom Pedro V, 89–91

'Ye Olde Curiosity Shoppe' would be a more appropriate name than 'Chinese Pavilion', but even that Dickensian description doesn't come close to summing up the zany interior decoration of this extraordinary bar. With its eclectic collection of knick-knacks – everything from toy soldiers to pottery tankards – it's kitsch-meets-Art Déco with a generous dollop of Grandma's basement thrown in. Order a 'Lady Di' or 'Frank Sinatra' cocktail and settle back for a surreal night.

DÉCO DELIGHT
25 Café Nicola
Praça Dom Pedro IV, 24

The 18th-century poet Manuel Maria Barbosa du Bocage used to hang out at this café, which dates back to 1783, and he's still there in the form of a life-sized bronze statue and in the paintings decorating the place. The glamorous Art Déco revamp of 1935 is how this café institution appears today, and it is an ideal place for a drink or light meal, especially on Thursday evenings when live music performances often take place.

shop

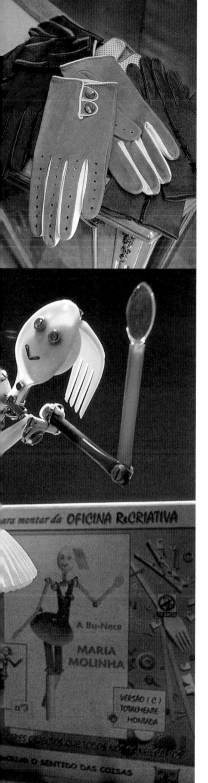

PORTUGUESE DESIGN DEPOT

26 Alma Lusa
Rua de São Bento, 363

A treasure trove of Portuguese design has been amassed by Ana Sousa Dias in this colourful boutique. Dias will wax lyrical about her favourite pieces, including the geometrically upholstered 'Formula 1' chair and the 'Carnivora' rocking chair by design duo Moio. Along with furniture, there are clothes, jewelry and accessories such as bags made of car-seat fabric by Yuki.

PARTNERS IN FASHION

27 Alves/Gonçalves
Rua Serpa Pinto, 15b

Of the two players in this enterprise, Manuel Alves came to Lisbon from Oporto while his partner-in-fashion José Manuel Gonçalves is a local lad. Their streamlined shop window displays key pieces of their designs for both sexes from their current collection, including sophisticated satin high-heeled shoes, as well as ceramics and other lifestyle accessories. Visit their atelier around the corner at Rua das Flores 105 by appointment only.

FASHION LEADER

28 Ana Salazar
Rua do Carmo, 87

Doyenne of the country's contemporary fashion scene, Ana Salazar began presenting collections under her own name in 1978. She has since acted as a mentor to a new generation of local designers, including Alexandra Moura and Filipe Faisca. At her boutique, you can choose from the full Salazar selection of dresses, tops and skirts, all to be accessorized with her own designs, from sunglasses to shoes and bags and her signature scent, Siléncio.

HAND IN GLOVE

29 Luvaria Ulisses
Rua do Carmo, 87a

This tiny shop, only a little wider than its doorway, is squished next to Ana Salazar (see above) and specializes in hand-made gloves. The soft leather is dyed in a bewildering range of colours, with gloves for both sexes and in a wide range of styles. In the unlikely event that the shop does not stock your size, gloves can be made in two days – even from a photocopy of your hand.

THE FAB FIVE

30 Nininha Guimarães dos Santos
Rua de São Julião, 7

Nininha Guimarães dos Santos is just one of a quintet of jewelry and accessories designers who show their work in this atelier. It's all highly original with necklaces, brooches, rings and earrings that appear in many different colours and are fashioned from a variety of materials such as plastic and wool, as well as the usual precious metals. International designers also exhibit here, including Marta Boino Eliseu from the Netherlands, whose tactile necklaces of woven cotton are covered with small clay balls.

LIGHT A CANDLE

31 Caza das Vellas Loreto
Rua do Loreto, 53

Candles in a spectrum of colours and a variety of shapes – including life-sized and amazingly life-like cabbages – are the specialty of this family-run concern that dates back to 1789. The carved wooden cases of the interior house many other wax offerings, and the kindly ladies behind the counter will offer up samples of their popular range of scented candles that feature aromas such as green tea, tomato leaves, coffee, jasmine, nougat and magnolia.

IN THE MIX

32 Mousse
Rua das Flores, 41–43

Like Alma Lusa (see left), Mousse acts as a showcase for Portuguese designers across a range of stylish products, including clothing, accessories, furniture and lighting – all displayed in the spacious premises of a former print shop. Along with gift boxes of bath goodies packaged in colourful graphic prints and retro magazines, you might pick up the collage-style T-shirts of Dino Alves or quirky, eclectic items from Designwise.

33 A Outra Face da Lua
WILD WALLPAPER

Rua da Assunção, 22

34 Fátima Lopes
FASHION HIGH FLYER

Rua da Atalaia, 36

35 Conserveira de Lisboa
SARDINES IN THE CAN

Rua dos Bacalhoeiros, 34

Half shop, half tearoom, 100 per cent funky – the 'Other Face of the Moon' could easily be a set from a Pedro Almodóvar movie. The walls are plastered with retro-patterned wallpaper, one of the trademark goods of the store, which also specializes in vintage clothes and kitsch toys. In the tearoom, become instantly refreshed with one of their special minty iced teas.

Is there nothing that Madiera-born designer Fátima Lopes had not done in the name of fashion? She's dressed the national football team, sauntered down the catwalk in a gold and diamond-encrusted bikini worth US$1 million, created a range of clothes for Barbie and collaborated with Portuguese porcelain manufacturer Spal on fine china tableware. View her latest collection, including diamanté-fringed bikinis, at her Bairro Alto base.

You didn't think you'd be shopping for tinned sardines or tuna in Lisbon, did you? But it's hard to resist picking up a brown paper and string-wrapped bundle of tinned goods at this charmingly old-fashioned shop, complete with a granny at the till and cabinets stacked with colourfully packaged goods. It specializes almost exclusively in tinned fish, which come in a variety of sauces and flavoured olive oils, including spicy tomato and lemon.

ON THE TILES

36 Fábrica Sant'Anna

Rua do Alecrim, 95 (showroom) and
Calçada da Boa-Hora, 96 (factory)

Ignore the ceramic lamps, pots and
other questionable knick-knacks and
zone in on the *azulejos*, both new and
antique, that can be purchased here.
Every piece is hand-made, from the
preparation of the clay to the painting
and glazing done according to the same
methods used in 1741 when the company was founded. You can also visit
the factory on Calçada da Boa-Hora on
your way to Belém.

CHINA IN YOUR HAND

37 Cutipol + Vista Alegre

Rua do Alecrim, 113–115 and Largo do
Chiado, 20–23

You're sure to notice Cupitol's distinctive cutlery on the tables of many of
Lisbon's finest restaurants. Their full
range can be viewed in this Rua do Alecrim store. Surprisingly affordable,
'Rondo' and 'Ikon' are the most popular
styles. For top-class porcelain plates,
it's a simple matter of crossing Largo do
Chiado to the showroom of illustrious
Vista Alegre, in business since 1824.
The patterns and designs range from
traditional to highly contemporary.

CONFECTIONERY CLASSIC

38 Confeitaria Nacional

Praça da Figueira, 18b

A red-packaged box of biscuits or pastries from this confectionery shop and
teahouse on the corner of Praça da
Figueira makes a lovely present. Little
seems to have changed in the shop
since its opening back in 1829, with its
mirrored ceilings, wall paintings and
grey marble counter to show off the
freshly baked goods. Climb the sweeping wooden staircase to visit the chan-
delier-hung tearoom upstairs.

see

39 Jardim Botânico da Ajuda + Estufa Real
Calçada da Ajuda and Calçada do Galuão

Laid out by Italian botanist Domenico Vandelli in 1768 at the behest of José I, the Jardim Botânico da Ajuda is Lisbon's oldest botanical garden and remains one of the city's most tranquil spots. The view from the upper terrace across the triangle-shaped hedges towards Belém is beguiling, while a gigantic *Schotia afra* tree from South Africa provides a shady canopy. Classy restaurant Estufa Real, located in the air-conditioned greenhouse, is only open for lunch. Join well-to-do families on Sundays for a splendid buffet that includes many Portuguese favourites.

40 Castelo de São Jorge + Casa do Leão
Largo do Chão da Feria

Phonenicians, Romans, Visigoths and Moors have all built their citadels here before Portugal's first king, Afonso Henriques, took control in 1147. Left to ruin after a new palace was built down the hill in the 17th century, the castle's battlements are today stormed on a daily basis by battalions of tourist. A brief multimedia romp through Lisbon's history entitled *Olisipónia* (the name given to the city by the Romans) is held in within one of the buildings. Also here is Casa do Leão, a surprisingly accomplished traditional restaurant given its touristy location. A table out on the patio with a view over the city is perfect for a lazy lunch or dinner.

41 Mosteiro dos Jerónimos
Praça do Império

Vasco da Gama is buried in the church attached to this magnificent monastery built in the Manueline style of architecture that was Portugal's version of late Gothic. It's an appropriate resting place for the navigator who discovered the sea route to India, since its construction was partly funded by taxes on the spice trade that de Gama's explorations opened up. The highlight of this UNESCO World Heritage site is the meditative cloister, where sculptural reliefs and intricate carvings cover practically every inch of the creamy sandstone.

42 Belém
- Centro Cultural de Belém, Praça do Império
- Bar Terraço, Centro Cultural de Belém
- Margarida Pimentel Jewelry, Centro Cultural de Belém
- Torre de Belém, Mosteiro dos Jerónimos, Praça do Império
- Padrão dos Descobrimentos, Avenida de Brasília
- Museu National dos Coches, Praça Afonso de Albuquerque
- Antiga Confeitaria de Belém, Rua de Belém, 84–92

Along with the Mosteiro dos Jerónimos (see left), there are many reasons for spending the day in the western suburb of Belém. Across Praça do Império is the Centro Cultural de Belém, a giant performing and visual arts centre built in 1992. Bar Terraço on the top floor provides a crowd-free view across the Targus, while back down at ground level you'll find several shops; of these, Margarida Pimentel's distinctive jewelry made with oxidized silver, gold, amber, pearls and diamonds is worth a look. The monastery used to be by the riverbank, which gives you an idea of how far the Torre de Belém, the area's other Maneuline masterpiece and another World Heritage site, was once out in the Targus. Today, a short raised platform across the murky river leads you into the watchtower; look out the slitted window in the northwest corner of the structure to see a rough carving of a rhinoceros, which would have seemed like a mythical beast when the tower was built in 1515. Eastwards along the riverbank is the striking Padrão dos Descobrimentos, built in 1940 to celebrate Portugal's Golden Age of Discovery (*descobrimento*); from the top you'll get the best view of the massive windrose set into the plaza below. Of Belém's several museums, the most unusual is Museu National dos Coches, a fairytale cavalcade of horse-drawn coaches assembled by the last Queen of Portugal and housed in a magnificent 18th-century riding school. Meanwhile at Antiga Confeitaria de Belém, you'll realize how the phrase 'selling like hot cakes' came to be coined while watching the crowds clamour for packets of their delicious custard tarts.

43 Museu Nacional do Azulejo
Rua da Madre de Deus, 4

From the Arabic *alzulaycha*, meaning 'little polished stone', comes the Portuguese word for tile – *azulejo*. This tile museum, housed in the former Madre de Deus convent, includes some spectacular examples of the art, including the 'Great View of Lisbon', a thousand-tile mural of the city prior to the 1755 earthquake, and modern examples of both ceramics and tiles by the likes of Maria Keil and Artur José. The convent itself is a delight and includes a Manueline-style cloister and a dazzling church, where a profusion of gilded Baroque carvings, paintings and tiles compete for attention.

44 Museu-Escola de Artes Decorativas Portuguesas
Largo das Portas do Sol, 2

In 1947, banker Ricardo do Espírito Santo Silva bought the 17th-century palace of the Duke of Azurara to house his collection of European decorative arts. Today the opulent palace, opposite one the city's best *miradouros* (vantage points), is not only a museum in which to find wonderful examples of the applied arts laid out as if it was still the home of the Duke, but also a school teaching all the traditional crafts. Call ahead to arrange to see the students at work. The museum's shop sells reproductions from the collection.

45 Museu Calouste Gulbenkian + Centro de Arte Moderna
Avenida de Berna, 45a and Rua Dr Nicolau de Bettencourt

Lisbon's reputation as a safe haven during the Second World War brought all manner of people to the city, including the oil magnate Calouste Sarkis Gulbenkian, who stayed here until his death in 1955. The museum that bears his name today presents items from his collection of over 6,000 pieces, including a terracotta Grecian urn (*c.* 440 BC), a 15th-century white jade tankard made for the Timurid ruler Ulug Beg, illuminated manuscripts, Old Master paintings and glass by René Lalique. A labyrinthine garden spreads between the museum and its offshoot, the Centro de Arte Moderna.

LONDON

Like many cosmopolises, London is heterogeneous and multilayered, complex and contradictory. According to a 2000 United Nations census, London's greater metropolitan area included around seven and a half million inhabitants, making it the twenty-sixth largest city in the world. Although it may not be one of the globe's top ten most populous cities, it is arguably the most diverse and among the most culturally influential. Bridging the United States and Europe in many, often conflicting, ways, and being the capital city on an island, has imparted to London a number of qualities that have often insulated it from the larger continental forces across the Atlantic and the English Channel.

Intensified by a dense historic urban fabric that has been fractured by the Great Fire of 1666 and the Second World War, London's political, cultural and social spheres have a potent way of inter-secting and mixing. Unlike many larger European cities, which have grown concentrically out from a historic (usually medieval) centre of power, and American cities based on the democratic grid, London is a concatenation of essentially autonomous villages that have merged over time. What were once royal hunting grounds in the 17th century or new suburbs in the 19th century have been sub-sumed into the greater whole that is London today. The result is that London has not one heart but many. With the exception of the Mall, it is unmarked by the grand urban gestures of Pope Sixtus V's Rome, Haussmann's Paris or Cerda's Barcelona, which created axes rather than centres. London's composition of mainly smaller streets and lanes feels distinctly unmodern, unimposing and accessi-ble. Whereas most visitors regard the main tourist sights – Trafalgar Square, Buckingham Palace, St Paul's cathedral – as central London, for Londoners there is no true centre, except perhaps the high street of their neighbourhood. There are financial centres (the City) and cultural magnets (the West End), but in the main London is everywhere and the best way to experience it is in its villages.

The millennium has seen an efflorescence of *grands projets* in the capital, which has revivi-fied the worlds of the arts, design and fashion and substantiated the 'Cool Britannia' image beyond the media. Yet while its public face may be enjoying a restoration, the city's most dynamic element remains its thriving, though less visible, underground scene. New trends in music, fashion and art that gain global popularity are often the product of London's subcultures rather than its estab-lished institutions. In the Noughties, London images of 'street style' have as much influence on the world as they did in the 1960s. Inspired by an edgy youth culture and the broad spectrum of ethnic influences, London's creative scene continues to confirm the city's position as a world leader. As with any great city, it is impossible to distil London's essence; even lifelong inhabitants are unable to characterize its complexity, to reconcile what is English with what is international. But London thrives on the contradictions it creates, the very borders that it blurs.

Primrose Hill

Camden Town

St John's Wood

Regent's Park

Fitzrovia

35

Paddington

Marylebone

2, 7,
42,

Soho

Westbourne Green

Bayswater

11, 33, 41,
47, 59

Notting Hill

5, 25, 38, 39, 40

Mayfair

18, 1

Shepherd's Bush

Hyde Park

Holland Park

10, 29

Kensington

Green Park

St Jame

4, 31, 32

Hammersmith

9

South Kensington

58

Knightsbridge

Pimlico

Earl's Court

6, 15, 16, 26, 37, 51

Chelsea

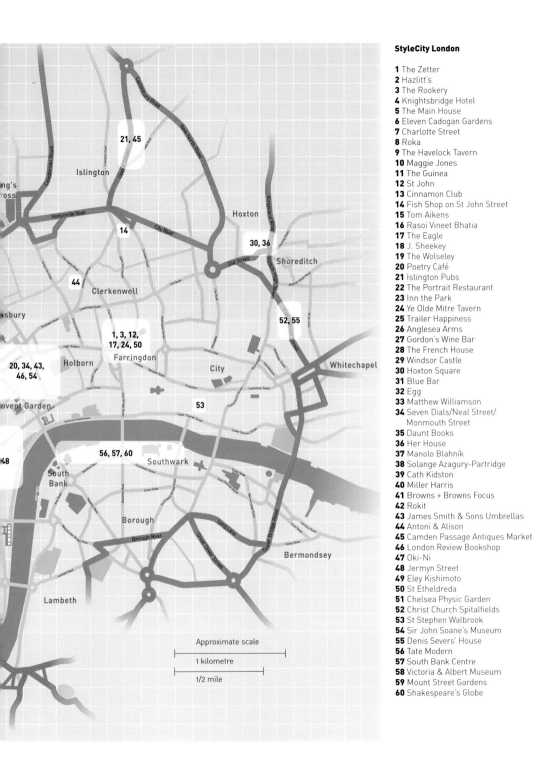

StyleCity London

sleep

URBAN INN

1   The Zetter

86–88 Clerkenwell Road

Rooms from £150

Period architecture with contemporary design flair, all mod cons and an environmental conscience, hip location and reasonable rates: the Zetter is a host of lively contrasts. Michael Benyan and Mark Sainsbury, the duo behind the Zetter, have had a string of restaurant successes, including the Quality Chop House and Moro. With the Zetter they combined a stylish bar and restaurant on the ground floor with rooms located around an atrium above, in their words, 'a modern-day urban inn'. Beyond that they managed successfully to integrate the historic architecture of a Victorian warehouse building with minimal but striking elements of new design. With fifty-nine rooms on five floors, the Zetter maintains a high level of quality and comfort on a relatively small scale. At the top of the building, seven rooftop studios have been added with floor-to-ceiling windows and French doors leading to patio spaces.

Design touches such as art pieces, textiles and wall panels add glamour, while home comforts include hot-water bottles and books for borrowing. The Zetter also has eco cred: the bathroom basins are made from recycled plastic; the atrium provides natural ventilation; and the hotel has its own well, which provides water for air conditioning and the source for the still and sparkling drinking water on offer. Situated near the confluence of the financial centre of the City, the cultural hub of Bloomsbury and the bohemian base of Clerkenwell, the Zetter is a starting point for a range of London experiences. Crafts by local makers are available at the Pennybank studios just behind the hotel in St John's Square, new British design objects can be sampled at Her House (p. 213) around the corner, and some of London's best new British cuisine is to be had at St John (p. 205), just a few minutes' walk away.

'In art, in taste, in life, in speech, you decide from feeling, and not from reason.' So wrote the great essayist, critic and Napoleon biographer William Hazlitt in 1822. With such inspiration in mind, Douglas Bain and Peter McKay set out to create a home away from home in a set of three of Soho's most characterful houses, built in 1718 and where Hazlitt died, purportedly of drinking too much tea, on 18 September 1830 in what was then a boarding house. Set on a bustling street and surrounded by creative agencies, restaurants and bars, Hazlitt's is a world away from 21st-century global London, a discreet and intimate hideaway from the modern world. Guests who desire a long-lost quintessentially English experience will experience the words that Hazlitt requested for his gravestone, 'grateful and contented'. But don't let the twenty-three rooms' carved mahogany four-poster beds, Victorian claw-foot tubs (some original to the house), the rich, bold colours of the walls and fabrics (the hotel was completely remodelled in 2001), the small sitting rooms and wonky floors and the absence of elevators fool you, this is the haunt of the media, antiques collectors and dignitaries who sense that there is something very special about Hazlitt's and far removed from corporate modern. The staff might be stylish and amenities contemporary, but the contrast wouldn't have bothered Hazlitt, who observed, 'We are not hypocrites in our sleep.'

3 The Rookery

Peter's Lane, Cowcross Street
Rooms from £270

It is hard to say what delights most about this hidden gem. After negotiating the tricky access off a pedestrianized alley near Smithfield Market, you step across the threshold of what seems like someone's private house. Once inside, there are the thirty-three eccentrically appointed bedrooms, each named after a local character and thus imbuing the four Georgian houses with period charm and real personality. Smithfield is an area that was once known for lawlessness (Fagin is said to have haunted its streets) as it was outside the City's jurisdiction. Areas such as these were known as 'rookeries', and though Smithfield is now full of City workers, clubbers and restaurant patrons, the edgy atmosphere has not completely disappeared. Douglas Bain and Peter McKay (see Hazlitt's; p. 199) have combined the old and new in a romantic but detail-conscious atmosphere. All of the modern amenities are on tap, while a careful refurbishment and restoration of the original furnishings and fittings have taken place with the idea that 'history is always more appealing when it has been cleaned up a bit'. The hotel's *pièce de résistance* is the 'Rook's Nest', a top-level suite with the same carefully honed period feel, enhanced by a restored Edwardian bathing machine.

'Affordable chic in the heart of Knightsbridge' is how hoteliers and interior designers Tim and Kit Kemp describe this new take on the usual B&B. Kit Kemp is no amateur designer, having imbued the Covent Garden, the Charlotte Street and the Pelham hotels with her particular blend of modern and traditional English style. The Knightsbridge she describes as 'fresh, modern English', which is discerned through the specially commissioned fabrics and artwork set off by comfortable sofas, chairs and tables. The forty-four rooms have been individually designed by Kit, so they are rich in colour, pattern and texture. There is the 'fuschia room', draped in pale greens and deep purples, as well as some with more neutral tones but still bearing light floral touches. Kit's trademark retro-design Roberts radios are in every room. Her quirky dress mannequins, which she upholsters in varying fabrics, appear in large and small versions, adding to the overall character and charm. Although there is no restaurant on-site, there is 24-hour room service with a gourmet menu. Continental breakfast is usually taken by room service, though guests can choose to eat in the jungle-themed drawing room or the library, both of which feature outstanding works of British art commissioned for the hotel.

HOME FROM HOME
5 The Main House
6 Colville Road
Rooms from £100

Caroline Main isn't exactly rushing around trying to fill her four-room/three-suite hotel located around the corner from what is probably Notting Hill's most fashionable 200-metre stretch. In fact, she has never advertised at all during the years that she has been operating the Main House hotel. She hasn't needed to. Word of mouth is enough to keep this spacious Victorian house, with unmarked entrance, relatively full for most of the year. But it's hard to keep a secret, especially the one about very reasonably priced, roomy, stylish accommodation in London with personalized service that makes you wonder why you ever settled for less. 'Simple and professional' is Main's mantra and it applies to everything from the furnishings to the taxi service, for which you pay only the fee to the taxi company. She is equally strict about the running of the Main House, whose rooms have been stripped of fussy decoration but retain period details and generous proportions. These are not highly kitted-out boxes but airy spaces with large windows, polished wood floors, a few choice antique furnishings and rugs and lots of fresh white linens. The first- and second-floor rooms, true to their Victorian design, are the grandest in terms of space and include separate sitting and bath areas, one suite per floor. The top floor is given over to two rooms and a smaller shower room, usually let as a suite for families or people travelling together. Main herself is often on call, along with manager Beatta, to bring tea, biscuits, wine, give local advice and arrange taxis. Guests are free to entertain their own visitors, and a separate doorbell even allows them to answer the door themselves – just like home. This and the lack of signage means that it feels more like a house, says Main. So there, the secret is out.

ENGLISH UN-DESIGN

6 **Eleven Cadogan Gardens**
11 Cadogan Gardens
Rooms from £240

A stone's throw from Sloane Square, marked only by a single sign 'No. 11', Eleven Cadogan Gardens is a genuine late-Victorian testament to what makes the English hotel unique: understatement, discretion, an apparently undesigned interior that works wonderfully, and just a hint of the aristocratic. It's not hard to understand why it is reportedly design guru Philippe Starck's favourite London hotel. Though one must resist the urge to use superlatives (particularly inappropriate in this context), there is an authenticity, warmth and ease that makes a stay at Eleven Cadogan Gardens an experience you would have only here, in the heart of Chelsea, which means that the high volume of loyal repeat guests can make getting a room tricky at times. Today's establishment began life in the late 19th century, when Lord Chelsea built four mansions on his cricket ground near Buckingham Palace, which soon became London's first private townhouse hotel. Today, there remain sixty rooms (ask for one of the ones at the back, which overlook beautifully manicured gardens), rich wood-panelled walls, oil paintings, an oak staircase and countless antiques, along with two Garden Suites, one that offers a private entrance and the other featuring a large drawing room that overlooks the garden. There is no reception desk, but a butler greets visitors at the door, signifying the level of service to follow. Guests sign a well-worn ledger before being escorted to their premises. Tucked discreetly away in the building are modern amenities, such as a gym and beauty treatment room; reluctant concessions, no doubt, to contemporary travellers. To round out the picture, guests are offered afternoon tea in the dining room, along with fresh cakes, sherry and canapés – what else?

eat

7 Charlotte Street

- Fino, no. 33
- Pied à Terre, no. 34
- Passione, no. 10
- Bam-Bou, 1 Percy Street
- Rasa Samudra, no. 5

This Fitzrovian throughway has become a hub of high-style international cuisine. Choose from a fine selection of modern tapas-style dishes at Fino or consistently well-prepared haute French cuisine at Pied à Terre, recently renewed after a kitchen fire. Updated and upmarket Italian fare is always on offer at Passione, where chef-proprietor Gennaro Contaldo serves the classics with quality. For French-Vietnamese fusion, Bam-Bou continues to please with spicy additions to trad- itional dishes. Upstairs, the Lotus Rooms offer cocktails in a cool, elegant Vietnamese atmosphere. Chef Das Sreedharan has made Indian seafood an art at Rasa Samudra, where fish, curry and chilli combinations are pleasantly inventive and well matched.

GRILL AND SPIRITS

8 Roka
37 Charlotte Street

Partner to Zuma in Knightsbridge, Roka has at its heart the robata grill used for a Japanese cuisine that involves searing and roasting hand-crafted portions of beef, chicken, pork, fish and vegetables. Seats at the robata bar are first come, first served, but tables in the dining area can be reserved. In the more intimate Shochu Lounge downstairs, dark wood, soft chairs and banquettes upholstered in perky Japanese prints provide a sultry atmosphere for sipping *shochu*, a vodka-like drink that comes in a variety of flavours, such as lemon, plum and strawberry, and is served as an aperitif in rippled glasses. Sushi, sashimi, tempura, rice and noodle dishes are all constructed with just the right amount and range of ingredients.

PLEASANTLY CROWDED

9 The Havelock Tavern
57 Masbro Road

This popular pub restaurant is somewhat off the beaten track, but it shows how consistently good food and a lively atmosphere can maintain a success story. The staff are relaxed, the interior doesn't try too hard, and everything from the steak and chips to the fried monkfish is fresh. Be warned, however: fresh food runs out, and they do not accept credit cards.

TIMELESS CLASSIC

10 Maggie Jones
6 Old Court Place

In the face of the epicurean revolution that has taken hold in London over the past decade, Maggie Jones's menu, which has changed little over forty years, is something of an institution. Thankfully, this has less to do with tradition and more to do with how reliably good the food is. Prawn cocktail, avocado and smoked chicken for starters, and fish pie and poached salmon are among the regulars on the menu, with specials that change daily. With the charm of fresh flowers, colourful funky crockery and well-worn wood furniture, it's hard not to feel comfortable here.

OLD AND RELIABLE

11 The Guinea
30 Bruton Place

Bruton Place is a quaint little mews off moneyed Berkeley Square, and the Guinea, tucked away down the mews, is a reminder of days past, before the looming buildings surrounding the square were built. The pub, dating back to the 15th century, has a modern restaurant addition that is famous for its classic grills. The small, dark and atmospheric bar is loved by high-flying locals and lucky wanderers alike for its Young's brews, award-winning steak-and-kidney pies and fine cuts of beef. If the glittering modernity of Mayfair becomes too much, the Guinea is a welcome old-world refuge from the haute cuisine and couture, but not from high standards.

'NOSE-TO-TAIL DINING'

12 St John
26 St John Street

Located a stone's throw from Smith-field Market, where livestock was traded for some 200 years, St John is a symbol of the British love affair with meat. This association, according to Trevor Gulliver, who started the restaurant with chef Fergus Henderson in 1994, happened somewhat by accident. True, one of the most famous and photographed items on their menu is bone marrow served with toasted flat bread and parsley salad, but this is more a reflection of the quality of the cuisine than a commitment to meat-eating. The restaurant also prides itself on its relationship with farmer-producers. Their fresh-baked bread can be bought from the bakery and the fact that they butcher their own meat gives them the opportunity and, they feel, an obligation to use all the parts. With a staunchly loyal following that includes dozens who ask for the menu to be faxed to them daily (some just so they can find out when tripe is being served), it is not hard to be won over by Gulliver's belief that 'a good restaurant is like a good friend'. The stark, white-washed premises – which include a former smokehouse – complement the food perfectly.

INDIAN NIGHTS

13 Cinnamon Club
30–32 Great Smith Street

All-white tablecloths and high-backed chairs arranged against magnificent soaring white walls in what used to be the 1897 Westminster Library, the Cinnamon Club is the modern, upscale face of Indian food as envisioned by owner Iqbal Wahhab. Original bookshelves, wood screens and parquet flooring have been retained, while Indian marble and stone have been incorporated into a clean-lined fusion of colonial convergence. Under chef Vivek Singh, with the help of Michelin-starred French chef Eric Chavot, contemporary Indian cuisine reaches new heights of sophistication and refinement, served to a public ranging from Westminster politicians to jet-setters. Traditional techniques are applied to unconventional ingredients and vice versa, producing acclaimed dishes such as sweet potato cake with crispy okra and spiced yoghurt, duck breast with sesame tamarind sauce, and spinach dumplings with chickpea cake, all suggesting that this is a place with staying-power. The downstairs late-night members' bar and lounge serves Indian-tinged cocktails and dance music to ensure your evening ends on a cool note.

14 Fish Shop on St John Street

RETURN OF AN OLD FAVOURITE

360–362 St John Street

The owners of the former Upper Street Fish Shop (whose departure was much-lamented by Islingtonians several years ago) have gone one better by opening a more upscale version of their beloved fish-and-chips restaurant. The Fish Shop on St John Street serves fish and shellfish fresh for the day from Billingsgate Market in mostly unadulterated forms that leave the creativity in the chef's selection. The standard battered plaice, cod and haddock are still on the menu, as are things like Cornish crab (served half or whole), rock oysters, langoustines and native lobster. The focus is on the variety of fresh fish simply pan fried, seared or cooked in batter (or egg and matzo).

15 Tom Aikens

REFINED DINING

43 Elystan Street

With a television documentary chronicling the daily grind of running his own restaurant in pursuit of a Michelin star, Tom Aikens seemed to run the risk of eclipsing his own gastronomic achievements with the entertainment value of personal struggle. What Aikens really dishes out, however, is worth talking about. From the black-painted façade on a Chelsea side street to the crisply white-clad waiters and simple floral displays, the feeling is one of serene sophistication. The menu follows suit, promising things that sound only mildly exotic but tempting enough and delivering a range of flavours that give credence to that Michelin rating. Choose duck foie gras and fig purée followed by turbot with langoustine ravioli or, for the more adventurous, the lauded braised pig's head with pork belly and stuffed trotter, and prepare for a memorable experience all around.

16 Rasoi Vineet Bhatia

DELHI STAR

10 Lincoln Street

Dehli-trained chef Vineet Bhatia brought the status of Indian food up a notch with Zaika, where in 2001 he earned a Michelin star, the first ever for an Indian chef. In 2004 he left Zaika and moved to these premises, where the rooms are more intimate, the décor more luscious, and the menu resembles poetry. Once on the plate, the choices aren't any less lyrical. The name translates to 'Vineet Bhatia's kitchen', and it is a proudly family operation, with Bhatia's wife, Rashima, running the dining room, which only seats thirty-five. Upstairs, two small private dining rooms are available, one of which includes a roof terrace. Bhatia claims to have accomplished his dream in having his own restaurant in which to continue refining and experimenting with his native cuisine. You can also enjoy his cooking on British Airways First or Business Class flights.

THE ORIGINAL GASTROPUB

17 The Eagle

159 Farringdon Road

THE FRESHEST FISH

18 J. Sheekey

28–32 St Martin's Court

OH, VIENNA

19 The Wolseley

160 Piccadilly

Hailed as London's first gastropub, the Eagle began in 1991 what many modernized pubs are now trying to do with widely varying degrees of success. As owner Michael Belben, who started the Eagle with its first chef David Eyre, says, 'we weren't the first pub to serve good food, but we were probably the first pub to serve extremely good food in casual surroundings.' What they did not want to do was 'exclude traditional drinkers'; nor did they want to include a lot of 'unnecessary trimmings'. So you won't find table linens or complicated selections of courses or even a tab (you pay when you order), but you will find a place that's welcoming for a long drink or a very good dinner, as enjoyed by the local journalists and creatives. Wood details and an eclectic mix of well-worn leather sofas, old bar stools and mismatched dining chairs contribute to the casual atmosphere.

Something of an enigma among the tourist-laden streets of Covent Garden, J. Sheekey has the high-powered provenance of being under the guidance of Jeremy King and Christopher Corbin, the founders of star-attractors Le Caprice and the Ivy, along with a plain and simple approach that puts quality above frills. So while the décor is plainly pleasant, there is a sense of understated glamour here, as the clientele include theatre producers, directors and actors. More importantly, this just might be the freshest seafood to be served in central London. And whether you go for caviar and lobster, scallops and black pudding, fish cakes or good old fish and chips, it's doubtful you'll be disappointed.

The Wolseley opened in 2003 to instant acclaim and doesn't seem to be losing any popularity. Jeremy King and Christopher Corbin of J. Sheekey (see left) took over the former Wolseley car showroom to open an old world-style café, designed by David Collins (see Blue Bar; p. 210). The brass-lined bar, reading lamps, pastry counter, starched table cloths and formal but friendly service staff make the Wolseley popular with both famous and casual diners. The menu is also old-fashioned, offering steaks and chips presented in a jolly paper-wrapped parcel. Chris Galvin, who once presided over the Orrery, also oversees omelettes, bratwurst, goulash, oysters and caviar, all conspiring to make customers feel like a Habsburg on holiday. Alas, you have a much better chance of getting in for lunch or breakfast than for dinner, which is sometimes booked weeks in advance.

drink

POETIC LITTLE LUNCHES
20 Poetry Café
22 Betterton Street

There is more poetry to this little café than the parchment-style lampshades with inked verses scrawled across them. This is the café of the London Poetry Society. By day it's a pleasant but unassuming little eatery – away from the madding crowd coursing through Covent Garden's nearby pedestrian zones – where light and inexpensive vegetarian lunches are served. There's plenty of coffee and tea, as well as a full bar. At night it becomes the venue for poetry readings, workshops and music. Tuesday nights feature open-mike poetry; on Saturday evenings, it's poetry and jazz.

CIVILIZED DRINKING
21 Islington Pubs
- The Crown, 116 Cloudesley Road
- The Draper's Arms, 44 Barnsbury Street
- The Duke of Cambridge, 30 St Peter's Street

As increasingly ubiquitous gastropubs go, the Crown is an old favourite. Established several years ago on a quiet street away from the traffic and in the heart of the Barnsbury conservation area, it can be relied upon for pleasant food and atmosphere, a clever selection of wines, Hoegaarden blond beer and Czech pilsner Staaropramen on tap. The Draper's Arms has been winning accolades from London pundits and Michelin critics alike for its menu, but popularity from the locals also comes from the very comfortable, slightly upscale atmosphere that's just as good for a pint as for a bottle of wine. Meanwhile in Islington's genteel Canonbury neighbourhood, the Duke of Cambridge, Geetie Singh and Esther Boulton's revamped corner pub, continues to attract organic foodies from all over the city.

TEA WITH A VIEW
22 The Portrait Restaurant
The National Portrait Gallery, St Martin's Place

The National Portrait Gallery has always been one of London's must-see museums, but a recent extension and refurbishment have given it one of the best views in London. On top of the new Ondaatje wing, just behind the National Gallery on Trafalgar Square, the gallery's rooftop restaurant has magnificent views across London – the ideal place for an afternoon tea or late afternoon cocktail. With Nelson's Column rising up from a roofscape of white and verdigris domes, and Big Ben in the distance, the true drama of London's architecture is revealed in full.

BUCOLIC BANQUET
23 Inn the Park
St James's Park

Restaurateur Oliver Peyton, founder of such swanky London establishments as the Admiralty and Isola, has gone one better with Inn the Park, a stylish restaurant set in the bucolic beauty of St James's Park, overlooking the duck pond and just a stone's throw from Buckingham Palace. The building by architect Michael Hopkins and interior by Tom Dixon remind visitors that they are in one of the most design-conscious cities in the world. Good for both high quality British food and just a drink outside or on the roof terrace.

ANOINTED PUB
24 Ye Olde Mitre Tavern
1 Ely Court

The Mitre's history goes back to 1546 when it was built by Bishop Goodrich for the servants of Ely Palace. The palace appears in Shakespeare's *Richard II*, Dr Johnson is said to have visited the tavern itself, and today you can still see the trunk of a cherry tree around which Queen Elizabeth I is said to have danced on May Day. Probably the most attractive pub in London – and the hardest to find – the Mitre's small rooms and dark wood panelling retain a pub atmosphere almost impossible to find elsewhere: no music, just the pleasing din of people chatting.

HIP AND HAPPY
25 Trailer Happiness
177 Portobello Road

New bars come and go, but in this area of Notting Hill a new venue that is trendy but friendly, noteworthy but welcoming, is something to be pleased about. Sitting a mere stone's throw from the Electric Cinema and in the heart of the market shopping district, Trailer Happiness offers a comfortable, kitschy atmosphere with a tropical-themed décor and drinks to match. Its trailer-home vibe and cocktails, created by drinks guru Jonathan Downey (who also launched the Matchbar) attract interested locals and hipsters alike.

SHABBY GENTILITY
26 Anglesea Arms
15 Selwood Terrace

Just north of the shopping highway that is the Fulham Road, the Anglesea Arms sits in quiet repose, offering a welcoming embrace with outdoor tables in leafy shadows and a discreet period air that bespeaks the days when it was presented as a gift to Lady Joseph from her husband, Sir Maxwell Joseph. This is a pub whose early Victorian charms are well preserved, along with such decorative details as framed old photographs and historic engravings, shaded chandeliers and velvet swag draperies that provide a reliably pleasing encounter every time.

DRIPPING WITH HISTORY
27 Gordon's Wine Bar
47 Villiers Street

If there ever was a truly down-to-earth wine bar, Gordon's is it. From 1364 it was a warehouse for cargoes of sherry and port coming off the busy River Thames. Its origins as a wine bar date from around 1870, and it has been in the hands of its current owner for more than thirty years. Today, you can still enjoy a glass of one of eighty wines in the subterranean medieval vaults that literally drip with ambience. The incomparable interiors, teeming with loyal customers (especially after work), bring alive another time that couldn't be re-created anywhere else.

VIVE LA FRANCE
28 The French House
49 Dean Street

This small, unpublike bar is a Soho standby. Though it serves beer only by the half-pint, encouraging the consumption of wine instead, it is often too crowded to move your elbows in the late-week evenings and is amicably full the rest of the time. Legend has it that this was a hangout of London members of the French resistance and, sitting as it does surrounded by traditional old pubs and trendy new cafés, it retains the aura of stubborn pride, much like its home country. Delightfully shabby, it has more character in one scratched wine glass than most of the new places put together. The upstairs restaurant is intimate and off-beat, but the food varies with the chef.

PLEASING DECAY
29 Windsor Castle
114 Campden Hill Road

There's simply no modern way to create an interior that exudes the welcoming, gently time-worn ambience of the Windsor Castle, built in 1828, which appears to have remained virtually untouched for almost two centuries. Far from feeling rarefied, the pub – once an inn – seems as though it has always been an integral part of the quiet residential area in which it is set. While the deep wood atmosphere warms in winter, a large, tree-shaded garden invites pleasurable drinking in the summer. A place for quiet conversation or contemplation, whatever the season.

REBIRTH OF COOL
30 Hoxton Square
- Electricity Showrooms, no. 39a
- Bluu Bar, no. 1
- Hoxton Square Bar & Kitchen, nos 2–4
- Liquid, 8 Pitfield Street
- Medicine Bar, 89 Great Eastern Street
- Great Eastern Dining Rooms, 54–56 Great Eastern Street

Well within the last decade, Hoxton Square has become synonymous with hip art and craft studios during the daytime and groovy bars at night, largely supplanting Soho as a nighttime destination. Inevitably, with the discovery of the area, many of the creatives who made the neighbourhood what it is today have moved on – but the vibe, day and night, remains intact, if made up more of visitors than with locals. Interestingly, most of the places that formed the early nightlife are still there, and still draw a crowd. Slightly off the square, a large, minimally furnished space with plate-glass windows, aglow with neon, announces what used to be electricity showrooms but has been for the last several years one of the area's principal watering holes. With a prominent but not prepossessing position on the southwest corner of Hoxton Square is Bluu Bar, formerly the Blue Note club, which many would argue was the epicentre of drum 'n' bass dance music. Five years later it features a modern stainless-steel-trimmed interior and DJs who continue the tradition of its predecessor. Next door and down one level, this time lacking in signage, is the Hoxton Square Bar & Kitchen, another local standby. The open interior, set slightly below ground level, is animated at night by the eerie sensation of car headlights as they turn just before the bar. A few blocks away is Liquid, a small but vividly coloured venue that comes alive at night. Heading somewhat south to Great Eastern Street are Medicine Bar and the Great Eastern Dining Rooms, which in addition to its bar and downstairs lounge serves respectable pan-Asian food.

FASHIONABLE SCENE
31 Blue Bar
The Berkeley Hotel, Wilton Place

A new take on the hotel bar, sensuously reimagined by designer David Collins (see the Wolseley; p. 207), the Blue Bar takes the Regency interior to a new level of chic. Vivid blue – what Collins calls 'Lutyens blue' – and a white onyx bar and crocodile-leather print floor set the scene, with bull's-eye mirrors, Art Déco-style chairs and tasselled hanging lamps adding appropriate flourishes. Reflecting surfaces shine, as does the sparkling service. The cocktail selection, served with honeyed nuts, is civilized – no silly concoctions – mainly Martinis, Champagne cocktails and grown-up drinks.

shop

32 **Egg**
37 Kinnerton Street

Designers Maureen Doherty and Asha Sarabhai create clothing that can be worn by young and old in relaxed styles that are luxuriously well made in India using traditional weaving and stitching techniques, from designs based on work garments to those inspired by 17th-century Indian menswear. They also have exhibitions of largely British contemporary craftspeople.

COLOURFUL CHARACTER
33 **Matthew Williamson**
28 Bruton Street

Nearly next door to fellow British fashion designer Stella McCartney's own designer shop but a world away in terms of style and approach, Matthew Williamson's flagship store is marked by the hot-pink signage on the outside and streaks of bright colour that enliven the cool, white space within. Since launching his debut collection 'Electric Angels' in 1997, which featured bias-cut dresses and separates in tangerine, magenta and fuchsia, he has become known for his sexy, sweeping designs in bold hues. The store, which opened in 2004, features ready-to-wear separates as well as products from Williamson's 'lifestyle' range, including candles, the eau de parfum 'Incense' (produced with Lyn Harris; see p. 214) and his eponymous new fragrance.

FASHIONABLE DIRECTIONS
34 **Seven Dials/Neal Street/ Monmouth Street**
- Coco de Mer, 23 Monmouth Street
- Monmouth Coffee Co., 27 Monmouth Street
- Koh Samui, 65–67 Monmouth Street
- Aquaint, 38 Monmouth Street
- Neal's Yard Remedies, 15 Neal's Yard
- Neal's Yard Dairy, 17 Shorts Gardens
- Magma, 8 Earlham Street

This small quarter of narrow, cobblestoned streets and restored buildings has become one of London's hippest shopping areas. Fashion shops and quirky boutiques are interspersed on the streets radiating from the the circular intersection of seven medieval roads. A short walk along Shorts Gardens takes you to Neal Street, a parade of shops that specialize in weird and wonderful shoes, from trainers and rock-climbing slippers to patent-leather stilettos. Monmouth Street, running north from Seven Dials, and Upper St Martin's Lane, running south, are pockets of design-label boutiques. Coco de Mer, the brainchild of Sam Roddick (daughter of Body Shop entrepreneur and fair-trade pioneer Anita Roddick), offers high-fashion lingerie and erotica. Continuing along the east side of the street, you can stop at Monmouth Coffee Co. for a cup of freshly ground dark stuff before heading to Koh Samui, which features a well-chosen selection of top new labels. Across the road, Aquaint, run by designer Ashley Isham, stocks the entire collections of a smaller number of mainly British designers. Neal's Yard, sandwiched between Monmouth Street and Shorts Gardens, and entered by way of small alleys, is a centre for organic eating and holistic treatments – Neal's Yard Remedies sells tonics, creams, oils and aromatherapy ingredients all bottled in the distinctive old-style blue glass. Just outside the courtyard, Neal's Yard Dairy is full of gorgeously pungent cheese. Nearby Magma is London's leading store for graphics, design and architecture publications, from local rags to obscure imports.

A WORLD OF TRAVEL BOOKS
35 **Daunt Books**
83 Marylebone High Street

Marylebone High Street has a surprisingly pleasant village atmosphere, but Daunt Books would be enough to lure travellers here even without the surrounding shops and cafés. There are many who consider its Edwardian rooms to house London's most beautiful bookshop. The *pièce de résistance* in both character and design is its foreign section, where Daunt features not only guides and maps but histories, fiction and cookery titles – all helpfully arranged by country. The travel section is housed in the beautiful atrium space with a gallery running along both walls.

HOME FOR DESIGN
36 **Her House**
26 Drysdale Street

Morag Myerscough invites you to visit her at home, wander around her kitchen, sit on a sofa, and perhaps buy a design object or two. At Her House, Myerscough presents contemporary design objects from a number of British makers, all arranged much as they would be in the home – albeit a particularly style-conscious home. A patron of emerging artists and designers, Myerscough also helps develop new products under the Her House brand. A recent collaboration with designer Luke Morgan produced the successful range of 'shoe plates', which might be set out on the glass table overhung with a lamp by Myerscough and Morgan. And don't forget to visit the bathroom, where a claw-footed bathtub keeps company with a range of tempting oil paintings.

THE FINEST POINT
37 **Manolo Blahník**
49–51 Old Church Street

Manolo Blahník's gold-accented shop is a must-see for any lover of footwear, with dramatic displays that raise shoes to the level of art objects. Many are just that, as his customers around the world are fully aware (Madonna says they're 'better than sex'). There is a high degree of concept, design and craftsmanship behind each pair of 'Manolos', whose lasts are carved by Blahník himself. Leathers are dyed in bright colours like pink and yellow or turquoise and lime. Despite his now firmly established fame, since first being 'discovered' by the legendary Diana Vreeland in 1970 and more recently brought into public consciousness by *Sex And The City*, Blahník is still the perfectionist who controls every aspect of design and manufacture. This is the place to find the genuine article.

MAGICAL JEWELRY
38 **Solange Azagury-Partridge**
187 Westbourne Grove

Westbourne Grove is chock-a-block with designer boutiques, but this gem of a bespoke jewelry shop is slightly removed from the fray. Despite the ruby-red front, it doesn't announce itself, and though you are welcome to drop in, you must make an appointment if you want a consultation with the lady herself. Having worked for costume jewelers Butler & Wilson, Azagury-Partridge is one of Britain's most inventive jewelry designers, whose bold, baroque creations in 18-carat yellow, white and rose gold and platinum are full of shape, colour and wit.

39 Cath Kidston
8 Clarendon Cross

British designer Cath Kidston's Notting Hill shop is a bower of bright prints and flowers in a distinctly crisp English style that has been much praised for its witty and nostalgic appeal. Vivid floral patterns, as well as bold polka dots and stripes, are splashed across everything, from aprons to ironing-board covers, pillows to tablecloths. Her fabrics are also available.

SCENT-SATIONAL
40 Miller Harris
14 Needham Road

Lyn Harris is the young perfumer behind this highly regarded line. After working with perfume-makers in Paris and Grasse, she launched her own range with the help of perfume house Robertet, who helps manufacture her distinctive collection. Basing many of her scents on 'old-fashioned, naturally derived' aromas, she creates such complex concoctions as 'Coeur Fleur', a mix of sweet pea, mimosa, Egyptian jasmine, raspberry, peach, Florentine iris, amber and Madagascan vanilla. The beautifully designed shop also houses her scent garden, which customers are encouraged to visit. Harris offers a consultancy service, too, inviting clients to access her fragrance library and laboratory to create their own personal scents. Another shop is located in Mayfair's Bruton Street.

BRITISH FASHION IN FOCUS
41 Browns + Brown Focus
24–27 and 38–39 South Molton Street

There are many places to buy designer wear in London, but few have the cachet that Browns has achieved over the past three decades. Joan Burstein and husband Sidney opened the shop in 1970, and since then it has become a revered name in London fashion. Browns features well-known designers from all over the world, while across the street Browns Focus demonstrates Burstein's prescient eye for young innovators, evidenced in the shop's design by one of Britain's most in-demand architects, David Adjaye. Fake London, Frost French, Hussein Chalayan and Maharishi are just a few of the talents showcased.

VAST COLLECTION OF VINTAGE
42 Rokit
42 Shelton Street

Having begun life trading in the Bohemian streets of Camden in 1982, the current growing taste for vintage has brought Rokit into the big time. With shops in Brick Lane and Brighton and fashion stylists from the likes of *iD*, *Dazed & Confused* and the *Sun* newspaper plundering their racks for photo shoots, Rokit are set to launch their own label. But you will still find that vintage prom dress or Hawaiian print shirt, as well as classic army-issue items and nearly new denim all looking crisp, and at prices more down-to-earth than you might think.

SINGIN' IN THE RAIN
43 James Smith & Sons Umbrellas
53 New Oxford Street

The exterior of this shop makes such a wonderful backdrop for photographs that too many people forget to go inside. Yet James Smith & Sons really is the ultimate in umbrellas. The first Smith set up shop in 1830 and his son moved the business to these premises in 1857, which have been maintained by the family ever since. This was the first company to make use of the Fox steel frame, which distinguishes the Smith & Sons umbrella as the finest in the sky. The company continues to produce walking sticks, though they may be more at home in the country than in the city. Umbrellas range from those created for ceremonial purposes to the everyday, in either solid, sombre tones or explosions of vivid colour, and all are working symbols of an era of fine workmanship – and a necessary London accessory.

'FACTORY OF LIGHTS AND EXPERIMENT'
44 Antoni & Alison
43 Rosebery Avenue

Known for their quirky and wry photographic-print T-shirts and whimsical accessories, Antoni Burakowski and Alison Roberts gained notoriety with their refreshingly humorous catwalk shows. Now their energy and bravado have been channelled into creating a full-blown collection of street-savvy ready-to-wear pieces, including knitwear, dresses, skirts and trousers.

ANTIQUES EMPIRE
45 Camden Passage Antiques Market
Off Upper Street
• The Mall, 359 Islington High Street
• Frederick's, 106 Camden Passage
• Annie's, 12 Camden Passage
• Tadema Gallery, 10 Charlton Place
• Elk in the Woods, 39 Camden Passage

Revived from the doldrums in the 1960s, Camden Passage is a hive of antiquarian activity on Wednesdays and Saturdays that is almost hidden from the many shoppers who come to Islington's busy Upper Street. The Mall is full of tiny spaces selling everything from antique tiaras and tea services to Art Déco ceramics and wooden sailing ships. Nearby Frederick's is an Islington institution, featuring a large conservatory and post-hunting luxuries like lobster and beef. In Camden Passage look for Annie's vintage clothing, filled with extravagant beaded flapper dresses and lacey Victorian linens. Tadema Gallery has immaculate Art Nouveau, Jugendstil and Arts and Crafts jewelry. Be sure to check out the overflowing rooms of the Pierrepont Row. A recent, welcome addition is Elk in the Woods, a homely and upbeat bar and restaurant for earthy gourmands. The log cabin-style décor brightened with low lighting beckons wanderers in for a drink and a warm chat.

LITERARY LIGHTS
46 London Review Bookshop
14 Bury Place

It is ironic that despite the great literary traditions that have emanated from Bloomsbury's intellectual and cultural centres of University College London and the British Museum, there isn't a decent independent bookshop in the neighbourhood (those surrounding the British Museum are highly specialized or aimed at tourists) – until now. An extension of the esteemed *London Review of Books*, perhaps the English-speaking world's greatest periodical of literary reviews, this modern shop follows the dictum 'If a book is interesting, it will find a place on the shelves.' In addition to the 20,000-volume stock, the shop also hosts literary talks, poetry and author readings and debates. Local resident Virginia Woolf would have been proud.

Oki-Ni is a high-concept store, not just in the sense of offering a range of products aimed at a particular design 'lifestyle', but in that you cannot actually take anything away from the shop. Everything from trousers and trainers to jackets and tops is there to be ordered through oki-ni.com. This is no clearing house for designer gear, however; the London-based design group works in collaboration with select brands and clothes designers to create items that are produced in limited numbers, all of them unique to Oki-Ni and only available online from their website. Designers for their exclusive range include Adidas (p. 109), Evisu, Levis, Fake London, Cockfighter, Dennis Morris, Motorola and Paul Smith. So while the satisfaction of actually walking away with a one-off piece in hand is not there, the knowledge that you are getting something very special and possibly unique is, even if you have to wait for it to arrive in the post.

This street of shirtmakers is a must-see for anyone looking to procure the genuine English article. At nos 96–97 with its Victorian shopfront is the epitome of traditional style, Harvie & Hudson, founded in 1929. Turnbull & Asser is probably the street's best-known shop and is where Prince Charles gets his shirts. Mother-of-pearl buttons, specially woven Sea Island cotton and three-button cuffs are among its trademarks. Nearby is Floris, the oldest perfumer in London, established as a barber shop in 1730 by Juan Famenias Floris. The interior is bejewelled with bottled essences, soaps and lotions, some displayed in cabinets obtained from the Great Exhibition of 1852. Dunhill started out as Alfred Dunhill the tobacconist before becoming the global purveyor of fine menswear and accessories that it is today, albeit with a decidedly modern edge.

Eley Kishimoto has become one of the hottest names in London fashion, despite being so little publicized. Mark Eley and his Japanese wife, Wakako Kishimoto, both trained in England. Formerly located in an old jam factory in Bermondsey that served as their workshop, factory and showroom, the duo have since moved their office to Brixton's Lyham Road and opened a shop in Soho's Greek Street. Known for their unique printed designs, which are mostly hand-drawn by Kishimoto and applied to everything from textiles to luggage and wallpaper, the two got their start producing patterns for top designers such as Alexander McQueen, Nicole Farhi and Hussein Chalayan. They then began producing their own ready-to-wear collections twice a year, and have been consistently successful ever since with their striking designs that border tantalizingly on the kitsch. Accessible to more than just the fashion élite, they are certainly set for bigger things, so get them while you can.

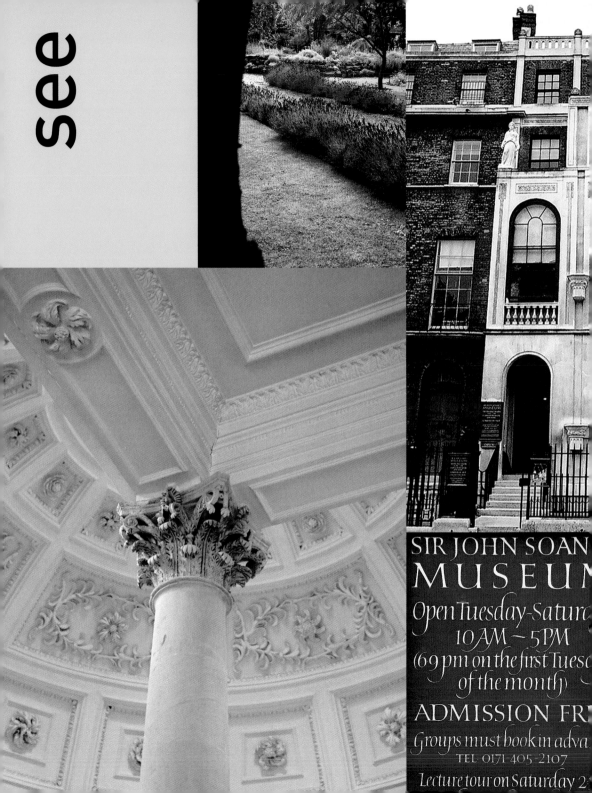

see

SIR JOHN SOAN
MUSEUM
Open Tuesday-Saturd
10AM ~ 5PM
(6-9 pm on the first Tues
of the month)
ADMISSION FR
Groups must book in adva
TEL 0171-405-2107
Lecture tour on Saturday 2

SANCTUARY OF AGES
50 St Etheldreda
14 Ely Place

One of London's most intimate and atmospheric churches, St Etheldreda was built in about 1293 during the reign of Edward I, and is the oldest surviving Catholic church the city. It was the private chapel of the Bishops of Ely, whose palace stood on the site of the present street, and in the early 17th century it was a place of refuge for persecuted Catholics. Although much of the church was damaged in the Second World War, the walls of the undercroft, once used as a tavern, survived and still contain Roman foundations that date from the third century.

A SPECIALIST GARDEN
51 Chelsea Physic Garden
66 Royal Hospital Road

A delicate and unusual green space, the Chelsea Physic Garden has been a home to specimen and medicinal plants since 1673, when it was planted as the Apothecarie's Garden for educating apprentices in the identification of plants. The riverside setting was chosen for its milder climate, which would support non-native species, and the first greenhouse in England was built here in 1681. Though set away from tourist attractions, the garden is well worth a detour, especially when combined with a walk along the Embankment or a look at the nearby Chelsea Royal Hospital, designed by Sir Christopher Wren, the architect of St Paul's cathedral, in 1692.

HAWKSMOOR'S TRIUMPH
52 Christ Church Spitalfields
Commercial Street

Built in 1714, Christ Church Spitalfields is considered one of the best churches designed by Nicholas Hawksmoor, the eccentric successor to Sir Christopher Wren. Located directly opposite Spitalfields market, it has an outsized tower and sober spire that are classically idiosyncratic Hawksmoor features in what is often called the English Baroque. The church is largely intact, despite having been struck by lightning in 1841 and subsequently 'repaired'. With its four great Tuscan-style columns, the portico makes a grand entrance, while the interior follows a simple, graceful design.

CHRISTOPHER WREN CHURCH
53 St Stephen Walbrook
39 Walbrook

There has been a church on this site since before 1096; the previous one, built in 1439, burned down in the Great Fire of 1666. Wren rebuilt the current church in 1679 using methods that he would later employ in the great cathedral, including the large central dome, described by one observer as 'a bubble of light'. Although damaged during the Second World War, it retains such 17th-century features as the communion rails, pulpit and font. A fascinating glimpse into the mind and career of one of London's greatest architects.

AN INDOOR FOLLY
54 Sir John Soane's Museum
13 Lincoln's Inn Fields

Sir John Soane (1753–1837) was a distinguished architect (most notably of the Bank of England) and collector of art and antiquities. The house was completed in 1824, and upon his death in 1837 Soane bequeathed the house and its contents to trustees with the mandate that it be preserved in its original condition. A visit to the Soane, a jewel box of delights and surprises, is a trip into one man's obsessions and love. And if that weren't enough, there are paintings by Canaletto, Turner and Reynolds, and two series by Hogarth. A particular treat is the first Tuesday of each month, when the museum is open in the evening and rooms are lit with candles.

PERIOD DRAMA
55 Dennis Severs' House
18 Folgate Street

California artist Dennis Severs fell in love with Spitalfields and its history, but his re-creation of 18th-century life in a London townhouse is an experience unlike any museum study. Severs saved the house from dereliction, and until his death in 1999 personally escorted guests around the house in a complete sensory experience. Using everything from period furnishings and art, clothes, utensils and food, he aimed to 'bombard the senses'. The house remains open to tours, and each one is like a journey into an Old Master painting. Moving silently through the candlelit rooms, you are transported far beyond historical reconstruction.

THE POWER OF ART
56 Tate Modern
Bankside

The former Bankside Power Station designed by Giles Gilbert Scott opened in 1963, but by the 1990s was disused and regarded by many as an eyesore. Through the vision of Tate director Nicholas Serota and Swiss architects Herzog & de Meuron, the massive building was transformed to house the collections that make up Tate Modern, international art from 1900 to the present, including important works by Dalí, Picasso and Matisse, as well as contemporary artists. The former Turbine Hall, which runs the whole length of the vast building, makes a grand gallery entrance not unlike a cathedral space. In addition to the galleries, which feature permanent and temporary exhibitions, a café and art bookshop – the largest in Europe – are located on the ground floor. The top-floor restaurant, serving modern British cuisine, has glorious views over the Thames.

MAGNET FOR THE ARTS
57 South Bank Centre
- Hayward Gallery, Belvedere Road
- Royal Festival Hall, Belvedere Road
- People's Palace, Royal Festival Hall

Although many decry the concrete brutalism of the South Bank Centre, built as the centrepiece for the 1951 Festival of Britain, its position today as one of London's most important attractions is undisputed. The exhibition spaces of the Hayward Gallery are dedicated principally to shows of modern and contemporary art. With three auditoriums and outdoor performances, the South Bank Centre is a constant hive of activity. On the third level of the Royal Festival Hall is the dramatic and minimalist People's Palace restaurant, which includes a bar and has stunning views of the river and the city beyond along its 36-metre-long glass front.

GARDENS OF DELIGHT
58 Victoria & Albert Museum
Cromwell Road

The largest museum of applied and decorative arts in the world needs little introduction. You might see only one collection – 'Clothing through History' in the Dress Gallery, for example or the splendours of the Asian and Islamic Art collection. You might spend a lot of time staring at the Great Bed of Ware in the recently refurbished and not-to-be-missed British Galleries (1500–1900) – with pieces by Chippendale, Morris, Mackintosh, Wedgwood and Liberty – or Lord Leighton's frescoes after having visited his astonishing house in Holland Park or the magical Glass Gallery. Whatever you manage to see, no visit should be without a stroll through the Pirelli Garden, an Italian-style piazza garden set within the late 19th-century walled courtyard. A large central fountain gurgles beneath grand, swaying trees, and in summer a tented enclosure serves refreshments. Visitors can enjoy both the garden and museum until 10 p.m. on Wednesdays.

PEACEFUL RESPITE
59 Mount Street Gardens
South Audley Street

This wonderfully secret, enclosed green space laid out as a public park in the late 19th century is surrounded by grand Queen Anne-style houses and shaded by giant plane trees. Small and discreet wrought-iron gated entrances near Carlos Place mean that the gardens are usually a peaceful, unpopulated place in which to sit on a wooden bench and to take in the scenery. In the southeast corner is the Church of the Immaculate Conception, known as the Farm Street church, built in 1849 for English Jesuits and containing a high altar by A.W.N. Pugin, architect of the Houses of Parliament.

HAPPY RECREATION
60 Shakespeare's Globe
21 New Globe Walk

American actor Sam Wanamaker's dream to re-create the Globe Theatre was realized in 1997. With its open-air wood stage and galleries, thatched roof and uncovered 'yard' – the standing area where the 'groundlings' who paid a penny for their entry would have stood while drinking beer, munching peanuts and heckling the actors – the Globe is a faithful reconstruction of the original Elizabethan theatre. Visitors today can stand in the yard for around five pounds. Performances, many of which are true to their Elizabethan originals and highly regarded by critics and public alike, take place in all weathers, despite the lack of a roof.

PARIS

In the hearts and imaginations of people around the world, Paris, of all the great cities, hardly needs introduction. Even in those of us who have yet to set foot in the City of Lights, it is remembered as a beacon of artistic and literary endeavour after the war, a place where creativity and philosophy emanated from the cafés of the Left Bank like so much Gitanes cigarette smoke. 'Like Paris in the Twenties', people say of any city drawing an international bohemian crowd with high culture on the cheap and high-intensity living to match. And no other city quite captures the particular 'romance' of Paris. This ineluctable appellation has perhaps become cliché, overused, commercialized, trivialized, but the real thing is still there for the savvy visitor.

Like any ancient city, modern Paris is built on many layers and exists on many levels of perception: physical, historical, emotional. One reason that Paris retains its aura is, of course, its survival – more or less intact – through the great wars. Coveted by invaders who would rather own it than destroy it, it is a city marked by large personalities and grandiose expressions, from King Philippe-Auguste, who chartered the first university in the 13th century, and the spendthrift François I, who rebuilt the Louvre in Italian Renaissance style and promoted humanism, to the even more ostentatious Sun King, who left the Louvre in favour of Versailles, and Napoleon, who added his own imperial monuments (the Arc de Triomphe, the Arc du Carrousel, the column in the place Vendôme). It was his nephew, Napoleon III, who left probably the most visible urban legacy through the work of his urban engineer, Georges (later Baron) Haussmann. Haussmann 'modernized' Paris, clearing away vast areas of medieval buildings (which urban historians decry to this day) to make way for the grand boulevards that give Paris so much of its opulent character.

What visitors will find in Paris today is a city bursting with creative energy. The most talked-about hotels are lavishly decorated in the spirit of the Empire or in a particularly French brand of minimalism, the best restaurants combine the talents of the most innovative designers with young chefs trained in traditional French methods but who are willing to experiment with global cuisines. The grand old fashion houses are still lined up around the Faubourg St Honoré and the Champs-Élysées, but so are the new names, and in pockets around the Marais, the Bastille and Montmartre young designers with backroom ateliers are producing clothing, objects and furniture that one day may be the next big thing, but for now are wonderfully unique creations you won't see anywhere else. Paris, as writer Edmund White contends, is truly the city of the *flâneur*, where an aimless wander can bring unexpected rewards: the glimpse of a medieval square, an exquisite boutique, an enticing café or one of those grand architectural gestures in which Paris's place in history and the imagination is writ large.

StyleCity Paris

sleep

GOTHIC REVIVAL REVISITED

1 Hôtel Bourg Tibourg
19, rue du Bourg-Tibourg, 4e
Rooms from €200

A velvet-lined lift, striped silk-lined walls, a forest of textures and colours set off with fringes – so much dramatic embellishment packed into such a small scale is very much part of the cozy charm of the Bourg Tibourg. Paris's pre-eminent design family, the Costes, have pulled out all the stops in this thirty-one-room hotel, formerly the Rivoli Notre Dame, in the heart of the Marais. Famed designer Jacques Garcia (see L'Hôtel; p. 231) has combined Gothic, Oriental, French Empire and a bit of Victorian to ensure that this is an intimate hotel experience that will leave a lasting visual and sensuous impression. Every room is a unique pleasure, with beds draped in taffeta or silk, complete with giant tassels. Low lighting and deep hues give the rooms the feeling of a richly appointed medieval garret or the tent of a desert prince. The castle theme is even more apparent in the cellar breakfast room, with its stone walls covered with tapestries and velvet curtains. Here, in some of the most atmospheric surroundings in Paris, you can enjoy a candlelit drink, play a game of chess or retreat up the blue-walled staircase to the plush comforts of your room, rather anachronistically equipped with an Internet connection. A garden, designed by Camille Muller, extends the richness out of doors. None of the extravagance will surprise those who have had the chance to visit another collaboration between the Costes family and Garcia, the Hôtel Costes, but it is the difference in scale that makes the rue du Bourg-Tibourg's embrace all the more alluring. And its location in the Marais, packed with restaurants, bars and ambience, is alluring, too; of note along the rue du Bourg-Tibourg are jewelry designs by Philip Cardon (no. 21) and the imported teas at Mariage Frères (no. 30).

This recently renovated three-star hotel set within an 18th-century townhouse has the look and feel of a contemporary classic with a degree of Empire luxury and without the grandiose price tag. The setting at the end of a small street with a view of the city hall and its lovely flower-filled courtyard is surprisingly quiet for this part of town. The colours of the public spaces – dark pinks and warm greens – reflect a sense of style that is more subdued and less flamboyant than some of the noisier arrivals to the Parisian hotel scene. The décor is just one sign of an establishment that wears its 1st arrondissement address (a stone's throw from the Palais Royal and easy walking distance to the Louvre) with solid confidence. There are the services and amenities you would expect, with little touches that let you know this is an independently run place with its own set of high standards. There are forty rooms and three junior suites; the top two suites have sweeping views, though without terraces. Even the small rooms have been fitted with bed surrounds and panel detailing in real wood and decorated in a tasteful mix of carefully selected colours and high-quality fabrics – heavy velvet, rich wool, thick cotton and canvas. The smallest rooms can be fairly *intime*, so it's worth requesting something slightly larger if you like to spread out. A 'superior' room on the back overlooks the private courtyard. Gleaming tiled baths with twin basins are totally modernized and feature lighting fixtures by Philippe Starck. Even rooms on the front are quiet, however, and look onto the serene little rue Thérèse. Breakfast is served buffet-style in the vaulted, stone basement, while other meals will need to be sought out. Try a wine stop at Juvenile's (p. 237), lunch at Le Café Marly (p. 238) or dine in splendid Napoleonic style at Le Grand Véfour. In the heart of one of Paris's most famous and upscale neighbourhood, with shops like Pierre Hardy and Martin Margiela (p. 123) around the corner, what you save on the hotel you can easily spend just by walking out the door.

3 **Murano Urban Resort**
13, boulevard du Temple, 3e
Rooms from €350

The name refers to the Venetian island not because of all the Murano glass in evidence, but because of director Jérôme Foucaud's intention to create a secluded 'island' of luxury between the bijoux streets of the Marais and the gritty style of République. From your first glimpse through the sliding-glass doors past the gleaming, glass-roofed entrance into the rich red dining room, you'll see that no spot has been overlooked in this Austin-Powers-meets-Space-Odyssey design scheme worked by Christine Derory and Raymond Morel. Guests can also surprise themselves by changing the lighting scheme and colour in their rooms, which are decked out in white with bold floral motifs and modern design objects to keep up with the cutting-edge creative types who stay here. There are twenty-three rooms and nine suites stacked up and around the courtyard bar space, including two suites that feature private swimming pools, defiantly cantilevered over the courtyard. Not for the fainthearted, and neither are the prices, but the Murano Urban Resort is offering a holistic luxury experience, further enhanced by the basement spa facilities and a restaurant under the direction of Pierre Auge (formerly of Sketch in London) and Julien Chicoisne.

4 **Azzedine Alaïa Hotel**
5, rue de Moussy, 4e
Apartments from €400

He doesn't advertise and there isn't any brochure, but designer Azzedine Alaïa hasn't had any trouble in getting people to sample his new venture into élite Parisian accommodation. Having converted a 17th-century building near his loft-like boutique in the Marais into three separate apartments, Alaïa maintains the same understated approach as he does with his retail space: no banners, no lighted sign, just a simple address and phone number opens the gate to his world of refined living. The design for each apartment was conceived by Alaïa himself and each is furnished in modern and Modernist style with pieces from the designer's own private collection. The furnishings by Jean Prouvé, Jean Nouvel and Arne Jacobsen, objects by Marc Newson and lighting fixtures by Serge Mouille make you feel as if you are in your own private design haven in the centre of Paris, at least for a while. Floor-to-ceiling windows make the already airy, white spaces lighter and brighter. Each 100-square-metre apartment is fully self-contained with complete kitchen facilities, so clients from fashion models to conscientious weight-watchers can create cuisine to their own specific requirements, or just make their own coffee and keep the wine chilled.

5 L'Hôtel de Sers

41, avenue Pierre 1er de Serbie, 8e
Rooms from €450

Tucked away from the frenzy of the Champs-Élysées, the laser-etched sliding-glass doors welcome you to the former pied à terre of the Marquis de Sers, a 19th-century townhouse brought forward into the 21st century with all the elegance of its Second Empire beginnings. The period interiors have been left open and uncluttered in architect Thomas Vidalenc's design for this new, privately owned hotel. Sitting happily near the border of the 16th arrondissement, it gives easy access to the Eiffel Tower and attractions farther afield, such as the Palais de Tokyo (p. 245) and the Bois de Boulogne, while still being centrally oriented toward the luxe shopping and dining of the 8th. Inside the soaring entrance, a cerise ribbon of carpet welcomes guests up the stairs to the lounge where there is an open bar from teatime until 1 a.m. Downstairs is a bright, modern restaurant serving French cuisine,

and a patio garden with ample wood seating. Fifty-two rooms are arranged over eight floors with two panoramic and four junior suites. The panoramic suites take in a stunning view of the Eiffel Tower, Arc de Triomphe and other splendours of the Parisian skyline. Double superior rooms have partially enclosed stepped-up terraces that overhang the private garden. White interiors avoid being stark with the use of rosewood furnishings, gauzy draperies and a few boldly coloured touches. Clean white, dark wood, stone and bright red combine throughout to create a style of embellished minimalism. Sitting in the neighbourhood of flagship stores for high-end shops like Balenciaga and Jean-Paul Gaultier, as well as the glamour that surrounds the Champs-Élysées, the Hôtel de Sers manages to fit right in without announcing itself too proudly. Its own glamour is to be found on the inside.

THE QUINTESSENCE OF ROMANCE
6 L'Hôtel
13, rue des Beaux Arts, 6e
Rooms from €280

Dramatic, luxurious, historic and with a fabulous location in the heart of St-Germain-des-Prés, L'Hôtel is a complete experience in the way that a small luxury hotel should be. Its Directoire period elements have been meticulously restored down to the last plaster detail in the neoclassically inspired cupola, with its galleried walkways overlooking the hall from all six floors. The themed bedrooms have the plush combinations of the fabrics and furniture for which designer Jacques Garcia (see Hôtel Bourg Tibourg; p. 226) has become famous, and he has lavished the same treatment on the public rooms. The restaurant is full of swags and mirrors, period pendant lamps, a fountain and thickly upholstered seating in bohemian patterns and striped taffeta. Oscar Wilde, who died in the hotel in 1900, has a room dedicated to his luxurious tastes with letters from him scattered throughout (as well as letters to him asking for payment of debts). The room labelled 'Mistinguett' is an essay in Art Déco, with plenty of boldly coloured velvet and decorative objects honouring the singer's heyday in Paris. Other rooms – the 'Marco Polo', the 'St Petersburg', the 'Pompéienne', the 'Reine Hortense' – are decorated in similarly extravagant fashion. The 'Cardinal' room is particularly provocative in varying shades of purple. A hotel since 1825, the recent incarnation is only a few years old and gives the place real star quality. The once abandoned underground cellar has been reclaimed and now houses a tiled sauna and intimate swimming pool lit by candelabras on the walls and surrounded by tea lights. Two bars have been decked out in Garcia's Belle Époque fantasy dressing, as has the restaurant Le Bélier, where the cuisine is well prepared with a small and well-considered wine list.

eat

7 L'Avant-Goût

LINING UP IN THE BUTTE AUX CAILLES

26, rue Bobillot, 13e

For great contemporary French cooking at reasonable prices (though the price of the *prix fixe* menu nudges gently upwards, it remains one of the city's best bargains), it's worth seeking out this tiny, warm bistro near the Butte aux Cailles. There's no point in showing up without a booking, unless you're willing to start queuing outside two hours ahead of time for lunch or even longer for dinner. The place is always crowded, for everybody knows that chef Christophe Beaufront's market-bistro cuisine is both artful (the spicy *pot au feu* is the classic) and tasty, and that the welcome is always excellent.

8 L'Astrance

SMALL BUT PERFECTLY FORMED

4, rue Beethoven, 16e

It was something like love at first sight. When chef Pascal Barbot and maître d' Christophe Rohat (both formerly at L'Arpège, see right) opened their tiny, elegant restaurant in 2001, every food lover in Paris begged for a table. L'Astrance, named after a flower from Auvergne, instantly became the city's best newcomer for years with its modern and creative cooking (avocado and crab ravioli is one of their most famous dishes). Make sure to let them handle your meal and you'll most certainly have a great time. Adopt the same attitude with wines; Monsieur Rohat knows best. Reservations should be made at least one month in advance.

9 Le Pré Catalan

SYVLAN SPLENDOUR

route de Suresnes, Bois de Boulogne, 16e

Dining on the terrace of the Napoleon III pavilion underneath the chestnut trees is pure bliss. Set in the heart of the Bois de Boulogne, Le Pré Catalan is a culinary journey into nature not far from the city centre. Chef Frédéric Anton has brought something essential to the place with his new classic cuisine. Try the small jellied crabs, the baby carrots with ginger sauce, or the John Dory glazed with maple syrup and you'll understand that this man is simply a master. Le Pré Catalan also has a great wine list with some clever selections, and near-perfect service.

10 Pierre Gagnaire

SURPRISING DELIGHTS

Hôtel Balzac, 6, rue Balzac, 8e

When staff bring six or seven small dishes to your table, that's just the beginning at Pierre Gagnaire – creative tapas are offered as a kind of welcome present, to give you a first glimpse of his kind of cooking. The intuitive and spontaneous Gagnaire is also capable of surprising even those who are frequent visitors to this modern dining room, blending unexpected flavours and textures. One can never tell what a meal will be like here, as he sometimes changes his menus or recipes on the same day as he presents them. Just let the staff handle your journey; it could very well be an unforgettable one.

11 L'Arpège

VEGETABLE ARTS

84, rue de Varenne, 7e

Even its biggest fans will tell you that this restaurant is one of the most expensive in Paris; the exciting *menu dégustation* is to blame, as is the ambitious wine list. But if money is no object, L'Arpège is a must-go, particularly if you have vegetarian inclinations. Chef Alain Passard's menu focuses on vegetables, which he grows in his vegetable garden in Anjou, but also includes seafood and poultry. Try the sweet onions with parmesan and black pepper, beets with balsamic vinegar and black truffles, or carrot and verbena consommé for a bold and unique gastronomic experience that is worth every Euro.

12 Ze Kitchen Galerie

RAW ARTISTRY

4, rue des Grands Augustins, 6e

Ze Kitchen Galerie is something entirely new, with a white-washed loft-like décor and an open kitchen you can peer into through a glass panel (a novelty in the city). Located in the 6th arrondissement's high concentration of antiques and furniture galleries, it has a relaxed and peaceful atmosphere. The food created by chef William Ledeuil complements this mood with a vocabulary of its own: playful, sharp and open-minded (plenty of Asian herbs and spices), with a destructured *carte*, allowing one to choose pasta and soup instead of the traditional progression of starter–main course–dessert.

13 L'Ami Jean

FRIEND FROM THE SOUTH

27, rue Malar, 7e

The straightforward sign outside reads *Cuisine basque*, a statement confirmed inside by the pepper braids and rugby paraphernalia on the walls, both typical of southwestern France. But you can expect far more from chef Stéphane Jégo than the local *piperade* (a tomato and pepper-based dish) followed by ewe's-milk cheese. Instead, he continually makes the most of seasonal produce in accordance with his regional origins, stuffing piquillo peppers with crab or serving black pudding in a salad. Connoisseurs will recognize a cooking style reminiscent of La Régalade, where Jégo trained for several years.

14 Chez Jean

PRIDE OF PLACE

8, rue St-Lazare, 9e

Nowadays, talented and ambitious restaurateurs normally wouldn't even think of taking up business anywhere else than on the Left Bank. Yet Frédéric Guidoni, ex-maître d' at the famous Taillevent, has made a striking debut with this wood-panelled brasserie near the rue des Martyrs. Chef Benoît Bordier, too, has proved an imaginative young recruit. His snail and asparagus monkfish with rosemary lettuce, confit of free-range pork with carrots and cocoa-lychee-red-grapefruit milkshake are definitely worth crossing the Seine for. The wine list as well bears absolutely no reproach.

15 La Famille

FAMILY FUSION

41, rue des Trois-Frères, 18e

A new restaurant on the Butte Montmartre is a rare thing, and a good restaurant even more so. But La Famille's relaxed and friendly atmosphere, trendy crowd, funky music and out-of-the-ordinary food cooked up under southeast Asian, Spanish and French influences by a self-taught chef from the Pays Basque make a successful combination. The menu changes almost every week and may feature foie gras in miso soup, coffee-flavoured entrecôte, seared tuna with dried fruit and citrus peel, or Espelette pepper-infused chocolate pot. A huge hit; bookings are a must, but worth the trouble.

16   La Table du Joël Robuchon
AT TABLE
16, avenue Bugeaud, 16e

Critics favour Joël Robuchon's second restaurant over his much publicized Atelier, which serves smaller portions in a less formal atmosphere. Firstly, it is possible to book a table here (unlike at Atelier), and secondly, there is a brilliant pastry chef, whose imagination stretches well beyond the familiar repertoire of fruit tarts. And finally, while the classic food strikes just the right chord, the sommelier offers about twenty different wines by the glass, enabling you to dine to a Latour 1990 without having to buy the full bottle.

17   Les Ambassadeurs
HIGH TABLE
Hôtel de Crillon, 10, place de la Concorde, 8e

Chef Jean-François Piège, a former pupil of Alain Ducasse, is the master of command on board this magnificent dining room reminiscent of the famous Galerie des Glaces at Versailles. With the profusion of crystal, splendid view onto the place de la Concorde and the staggering bill, you'll quickly grasp that an evening here is a special occasion. Pigeon with foie gras and olives, crayfish in a spicy broth, or Bresse poultry with spaghetti carbonara are washed down with equally exceptional wines.

18   Le Baratin
ARGENTINIAN JIVE
3, rue Jouye-Rouve, 20e

Take no notice if you hear a Spanish-accented woman's voice yelling from the kitchen – that's Raquel, the cook, from Argentina. Le Baratin ('jive') is one of Belleville's most famous wine bars: unexpected, unusual, bohemian and engaging – definitely the place to go if you want to grasp something of the eastern Parisian state of mind. Don't forget to book a table (the place is always full and smoky) to try one of the numerous wines by the glass (the wine list is remarkable) and one of Raquel's Franco–Argentinian dishes.

19 Spoon, Food & Wine

GLOBAL FUSION COMES TO PARIS

14, rue de Marignan, 8e

When Alain Ducasse opened this bistro in 1998, he (unusually) introduced a DIY fusion menu from which patrons could mix and match dishes, something that had never been done before in Paris, perhaps in the world. The place became immediately popular among the fashionable set, drawn by the playful Asian-, French-, Italian- and American-inspired menu that featured everything from Thai soup to pasta with tomato marmalade, pan-seared squid with satay sauce and sautéed vegetables to bubble-gum ice cream.

20 Le Villaret

NEIGHBOURHOOD STAR

13, rue Ternaux, 11e

What used to be a neighbourhood bistro with clever cooking is becoming a truly ambitious restaurant. Though prices have risen in recent years, the place still has a laid-back atmosphere and a funky clientele who know that quality and taste will be part of the deal. Self-taught chef Olivier Gaslain likes tweaking classic French cooking, though there's little likelihood you will bump into a Camembert pizza or other such fusion silliness here. It also benefits from being open until very late at night. Reservations are essential.

21 L'Ambroisie

ÉLÉGANCE SUPRÊME

9, place des Vosges, 4e

Chef Bernard Pacaud runs one of Paris's best restaurants (some would even say *the* best) set in one of the city's best locations. The moment you arrive under the magnificent arcades of the 17th-century place des Vosges and step into the hushed elegance of the Viennese-inflected interior designed by François-Joseph Graf, you will begin to sense what makes this place so special. L'Ambroisie is the epitome of classic French cuisine, but with a twist of modernity. Sharp flavours, high prices, a truly memorable experience.

drink

Pétrissans

22 Caves Miard
9, rue des Quatre-Vents, 6e

Yes, another wine bar and shop. Yet you should take a closer look – the place is simply beautiful. Picture a seventy-year-old ham slicer set in a splendidly preserved 19th-century décor. Imagine top-of-the-crop wines at their unsulphured, healthy and nature-friendly best. Add a charming young owner wearing a funky cap, and top it all off with exceptional Italian cured meats such as *culatello, coppa* or *lardo di Colonnata*. Now you'll understand why the few tables are constantly taken over by a pool of enthusiastic customers.

MODELS ON ICE
23 Bar du Plaza Athénée
25, avenue Montaigne, 8e

Some, even some Parisians, describe the Bar du Plaza Athénée as the most beautiful bar in Paris. Beneath Murano glass chandeliers, high, grey Louis XV-style stools line the long, transparent bar that glows like a slab of blue ice. The décor is the work of Patrick Jouin, who redid the interior after the bar was destroyed by fire in 2000 – one reason, perhaps, for the icy feel. The wood panelling and chandeliers survived, and the stage was set for the models, actresses and rock stars who like to revel in its glory. Sip a Champagne Mojito and watch the limousines arrive; save the jelly shots for later.

THE HIPPEST HAPPENINGS
24 De la Ville Café
34, boulevard Bonne-Nouvelle, 10e

This new addition to the café-bar-restaurant scene on the border of the 9th and 10th arrondissements is attracting diners, drinkers and pre-club hangers-on in droves. The design by Périphériques swings from cool, orange-and-black plastic chairs on the deck terrace to the odd geometric forms of the wood furnishings to candelabras and velvet upholstery. The ceiling mosaics in the lounge are worthy of a reclining gaze and may be a holdover from the building's previous incarnation as a brothel, or some other glimpse of Parisian history. Come for a drink, stay to watch the crowds.

FAR OUT, BABY
25 Murano Urban Resort Bar
13, boulevard du Temple, 3e

You may feel the need to utter something about 'Bond, James Bond' when you walk through the door of this fun and futuristic watering hole set in the ultra-mod lobby of the new hotel (p. 228). As if the shiny white space, complete with white Chesterfield sitting nonchalantly near the block fireplace isn't chic enough, the bar, with walls upholstered in fuchsia and plum, zinc tables and stools and a range of 100 types of vodka, signals a new high in decadent drinking. In the early evening, piano music provides a civilizing touch, while later on the DJs take over to add vibe to vibrancy.

TO DRINK LIKE A …
26 Fish/La Boissonnerie
69, rue de Seine, 6e

If you've already been to Paris with a hip travel guide in your pocket, you might have run into this wine bar owned by a young American named Juan Sanchez (ask for the address of his wine shop), who knows French vineyards better than most French. Each week he changes the ten wines served by the glass, a clever means to ensure that oenophiles return. His viticultural *coups de cœur* often take him to the Rhône valley, the Languedoc-Roussillon and the Riviera (check out the fantastic Côtes de Provence Château de Roquefort, for instance). And to fill stomachs, the food, mainly based on pasta and vegetables, is just right.

CAFÉ OF THE ARTS
27 La Palette
43, rue de Seine, 6e

As the name suggests, La Palette is a café with genuine artistic leanings. Its proximity to the École des Beaux Arts and setting in an area filled with galleries mean that it draws clientele from both. Large, colourful oil paintings and exhibition posters contribute to the arty Parisian stereotype. This is a traditional French café with all the classic offerings, occasionally brusque waiters and a fine corner spot for outdoor tables. The daily specials are fresh, well prepared and worth trying, even if you don't completely understand the description.

WINE BAR TRÈS CHIC
28 Les Caves Pétrissans
30 bis, avenue Niel, 17e

There are some wine bars where you bump into more Hermès ties than Nikes, and Les Caves Pétrissans, with its chic atmosphere and clientele, is one of them. But you'll never feel uncomfortable, since conviviality is this bistro's buzzword and people of all kinds rub shoulders around the bar. The décor (worth a visit in itself) is as ageless as the food – perfect bistro and home-cooking fare with set pieces of steak tartare (superb), calf's head with shallot sauce, and kidneys, to name a few. And since the place doubles as a vintner's, have a look at the remarkable wine list and then go next door and buy a bottle of your own.

WINE AND SCOTS
29 Juvenile's
47, rue de Richelieu, 1e

You might not want to come to Paris to meet English-speaking tourists. But what you might want to find is a wily wine bar, even if it's run by a Scot called Tim Johnston. Therefore, sieze the occasion to ask the owner (in English, obviously) what's worth looking at from the French vineyards. He might have you start with a glass of Purple Four (a Rhône valley vintage specially blended for him), then take you to the Barossa valley (the international wine list is clever, though a bit expensive). Meanwhile, you'll be pecking at some nice tapas (hot chorizo included) or cheese plates. Wine can also be purchased to take home.

TEA CEREMONIES
30 La Maison des Trois Thés
33, rue Gracieuse, 5e

Tea is becoming more popular in Paris, although, as you might expect, in a refined and sometimes even haute manner. At La Maison des Trois Thés, Taiwanese proprietress Yu Hui Tseng, one of the leading tea-masters in the world and an official expert for the Chinese government, is on a mission to promote the ancient *gong fu* ceremony in Europe, along with a genuine appreciation of tea. Offering more than a thousand varieties of teas, from the humble jasmine to the rare (and dear) oolong, her teahouse has the largest selection in the world, but the setting is pleasantly intimate, modern and serene.

FUGITIVE OENOPHILIA
31 Le Verre Volé
67, rue de Lancry, 10e

Wine bar, wine shop and microbistro rolled into one – this is what makes 'the stolen glass' such an unusual place. Since the word has begun to spread out of the Canal St-Martin area and across Paris, you'll need to book one of the four or five tables if you want to eat or be seated to enjoy some of the finest wines of the moment (the white Coteaux d'Aix from Château Bas, or the Vinsobres from the Domaine Gramenon in the Rhône valley) with a simple plate of cheese or some oysters. The tiny locale doesn't inhibit enjoyment, however – it can be wild from time to time.

HAMMAM AND MINT TEA
32 La Mosquée de Paris
39, rue St-Hilaire, 5e

If you're already planning a visit to the spectacular Jardin des Plantes, then it's also a good time to take in this 1920s mosque built in Hispano-Moorish style by three French architects and decorated by numerous North African artisans. Featuring lacey Moorish patterns in intricately carved wood screens, decorative tilework and lighting and ornate cupolas, the mosque also has beautifully kept patio gardens. You might enjoy the hammam or have traditional mint tea at the café/tea-room in a plant-filled courtyard, itself reminiscent of a Mughal palace.

MUSEUM OPULENCE
33 Le Café Marly
93, rue de Rivoli, 1e

Some say you cannot get a feel for Paris without sitting at least once on the terrace of the Café Marly, facing I.M. Pei's beautiful glass pyramids at the Musée du Louvre. There is a lot to see while sipping a coffee: models, Gucci worshippers, actors you haven't yet heard of, armchairs designed by Olivier Gagnère. The Marly is one of the Costes brothers' (see Hôtel Bourg Tibourg; p. 226) major successes of the 1990s. Knowing that, you should not complain about the fashion food (chicken with Thai basil, gazpacho, duck brochettes with caramel and coconut) – nor the prices.

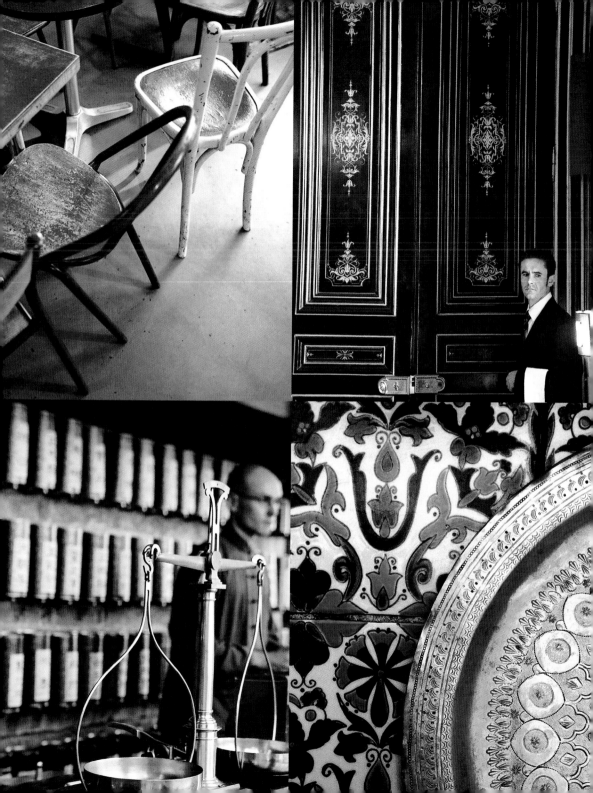

shop

A WORLD-CLASS NOSE

**34 Editions de Parfums
Frédéric Malle**
37, rue de Grenelle, 7e

When Frédéric Malle wanted to revolutionize perfume-making, he hired nine reputable perfume-makers and gave them carte blanche to produce original, complex scents. These mystery 'noses', formerly unknown because of their associations with large perfumeries, now have their names attached to the scents created under the auspices of Malle's Editions, which he says he produces like a publisher. Interiors were designed by Malle with his friend and 'the godmother of the shop', Andrée Putman, together with her protégé, architect Olivier de Lempereur.

SEDUCTION ZONE

35 Iunx
48–50, rue de l'Université, 7e

The name is as enigmatic as the seductive Zen-toned black and white space with rectangular lily pond lapping at the centre. Entering the shop is like stepping into a world where the calm and the aromatic prevail. Seductively lit, it is lined with slim, cone-shaped bottles of perfumes, shower, hair and beauty products, as well as scented candles and blocks of fragrant wood. It was created by Fabienne Conte-Sévigné and Francis Giacobetti to stock the eighty scents compiled by Olivia Giacobetti, formerly a nose for other grand perfumers and now a creator in her own right.

SHOE FETISH

36 Christian Louboutin
19, rue Jean-Jacques Rousseau, 1e

This young designer trained under master Roger Vivier, but quickly made a name for himself with his outrageous concepts, including heels made of beer cans. Though Louboutin now claims to be toning down his oeuvre, it's hard to imagine that the man who popularized scarlet soles and heels of Lucite with flowers or bits of fashionable rubbish trapped inside will ever become pedestrian. Celebrities from Cher and Madonna to Princess Caroline of Monaco are fans. The shop is like a mini gallery, each shoe lovingly displayed against gilt foil or in a cubby-hole.

ARTISAN-MADE BAGS AND SHOES

37 Jamin Puech
68, rue Vieille du Temple, 3e

Tied to a 'respect for tradition and a belief in artisanal manufacture', Benoît Jamin and Isabelle Puech's experimentation with materials 'never before seen in the leather industry' quickly brought them to the fore of the fashion world. Their first collection went on sale at Bergdorf Goodman in 1992 and in the following years they created accessories for Chloé, Karl Lagerfeld (p. 246), Balmain and Ally Capellino. The duo's eclectically decorated original shop in the rue d'Hauteville is comfortable and welcoming, with its antiques-market furnishings, bright colours, and leather, beaded, stitched and flower-studded handbags and coordinated footwear. Previously located in the area around the Canal St-Martin, the pair moved house to the boutique-laden Marais.

PIÈCE UNIQUE

38 A-poc
47, rue des Francs-Bourgeois, 4e

'A-poc' stands for 'a piece of cloth' and is one of Issey Miyake's experiments in textile design. Like 'Pleats Please', it takes a concept of fabric design – here, the cutting and assembling of one piece of cloth made from a single thread – and displays it in variation and as art. The concept has a showroom and workshop in the Marais by designers Erwan and Ronan Bouroullec, who have created white polystyrene circular display units to cradle coordinating sporty footwear and accessories. Some articles can be tailored to fit.

PASTRY ARTS

39 Sadaharu Aoki
56, boulevard de Port Royal, 5e

Where else but in Paris would you find the Japanese skill of fine detailing turned to the art of pastry-making? Chef Sadaharu Aoki delights in what he calls France's 'treasure house of fruits', which he incorporates into his artful little delicacies, all set out in a suitably trim and elegant boutique of a shop that you would easily miss if you weren't looking for it. Minute sketches that are works of art in themselves diagram the contents of some of the carefully stacked layers and swirls. Sesame and green tea are among the exotic flavours arranged in picture-perfect parcels. But he also turns out a number of more traditional items such as cheesecakes, millefeuille and a 'Japon', which features strawberries and Chantilly cream. Aoki's confections are served in a number of top Parisian teahouses, but there is a diminutive seating area here, as elegant as the pastries.

CLASSIC MEN'S SHIRTS

40 Charvet
28, place Vendôme, 1e

'Trendy' is not a word you associate with this, one of Paris's last surviving traditional shirtmakers, but if you are looking for something with that quintessential Parisian gentlemanly air, then this venerable institution is a worthwhile stop. Made-to-measure shirts (still sewn one at a time in their workshop) as well as ties and handkerchiefs in dozens of fabrics and patterns and a selection of classic pyjamas and toiletries are all on display in the reassuringly old-fashioned premises. The inventor of removable collars and cuffs, Charles Charvet, opened shop in 1838 and was soon shirtmaker to royalty and nouveau riche alike.

PREMIER CONCEPT STORE

41 Colette
213, rue St-Honoré, 1e

The woman who created this early 'concept store', mixing design, art, fashion and books on the subjects in a high-design backdrop, did it fashionably on a first-name basis. Now when such holistic blends have become much more commonplace, Colette still holds the reins with this original and still top-notch fashion emporium. The three floors of minimally designed premises feature an international collection of clothing and accessories, art objects, electronic gadgetry and cosmetics from the pantheon of designers. Downstairs everything from designer furniture to toiletries is on offer, as well as a restaurant and the refreshment of the famed 'water bar', where you can sample from around eighty brands from all over the globe. Despite its high profile, this is a shop where browsing is part of the experience, with a photo gallery and bookshop on the mezzanine level, as well as space for temporary exhibitions.

SWEET ARTS
42 Pierre Hermé
72, rue Bonaparte, 6e

To know him is to love his creations: melt-in-your-mouth macaroons, apple-and-almond milk tart, 'velvet heart' cake – all like beautiful still lifes that you can eat. All Paris is wild about Pierre Hermé, as you can tell by the queue stretching out from his tiny jewel-box shop designed by Yann Pennor, especially on a Friday afternoon. Uniquely creative with chocolate, Hermé works like a fashion designer, creating 'collections' by the season, and has recently opened a tearoom off the Champs-Élysées.

COOLEST CASHMERE
43 Lucien Pellat-Finet
1, rue Montalembert, 7e

Christian Biecher, the designer's interior designer of the moment, has worked his bright magic to create an appropriately striking backdrop for Lucien Pellat-Finet's famed cashmere creations. A glass front marked by a pink awning and bright-red display shelves inside announce knitted wonders, T-shirts, pullovers and belted, tunic-length cardigans. The mere luxury of 100 per cent cashmere is not enough for the designer, who adds stripes, patterns and whimsical cut-out motifs to make eye-catching pieces that range from sporty to sophisticated.

TASTEBUDS IN ECSTASY
44 Les Papilles
30, rue Gay-Lussac, 5e

Bertrand Bluy, former pastry chef at le Bristol and Taillevent, left behind the world of Michelin two- and three-star enterprises to open this warm and inviting gourmet shop and restaurant. The shop is filled with luxury foods sourced from around the country and well-chosen wines, while the restaurant serves up a menu of modern neo-bistro food, all much tastier than any of us could actually do at home. Dishes like Basque goats' cheese with black cherry jam and Espelette pepper jelly, duck breast with butter-encrusted new potatoes, oysters and charcuterie are prepared and presented in copper pots. In a neighbourhood somewhat lacking in inspired choices, this is the choice of foodies in the know.

GOURMET COOKBOOKS
45 Librairie Gourmande
4, rue Dante, 5e

In the city long thought to be the world's culinary capital, it makes sense to have a look at what Parisians consider a good cookbook. The problem at the Librairie Gourmande is that there are so many to choose from, and not just the latest titles. There are old editions of some American and British cookbooks, as well as the full stock of French titles. The small, cramped space and tables outside are brimming with traditional and modern fusion recipes, from Escoffier to Pierre Hermé (see left) to Jamie Oliver.

SOPHISTICATED FOLK
46 Vanessa Bruno
25, rue St-Sulpice, 6e and
12, rue de Castiglione, 1e

Vanessa Bruno's clothes have something of a 1970s gypsy look about them, but with a definite contemporary style. Blouses with lacey bodices, high necks and gathered sleeves are paired with bias-cut cardigans and flounced skirts. The chunky leather boots and bags, along with the more streamlined footwear, all have a relaxed attitude that's more folk than fashion. Bruno's first shop on rue St-Sulpice has homey wood floors, along with a cut-out purple wall and funky ornamental chandelier to signal an all-over sense of design. Her newer shop on the pricey rue de Castiglione goes more chic and modern with glossy enamel fixtures contrasting with the fresco-style wall treatments.

GLORIOUS FABRICS
47 Dominique Kieffer
8, rue Hérold, 1e

Dominique Kieffer designs fabrics and objects to do with fabric, such as cushions and throws, but that doesn't begin to describe the visual and tactile richness of colour and texture of the velvet, raffia and feather trim, or the fabrics that are sometimes a patchwork of different luxurious weaves. Her interest is in 'natural materials, particularly linen'. By 'developing soft, heavy fabrics and using special finishes to give them an antique look', Kieffer explains, she 'gives them a soul'.

see

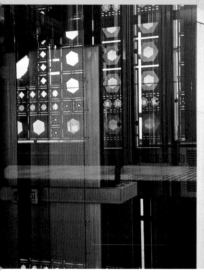

48 Institut du Monde Arabe
1, rue des Fossés-St-Bernard, 5e

This centre for Arabic arts and culture was designed by Jean Nouvel in 1987 around the concept of a *moucharabieh* but used in a distinctly modern way with photo-electric cells in the exterior cladding that adjust the amount of light entering the building to protect the museum pieces inside. The building itself is a graceful piece of architecture with Islamic elements and patterns woven into the façade. The institute hosts temporary exhibitions, films and lectures, while the stylish café Loubnane serves sandwiches and drinks.

HIGH-TECH LANDMARK
49 Centre Pompidou
place Georges Pompidou, 4e

Some find it amusing that a conservative politician like Georges Pompidou has fostered such avant-garde architectural projects as this extraordinary work by Richard Rogers and Renzo Piano. As striking as it is today, it certainly caused a few jaws to drop when it opened in 1977, with its exposed pipes and framework jutting up from the old Beaubourg neighbourhood. But the building has lived to be loved and a revamp in 2000, which included the addition of a rooftop restaurant (see right), has given it a new lease of life.

AN EVEN NEWER TWIST
50 Georges
place Georges Pompidou, 6th floor, 4e

With breathtaking views over the city's rooftops, Georges, located on the sixth floor of the Pompidou, is another piece of the Costes brothers' empire. Most interesting is the unusual architecture, designed by Brendan MacFarlane and Dominique Jakob, a strange mixture of space-age influences and hollowed-out shapes, alternating with icy aluminium and splashes of colour. Booking is a good idea for dinner, but you can just turn up and have a drink in one of the organic-shaped pods, or, early on, a cocktail on the roof terrace.

Jean Nouvel (see opposite) has once again created a stand-out structure for a cultural centre, this time for the Fondation Cartier *pour l'art contemporain*, an organization created in 1984 according to the vision of Cartier president Alain Dominique Perrin, which moved into this space of shifting glass panes in 1994. With the stated aim of 'building up a collection of work by living artists that is a reflection of the age', the foundation buys, commissions and exhibits works of art, as well as staging theatre, music and dance performances.

The Musée d'Art Moderne already occupied one wing of the Palais de Tokyo, but the need for more flexible space was behind the new interior designed by Anne Lacaton and Jean-Philippe Vassal. Inside they have created an open-plan space by ripping out beams and floors to create a hangar-like backdrop for exhibitions, open from noon until midnight. Downstairs the tabula rasa has been livened up in the colourful café area that spills out onto the terrace, where the view over the Seine is art of a different nature.

The Musée Nissim de Camondo is an exuberant celebration of 18th-century French decoration and craftsmanship. Jacob, Sèvres, Meissen, Huet and a host of other names linked to the golden age of French decorative arts fill the meticulously laid-out rooms. The banking family de Camondo were known as 'the Rothschilds of the East', coming from Constantinople to establish branches in Paris. Moïse de Camondo tore down the family house on this site in 1910 and erected a new building inspired by the Petit Trianon at Versailles.

DESIGNED AFTER A FASHION
54 Lagerfeld Gallery
40, rue de Seine, 6e

Not so much a gallery as a place for the slow, boutique style of shopping that's become popular with designers of late, though the title is appropriate enough in a neighbourhood filled with art and antiques showrooms. Lagerfeld Gallery is actually the name of the particular line of prêt à porter that is showcased in this shop decorated in Andrée Putman's signature luxurious minimalism – dark wood and rich-coloured fabrics, all streamlined against pure white. This isn't all about clothes, as the design objects, books and photographs of buildings by Tadao Ando make clear. There is even a room at the back to sit and read the latest fashion magazines between couture decisions, or while you wait for that Lagerfeld fan to emerge from the changing room.

HOUSE OF ART
55 Musée Gustave Moreau
14, rue de La Rochefoucauld, 9e

Born in Paris in 1826, Gustave Moreau was a prolific painter who helped to usher in the Symbolist and Surrealist movements. Moreau intended that the house and studio where he worked with such great intensity should be preserved as a museum, to 'give a small idea of the person I was and the atmosphere in which I liked to dream.' Thousands of works, from delicate sketches of animals and plants to monumental canvases depicting scenes from the Bible, myth and fantasy, are displayed in two large, light-filled studio rooms joined by a spiral iron staircase. Domestic rooms, including one devoted to his student and mistress, present an intriguing glimpse of late 19th-century French bourgeois life.

PARTERRES AND PAVILLONS
56 Parc André Citroën
quai André-Citroën, 15e

One feels a little like a modern-day Alice in Wonderland here, especially when entering from the north end at rue Cauchy and encountering the allée formed by stepped concrete cubes, wrapped in box hedges, leading to a tunnel of trees and beyond to other wonders both formal and wild. In the land where the formal garden was invented, it's no surprise that the 20th-century version is something to behold. Three-storey greenhouse towers on one side of a path are countered by small, shaded pergolas. A *jardin en mouvement* contains bamboo and other plants that rustle in the breeze, while other areas are planted by colour or form, all divided by low stone walls and walks. Pavement fountains dance in front of the two great glassed conservatories. Landscape artists Gilles Clément and Alain Provost completed work in 1992 on former Citroën factory land. Until the Bercy park was completed, it was the largest Parisian park project of the 20th century.

MUSEUM FOR AN ENIGMA
57 Musée Rodin
Hôtel Biron, 79, rue de Varenne, 7e

The Hôtel Biron was known as a fine house and garden even before Rodin took up residence, in the wake of artists like Henri Matisse and Jean Cocteau, in 1908 at the age of sixty-eight. A masterpiece of rocaille architecture completed in 1730, the house later fell on hard times, but the museum has brought back much of the original décor, including some fine painted overdoors by François Lemoyne. Inside are numerous busts, drawings and paintings by Rodin and others, while in the restored gardens are such masterworks as The Thinker, Ugolino, The Gates of Hell and The Burghers of Calais.

NOTES ON THE MASTER
58 Fondation Pierre Bergé, Yves Saint Laurent
5, avenue Marceau, 16e

Opposite the grand wooden doors marked with the large 'YSL' is the entrance to the exhibition space and archives. The more extraordinary of YSL couture designs are displayed on mannequins set on a ribboned catwalk, which scrolls through the two rooms while video screens play footage of vintage fashion shows and preparations, and interviews with the man himself serenaded by the likes of Lou Reed and the Beatles. The whole presentation is lively and vivid, if limited. Upstairs a small bookshop has titles on Yves Saint Laurent and fashion, and colourful postcards by the designer. Access to the 5,000 haute couture garments and 15,000 accessories in the archives on the second and third floors is by appointment only.

CREATIVE CAVERNS
59 Viaduc des Arts
avenue Daumesnil, 12e
- Créations Chérif, no. 13
- Maison Fey, no. 15
- Malhia, no. 19
- Via, nos 29–35
- Le Viaduc Café, no. 43
- Vertical, no. 63
- Cyrille Varet, no. 67
- Marie Lavande, no. 83

The arches of a disused railway viaduct have been cleaned up and glassed in and now house a parade of craft shops and ateliers. Tapestries, furnishings and lighting are prominent as are gallery spaces and exposition/showrooms. Some good stops are Créations Chérif, which features purple, orange and red curvy velvet sofas and chairs, Maison Fey, which carries leather-covered, stamped and embossed books, frames and furnishings, and Malhia, a shop overflowing with gorgeous fabrics that are woven on site and in full view and are available as sweaters, scarves, coats and shawls. Buy one of their reasonably priced pieces and come away with a hand-decorated Malhia bag. Via (Valorisation de l'Innovation dans l'Ameublement), which promotes communication between designers and manufacturers, has offices and a permanent exhibition of furniture, textiles and home accessories. Le Viaduc Café has lots of pavement tables and jazz brunches on Sundays. Nearby Vertical features sculptural wood and vegetation, while no. 67 houses the wild nouveau-baroque designs of Cyrille Varet, who produces curving brushed steel in asymmetrical shapes and upholsters it in jewel tones. Marie Lavande specializes in the conservation of fine linens using soap flakes, lavender oil and rice starch. You can watch the white-coated women, experts in the 17th-century technique of 'breaking and folding' table linens, at work hand-stitching and ironing.

ROME

Mesmerizing Rome, hub of an ancient empire. Medieval and baroque, piled on a vision of crumbling antiquity and decadence; aged political city, seat of papal power; hip epicentre of swinging postwar Europe: history marks Rome at every turn, oozing from the rambling succession of cobbled alleyways, squares and palaces that weave through its largely unspoiled historic centre. The capital of modern Italy and host to the Vatican – the city within a city – Rome's population is around four million, but it feels distinctly unmodern and barely a metropolis. The wealth of centuries-old art and architecture seems to ward off even the tiniest modern advance. Rome still lives a village life: food and vegetable markets appear in every neighbourhood; craft shops, bars and piazzas act as community meeting points; cars creep around narrow streets best suited for walking. Rome has none of the boulevard ostentation of its European counterparts. Instead, the atmosphere of a thriving, social, medieval city remains intact.

Founded on seven hills and now spread into a well-contained suburban sprawl, Rome is defined by its ancient centre, itself divided into quarters. Its many churches and palaces were restored to the authentic reds, pale blues and ochres of Pompeii during the massive Millennium facelift that spruced up much of the city. Modish areas like Trastevere and Campo de' Fiori are the crowd-pullers, but they are gradually being usurped by Testaccio, the former slaughterhouse area now revitalized by a bustling nightlife scene, and San Lorenzo, home to the city's students and a thriving artist community. A steady rise in property prices has pushed young bohemians into neighbourhoods like il Pigneto and Ostiense, now poised to become the creative and nightlife hotspots in the coming years. A political city since the days of the Roman Empire, Rome bears its *Caput Mundi* status lightly. Its citizens display a healthy disrespect towards the ruling class and use jaded sarcasm against excessive displays of wealth. Unlike Milan, Rome's inhabitants traditionally resist the northern European work ethic, something that has always given the city a reputation for being relaxed, if not cheerfully chaotic. An afternoon siesta is not as common as it once was, but most workers (including shopkeepers) still take a leisurely lunch. *La Dolce Vita* might have just been Fellini's idealization of a particular era, but it undoubtedly captured the heady mix of hedonism, laziness, and the ability to reinvent oneself daily (*l'arte di arrangiarsi*) that defines the Roman way.

Rome's rich melting pot of culture can sometimes be overwhelming, but luckily many of the sights are easily accessible on foot. And can there be a city more photogenic than Rome? It has a slow-paced beauty that lends itself to a cinematic backdrop: a creeper-clad wall, a sunset-tinged dome across the river at St Peter's, lovers perched on a sky-blue Vespa. Even through the snap of a digital camera, Rome is a vision steeped in antiquity and frozen in time.

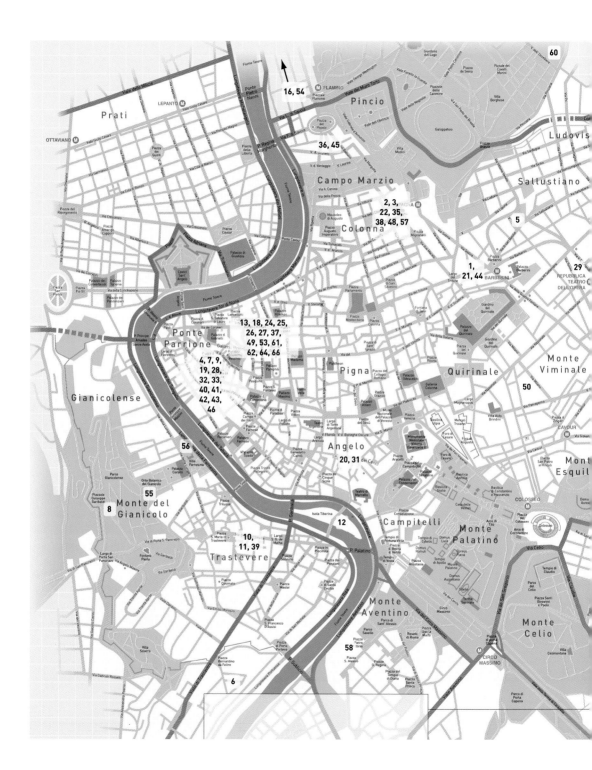

sleep

AN ECCENTRIC GUESTHOUSE

1 Casa Howard
Via Capo le Case 18 and Via Sistina 149
Rooms from €160

This quirky guesthouse, whose name is a play on the Italian translation of E.M. Forster's novel *Howard's End*, is actually two separate *palazzi*, perfectly located a stone's throw from shopping heaven in the form of the Piazza di Spagna. An intimate and luxurious residence, Casa Howard's owners are Jenifer Howard Forneris, originally from Britain, and her husband Count Massimiliano Leonardi di Casalino. The *palazzo* in Via Capo le Case has only five guestrooms, each with parquet floors, coffered ceilings, oil paintings and antiques. The rooms are named after their decorative schemes: the 'Chinese Room' has fabrics sourced from Shanghai Tang in Hong Kong, while the 'White Room' is decorated with pretty black-and-white Toile de Jouy with red trimmings. Not every room in Capo le Case has an en-suite facilities; those who must venture down the hall are supplied with dainty slippers and a kimono. A small Turkish hammam provides welcome respite after a day of sightseeing. The second property in the Via Sistina was designed by Tommaso Ziffer, who was also responsible for the nearby Hotel de la Russie. Ziffer's mark can be found in the unashamedly maximalist style of the rooms, which still remains true to the hotel's essentially cozy feel. The 'American Cousin Room' is a true bachelor pad, with flat-screen TV, Internet connection and shiny black furniture, while the 'Zebra Room' is a sensory overload of black-and-white prints and red floors and walls. Breakfast is served in your room, with warm croissants and jam from the Leonardis' farmhouse in Tuscany. A well-stocked fridge in the hallway is there for everyone to use. In addition to the two Roman locations, Casa Howard Florence recently opened in the Via della Scala.

2 **Palazzetto at the International Wine Academy**
Vicolo del Bottino 8
Rooms from €210

A four-storey, turn-of-the-20th-century honey-hued building perched on the Spanish Steps, the Palazzetto has just four luxurious rooms. Owned by Roberto Wirth, of nearby Hotel Hassler Villa Medici, it is a bolthole for those attending the International Wine Academy, with early evening tastings on the superbly located roof terrace. Other customers come to this townhouse hotel for its intimate surroundings and pared-down décor. Each bedroom is individually decorated with pale and neutral tones, although the beds are a display of indulgence with their printed velvet covers, linen sheets and tiers of taffeta silk pillows. The mini-bars are well stocked with Italian wines. Guests have a number of different dining options. The wood-panelled Library provides food for thought with its impressive wine book collection; the display cases are packed with bottles from all over the world. On the first floor, the wine bar/salon is a more informal affair, where chef Antonio Martucci will rustle up a plate of mozzarella, Roman ham (*coppa*) or an artichoke salad. A fireplace, comfy armchairs and a chess set give the area a warm, clubby feel. In fine weather, breakfast is served in the ivy-clad garden, next to a statue of Bacchus. Visitors are also given their own set of keys so that they can come and go at all times via the roof terrace, and the service is relaxed, materializing only at times of need. The circular wrought-iron staircase may remind film lovers of Bernardo Bertolucci's film *L'Assedio*, which was filmed here. Whether you wish to meander through the smart shopping streets around the Spanish Steps or just live out your own *Roman Holiday* fantasy, this is the ideal private *palazzo* experience.

3 Hotel Art

Via Margutta 56
Rooms from €340

The peacefully pedestrian Via Margutta has been famous since the 1950s for being where many artists had their studios and where Federico Fellini lived. Hotel Art takes its name from the street's reputation and from the works of art that decorate the public areas, such as Enzo Catellani's light installation at the entrance. Inside, two futuristic white bubbles function as reception and office, while the vaulted ceiling is frescoed a deep cobalt blue with golden stars. Because the listed building was originally a chapel, architects Sycamore had to blend the period features with their particular style of understated design. The marble altar is enshrined by a glass panel and is located just behind the bar counter, which serves breakfasts and light meals. For heartier fare, both Margutta Vegetariano and Osteria della Frezza (p. 261) are conveniently nearby. Colour is the other theme of the hotel; corridors leading to the guest-rooms are blue, orange, green or yellow, and in the bathrooms the brightly coloured tiles reinforce the chromatic link with the corridors. On the floor, narrow light strips are etched with verses by poets Garcia Lorca and Octavio Paz. The forty-six rooms are all decently sized and combine attention to detail with an atmosphere of intimacy.

4 Relais Banchi Vecchi
Via dei Banchi Vecchi 115
Rooms from €125

Finding a reasonably priced place to stay in the historic areas of the city can be a challenge, so newcomer Relais Banchi Vecchi is a welcome addition to Rome's hospitality map. The hotel is hidden behind a solid wooden door on a lovely street lined with artisans' workshops, not far from Via Giulia. The official entrance is tucked away in tiny Via del Pavone. Housed in a *palazzo* owned by the Sforza Cesarini family, the hotel combines the intimacy of a B&B with the grandness of past Roman aristocratic life. The multilayered history of the building is evident in the small but atmospheric rooms with exposed masonry, medieval beams and large windows overlooking Via dei Banchi Vecchi or the courtyard off Vicolo del Pavone. Bathrooms are spacious with marble-topped basins and terracotta-tiled floors. The furnishings are unfussy – draped red curtains, embroidered bedspreads and a couple of 19th-century antique chairs are as far as it goes. On the walls, Piranesi's prints of ancient Roman ruins are appropriate adornments. This isn't a glamorous hotel, but it has an authenticity that is charming and is in a superb location. Bonus points come from being next door to top drinking den Il Goccetto (p. 264) and cheap and cheerful restaurant Boccondivino.

SEVENTH HEAVEN
5 **Aleph Hotel**
Via di San Basilio 15
Rooms from €350

'A journey filled with heavenly places and sinful delights' is how American designer Adam Tihany describes the hotel that he created for the Boscolo Group in 2003. Tihany, who is also responsible for restaurants Le Cirque 2000 in New York and Foliage in London, created the Aleph in his signature lavish style, combining contemporary design with sensuous overtones. It is one of Rome's most atmospheric boltholes, a place to get lost in for a couple of hours, or even days, and is popular with the most glamorous Italians (the son of the exiled heir to the throne chose it for his wedding reception). A strong heaven-and-hell theme dominates the public areas. Guests entering the black-and-red lobby are greeted by two oversized samurai, while a plasma screen plays back a video of their entry. Rich red drapery conceals mysterious dark corners, and huge white sofas are a focal point for the black-

clad staff on call to satisfy your every whim. A giant bell hangs from the ceiling, and two sculptural dice dangle in the courtyard, an ironic reminder of the perils of falling into temptation. In the blue-and-cream guestrooms the emphasis is on relaxation, with photographs of Roman street scenes (taken by Tihany's son, Bram), Murano glass chandeliers and window blinds made from strings of metal beads. In addition, there are six suites that represent complete indulgence, with bathrooms in onyx marble, private roof terraces and outdoor Jacuzzis. The hotel was formerly a bank, and a giant safe downstairs has been converted into a relaxation room; you will find it next door to the small Paradise spa room. Tucked just behind Via Vittorio Veneto, the road immortalized in Federico Fellini's film *La Dolce Vita*, the Aleph seems to have kick-started a small design renaissance in the area.

6 Ripa Hotel
Via degli Orti di Trastevere 3
Rooms from €420

Before the arrival of Aleph Hotel (see opposite), ES Hotel (now the Radisson SAS) and Hotel Art (p. 254), the Ripa, patronized by design-conscious travellers, was the only aesthetically challenging hotel to be found in Rome. Fast-forward a couple of years and Jeremy King and Riccardo Roselli's boldly designed hotel still holds its own, thanks to a successful blend of futuristic forms and comfortable, pared-down environments. Grey and white-toned bedrooms have pebble-patterned carpets, ample beds and no closet space, so that guests' clothes are on display. The all-white, 1960s-inspired curvaceous bathrooms are functionally high-tech and stylish. The look is a far cry from the more conventional gilded and decorative Roman options, but then the clientele is not your average crowd. Party people love to check into the new Presidential Suite, with its cocoon-shaped silver and white

sleeping area, two balconies and an unashamedly large Jacuzzi. At the 150-seat 'risto-bar', Riparte Café guests sit on blond timber chairs to sample a sophisticated and light menu that offers options created with produce from the proprietors' farm, Le Roscioline. The atmosphere in the bar is decidedly warmer as the terracotta and white walls are covered with displays of contemporary art and the floors and panelling are decked out in dark wood. Next door, Suite is one of the city's favourite addresses for discerning clubbers. Although officially still in Trastevere, Ripa's location is off the beaten track, and sports views of highrise concrete blocks rather than of Baroque churches. But it is convenient for Porta Portese flea market and is just a short stroll away from the historic heart of the city.

eat

7 L'Altro di Mastai
Via Giraud 53

Having already worked with Heinz Beck of Michelin-starred La Pergola and Raymond Blanc of Oxford's Le Manoir aux Quat' Saisons, chef Fabio Baldassare is a star in the making. The menu at L'Altro di Mastai, with its formal service and luxurious interior, changes according to seasonal produce, and most dishes are small but intensely flavoured. A tender swordfish fillet is teamed with cauliflower purée, orange sauce and marinated sea-bass eggs, while spaghetti is tossed with a sauce of wild asparagus and shrimps. The cellar is also impressive – let the sommelier guide you through the 1,000 Italian and French labels.

SMOOTH OPERATOR

8 Antico Arco
Piazzale Aurelio 7

Perched atop the Gianicolo hill, just behind the arch of San Pancrazio, Antico Arco can be reached via one of the most evocative climbs in Rome. Once there, you are rewarded by the serene atmosphere, friendly welcome and food to die for. Owners Patrizia Mattei, Domenico Calio and Maurizio Minore all come from a non-restaurant background, but have turned Antico Arco into an essential destination. Roman classic *cacio e pepe* (cheese and pepper) spaghetti is teamed with a sauce made from courgette flowers, while a warm lobster and prawn salad is tossed over gazpacho and rice. The interior by Tatà Gallo features bespoke furniture, while the wine cellar boasts 1,200 labels from around the world.

ESTABLISHED ENOTECA

9 Cul de Sac
Piazza di Pasquino 73

More of an eye opener than a dead end, this Cul de Sac offers an assortment of cold cuts, paté, cheese, soup and pasta, served with one (or more) of the *enoteca*'s 1,500 wines. Cul de Sac is all snug seating and marble counters, with the racks of wines overhead giving it a retro feel. The wines are the real stars, and staff are on hand to recommend the best pairings. Vintages are from Piedmont and Tuscany as well as Bordeaux, though do try the best from the nearby vineyards of Lazio.

TRASTEVERE'S BEST

10 Enoteca Ferrara
Piazza Trilussa 41

Enoteca Ferrara, occupying the entire building between Piazza Trilussa and Via del Moro, knocks spots off the multitude of mediocre establishments in Trastevere. Sisters Lina and Maria run the place with some flair, the first as an established sommelier and the second as a cook who knows how to play with tradition. A typical evening kicks off with fish soup with Vesuvio cherry tomatoes, stewed rabbit and swordfish rolls. In the summer, the few outdoor chairs make it an ideal spot for an *aperitivo*. On the counter is a selection of *stuzzichini*: morsels of pizza, fried polenta and cold cuts of ham and olives to whet your appetite.

SHOP AND DINE

11 Roscioli
Via dei Giubbonari 21–22a

Coming from a family of bakers, Alessandro and Pierluigi Roscioli's latest venture is an *alimentari* (deli) that is also a wine bar at lunchtime and a restaurant in the evening. The shop counter has goodies from all over Italy: juicy hams from Parma, ricotta from the neighbouring countryside, and huge shapes of *caciocchiato*, a cheese from the Irpinia region that is then seasoned in Roscioli's own caves in the Marche for another four months. Menu favourites are the broad bean and mushroom soup served with Pecorino cheese, stuffed celery with fondue, foie gras with grilled pears and marsala and, to top it all, the famous *cappuccino di ricotta*, which is pure bliss.

RESTAURANT WITH A VIEW

12 Sora Lella
Via di Ponte Quattro Capi 16

Wedged between the Trastevere and the old Jewish Ghetto is the secluded island of Tiberina, now a gourmet destination thanks to Sora Lella, one of the city's most celebrated (and pricey) establishments. Sora Lella was the sister of actor Aldo Fabrizi and a formidable cook; her son Aldo Trabalza later took over the restaurant. House specialties include *tonnarelli alla cuccagna* (pasta with sausage pancetta and nuts) and *maialino in agrodolce Antica Roma* (roast pig in sweet-and-sour sauce with prunes, pine nuts and raisins).

A SHRINE TO SEAFOOD

13 La Rosetta
Via della Rosetta 8

Opening forty years ago, La Rosetta was the first restaurant in Rome to serve exclusively fish. Other restaurants have adopted many of its recipes, including a warm salad of rocket and prawns. Chef Massimo Riccioli, the celebrated and charming talent behind La Rosetta's success, describes his inventive cooking as 'an act of improvisation'. The results include tuna tartare, baby squid and mushy peas, home-made pasta with aubergine, and black olives and sea bass cooked under a coarse crust. A French pastry cook bakes chocolate cakes and other sweets, while the service is a master class in discretion and professionalism.

STREETCAR STYLE

14 Tram Tram
Via dei Reti 44–46

Named after the tramline that runs along the Via dei Reti, family-run Tram Tram was one of the first restaurants to open in San Lorenzo in the 1980s, serving innovative yet traditional cuisine. Starters have a southern Italian flavour, such as broad bean mash with chicory, while mains are inspired by Roman cuisine, including *Pugliese orecchiette* with broccoli and clams, swordfish rolls and anchovies, and endive salad terrine. The décor employs disused train parts that have been converted into wine racks and banquette seating in the bar area, a reference that dates back to the early 19th century when San Lorenzo was home to the railway workers' housing associations.

VEGGIE DELIGHTS

15 Arancia Blu
Via dei Latini 55/65

Since 1993, Fabio Bassan has been serving vegetarian fare to the trendy inhabitants of San Lorenzo, no doubt converting a few meat-eaters along the way. The innovative menu includes a salad of artichokes served on a bed of creamed chickpeas, followed by *maccheroncini* with truffles. For those who still have an appetite, there is *zabaione* with a crunchy toasted pine-nut topping for dessert. The homey décor makes it an excellent place for lunch before a visit to nearby Galleria Pino Casagrande (p. 272).

COUNTRY STYLE IN THE CITY
16 Baba
Via Casale di Tor di Quinto 1

You will need a taxi to get there, but the truly original experience is well worth the expense. Set in a tiny medieval hamlet, Baba is in an old *casolare*, a traditional farmhouse with outdoor patio. Baba herself is a formidable cook and a larger-than-life character; be sure to arrive before 9 p.m. so as not to miss Baba's ringing of the bell to kick off dinner. The reasonably priced fixed menu offers soup and buffet-style dishes such as gnocchi with courgettes, veal meatballs, and risotto with melon and ham. The restaurant is only open for dinner; booking a week ahead is essential.

NO-FRILLS TRATTORIA
17 Uno e Bino
Via degli Equi 58

Set up by brother and sister Gianpaolo and Gloria Gravina in 1997, this unpretentious establishment is part of the *enoteca* movement that has changed the city's gastronomic map for the better. An excellent wine list (try any wine from Sicilian producer Planeta) complements the seasonally changing menu. Classics that are available year-round include *paccheri* with pork sauce and marjoram ricotta, braised beef cheeks with cocoa and red wine, and chef Andrea Buscema's divine *tortino di cioccolato*. With its wooden tables covered in waxed paper and wine guides lining the bookshelves, Uno e Bino does not do cool interior design, but it is a little gem not to be overlooked.

SICILIAN CHIC
18 Trattoria
Via del Pozzo delle Cornacchie 25

Native Sicilian and self-taught chef Filippo La Mantia was a reporter before turning his enviable culinary skills to cooking. At Trattoria, a stylish den designed by Marco and Gianluigi Giammetta, La Mantia prepares Sicilian classics that have been updated for the modern palate from his open kitchen. Dishes include *caponata* (a sweet-and-sour stew of aubergines), rigatoni with a pesto of almonds, capers, anchovies and breadcrumbs, tuna with lemon-and-orange couscous and Sicily's most famous sweet, *la cassata* (ice cream peppered with candied fruit). Wines are primarily Sicilian.

FISH FANTASY
19 Hosteria del Pesce
Via di Monserrato 32

A favourite of the wealthy clientele who live around the Campo de' Fiori, Hosteria del Pesce is a mecca for those who love fish. Owners Johnny and Giuliano Micalusi are former fishermen and buy all their seafood at the nearby Terracina market. At the entrance to the restaurant, lobsters, clams and sea bass are displayed on ice; just choose your fish and chef Franco will cook it for you. Starters include salt cod with potatoes, clam and langoustine *carpaccio* and stewed octopus; for mains there is grilled red snapper, Catalan-style lobster, or sea bass baked in a salt crust.

DINING UNDER THE ARCH
20 Giggetto
Via del Portico d'Ottavia 21a–22

Although its owners are Catholic, Giggetto is known for its crunchy *carciofi alla giudia*, a Jewish dish in which whole artichokes are flattened into the shape of a chrysanthemum and deep fried. Other delicacies include spelt soup, fried calamari, battered salt cod and pasta carbonara. The owner Luigi Ceccarelli, also known as 'Giggetto', founded this *hostaria* in the 1920s when his dislike for Fascist politics led him to switch from a career as a train master to one in catering. His son Franco and nephew Claudio continue to run Giggetto with the same sense of hospitality. Outside, tables are placed under the Portico d'Ottavia, which Augustus dedicated to his sister in 23 BC.

COMFORT FOOD
21 Colline Emiliane
Via degli Avignonesi 22

Those nostalgic for north Italian fare come here to sample dishes like *tortellini in brodo* (tortellini in broth), *bolliti* (boiled meat) and pumpkin-stuffed pasta. The wooden décor is reassuringly rustic; this place is about satisfying the stomach rather than the eye. The restaurant has been here since 1931 when Bologna-born Mario Falchieri opened an establishment that focused on the cuisine of the Emilia region. It was bought by the Latini family in 1967, who still run it today. Since then nothing has changed, from the menu to the discreet service offered by white-jacketed waiters.

22 Osteria della Frezza
Via della Frezza 16

Not content with owning Gusto next door, the Tudini family opened Osteria della Frezza, a smaller, brasserie-style restaurant with a modern take on Roman cuisine. Chef Marco Gallotta runs both restaurants but has a particular attachment to La Frezza, where he serves up classics like *polpette al sugo* (meatballs with tomato sauce) or *rigatoni alla matriciana* (pasta with a spicy bacon sauce). La Frezza's main claim to culinary fame is having introduced the notion of *cicchetto*, a selection of small dishes like tapas. Depending on what the kitchen is preparing, waiters will suggest a series of dainty portions of pasta, meat or vegetables to give customers a varied eating experience. A further temptation is the cheese board; with over 200 types, it is hardly surprising that the restaurant employs a cheese master to turn them regularly and keep an expert eye on temperature and level of seasoning. Leather banquettes and black-and-white photography create a warm and comfortable environment.

23 Agata e Romeo
Via Carlo Alberto 45

A few intimate tables are what you'll find at Agata e Romeo, semi-hidden behind the majestic basilica of Santa Maria Maggiore. Inside, the décor is reassuringly understated, perhaps to focus attention on the celebrated cooking of Agata Parisello. A cookery writer, teacher and broadcaster as well as talented chef, Parisello's passion for traditional Roman cuisine and her desire to update it through constant experimentation has become a blueprint for a younger generation of chefs in the city. Parisello took over the restaurant from her father in 1980 and now runs it with her husband Romeo, one of Rome's more knowledgeable sommeliers. Since then, Agata e Romeo's success story has been consistently sanctioned by the best food guides, and rightly so. Be prepared to be surprised by the delicate oxtail and celery terrine, *cacio e pepe* pasta made with Sicilian saffron cheese, and Parisello's specialty, *millefoglie al cucchiaio* (millefeuille with a rich, runny cream).

drink

24 Bar della Pace
Via della Pace 3/7

Seasons may come and go, but Bar della Pace's reputation as one of Rome's sexiest bars remains. Framed by a wonderful climbing vine, the bar sits on the corner of Via della Pace, just next door to Bramante's beautiful cloister. La Pace's interiors are dark and cool, with Art Déco statues, large mirrors and vases overflowing with decadent lilies. During the day the bar is a local café, but after dinner it comes into its own, serving cocktails to the young crowd spilling into the street.

25 Casa Bleve
Via del Teatro Valle 48–49

Anacleto Bleve knows a thing or two about wine; for years he ran his tiny shop in the Old Jewish Ghetto, effectively spearheading the *enoteca* movement in Rome. Now that he has moved to more palatial premises (a 14th-century coach house in front of the Teatro Valle), he can afford to indulge in equally grand crus. From Tuscan red Sassicaia to Trentino's Saint Michel's Epan Sauvignon, the excellence of Italian producers really shines. The high ceilings, arches and restored wooden stable doors provide an airy ambience, while faux Roman statues set the mood for a light lunch or a glass (or bottle) after dinner. Downstairs, remnants of a Roman wall are visible, along with two cellars packed with covetable wine labels.

26 Il Caffè di Sant'Eustachio
Piazza Sant'Eustachio 82

Since its invention in 1938, customers have debated what makes Sant'Eustachio's secret *gran caffè* so special, and while many myths have spread around town, the reason is probably the blend, which is made from a blend of different South American beans. Despite the long queues outside, this specialty (a creamy and frothy cappuccino without the milk) is worth the wait. Named after the Roman general Eustace, who paid for his conversion to Catholicism by being roasted alive, Sant'Eustachio is run by Raimondo and Roberto Ricci, who also sell honey, biscuits, chocolates and coffee to try at home.

27 Riccioli Café
Via delle Coppelle 13

This is Massimo Riccioli's – of La Rosetta (p. 259) fame – funkier outpost: a lounge bar, tearoom and restaurant that specializes in top sushi and oysters. Open from breakfast until 1 a.m., Riccioli caters to a discerning crowd – trendy shoppers by day and beautiful *prosecco*-sipping locals by night. Renaissance vaults prop up the ceiling, while the walls are covered with blue neon installations by Massimo himself. The blue-and-red theme is carried across the velvet furniture, steel counters and funky lamps. During happy hour, the outside covered lounge area provides a vantage point for people-watching. This is a great place to start an evening.

28 La Vineria Reggio
Piazza Campo de' Fiori 15

Run by the Reggio family for over thirty years, La Vineria, perched on the edge of the bustling Campo dei Fiori (one of Rome's oldest fruit and vegetable markets), has evolved from an edgy wine bar in the 1970s, frequented by local bohemians and the odd celebrity like Beat poet Gregory Corso, into one of the city's most popular destinations. At sunset, Rome's beautiful people flock here for an *aperitivo*, while later in the evening the atmosphere becomes rowdier as the music is turned up. There is an extensive selection of wines by the glass, along with a very good own brand of *Prosecco Conegliano*, and the cellar is priced affordably enough to function as a wine shop for locals.

29 Angelo Lounge Bar
Aleph Hotel, Via di San Basilio 15

Sipping a cocktail in a hotel bar has yet to become a Roman habit, but Angelo Lounge Bar, where devilishly good Martinis are prepared by the resident barman, in the Aleph Hotel (p. 256) might change all that. A small island amid designer Adam Tihany's maximalist décor, the Angelo bar feels intimate yet sophisticated, with the wood panelling and library adding to the clubby atmosphere. Angelo's appeal lies in the fact that although hotel guests drift by, it has yet to be fully discovered by the city's glitterati. A drink here feels like a small, shared secret.

30 BAR STRIP
Via Galvani
- Joia Music Restaurant, no. 20
- Ketumbar, no. 24
- Bush, no. 46
- Letico, no. 64

Over the past ten years, Testaccio has evolved into a hedonistic hotspot clustered around the old slaughterhouse area. Watering holes include Joia, whose baroque lounge provides a decadent setting for cocktails; Ketumbar, one of the first bars to attempt an local version of Paris's Buddha bar; disco bar Bush, decorated with photos of celebrities; and restaurant-bar Letico, another of the area's stand-bys.

31 KALEIDOSCOPIC BAR
Bar Taruga
Piazza Mattei 8

Those with idiosyncratic tastes will love the eccentric ambience of Bar Taruga. With its plush sofas, bordello-red walls, faux crystal chandeliers, plastic flowers and draped curtains, it transports nocturnal visitors to somewhere near Marrakech, c. 1974. The bar is a magnet for late-night drinkers who sip their cocktails to jazz songs or a Roman-style cabaret. A row of outdoor seats in the square allows revellers to contemplate life while gazing at the wonderful fountain decorated with turtle shells in the Piazza Mattei.

32 NEIGHBOURHOOD BAR
Il Goccetto
Via dei Banchi Vecchi 14

On balmy evenings, customers spill out of Il Goccetto onto the narrow street, balancing a glass of wine and resting a foot on a parked Vespa. The cool and dark interior of this listed building, with its frescoed ceilings and rustic wooden chairs and tables, make it an informal retreat for an *aperitivo*. One of the precursors of the *enoteca* movement, Sergio Ceccarelli serves twenty wines by the glass and stocks hundreds of bottles, all carefully selected with a particular emphasis on smaller, independent producers.

33 Caffè Farnese
CAPPUCCINO CENTRAL
Piazza Farnese 106/107

Affluent locals, tourists and the odd dog walker are among those who enjoy Caffè Farnese's exceptional location, facing one of the finest Renaissance palaces in Rome. The rows of tables spilling into Via dei Baullari are always packed, especially during sunny weekend mornings, but while you are waiting you can always buy the papers at the next-door newsstand. Breakfast is traditionally Italian, with *cornetti* filled with jam, cream or chocolate, while *tramezzini* (triangular sandwiches) make a perfect lunchtime snack.

34 Ferrazza
WINE CORNER
Via dei Volsci 59

Local artists make this *enoteca* their favourite spot for an *aperitivo*; for the price of a glass of *prosecco* you, too, can savour a vast selection of pizzas, olives and miniature sandwiches. The wine cellar has over a thousand Italian labels, plus a good selection by the glass. Oysters and raw fish dishes are among the choices on the light menu served in the narrow dining section. The interior is minimal and stylish, with the attention focused on the bottles on display. Ferrazza is always packed, so arrive early.

35 L'Enoteca Antica
WINE AND FOOD
Via della Croce 76b

Inscriptions on amphorae lining the shelves remind visitors that this small, crowded wine bar has been trading in *vini e olii* since 1726. Transformed into an *enoteca* twenty years ago, the front area now functions as a wine shop. In one corner, a marble counter is where you get light snacks from the bar's menu, including Roman favourites like *frittata di patate* and *mozzarella di bufala*, and in the back room a sit-down restaurant offers dishes like *vitello tonnato* (veal in a tuna and mayonnaise sauce) at reasonable prices.

shop

MULTICOLOURED MINIMALISM
36 Bomba Abbigliamento
Via dell'Oca 39

Roman women come to Bomba for designs that combine understatement with a splash of colour. Cashmere children's dresses by Ang e un Bebe and beaded bags hang on the walls as installations, while a specific area is devoted to small designers, among them shoes by Henry Beguelin, jewelry by Donatella Pellini and Mother Superior T-shirts by Bettina Pontiggia. The menswear section is a kaleidoscopic display of ties, some even designed by architects Scarpa and Lapadula. Suits and dresses can be made to order in the upstairs workshop. A recent addition is the small gallery-cum-tearoom that provides an exhibition space for emerging Roman artists as well as the occasional catwalk show.

LOFT LIVING
37 Magazzini Associati
Corso del Rinascimento 7

The atmosphere of this stunning interiors shop – all concrete floors, flights of stairs and recessed backlit rooms – is calm and uncluttered. Magazzini Associati is the exclusive agent for Rome's De Padova line, and also stocks wicker creations by Gervasoni and lights by FontanaArte. Smaller items include Hickman Tools kitchenware designed by Antonio Citterio and Boffi's bathroom fittings, as well as a linen nightwear and daywear collection. Most items will be too big to fit into a suitcase, but the shop deserves a visit if only for its uncompromising devotion to contemporary minimalist living.

TOOLS FOR COOKS
38 C.U.C.I.N.A.
Via Mario de' Fiori 65

C.U.C.I.N.A. caters to cooks who delight in ceramic knives and Alessi cafetières. The original flagship store was located in Via del Babuino, and for years discerning shoppers would flock here to snap up the latest in aluminium salad spinners. There are no big brands here, rather a functional selection of kitchenware to serve all purposes. Funky flatpack laundry bags that open up in the shape of a washing machine, elegant linen aprons and tea towels, chunky glassware and white china plates are among the shop's finds.

TAILORING TALENTS
39 Scala Quattordici
Via della Scala 13

The attraction of Scala Quattordici, a semi-hidden womenswear boutique in the heart of Trastevere, is undoubtedly its attentive and personalized service – 'no rush' seems to be the owners' mantra and there is plenty of time for fittings, choosing favourite styles and even to have a leisurely chat on the sofas. The look is pretty and feminine rather than cutting edge, and suits those looking for an outfit for a romantic or special occasion. Next door is the tailoring workshop, with its mannequins and piles of materials just waiting to be rustled up into memorable creations.

SWIMWEAR SPOT
40 Laura Urbinati
Via dei Banchi Vecchi 50a

Laura Urbinati is the ultimate queen of the bikini. Step inside her small, white box of a shop and a riot of acid green and shocking pink models hanging from the rails will deluge your senses. Her swimwear designs have been collectable items for some years, so news that the Milan-based designer's second Italian shop would be in Rome was celebrated by her fans. Urbinati's kaftans from Attik Battik, leather flip-flops and embroidered sheer dresses are essentials for every true Italian beach babe.

OPULENT STYLE
41 Fabio Salini
Via di Monserrato 18

A bank vault with protective walls and a secretive atmosphere is the inspiration behind Fabio Salini's atelier, created by the jewelry designer himself with help from architect Massimo d'Alessandro. The interior has sumptuous Art Déco-style woodwork and furnishings, with silver-leaf walls, white leather daybeds and cabinets encasing his precious necklaces and bracelets. Nothing is too opulent for Salini, whose work is featured regularly in *Vogue Gioiello* and at Rome's fashion shows. Classic pieces include jade chokers encrusted with diamonds, earrings dripping with rubies, sapphires and emeralds, as well as bracelets in semi-precious stones. Queen Rania of Jordan is a fan of his delicate silverwork and lavish use of precious gems.

PRETTY PURCHASES
42 Baullà
Via dei Baullari 37

Everything in Baullà's cramped premises has a story to tell, from the silk travel sheets sourced in Cambodia to the 1950s-style Vietnamese print fashioned into a one-off skirt. The textiles of the Far East are certainly an inspiration, as are the crafts of rural northern Italy. The shop sells stacks of the soft velvet slippers produced in the Veneto region and traditionally worn at home or during Carnivale, which you can get in every colour combination possible. From natty wicker bags with pink handles to linen hats and caps in soft wool, Baullà is a treasure trove for quirky, individual pieces.

TROTTER'S DELIGHT
43 La Libreria del Viaggiatore
Via del Pellegrino 78

The shelves at Bruno Boschin's travel bookstore positively groan with publications about countries in every corner of the globe. Among the lavishly illustrated coffee-table books and food guides are titles on Rome that feature watercolours by Boschin's wife, American artist Wendy Artin. Battered old leather suitcases and globes add to the atmosphere of the place. At the front, there is a selection of vintage maps, first editions by travel writers such as Pierre Loti (see p. 163) and rare finds like a manual of Neapolitan sign language, along with an extensive selection of vintage maps and prints. Boschin advises adventure seekers and armchair travellers alike on what to read, however far away they want to go.

PRETTY CHILDREN'S WEAR
44 Lavori Artigianali Femminili
Via Capo le Case 6

In a world saturated by chains, it is refreshing to find a shop selling handmade and one-off children's clothes. The items are so pretty that just a glimpse at the old-fashioned window display could distract mothers from their Prada account to invest in a new wardrobe for their offspring. Lavori Artigianali Femminili carries household linens, exquisitely embroidered baby clothes and smocked christening dresses. These are precious clothes for special occasions, well worth the expense.

A TAD TRENDY
45 TAD
Via del Babuino 155a

Rome's very personal spin on a concept store, TAD stands for *tendenze e antiche debolezze* ('trends and old weaknesses'). Indulge in this large retail heaven, which offers covetable creations by Alessandro Dell'Acqua, Alexander McQueen, Alberto Biani and Balenciaga, among others. There is homeware inspired by the Far East by Marina Coffa and teak, mahogany and wicker furniture. Foreign magazines, art books and a selection of trip-hop, soul, Latin, house, garage and lounge compilations grace the shelves. There is also a Nu-Yorica shoe concession, a flower shop and a small hairdresser's. Exhausted shoppers can stop for a *macchiato* at the TAD Café, which has a refreshing outdoor courtyard space with seating by Philippe Starck and lighting by Ross Lovegrove. Lunch is also popular, with its Asian-Mediterranean fusion cuisine supervised by chef Anthony Genovese.

FUN AND FUNKY
46 Sisters
Via dei Banchi Vecchi 143

Sisters Eleonora, Emanuela and Veronica Nobile Mino have made this store-cum-gallery an essential stop for anyone interested in contemporary Italian art and over-the-top decorative lamps, tables and mirrors. 'Our father is a collector and we grew up in his villa surrounded by busts, antiques and other eccentric finds,' explains eldest sister Eleonora. Quirky 1950s chairs found at flea markets around Italy sit incongruously next to lights by designer Angela Ardisson, while sculptural wrought-iron lamps and stuffed birds are mixed with large antique mirrors. Every couple of months, Sisters in Art promote a range of contemporary Italian artists, whose work is shown within the 'furnished' environment of the shop. Exhibitions of up-and-coming artists have included Giorgio Sabbatini, Daniela Perego and Michele de Andreis.

GOURMET DELI
47 Volpetti
Via Marmorata 47 and Via Alessandro Volta 8

Customers complain that they can never leave Volpetti without buying much more than they bargained for; certainly the staff here excel at persuading you to buy delicacies from all over Italy. Owners Claudio and Emilio Volpetti have run the place since 1973, gradually transforming it from a local *alimentari* into a gourmet pilgrimage site. The shop prides itself on specializing in several types of hams, including *Prosciutto di Norcia* and *San Daniele e di Montagna*, as well as Parmesan, *mozzarella di bufala* and goats' cheese. Their Pecorino Romano comes from sheep that graze the local countryside, and specialty breads are delivered daily; sample their fragrant bread from Altamura in the Puglia region on Tuesdays and Fridays. Their *tavola calda* (a lunchtime, paper-tablecloth food joint) is in Via Alessandro Volta.

This global brand started small when Sotirio Bulgari arrived from Greece in 1895 and set up shop in Via Sistina. The Via dei Condotti shop opened in 1905 and features palatial architecture that reflects the jeweler's opulent style. Old coins set in gold, cabochon-cut precious stones and lots of glittering metal are the trademark of this iconic name, which with its collections 'Parentesi', 'Tubogas' and 'Spiga' became a firm favourite of the fashionable jet set in the 1960s. Today the business is still family run, with Giorgio and Paolo Bulgari at the helm and nephew Francesco Trapani steering it in a design-led direction. After expanding into watches and perfumes, Bulgari recently forayed into the world of boutique hotels, with one designed by Citterio in Milan and two more in the pipeline.

Diego Percossi Papi has been making bespoke jewelry for Romans-in-the-know for over twenty years. Indeed, his work is so highly regarded that recently he was made a *Cavaliere del Lavoro*, one of the highest honours that Italy can bestow on a working professional. European aristocrats often drop by his tiny jewel box of a workshop, tucked beneath a vine-covered *palazzo* behind the Pantheon. What attracts them is his talent for unpicking family heirlooms and vintage jewelry and combining them with coloured gemstones, jade, opals and patches of enamelling. The design follows a long consultation with the customer, and the results are opulent necklaces and bracelets filled with personality and imbued with the style of the Renaissance.

Over the years Le Gallinelle has successfully graduated from a second-hand shop into a fully fledged own label, while still keeping the retro spirit alive with its quirky materials and shapes. Wilma Silvestri's Greek goddess-inspired evening dresses, paisley-patterned sundresses and floral skirts are just some of the designs on display. A small selection of vintage Gucci bags, Valentino belts and Ben Sherman shirts for men make it a destination for bargain hunters and fashion stylists. The store's name is both a play on the common name for the star constellation Pleiades, and a reference to its previous incarnation as a butcher's shop. The original marble counter engraved with chickens, the meat hooks and the tiled floor have all been kept in their original condition, blending seamlessly with the multicoloured garments hanging from the rails.

see

CULTURAL CENTRE
51 Macro
Via Reggio Emilia 54

At Macro, Rome's first museum dedicated to contemporary art, artworks blend with the high-tech architecture, while glass lifts and bridges connecting the two original buildings lend an industrial feel. The collection includes pieces by the Scuola di Piazza del Popolo and Arte Povera members Mario Ceroli and Pino Pascali, as well as by Piero Pizzi Cannella, Gianni Dessì and Bruno Ceccobelli, a group known as the Nuova Scuola Romana. A new wing by Decq features a roof terrace, garden and galleries.

THREE CHURCHES IN ONE
52 Basilica di San Clemente
Via Labicana 95

Located on top of three successive sites of Christian worship, this church is something special. The top church contains the chapel of St Catherine of Alexandria with frescoes by Masolino and Masaccio, while the 4th-century basilica below features one of the earliest examples of the Italian language. Further down is a Mithraeum, the focus of an ancient cult devoted to Mithras. The running water of a stream 9 metres below, used by Irish Dominicans during World War II, reminds visitors of Rome's mysterious subterranean life.

MASTER AT WORK
53 San Luigi dei Francesi
Piazza di San Luigi dei Francesi 5

Around the corner from the Senate is the French national church, San Luigi dei Francese, built in 1589 by Domenico Fontana and dedicated to Louis IX of France, who led two crusades in the Holy Land in the 13th century. Inside is the Contarelli chapel, famous for housing Caravaggio's painting cycle of the life of St Matthew: *The Calling of St Matthew*, showing the pre-sainthood tax collector in his counting house, *St Matthew and the Angel* and *The Martyrdom of St Matthew*.

RENAISSANCE VILLA

56 Villa Farnesina
Via della Lungara 230

Designed by Baldassare Peruzzi between 1506 and 1510, Villa Farnesina, once the home of 16th-century banker and art patron Agostino Chigi, is renowned for its exquisite frescoes by Raphael and Peruzzi. In the Loggia of Cupid and Psyche, the ceiling decoration is a pergola of fruit and flowers. Raphael's stunning *Triumph of Galatea* in the loggia of the same name features the nymph driving a scallop-shell chariot pulled by dolphins. Popular legend claims that Chigi allowed Raphael's mistress, La Fornarina, to live here while he worked so that the painting would be completed more speedily. Today the villa is the seat of the Accademia dei Lincei, one of Italy's most distinguished centres of learning; it also houses the Department of Drawings and Prints.

AN ARTISTS' SQUARE
57 Piazza di Spagna
• Museo de Chirico, no. 31
• The Keats–Shelley House, no. 26

Opening in 1998, the Museo de Chirico occupies the three upper floors of the 17th-century Palazzetto dei Borgognoni and faces onto the Piazza di Spagna, overlooking Bernini's fountain. At the back, there are views of Trinità dei Monti and Villa Medici, the gardens of which feature in a number of de Chirico's paintings. On the top floor is the studio, and a few of the plaster models that the artist used are scattered about in an attempt to re-create the working atmosphere. Furnished during the 1950s, the rooms have been kept as they were, although the museum occasionally rotates its collection of some sixty artworks. Nearby is the Roman residence of the English poet John Keats, a pale pink building that is now the Keats–Shelley Memorial House. Keats died here in 1821 of consumption, just four months after his arrival in Italy, and is buried in the Protestant cemetery in Testaccio. The residence was bought in 1906, largely due to the efforts of a group of American and English poets. Included in this amazing collection is the locket that Elizabeth Barrett Browning gave to her husband.

ARCHITECTURAL JEWEL
54 Auditorium Parco della Musica
Viale Pietro de Coubertin 30

Designed by Renzo Piano, the auditorium is wedged between the 1960s Olympic village and the Corso Francia flyover. Finally providing the city with a venue for classical music, this is where the National Academy of Santa Cecilia has taken up residence. Conceived as a 'park of music', the Auditorium comprises three music halls, each specifically 'tuned' for a different type of performance; there is one for chamber music and small concerts, another for symphonies and ballets, and a larger hall for opera performances.

GREEN OASIS
55 Orto Botanico
Largo Cristina di Svezia 24

At the foot of the Gianicolo hill, the botanical gardens are filled with tropical palm trees and greenhouses containing all kinds of prickly cactus species, while uphill is a rose garden filled with old-fashioned varieties. Children are attracted by the central fountain, lovers lose themselves in the zig-zagging paths of the bamboo forest, and botanical enthusiasts spot the rare medicinal plants that flourish here. The gardens are a secluded spot lying right in the centre of this bustling and touristy part of Trastevere.

58 Santa Sabina
Piazza Pietro d'Illiria

Founded in 425 by Pietro D'Illiria on the site of a villa owned by Sabina, a Roman martyr, the church of Santa Sabina stands apart for being the most perfectly preserved example of an early Christian basilica. It was also the first Dominican church, dedicated by Onorio III to St Dominic in 1222. The façade is stark in its simplicity, with carved wooden doors that feature scenes from the Old and New Testaments, while inside the twenty-four Corinthian columns create a magnificent space. Next door is the Dominican monastery; on request, visitors may visit St Dominic's cell and the 13th-century cloister.

ART AT HOME
59 Galleria Pino Casagrande
Via degli Ausoni 7a

Located in an area favoured by the Scuola Romana, textile magnate Pino Casagrande decided to open the doors of his Art Déco-style townhouse to visitors. Over the years, Casagrande had amassed a collection of antiquities and contemporary art. American minimalism is well represented by Donald Judd, Sol Le Witt and Dan Flavin, while the constantly changing selection also includes the work of British artist Julian Opie and furniture by Ettore Sottsass, Alvar Alto, Mies van der Rohe and Le Corbusier. The beautiful, geometric garden contributes to an aesthetically pleasing moment.

FAMILY HEIRLOOMS
60 Galleria Borghese
Piazzale del Museo Borghese 5

Set in the green oasis of Villa Borghese, also home to Rome's much improved zoo, a visit to Galleria Borghese is an occasion to peek into the splendours of what has been described as the finest non-royal private collection in the world. Reopened in 1998, the gallery houses a remarkable collection of masterpieces, including Antonio Canova's *Paolina Borghese as Venus* (Paolina, or Pauline, was Napoleon's sister), Bernini's *David* (executed when the sculptor was only twenty-five years old), and paintings by Caravaggio and Raphael. Visits are limited to two hours and advance booking is essential.

FAMILY JEWELS
61 Galleria Doria Pamphilj
Piazza del Collegio Romano 2

No visit to Galleria Doria Pamphilj would be complete without Jonathan Pamphilj's audio guide, a delightful memoir of a childhood spent surrounded by paintings and sculptures steeped in history. The collection, begun in the 17th century by the influential Pamphilj dynasty, includes works by, among others, Caravaggio, Guido Reni, Velázquez, Titian and Raphael. Perhaps the famous member of the family was Pope Innocent X (1644–55), born Giovanni Battista Pamphilj and immortalized in Velázquez's portrait, on show here, famously the inspiration for Francis Bacon's version.

SPIRALLING BEAUTY
62 Sant'Ivo alla Sapienza
Corso del Rinascimento 40

Now home to the State Archives, the Sapienza was founded in 1303 by Pope Boniface VII as Rome's secular university. The church of Sant'Ivo, located within the Sapienza complex, was begun in 1642 by Borromini. The façade has two storeys of arches, which continue along the side walls, flanking a cobblestone courtyard and its stunning shell-shaped dome, crowned by a lantern and delicate spiralling tower, was inspired by a series of depictions of the Tower of Babel. Inside, the strong geometry and stucco decoration make it an exquisite example of the Roman Baroque. During the summer, Sant'Ivo comes alive with a festival of concerts.

CIRCLES OF BEAUTY
63 Santo Stefano Rotondo
Via di Santo Stefano Rotondo 7

Built in the 5th century on the remains of Nero's great market, the *Macellum magnum*, and restored in 1453 by Pope Nicholas V, the church of Santo Stefano Rotondo surprises visitors with both its circular architecture and its macabre contents. On the walls, thirty-four faded frescoes, painted by Pomarancio and Antonio Tempesta in the 16th century, realistically illustrate the tortures received by early Christian martyrs. Next door in the secluded garden is a small house thought to be where Giovanni Pierluigi da Palestrina (c. 1525–94) composed his music, surely inspired by the celestial atmosphere.

PRIVATE COLLECTION
64 Palazzo Altemps
Piazza Sant'Apollinare 44

Like many aristocratic homes in Rome, the 15th-century Palazzo Altemps languished for centuries. Now part of the Museo Nazionale Romano, after extensive restoration work it opened in 1997 and features what is left of the original collection of Greek and Roman statues. The interior frescoes that remain have been restored, and some of the rooms are remarkable in their size and grandeur, in particular the chamber with a fresco depicting the wedding presents given to Girolamo Riario and Caterina Sforza in 1477.

CHARMING COLLECTION
65 Centrale Montemartini
Via Ostiense 106

Inaugurated in 1921, Centrale Montemartini was the first electrical power plant in Rome and is a highlight of early 20th-century industrial architecture. Now it is the home of the superb collection of Hellenic statues from the Capitoline Museums. Marble sculptures stand among boilers, hydraulic pumps and steel tubes in an incongruous yet fascinating juxtaposition of the ancient and the relatively new.

STUNNING DOME
66 Pantheon
Piazza della Rotonda

Despite Agrippa's inscription on the portico, the Pantheon was built in AD 118 under Hadrian and may even have been designed by him. The building's dome, a feat of Roman engineering, is more than 43 metres high and was the largest dome in the world until 1436 when the Duomo in Florence was constructed. In 609, the Pantheon became the first temple in Rome to be consecrated and was renamed Santa Maria ad Martyres due to the many bones buried beneath the sanctuary. According to tradition, seven devils escaped the Christian site and a particularly large demon struggling to break free created the great oculus in the centre of the dome. Raphael is buried here, as are the kings of Italy. With the sheer size of its interior and opulent marbles, the Pantheon looks more like a monument than a church, except on Christmas Eve when a candlelit midnight mass is held, accompanied by Gregorian chants.

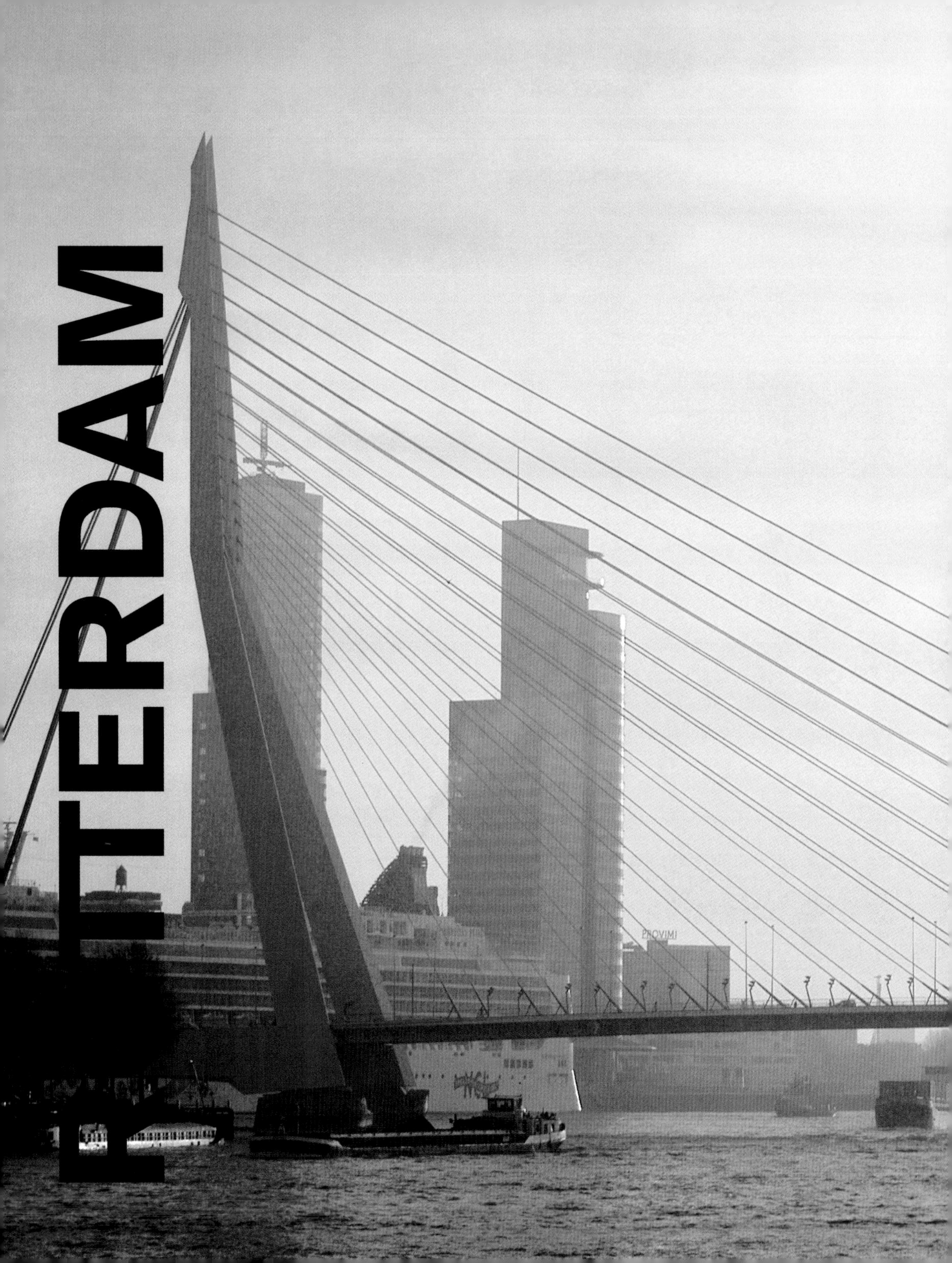
TERDAM

Rotterdam is in a state of flux, the status quo in this city; as a busy, industrial port, perhaps this has always been the case. But never more so than over the past sixty years, as Rotterdam rose like a phoenix from the ashes after a ten-minute aerial bombing on 14 May 1940 that razed nearly 30,000 buildings, covering 635 acres, to the ground. In fact, it was this flattened, empty canvas in the city centre that is responsible for Rotterdam's lack of resemblance to any other city in the Netherlands. Gone are the twee canal bridges and cobbled streets; instead, Rotterdam's skyline is an inspiring jagged range of architectural experiments that map the discipline's development like a three-dimensional reference book. No wonder then that the city named 2007 as its official 'year of architecture', and that it is a destination for architecture buffs from all over the world.

Yet civic pride is apparent in other creative aspects. Rotterdam has a buzzing club scene and its bars and restaurants are sophisticated, taking maximum advantage of the large-scale buildings. Its pedestrianized shopping arteries lead almost seamlessly into a generous museum park, home to four of the Netherlands' most important institutes for art, natural history and architecture: De Kunsthal (p. 288), Museum Boijmans van Beuningen (p. 287), Netherlands Architectuurinstituut (p. 288) and the Natuurhistorisch Museum Rotterdam. Local fashion culture is vibrant, reflected in countless visionary multi-brand concept stores, as well as in home-grown talent like Marlies Dekkers (p. 285), who has gone global with her lingerie lines. Even the most casual visitor can stumble across art and design enclaves in converted warehouses, such as the Westelijk Handelsterrein, where galleries, furniture stores and restaurants make glamorous neighbours.

The past decade has seen Rotterdam stretch itself along the River Maas, with investment in the former piers resulting in the rise of new hotels, theatres, office blocks and academies. The Kop van Zuid (p. 287) is the most developed, now boasting breathtaking skyscrapers by British über-architect Norman Foster (the World Port Centre), Renzo Piano (Toren van Zuid) and Francine Houben of Mecanoo (the Montevido building), with Rotterdam native Rem Koolhaas's thirty-seven-storey project in development. This, along with the Lloydkwartier and Maasvlakte I + II, are securing the future of what were recently defunct areas as fresh, hip places in which to meet, socialize and enjoy the views over the river and the ever-changing face of Holland's most dynamic city.

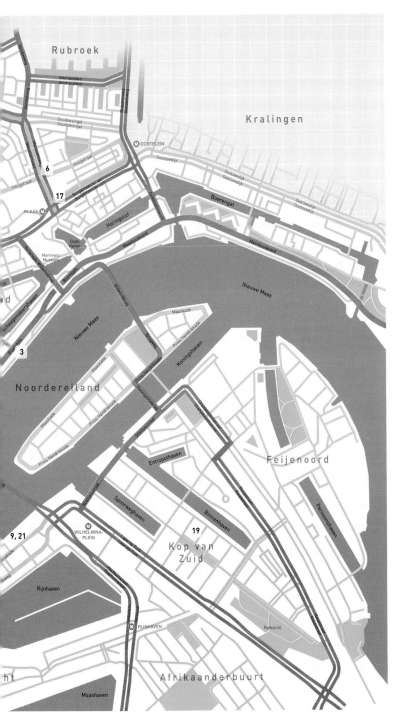

StyleCity Rotterdam

sleep

DESTINATION AMERICA

1 Hotel New York

Koninginnenhoofd 1

Rooms from €125

Sitting at the tip of the Wilhelmina Pier, now dwarfed by the landmark skyscrapers of the Kop van Zuid (p. 237), Hotel New York is one of Rotterdam's landmark buildings and a serious success story as a hotel. The former head offices of the Holland-Amerika Lijn were built by architects J. Muller, Drooglever Fortuin and C.B. van der Tak between 1901 and 1917. Its ships began carrying European emigrants looking for a better life in the United States in 1896. Service continued until 1984 as the Holland America Line, but in 1993 the grand Jugendstil head offices were converted into a seventy-two-room hotel. Hotel New York pays homage to its rich history by mixing maritime essence with modern-day style. Enigmatic graphics adorn the booklets, luggage tags and menus, and the former executive suites in the building have been lovingly restored, their rosewood and walnut panelling polished. Carpets designed by Theodoor Colenbrander still lie on the floors of most of the rooms. The Art Nouveau motifs were woven in the 1920s by the Deventer Carpet Factory and Tilburg's Textile Museum mended the weave. The façade is reminiscent of many grand hotels – two green towers thrust skyward, each housing a room with its own spiral staircase and views across the River Mass. The other rooms, including a penthouse, all vary in shape, size and colour. Hotel New York has captured the elegance of travel in days gone by and the result is a grand hotel with a cosmopolitan flavour. Visitors arrive by water taxi, crossing the Maas to arrive at the outdoor terrace before checking in underneath the shadow of a wrought-iron staircase. A bookshop containing a well-chosen selection of design and travel books complements the foyer.

2 Stroom Rotterdam
Lloydtstraat 1
Rooms from €145

The development of the Lloydkwartier, located on the former Lloyd pier, is testament to Rotterdam's expansion and development out towards the new harbour area (Maasvlakte I + II). Where once there was nothing but an empty pier, there is now a hotbed of creative talent working in the theatre and offices, living in new high-rise apartments, studying at the Scheepvaart en Transportcollege (the impressive gravity-defying maritime and shipping college by Neutelings Riedijk Architecten), and enjoying the view from restaurants and cafes on the Lloyd as well as the Muller pier. Stroom Rotterdam, an eighteen-room hotel housed in a former electricity factory (*stroom* means 'electric current'), was built for guests and locals alike. Opened in 2005, Stroom's public areas are light and bright: robust architecture belies its former industrial role. The bar is colourful and there are some 360 small mirrors stuck at angles above it, presenting interesting aspects of the crowd. A huge monitor in the restaurant allows diners to see what is going on in the kitchen as the chefs prepare an uncomplicated menu of fresh ingredients to be eaten at high tables. When designing the rooms, the hotel started from the premise that 70 per cent of time spent in a hotel room (apart from sleeping) is spent in the bathroom. As such, Stroom's bathrooms are fitted with all the luxuries and extras one could hope for. The duplex suites' bathrooms are located on the entry floor, with the bedroom on the mezzanine level upstairs. There are no poky interior bathrooms at Stroom, theirs boast sky views as well as baths sized for two and mega-showers with products from fun bath range Anatomicals. Attention to detail is apparent throughout: the overhead projector for TV and DVDs (with a collection to borrow from reception) is accompanied by Bose speaker systems, and the beds are by luxury slumber specialists Coco-Mat. For any lazy risers, breakfast is served daily till 2 p.m.

eat

The opening of this restaurant in 2005 transformed busy riverside highway, the Boompjes, into a destination rather than a drive-through. Brothers Aryan and Willem Tieleman acquired the site, which previously housed Brasserie de Boompjes, and gave Marcel Wanders (see The Lute Suites; p. 15) free rein to design the interior. The result is a restaurant to see and be seen in. Wanders, drawing inspiration from theatre, installed a 26-metre-long bar that stretches the full length of the restaurant: split levels appear as stages

witnessed by an audience on a lower floor. The use of warm tones – oranges, reds and yellows – imbue a celebratory atmosphere. There is even a love suite in which a couple can dine, isolated by curtains with their own private view through the floor-to-ceiling glass façade over the Maas. Wanders created heart-shaped cushions for this nook, perfect for a romantic tête-à-tête. Chef Glyn Stoker's menu consists of eighteen small dishes, a mix of Japanese, North African and South American cuisine, and changes daily.

After the retirement of Cees Helder (the first Dutch chef to receive three Michelin stars), Herman den Blijker stepped in to take the cooking crown. Den Blijker, the Dutch equivalent of Britain's Gordon Ramsay, hosts several cooking shows, including the successful 'Herrie in de Keuken' (*herrie*, as well as being a nickname for Herman, also means 'noisy'). De Engel is a cozy affair that serves a mix of French- and Italian-inspired dishes on the upper-ground level of one of the grand old houses overlooking the Westersingel canal.

5 ## Hotel Bazar
Witte de Withstraat 16

6 ## Proef
Mariniersweg 259

Once home to the largest port in the world, Rotterdam is recognized as a multicultural melting pot and has a large Moroccan population. The best of North African hospitality is celebrated at Hotel Bazar and its restaurant. Opened in 1997, the name is reflected by its joyous décor, reminiscent of a Middle Eastern *souk*. The colourful hanging lamps, bright tables and vibrant music combine to create an atmosphere that brings traditional Arabic courtesy alive in a fun environment. Dishes are tasty, portions are healthy and prices are low, ensuring Hotel Bazar's popularity with native Rotterdammers and visitors alike. Falafels, Turkish bread, Algerian pancakes and couscous are just some of the dishes that appear on the menu, to be enjoyed over a beer or fresh mint tea. The twenty-seven rooms of the hotel are equally vivacious in design and feature brightly coloured walls and carpets, along with beds wrapped in exotic fabrics.

At Proef ('taste'), self-styled 'food designer' Marije Vogelzand's approach to food is thorough. She considers its scent, colour and sound, how it is presented, even the ambience in which it is eaten. To eat from her selection is to taste dishes created by someone who is in tune with produce and diet. It is food just as it should be. Menus vary seasonally, and some dishes are designed to give energy or induce calming effects. Vogelzand also lectures and takes a responsible hands-on attitude to teaching her approach in cooking classes.

drink

CAKE AND ARCHITECTURE

7 Dudok
Meent 88

Created in the finest *grand café* tradition, Dudok is named for the famous Rotterdam architect who designed the building that now houses it. Willem Marinus Dudok's signature styles are apparent: large glass-panelled windows form the outside walls, as well as act to divide kitchen and café. The effect is at once open and inviting, and the huge space provides the right balance in a bustling catering environment. The building saw life as an insurance company office before it was transformed into a café by Dudok-groep, the same team behind Club Rotterdam (see right). The open-plan interior was retained. Today Dudok has a reputation as one of the best restaurants in the Netherlands at which to sample a traditional slice of apple pie (ask for *Appeltaart met slagroom*), and is a meeting place for locals and tourists alike. There is an imaginative à la carte menu and a patisserie serving cakes and pastries. And be sure to visit the toilets, where the sinks are complemented by beer taps for running water.

CREATURES OF THE NIGHT

8 Kruiskade
- Off_Corso, no. 22
- Thalia Lounge, no. 31
- De Beurs, no. 55
- Zin, Lijnbaan 40–42
- Catwalk, Weena Zuid 33
- Nighttown, West-Kruiskade 26–28

For two decades Rotterdam's most (in)famous night out was to be had at Nighttown. But all good things must come to an end, and today the crown is shared by several venues, all conveniently situated a stone's throw from one another. Located in the converted cinema Corso, Off_Corso attracts a twenty-something crowd. A more famous cinema, the Tuschinski (founded by cinema chain owner Abraham Tuschinski, who was killed at Auschwitz in 1942), has been divided into two clubs: Thalia Lounge in the former seating area appeals to a sophisticated international crowd, while De Beurs, located in the foyer, provides a top night out for the student posse. The most glamorous location on the Kruiskade strip is Zin, attracting an older group of party-seekers not afraid to spend on clothes and drinks. But all nights end

up at Catwalk, an underground tunnel with a DJ booth at one end where Carl Cox, Speedy J, Chris Leibing and Secret Cinema have all spun the crowd into a state of ecstatic revelry. Nighttown was acquired by Heineken and subsequently closed for refurbishment. Its scheduled 2007 reopening will give it the chance to take up its rightful place on the city's after-hours map.

A ROOM WITH A VIEW

9 Club Rotterdam
Wilhelminakade 699

This former arrivals and departures building, once owned by the Holland-Amerika Lijn and now part of the prolific Dudok-groep (see left), underwent a recent refurbishment resulting in one of the most stylish venues in the city from which to enjoy a view of the Erasmus Bridge and the River Maas. Enter at ground level to a contemporary bar popular for pre- and post-dinner drinks, with doors into the vast nightclub that opens after hours. The two upper levels, with their sublime vistas, house the restaurant and café so popular with Rotterdammers that booking is essential, especially at weekends. A brown, black and white minimal colour scheme is complemented with huge sofas on which to lounge while taking in the view. An extensive salad and breakfast menu is perfect for quick sustenance, while the restaurant offers European fusion dishes for those who want to take their time.

CAFÉ IN A CONTAINER

10 Wijn of Water
Loods Celebes 101

The exterior is striking as Wijn of Water ('wine or water') is located in nine former sea containers. Owner Bea Oomens combines her passion for Mediterranean cuisine with her work for the Bureau Medelanders, who instigate projects to aid the integration of immigrants into Dutch society. Located in the Lloydkwartier, which is fast becoming known as Rotterdam's centre for new media due to the presence of many film and IT offices, Wijn of Water appeals to its local patrons with a complete Wi-Fi network. Every seat, both inside and out on the terrace, provides a view over the River Maas. On offer is a range of global fingerfood or more substantial fare.

shop

MOOOI-TASTIC

11 Van Oosterom
Van Vollenhovenstraat 15

FRESH TALENT

12 NieuweOntwerpers
William Boothlaan 13a

By 2001 the thirty-six warehouses underneath the first-ever grass roof in the Netherlands (built by T.L. Kanters in 1894) were derelict, but luckily brothers Robert and Erik van Oosterom saw the potential of this unique site and moved into the vast space of the Westelijk Handelsterrein, with its super galleries, bars and restaurants (Italian Rosso is a local favourite) as their new neighbours. Their own space commands some 1,250 square metres, perfect for its role as the pilot store for Marcel Wanders' Moooi range. Moooi's success

has grown over the past five years, and Van Oosterom's has grown right along with it. Today the shop also offers a bespoke interior design service, and recently completed two 150-metre-high flats in the new Montevideo building on the Kop van Zuid (p. 287). The brothers have given their store the ambience of a dream home full of stunning design classics. Rotterdam's star chef Herman den Blijker (see p. 281) likes to cook in their fully operational Minotti Cuisine kitchen, and even filmed episodes for his TV shows here.

The literal translation of the shop's name is 'new designers', and this industrially minimal store provides a much-needed platform for young talent in Holland, stocking the work of students from the Rietveld Academie, the Amsterdam Fashion Institute and arts schools in Arnhem and Utrecht. It also carries pieces by its three founders: Henck Koers sources vintage fabrics to create his tailored menswear, Dick van der Vlies makes versatile dresses, and Maartje Versluijs designs collections for both women and men.

LOUD LINGERIE
13 Marlies Dekkers
Witte de Withstraat 2

Rotterdam native Marlies Dekkers' lingerie designs have proved so popular that they are now sold in some 850 outlets around the world. This flagship store in the Witte de With features a range of beach and swimwear called 'Sundressed' (complementing the lingerie line 'Undressed'). Her creations are renowned for their innovative use of high-tech fabrics and graphics, and some have found their way into the permanent collections of fashion museums.

ROTTERDAM CALLING
14 Zer010
Oude Binnenweg 122

With Zer010, Dennis Aarse and Richard Siebel have opened Rotterdam's first concept fashion store. By dedicating the top floor of the building to an Aveda hair and beauty salon and café run by Maastricht's organic eatery Simply Bread, Aarse and Siebel have secured a winning combination. Zer010 (a twist on Rotterdam's telephone dialling code) carries such labels as Kenzo, Diesel, Dolce & Gabbana and Alexander McQueen, as well as Dutch jewelry by Soon, including golden shoe accessories that read 'Max 20kg'.

FASHION FORWARD
15 Van Dijk
Van Oldenbarneveltstraat 105

Hailed as the 'Fashion Queen of Rotterdam', Wendela van Dijk likes to mix it up. Helping to transform the street into the high-end fashion destination it has now become, her style is feminine yet urban and glamorous, and she happily pairs stilettos with jogging pants. Van Dijk's fashion-forward vision saw her bring Martin Margiela (p. 123), Rick Owens and Paul Smith to Rotterdam, and she continues to design own-brand pieces but, with a young family, works to her own schedule rather than being seasonally collection driven.

see

16 Euromast
Parkhaven 20

The Euromast, built in 1960 by architect H.A. Maaskant and contractor J.P. van Eesteren, was the city's homage to the international flower show Floriade, first held that year. One hundred metres up the tower is the main viewing platform, a steel construction of 240,000 kilograms. Shaped like a crow's nest on a mast, it houses a restaurant offering unsurpassable views over the city and surrounding countryside. Since 2004, when Rotterdam's Brothers Tieleman acquired the management of this landmark site, the thirty-second elevator ride has opened into a glamorous white space created by Holland's favourite interior designer, Jan de Bouvrie. His signature blank canvas applied in the restaurant forces diners' attention to the panoramic floor-to-ceiling windows that gape over the city's skyline and far beyond (on clear days you can even see Delft and The Hague). One level up is an open balcony that wraps around the whole tower. Here de Bouvrie was invited to design two suites that can be rented for an unforgettable night. Upping the ante on the 'mile-high club', these are the ultimate luxury suites, complete with vast bedrooms and bathrooms, all facing out onto the stunning view which, once the tourists have gone home, you can call your very own. In the summer, visitors can abseil or slide down a rope to get off the Euromast.

LIVING IN A BOX
17 De Kijk-Kubus
Overblaak 70

A veritable testament to Rotterdam's reputation as an architect's playground, this cluster of thirty-nine yellow cube houses was built by Piet Blom between 1978 and 1984. All are distinctively tilted, seemingly balancing on the tip of one corner. The architect called them 'tree houses', and today the whole area is referred to as *het Blaakse Bos* (the Black Forest). Inside everything appears as normal in the three-storey homes. No. 70 is open to visitors as a showroom house and presents information on the housing project. Nearby is the Witte Huis (1898), which at 43 metres was Europe's first skyscraper and is now dwarfed by nearly every other building in the vicinity, including the distinctive

pencil-shaped Blaaktoren (1984), also by Piet Blom. Equally noteworthy here is Station Black, the subway and train station built by Harry Reijnders in 1993, locally referred to as the *vliegende schotel* ('flying saucer') as it resembles one hovering above the earth.

HISTORY HOUSED
18 Museum Boijmans van Beuningen
Museumpark 18–20

To wander the galleries of the Boijmans is to take a walk through time. Objects from the Middle Ages through to the present day sit comfortably in the Van de Steur building, first opened in 1935. You will come across familiar faces here: Rembrandt's *Titus* and Bruegel's *Tower of Babel* complement works by Mondriaan, Van Gogh, Monet, Bosch and Degas. There is an extensive Surrealist collection on display in the newest wing, featuring paintings by Dalí, Magritte, Max Ernst and Man Ray. The 20th century is further represented by Andy Warhol, Claes Oldenburg, Donald Judd and Joseph Beuys. This three-dimensional *Who's Who* also includes design classics, temporary exhibitions, a library and a statue garden. The Boijmans, as it is affectionately referred to, is a national treasure trove that has visitors coming back again and again.

THE SKY'S THE LIMIT
19 Kop van Zuid

Stand on UN Studio's iconic Erasmus Bridge, Europe's largest and heaviest bascule bridge, and witness the fierce young architecture that claws skyward, defying gravity and reinventing the profession as an experimental study. Architects from all over the world make inspirational pilgrimages to Rotterdam; it is no wonder that the city deemed 2007 its official 'year of architecture'. On the five-minute crossing to the Kop van Zuid peninsula look at Renzo Piano's Toren van Zuid (home to Dutch phone company KPN), the World Port Centre by Norman Foster and the Montevideo building by Francine Houben of Mecanoo. By 2009 this illustrious list of architects on the Kop van Zuid will be further bolstered by Rotterdam's own Rem Koolhaas when he completes the thirty-seven-storey De Rotterdam, which will house luxury apartments, shops and a hotel.

20 Witte de With Center for Contemporary Art + Centrum Beeldende Kunst
Witte de Withstraat 50

Housed in a former school building, Witte de With was established as a contemporary art centre in 1990. Its presence on the Witte de Withstraat underlines this street as a cultural hub of Rotterdam. The top two floors of the building are dedicated galleries, vast white cubes with striking views across the city. Throughout the year they become the backdrop for temporary exhibitions of contemporary art, from video to installations, sculpture to photography. Witte de With works predominantly with living artists from around the globe and prides itself on showing emerging talent alongside more established figures in a changing programme of thematic and solo exhibitions. The gallery's positive international outlook and staff means that all exhibitions and most publications are presented in English and Dutch. Located in the same building is the Centrum Beeldende Kunst, Rotterdam's centre for the visual arts.

21 Nederlands Fotomuseum
Wilhelminakade 332

Housing a treasure trove of Dutch photography, the Nederlands Fotomuseum is at once a gallery, shop, library and archive. Within its climate-controlled vaults are 129 archives that comprise some three million negatives, colour transparencies, prints and documents about the life and work of such photographers as Ed van der Elsken, Cas Oorthuys and Piet Zwart. The museum also collects amateur photography and administers the archives of, for example, Katharina Eleonore Behrend and Hein Wertheimer. Thanks to the profusion of subjects, genres and applications, the collection not only represents the history of Dutch photo-graphy but also provides a history of the Netherlands in pictures, dating back over a century. Past shows have included contemporary fashion photography as well as a Dutch press photo exhibition.

22 De Kunsthal
Museumpark, Westzeedijk 341

A quality of illusion pervades the city's most important contemporary art museum, designed by Rotterdam native and world-famous architect Rem Koolhaas. The entrance is via the auditorium, and the effect once inside is that of being outside; passersby can walk, cycle, even drive through the centre of the museum. The seemingly compact building actually houses three main halls and two galleries in some 3,300 square metres of space. Since its inception in 1992, the Kunsthal's mission has been to 'present culture in the widest sense of the word: old art, new art, design, photography – from élitist to popular'. The result is an unpredictable exhibition repertoire of about twenty-five shows a year that range from small, intimate shows to major installations, and has included such topics as lingerie, Impressionism, Leonardo da Vinci, Dutch favourite Escher and Pop Art.

23 Nederlands Architectuurinstituut
Museumpark 25

More than a museum for architecture, the Netherlands Architecture Institute exists as a communication conduit for examining the shaping of human space. Located at one end of the Museumpark – the Kunsthal (see above), the Boijmans (p. 287) and the Natural History Museum are the other players in this cultural heart of the city – the 1993 building designed by Jo Coenen contains four distinct spaces: the lobby and auditorium, accessed by a footbridge or from a sheltered arcade that is lit at night by Peter Struycken's light sculpture; the exhibition wing; the archives; and the library with offices above, home to a world-class archive of architectural texts and providing research facilities and a forum for discussion. Be sure to check out the adjacent Sonneveld House, on the corner of Jongkindstraat and Rochussenstraat. One of the only authentic houses in the *Nieuwe Bouwen* style (the Dutch interpretation of Modernism) of the 1930s, it was designed by architects Brinkman & Van der Vlugt, celebrated in Rotterdam for their Van Nelle Factory and Feyenoord Stadium.

Anke van Iersel

tot Zero

1965 - 1974

NAï

VIENNA

Vienna is forever associated with the *Kaffeehaus*, where the seductive link between architecture, the arts, music and ideas has given rise to some of the world's great creative achievements. Distilled into these often grand but congenial places are so many of the city's cultural and existential riches that they have imbued Vienna's very way of life for centuries. The coffee houses continue to be vital social gauges, places where tradition and the avant-garde percolate vigorously, a state described by the 19th-century Austrian writer Alfred Polgar as *Weltanschauung*. Vienna is a harmonious mix of the historic and the hip, the imposing and the modern, with Gothic, Renaissance, Neoclassical and Eclectic sandwiched between Biedermeier and Secessionism.

The musical, literary and design-centric culture of Vienna's past, which flourished over six centuries of the Habsburg empire, has seeped across terrible decades of destruction into new, freethinking generations. The imperial tradition and its trappings were so strong that it wasn't until the 20th century that fresh creative energies would emerge. More recently, the Millennium marked the beginning of Vienna's global self-awareness, symbolized by the opening of the MuseumsQuartier, one of the world's largest arts complexes. But even a century and a half before, Vienna had begun to shake off the conservative grip of the Habsburgs and entered a phase of liberalization under the Austro-Hungarian Empire's last ruler, Franz Josef. It was he, together with the 18th-century empress Maria Theresa and her son Joseph II, who really fostered Vienna's cultural high notes. From the mid-1800s, its modern look took dramatic shape; the Ringstraße, much like Haussmann's grand boulevards in Paris, imposed an iconic architectural style on the city. The medieval walls of the old city were demolished, and the 4-kilometre 'ring' was given a flamboyant facelift with its ornate, historicist buildings: showy touches of Flemish neo-Gothic (Rathaus), Greek Revival (Parliament Building) and neo-Renaissance (Kunsthistorisches Museum). Today they delineate the border between Vienna's largely pedestrianized *Innere Stadt* and its twenty-two other *bezirke* (neighbourhoods).

In 1897 a group of artists, including Gustav Klimt (see p. 309), Josef Hoffmann (see p. 305) and Otto Wagner (see p. 309), rebelled against the pomp and constraints of older architectural styles. The resulting Viennese Secession, along with the Jugendstil and the Wiener Werkstätte, the cooperative workshop of craftsmen who sought to turn everyday objects into *Gesamtkunstwerken*, was profoundly influential. Vienna's creative past is reflected in the name of its annual design exhibition, Blickfang, an eye-catching event that features furniture, fashion and jewelry. At street level, the continuing spirit of reinvention is captured in the ironic name of a budding atelier in the Spittelberg area, Werkprunk (p. 305), which can mean 'art-work splendour' or 'pomposity', depending on your taste. Either way, it sums up the rich and lively blend of Vienna's creative spirit.

StyleCity Vienna

1 Hollmann Beletage
2 Hotel Rathaus Wine & Design
3 Altstadt Vienna
4 Das Triest
5 Immervoll
6 Österreicher im MAK
7 Zum Schwarzen Kameel
8 Kantine
9 Café Amacord
10 Hansen
11 Huth Gastwirtschaft
12 Naturkost St Josef
13 Julius Meinl am Graben
14 Palmenhaus
15 Steireck im Stadtpark
16 Glacis Beisl
17 Café Central
18 Café Sperl
19 Café Korb
20 Das Möbel Café
21 Lutz Die Bar
22 Europa
23 Loos American Bar
24 Café Konditorei Gerstner
25 Sektcomptoir Szigeti
26 Stefan Pagacs Weinhandel
27 Spittelberg Design
28 Pregenzer Fashion Store
29 Kaffee Rösterei Alt Wien
30 Grüne Erde/Bio-Kosmetika & Wein
31 J. & L. Lobmeyr
32 Çombinat
33 R. Horn's Wien
34 Gatto Möbel
35 Mühlbauer
36 Schella Kann
37 Renate Asenbaum
38 Wagner:Werk Museum Postparkasse
39 3mpc (Third Man Private Collection)
40 Secession
41 Museum of Applied Arts (MAK)
42 Architekturzentrum Wien
43 Österreichisches Theatermuseum
44 Sigmund Freud Museum
45 Theater an der Wien
46 Naschmarkt

sleep

1 **Hollmann Beletage**
Köllnerhofgasse 6
Rooms from €130

The blackboard by each room welcoming each guest by
name typifies the hotel's ethos of personal touches combined
with intense privacy, a philosophy with echoes of Johann
Wolfgang von Goethe: 'Here I am human, here they let me
be.' Outside office hours, the sixteen rooms of the Hollmann
Beletage, owned by chef-turned-actor Robert Hollmann, seem
part of a swish private boarding house. The door code and the
key waiting on the counter of the orange-sorbet lobby, the
library books and CDs (to enjoy on the retro-style player on
the bedhead/workstation/wash basin) all add to the luxe feel.
Offered in two sizes, Residence L (20–25 square metres) and
Residence XL (35 square metres), the rooms provide everything from designer bathtubs to pistachio-dispensing machines.
All rooms are non smoking.

MESSAGE IN A BOTTLE

2 Hotel Rathaus Wine & Design
Lange Gasse 13
Rooms from €186

This most unusual hotel is definitely not for teetotallers; as the name suggests, most things here at the Hotel Rathaus Wine & Design are vinified. From the moment you enter through the doors decorated with wine-labels, it is apparent that each of the thirty-three 'wine and design' rooms is an homage to a different Austrian wine *Schloß,* which provide the wine for the mini bars. Add to that wine cosmetics, wine cheese, and *Gugelhupf* for breakfast, tastings and wine murals on the courtyard walls, and viniculture is decanted into every pore of Salzburg-based chef-owner Klaus Fleischhaker's hotel. No sour grapes here.

3 **Altstadt Vienna**
Kirchengasse 41
Rooms from €139

Upon entering the red portico of this Secession building, take the lift or the cast-iron stairway to reception, where the scarlet carpets echo the striking pieces of contemporary art. With forty-two rooms and suites secreted in various wings of the residential building, there is a tangible feeling of 'your private residence in Vienna'. For owner Otto Wiesenthal, a collector of art and furniture, variety is the spice of life: there are four breakfast rooms alone. The traditional parquet-floored suites sport names from 'Freud' to 'Bosendorfer', along with both Art Déco and modern furnishings and fixtures. Rooms recently designed by Italian architect Matteo Thun have a dark chocolate naughty-but-nice décor, redolent of the historic Spittelberg area's boudoir past.

4 Das Triest

Wiedner Hauptstraße 12
Rooms from €265

A revolving blue 'T' on the roof is all that identifies this establishment, and this aloofness is matched inside. Housed in a three-century-old building that formerly served as the Vienna–Trieste stagecoach depot, Das Triest was reimagined by architect Peter Lorenz and given the Terence Conran design treatment in 1996. Points of particular panache include its ship-shape spaciousness, cross-vaulted rooms that have been reworked with angular ceilings and port-holed 'decks', suites fitted out like home studios, an Italianate courtyard garden, and the piquant use of bright glassy colours in a sea of mint-green walls. There are seventy-two rooms and suites, with two non-smoking floors. Music available through LoungeFM provides 'the best of lounge music in Austria'.

eat

Schremser
Das Waldviertler **Bier** naturgebraut

NATUR-
HISTORISCHE
MUSEUM

2TER
GARTEN

ALWAYS PERFECT
5 Immervoll
Weihburggasse 17

When Immervoll ('always full') is just that, or when the weather is *immer schön*, devotees take to the terrace on Franziskanerplatz, 50 metres away, mingling with those of the Kleines Kaffée. Both are owned by actor-gastro-nome Hanno Pöschl, who has a predilection for small places and 'personal over perfect' service. The pretty vaulted bistro uses mirrors to create space and a cantilevered ceiling rack for wine bottles and glasses to save it. The menu includes at least three vegetarian dishes, which also account for one of two daily specials.

EXTRA ARCHITECTURE
6 Österreicher im MAK
Stubenring 5

The menu and design of this spaceship-lit chunk of history are impressively in two camps: classical and modern Viennese. Located in a former exhibition space of the MAK (p. 309), restaurant and bar flow into one other around minimal wine shelving. Architects Eichinger oder Knechtl wanted to reinvent the traditional *Gasthaus*, which includes a bar, dining room and *Extra-zimmer* in which guests relax or party. The coffered ceiling is offset by mod elements, including a 22-metre-long light sail, a wine-bottle chandelier and black benches with green, pink and blue underlighting. Chef Helmut Österreicher steadily produces local favourites, including pork with *Knödel* (dumplings) and sauerkraut.

JUST DESSERTS
7 Zum Schwarzen Kameel
Bognergasse 5

At this Jugendstil jewel, an elegant crowd sip cocktails and dine around diminutive wood-panelled bars, in lamp-lit booths and on the terrace. Opened as a spice shop in 1618 by Johan Baptist Cameel, this former haunt of Beethoven is a bar, delicatessen and *Weinhandlung* (wine store) with the best leg ham in Vienna and delightful displays. Under the whimsical black camel insignia, there is also an Alfred Loos-designed formal eating den with glass-beaded copper chandeliers and plaster friezes.

PITA FUNK
8 Kantine
Museumsplatz 1

The main courtyard of the MQ is one of the most exciting public spaces in the world, around which people gather to read, relax, rave, write and Wi-Fi en masse. Looking over it to the Kunsthalle contemporary arts space, Kantine serves up quality organic food (pita breads with Asian flavours and Mauritian fish soup) with a restaurant-sized drinks list. From the hologram tables and green plastic chairs outside, the mood within is of a different sort. With funky couches, a ceiling disco *Kugeln* and 'music buffet', it's both physically and psychologically between the Electric Avenue experimentation space and Prachner architecture bookshop.

CHESTERFIELD UNDERGROUND
9 Café Amacord
Rechte Wienzeile 15

'Dark, cozy, very good food and wine – typically Viennese,' is how one regular describes this den of wooden tables and Chesterfield sofas. The cooking is Viennese with a touch of the Mediterranean: risotto with pumpkin-seed oil from the Styria region (*Kürbisrisotto mit Steirisches Kürbiskernöl*), and pumpkin and lamb ragoûts (*Kurbisragout, Lamm-ragout*). The Styrian spirit belongs to owner Dieta Eder. In 1988 she opened the first restaurant along the right-hand border of the Naschmarkt (p. 309); it's now an institution loved by students, socialists and politicians.

POTTED TREASURES
10 Hansen
Wipplinger Straße 34

The closest thing to Viennese on the weekly Mediterranean-inspired menu is the Hokkaido-pumpkin *Strudel* or breakfast *Birchermuesli* and Wieser's jam from the Wachau region. But the location in the basement of the *Börsegebäude* (Stock Exchange building), is legendary. Named after Danish architect Theophil Hansen, who headed the monumental Ringstraße project (1874–77), the eatery shares a luxuriantly planted space with garden design store Lederleitner. Outside eating is all sandstone and terracotta, inside the skylit domed ceiling and milky-white arches are 'reminiscent of a Roman covered market'.

DESIGN SCHNITZEL
11 Huth Gastwirtschaft
Schellinggasse 5

WHOLLY PUMPKIN
12 Naturkost St Josef
Zollergasse 26

SULTANATE OF SWING
13 Julius Meinl am Graben
Am Graben 19

Gabriele and Robert Huth's *Gast-wirtschaft* (inn) is a devoted supporter of *Wiener Küche*, despite its modern bistro look. Loved by young and old in search of Viennese classics in a chic setting, the glass-fronted eatery with its terrace and overhanging loft is light, leafy and *lärche* (wooded); it is the larch tree, in fact, which provides the traditional dark, woody touch. The past makes an appearance on the menu in the form of *Schnitzel*, boiled beef and meatballs. Weekly specials include vegetarian pasta and seasonal dishes.

Pumpkins, plants, wooden tables and ingredients from long-established organic grocers all find their place at Naturkost St Josef health food store and its adjoining canteen. Lawyers, artists and wine merchants alike will recommend this hidden treasure, which says something about the ecological underbelly of the Viennese. Its reputation exceeds its vegetatively overwhelmed and unsigned entrance. Both eco-warriors and ladies-who-lunch come here for the seasonal range of organic salads and hot vegetable dishes.

The saffron window seats of this first-floor restaurant offer views onto one of the most beautiful pedestrian streets in the world. While the menu is creatively international (with the carrot mille-feuille an improvement on both the vegetable and the pastry), the milieu is totally Viennese. The 700-strong wine list is half that of the cellar wine bar, which serves cheese platters and wines by the glass. Finish off a meal with the house espresso (Meinl started out as a coffee roaster in 1924), served in exquisite red porcelain cups.

FLOAT LIKE A BUTTERFLY

14 Palmenhaus
Burggarten

Its hard to beat breakfast on the terrace of this glass-and-steel Jugendstil pavilion, a former greenhouse. Daytimes are breezy, with tables dotted between the ferns and a cozy nook with sofas looking into the next-door butterfly house. From 10 a.m. to 1 p.m., breakfast includes muesli and fresh fruit, vegetables with *Joghurtdip*, cheese, ham and home-made jam. At night, the long bar and red leather seats are boosted by two outdoor bars (one for BBQs, the other for cocktails) with DJs poised for action.

STYRIAN ROCOCO

15 Steirereck im Stadtpark
Am Heumarkt 2a

When the Reitbauer family opened their restaurant in the Stadtpark, they found somewhere as close to nature as possible in which to feature their Styrian cheese, beef and venison. The Jugendstil building, formerly a *Milch-haus*, has been transformed into a lavishly extravagant epicurean theatre, from the tangerine-tiled bar with a gold-leaf table and Murano-glass beer pumps, to the the river-facing location with its ceiling of Styrian 'leaves', to the downstairs milk and cheese bar with its white chairs and wall of milk bottles.

TWIST ON A TAVERN

16 Glacis Beisl
Breitegasse 4

Terrazzo floors, sea-green tabletops, booths and *Kugellampen* (orb lights), even an aquarium with live trout – these classic tavern elements take seductive form in this woody lair. With the owners desirous of leaving behind the look of a 1950s *Beisl*, part of the striking adaptation is the glassed *Wintergarten* area encased in ruby wood with leaf-shaped holes, through which diners can spy on the outdoor *Gastgarten*. Styrian *Krautfleckerl* (caramel-ized cabbage pasta), goulash and dumplings all feature on the menu.

drink

CELESTIAL CEILINGS
17 Café Central
Herrengasse 14

BOOKISH VELOUR
18 Café Sperl
Gumpendorferstraße 11

SOCIAL PALETTE
19 Café Korb
Brandstätte 9

Featuring on the tourist circuit has done little to diminish the appeal of this café. Housed in the Palais Ferstel, its soaring ceilings and baroque columns make Café Central a stirring spot in which to imbibe the *Kaffeehaus* tradition. The menu has expanded beyond the usual coffeehouse choices of *Bratwurst* and *Strudel* to sautéed vegetables with smoked tofu. A particularly delicious treat from the in-house *Konditorei* is *Esterházytorte* (made with layers of sponge and almonds). Start practicing your pronunciation now.

In a garden square dotted with green chairs, this neighbourly café wears its history with a relaxed elegance. Pewter pots of daisies and a black-and-gold sign precede a charming interior of banquettes and billiard tables. Built in 1880 in the Ringstraße style, members of the Viennese Secession frequented this arty café. 'Franz Lehár always sat in that corner', says owner Manfred Staub, pointing to a photo of the Austrian operetta composer. The food, including *Pflaumentorte* (plum cake) and *Tafelspitz* (boiled beef), is excellent.

Philosophical airs were fanned here by Freud when he met with the Vienna Psychoanalytic Society, and theatrical ones by owner Susanne Widl, a former actress-model who turned Café Korb into a stage for all. 'The art of taste and discussion should dominate in the coffee house,' she says. The mood among the 1950s fixtures is one of bohemian laissez-faire, with writers meeting in the Art Lounge basement and psychologists for the PsychArt series. Not to be missed on the menu are the yeast dumplings.

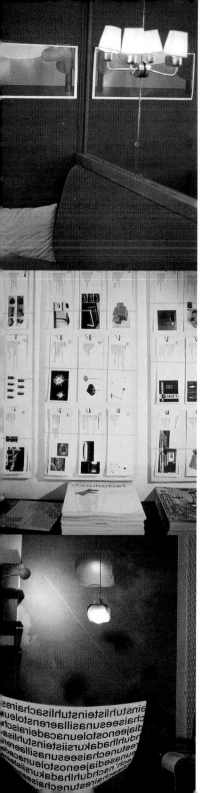

SITZ ON IT
20 Das Möbel Café
Burggasse 10

Viennese *Design Kultur* meets coffee culture in this changing furniture universe, where you can test-drive fabulous *Sitzmöbel* (sofas, seats, stools, hammocks) by young designers. The day-night venue has a supernatural capacity for sensational facelifts and mood changes with its quarterly furniture exhibitions, while the wall catalogue is an artwork in itself. Avant-garde design does not exclude hallowed traditions: newspaper racks, endless cups of coffee, lingering all day, and, insists owner Markus Luger, a true *Kaffeehaus* chill-out vibe that allows no noisy music.

PERSONAL EFFECTS
21 Lutz Die Bar
Mariahilfer Straße 3

In a stretch dominated by interior design stores, it seems appropriate to find a bar where you can try out the latest furniture designs while sipping a cocktail. Seriously lounge-worthy, if you took away the seating there would be little left apart from the large aquarium behind the bar. Rows of chocolate-coloured ottomans (in the dark, caramel and white varieties), club chairs and bench seats ring the walls of this smooth, minimalist lounge with its discreet entry of wrought-iron railing. The window seats make cushy nooks for nibbling bar snacks while people-watching.

CLUB LIBERTY
22 Europa
Zollergasse 8

'*Ein Wohnzimmer* called Europa' is how daily newspaper *Der Standard* described this retro-cool bar, a 'living room' with electro-funk music at times, jazz and blues at others, and a rainbow range of staff, flavours and behaviours. Owner Andreas Friesz backs a common European feeling of liberty for all, hence the name. Diversity has right of way: there's a coveted street terrace, two red rooms with a 1950s-style bar and several seating niches and a backroom nightclub (the *Hinterzimmer*). The Santora coffee is among Vienna's best, as are the Sunday breakfasts (served 8 a.m. to 3 p.m.).

OUT OF SPACE
23 Loos American Bar
Kärntner Durchgang 10

A dissonant mosaic façade, glowing octagonal tables and onyx wall tiles, Jugendstil booths and a wood-and-brass bar: Adolf Loos packed all of that in 1908 into this dense atmosphere of marble, mahogany and mirrored trickery. 'In 6 by 4.5 metres, we connect art and pleasure with classic cocktails and over 200 drinks,' says Marianne Kohn, manager of Loos American Bar since the early 1980s. The bar is renowned for its Martinis, which regulars sip on while warming the bar stools in this historic protected building.

ROYAL SWEETS SUPPLIER
24 Café Konditorei Gerstner
Kärntner Straße 13–15

The terrace of this former *Hofzuckerbäckerei* (confectioner to the Imperial Palace) makes for a sweet pit stop on the hectic main shopping stretch of Kärntner Straße. Bits of the past that are worth holding on to fortunately have been here, such as the 154-year-old recipe for *Haustorte*, a heavenly concoction of nougat, chocolate and almond. 'Many people come to Vienna just for this,' notes director Oliver Braun. A slice of one of the four dozen cakes that are baked daily with a glass of Veuve Cliquot on the terrace is the best antidote to an overdose of retail therapy.

TINY BUBBLES
25 Sektcomptoir Szigeti
Schleifmühlgasse 19

Regulars help themselves behind the bar of this button-sized *Sekt*-swilling cellar with its chandelier strung with wine glasses and Champagne flutes, also the work of an habitué. 'This place is Vienna,' says one. There's a chunk of bread on the counter, about a dozen stools moved around at will, and wooden alcoves containing displays of the 'Classic', 'Prestige' and 'Frizzante' varieties of *Sekt* made by brothers Peter and Norbert Szigeti. Set up in 1990 to promote a 'new sparkling wine culture', all the popped corks in this bubbly comptoir come from the Szigetis' vineyard in Gols, southeast of Vienna.

shop

Grüne Erde
KRÄUTERBAD
ART.-NR. 48 973

Kamille & Lavendel
Baby

Grüne Erde

GESUND & SCHÖN VON INNEN
FÜR HAUT & HAAR

NEU   **NEU**

Take the dainty Art Déco lift to this *Weinkontor* (an old word for a merchant who combines business and tasting in one place, off the main street), where Stefan and Michaela Pagacs welcome you into their select *Wein* world: two rooms of boxes and bottles, antique furniture, contemporary art and 'the smallest vineyard in Vienna', planted on the balcony with 1963 French grapes. The 'whole portfolio of Austrian wines' (150 producers) can be found at this 'oldest trader of quality Austrian wines in Vienna', along with organic Styrian pumpkin-seed oil.

Lindengasse and Kirchengasse are turning into virtual clothes-racks of the small ateliers of subversive and whimsical young designers. At Werkprunk, with its entry on Lindengasse, sisters Jasmine and Silvia König sculpt rings, clogs and belts in raw metals, silver, stone and leather. Pretty La Petite Boutique is home to the fetchingly French Nuit Blanche nightwear and the impeccably finished skirts and shirts of Sandra Gilles. Das Studio is part atelier of sculptor Igor Sapic, part showroom for labels Monikova, Milch and Göttin des Glücks, and home accessories by NoNo ('no-nonsense').

Owner Jutta Pregenzer's love of the exotic textiles gathered on her travels (Persian, African and Asian), was reflected in her first creations some twenty-five years ago. 'I am more practical now,' she says, 'some things you couldn't even wear, they were works of art.' The store carries a handful of chic brands from Italy and France, but it is Pregenzer's own designs that jump off the rack – and none more so than her deep orange, blue and raspberry Lodens, the famous Austrian coats.

The folks behind this venture once came second place in a coffee-tasting competition, just behind Julius Meinl (p. 300). A 100-year-old Guatemalan pedal-grinder demonstrates the company's philosophy of *die Poesie des Einfachen* ('the poetry of simplicity'), roasting the old-fashioned way in 12-kilogram batches. The aroma confirms that 'more than 800 flavours can be found in a single bean'. It stocks organic Zotter chocolate (including the Sunflower and Coriander and Edelbitter Pumpkin Seeds varieties) and there's a bar for chocolate and bean tasting.

In its fresh, white setting, lifestyle shop Grüne Erde stocks face and body products perfumed with lavender, lemon, rose and Aloe Vera, along with 'Frauenmantel' balsams for mums-to-be, 'Babypflege' baby products, and the fragrance-free 'Pur' series. Over at Bio-Kosmetika, Ingrid Schreier and Herbert Miksits tested their *Naturkosmetiks* on an online clientele before opening their Stiftgasse shop, a whimsical mix of wholly organic products from wines to hand-made fruit- and flower-infused *Blutenbaderiegel* (bath bombs) and 'Sanoll' creams enriched with poppy, sesame and jojoba oils.

Lobmeyr, established in 1823, produces hand-cut 'crystal for connoisseurs', along with tableware, light design, mirrors, vases and ornaments. 'In crystal lines our role is as an editor,' says general manager Andreas Rath, a great-nephew of Ludwig Lobmeyr, from working on designs with artists to commissioning glass blowers. But for the delicate process of engraving and cutting, Lobmeyr relies on its own workshops. The black-line drinking set by Josef Hoffmann remains an icon, but contemporary artists and designers are also called upon to inject new life into the 'Lobmeyr style'.

STABLE OF FASHION
32 Çombinat
Museumsplatz 1

EMPTY POCKETS
33 R. Horn's Wien
Bräunerstraße 7

FELINE FIFTIES
34 Gatto Möbel
Kettenbrückengasse 14

In a chalky cavern of the Museums-Quartier, several young and distinctive designers share a *Schauraum* (show-room) and *Werkstatt* (atelier). Today the venture is a pivotal part of the neighbourhood's mode zone Quartier 21, which provides a platform for new talent. All of the labels available here use highly original materials for their urban chic designs. 'Textile techniques' define the functional creations of Doppler & Michlmayr, while MeYoTa bags are for mums and movers by bike or by hike. Pitour has 'sporty fashions with a touch of elegance' such as easy-to-wear dresses with flower appliqués. Entry is in the Burggasse.

Though known primarily for its brief-cases, Viennese shoppers-in-the-know can't stop talking about Robert Horn's leather washbags and *Damentaschen* (handbags). Briefcases, agendas, wallets, boxes for tissues, nail kits, jewelry cases, keyring fobs and other leather accessories come in a variety of rich shades. For both the at-home and travelling perfectionist are silk tie holders and *vide poches* (change trays) for the contents of gentlemen's suit pockets, loved equally by twenty- to eighty-year-olds. The iconic briefcase, first made in 1989, has an identical lock to that originally made for Prince Klemens von Metternich to use at the Vienna Congress in 1815.

One wonders whether Martin Kristof-csak's Art Déco leather furniture was just put there to display his wife Kathrin's handbags, or whether it is the bags themselves that are the props. Either way, the Kristofcsaks' individual Art Déco-inspired creations are mutually enhancing. A vintage Vespa at the entrance delivers them from the 1980s-established *Werkstatt* at Spengergasse 49 to the 1950s-feel 'Riviera Bar' *Schauraum* on Kettenbrückengasse. Handbags stitched with droll feline emblems (the 'gatto' in Gatto Möbel) share space with more masculine crocodile wallets, binders and mobile phone cases.

35 Mühlbauer
Seilergasse 5

CYBER-ELASTICS
36 Schella Kann
Singerstraße 14

SWEET SCHMUCK
37 Renate Asenbaum
Tuchlauben 12

Family-run Mühlbauer has been in the millinery business since 1903. Some of the more whimsical designs by brother and sister Klaus and Marlies Mühlbauer (who belong to the fourth generation of hat-making Mühlbauers) include blue and black melusine bonnets in cheetah fur, men's caps in turquoise velvet, and hats in purple and pink merino wool. Fur features heavily at Mühlbauer (animal-rightsters, look away now): there are denim caps and earmuffs trimmed in possum fur, hamster cloches and yellow and ginger fox-trimmed hats.

First-time visitors to Schella Kann's showroom might find it rather bare. But 'it is an atelier, not a shop', reminds Anita Aigner, one of two designers behind the established label. Set up in 1985 at the vanguard of Vienna's fashion scene, Aigner previously worked for Helmut Lang. With two collections a year, the basic look of Schella Kann is elegant, high tech, easy to wash and easy to wear. The travel-friendly fabric sourced from Italy is used for everything from trousers to bathing suits. 'It's a shell,' explains Aigner, 'you can buy your accessories elsewhere'.

Alice would be happy to wake up in this deliciously dainty jewel-box wonderland. With a wave of her creative wand, Renate Asenbaum's atelier tools (paint brushes and a candle in a brass urn) are poised with romantic ease between displays of Art Déco jewelry and her own *Schmuck* (jewelry) designs in stone. Inside a raspberry-red painted chest-of-drawers are strings of translucent necklaces in the making; the front of the cabinet is pinned with rows of bon-bon coloured earrings. A true artist, in two decades of creation Asenbaum has 'never made the same design more than once.'

see

WAGNERIAN SPLENDOUR
38 Wagner:Werk Museum Postsparkasse
Georg Coch-Platz 2

Along with the Karlsplatz and other Art Nouveau railway pavilions, Otto Wagner's 1903 Post Office Savings Bank is a milestone of *Moderne Architektur*. Branded a 'box of nails', its functional aesthetic – as seen in the marble and granite façade fixed with 17,000 rivets and the steel-and-glass roof of the banking hall – illustrate the Hungarian-born Wagner's philosophy that 'What is impractical can never be beautiful.' This über-architect also designed the handsomely durable fittings, from floor coverings to clocks and counters and the Thonet-inspired chairs.

DOWN THE SEWERS
39 3mpc (Third Man Private Collection)
Pressgasse 25

Gerhard Strassgschwandtner spent a decade amassing records, posters and other memorabilia associated with cult movie *The Third Man*, which was filmed in Vienna in 1948, before going public in 2005. His biggest triumph was the discovery of the original zither played by Anton Karas (an instrument which led to a zither boom) in the actor's garden shed. Other highlights include a recorded interview with the film's only surviving star, Herbert Halbick, who played Hansel, and a short screening on a 1936 projector. Like the film, the visit ends in part of the 2,300 kilometres of Viennese sewers. Only open on Saturday afternoons.

SNUB TO PSEUDO-ECLECTICS
40 Secession
Friedrichstraße 12

In 1898, the Association of Visual Artists Vienna Secession commissioned Joseph Maria Olbrich to create a 'modern, functional' exhibition space. Its gold-leaf cupola and Art Nouveau façade is a landmark on a par with the spires of St Stefan's. The once controversial structure is now the oldest independent gallery in the world devoted entirely to contemporary art. In its basement lies a treasure: *The Beethoven Frieze*, a 34-metre-long fresco by the Secession's most famous son, Gustav Klimt, dedicated to the composer and inspired by his IX Symphony.

DESIGN ME A COFFEE SET
41 Museum of Applied Arts (MAK)
Stubenring 5

Silver and ivory coffee and tea services in organic shapes, candy jars, cutlery and chandeliers, table lamps, wine glasses, writing cases, brooches and astonishingly decorated secretaries are just a few of the everyday yet fantastic objects designed by Wiener Werkstätte craftsmen Josef Hoffman and Koloman Moser for private clients. Both the WW and Jugendstil occupy permanent spaces on the first floor of the forward-thinking MAK. Inspired by London's Victoria & Albert Museum (p. 220), this 1852 neo-Renaissance building melds applied and contemporary arts in a cool and dynamic exhibition space.

DEMYSTIFYING
42 Architekturzentrum Wien
Museumsplatz 1

The Loos House as 'a house without eyebrows', the MuseumsQuartier as 'a tumour', the Haas Haus as 'a glass monster in the historic ensemble of buildings': guided tours of such controversial buildings are among the many facets of the Architecture Centre's role as a feisty public platform for design discussion. Set up in 1993, its mission is to democratize the knowledge of architecture, 'to mediate it as a cultural discipline, an everyday phenomenon and complex process'. The centre is a 'living venue' for exhibitions about current and future trends in architecture, as well as the ongoing project, 'Architecture in the 20th Century – Austria'.

CHILD'S PLAY
43 Österreichisches Theatermuseum
Lobkowitzplatz 2

The baroque Palais Lobkowitz makes a splendid stage for the Theatre Collection of the Austrian National Library, which consists of costumes, stage models, marionettes, drawings and prints, all displayed with a refreshing emphasis on the illustrative over the interactive. Magic for children young and old are provided by the Javanese rod puppets and *Figurenspiegel* by Richard Teschner, and a stage of alternately spotlit costumes. Beethoven's 'Eroica' was performed here for the first time in 1805, during a private performance for Prince Lobkowitz.

VIEW FROM THE COUCH
44 Sigmund Freud Museum
Berggasse 19

Sigmund Freud spent forty-seven years living and working in this house before fleeing from the Nazis in 1938. Acquired in the 1980s, the museum mixes funky red-and-green seats and screenings of Andy Warhol films with the original books and somber waiting-room environment of his medical practice. The neurologist and father of psychoanalysis put diagnosis on the divan by analyzing dreams and the associations that arise in a state of repose. In the video room, you, too, can stretch out, while watching home movies of the Freud family.

MOZART ON THE RIVER
45 Theater an der Wien
Linke Wienzeile 6

This theatre on the banks of the River Wien opened in 1801 after Mozart's librettist, Emanuel Schikaneder (he penned *Die Zauberflöte*), was granted an imperial licence to build it. The Wienfluss, which once flowed nearby, is now covered over by the Naschmarkt area (see below). Beethoven lived in rooms here from 1803 to 1805 while composing his opera *Fidelio*, and ten of his symphonies had their premiers here. During *Wiener Festwochen*, the venue stages operettas and musical theatre performances.

SAUSAGES AND SUSHI
46 Naschmarkt
Linke Wienzeile and Rechte Wienzeile
• Gradwohl, stand 239
• Dogan & Acer, stand 358

With its stacks of sauerkraut, sausage stands and sushi restaurants, the city's largest open-air market must be experienced on the 'inside', within the hordes of people and the rows of stalls and eateries. These improve the further north you stroll, where the wine bars are frequented by locals and cafés turn into electronic music venues. Food highlights include the organic Gradwohl bakery, the Dogan & Acer stand selling Turkish delight and the *Kasehutte* (cheese hut). The northern end around Kettenbrückengasse is home to the Flohmarkt am Naschmarkt every Saturday from 7 a.m. to 5 p.m., a colourful bazaar of around 400 antique and bric-à-brac traders.

contact

All telephone numbers are given for dialling internationally. The number in brackets by the name refers to the page on which the entry appears.

AMSTERDAM

Altmann [17]
Amsteldijk 25
1074 HS Amsterdam
T +31 20 662 7777
E altmann@diningcity.com
W www.altmann.nl

De Bakkerswinkel [17]
Warmoesstraat 69
1012 HX Amsterdam
T +31 20 489 8000
W www.debakkerswinkel.nl

Bar ARC [21]
Reguliersdwarsstraat 44
1017 BM Amsterdam
T +31 20 689 7070
E info@bararc.com
W www.bararc.com

Café de Jaren [18]
Nieuwe Doelenstraat 20–22
1012 CP Amsterdam
T +31 20 625 5771
W www.cafe-de-jaren.nl

Café de Still [21]
Spuistraat 326
1012 VX Amsterdam
T +31 20 427 6809
E info@destill.nl
W www.destill.nl

Café-Restaurant Amsterdam [17]
Watertorenplein 6
1051 PA Amsterdam
T +31 20 682 2666
E mail@cradam.nl
W www.cradam.nl

Canal House Hotel [13]
Keizersgracht 148

1015 CX Amsterdam
T +31 20 622 5182
E info@canalhouse.nl
W www.canalhouse.nl

The College Hotel [14]
Roelof Hartstraat 1
1017 VE Amsterdam
T +31 20 571 1511
E info@thecollegehotel.com
W www.collegehotelamsterdam.com

Dekker Antiquairs [27]
Spiegelgracht 9
1017 JP Amsterdam
T +31 20 623 8992
E dekkerfa@xs4all.nl
W www.dekkerantiquairs.com

Droog @ Home [25]
Staalstraat 7b
1011 JJ Amsterdam
T +31 20 523 5059
E info@droogdesign.nl
W www.droogdesign.nl

The Dylan [12]
Keizersgracht 384
1016 GB Amsterdam
T +31 20 530 2010

Eduard Kramer [27]
Nieuwe Spiegelstraat 64
1017 DD Amsterdam
T +31 20 623 0832
E info@antique-tileshop.nl
W www.antique-tileshop.nl

The Frozen Fountain [24]
Prinsengracht 645
1016 HV Amsterdam
T +31 20 622 9375
E mail@frozenfountain.nl
W www.frozenfountain.nl

Gassan Diamonds [24]
Nieuwe Uilenburgerstraat 173–175
1011 LN Amsterdam
T +31 20 622 5333
E info@gassandiamonds.nl
W www.gassandiamonds.nl

Hester van Eeghen [23]
Hartenstraat 37 (bags)
1016 CA Amsterdam
T +31 20 626 9212
Hartenstraat 1 (shoes)
1016 BZ Amsterdam
T +31 20 626 9211
E info@hestervaneeghen.com
W www.hestervaneeghen.com

Hortus Botanicus [27]
Plantage Middenlaan 2a
1018 DD Amsterdam
T +31 20 625 8411
E info@dehortus.nl
W www.dehortus.nl

Huis Marseille [27]
Keizersgracht 401
1016 EK Amsterdam
T +31 20 531 8989
E info@huismarseille.nl
W www.huismarseille.nl

In 't Aepjen [21]
Zeedijk 1
1012 AN Amsterdam
T +31 20 626 8401

JOOT [23]
Hartenstraat 15
1016 BZ Amsterdam

T +31 20 688 1783
E info@joot.nl
W www.joot.nl

Kapitein Zeppos [21]
Gebed Zonder End 5
1012 HS Amsterdam
T +31 20 624 2057
E kapitein@zeppos.nl
W www.zeppos.nl

De Kas [17]
Kamerlingh Onneslaan 3
1097 DE Amsterdam
T +31 20 462 4562
E info@restaurantdekas.nl
W www.restaurantdekas.nl

The Lute Suites [15]
Amsteldijk Zuid 54–58
1184 VD Ouderkerk aan de Amstel
T +31 20 472 2462
E info@lutesuites.com
W www.lutesuites.com

Mart Visser Haute Couture [23]
Paulus Potterstraat 30a
1071 DA Amsterdam
T +31 20 571 2020
E info@martvisser.nl
W www.martvisser.nl

Menno Kroon [23]
Cornelis Schuytstraat 11
1071 JC Amsterdam
T +31 20 679 1950
E info@mennokroon.nl
W www.mennokroon.nl

Morlang [21]
Keizersgracht 451
1017 DK Amsterdam
T +31 20 625 2681
E mail@morlang.nl
W www.morlang.nl

The Nijntje Shop [23]
Beethovenstraat 71
1077 HP Amsterdam
T +31 20 671 9707
E winkel@dewinkelvannijntje.nl
W www.dewinkelvannijntje.nl

Paul Warmer [25]
Leidsestraat 41
1017 NV Amsterdam
T +31 20 427 8011
E paul@paulwarmer.com

P.G.C. Hajenius [24]
Rokin 92–96
1012 KZ Amsterdam
T +31 20 623 7494
E info@hajenius.com
W www.hajenius.com

Pol's Potten [23]
KNSM-Laan 39
1019 LA Amsterdam
T +31 20 419 3541
E info@polspotten.nl
W www.polspotten.nl

Pompadour [17]
Huidenstraat 12
1016 ES Amsterdam
T +31 20 623 9554

Puccini Bomboni [23]
Staalstraat 17
1011 JK Amsterdam
T +31 20 626 5474
E info@puccinibomboni.com
W www.puccinibomboni.com

Pygma-Lion [18]
Nieuwe Spiegelstraat 5a
1017 DB Amsterdam
T +31 20 420 7022
E info@pygma-lion.com
W www.pygma-lion.com

Seven One Seven [10]
Prinsengracht 717
1017 JW Amsterdam
T +31 20 427 0717
E info@717hotel.nl
W www.717hotel.nl

Spring [17]
Willemsparkweg 177
1071 GZ Amsterdam
T +31 20 675 4421
E info@restaurantspring.nl
W www.restaurantspring.nl

Supperclub Cruise [19]
Ruyterkade Pier 14
Amsterdam
T +31 20 344 6403
E info@supperclub.nl
W www.supperclub.com

De Taart van m'n Tante [18]
Ferdinand Bolstraat 10
1072 LJ Amsterdam
T +31 20 776 4600
E info@detaart.nl
W www.detaart.nl

Tempo Doeloe [19]
Utrechtsestraat 75
1017 VJ Amsterdam
T +31 20 625 6718
W www.tempodoeloerestaurant.nl

Torch [27]
Lauriergracht 94
1016 RN Amsterdam
T +31 20 626 0284
E mail@torchgallery.com
W www.torchgallery.com

Vakzuid [17]
Olympisch Stadion 35
1076 DE Amsterdam
T +31 20 570 8400
E info@vakzuid.nl
W www.vakzuid.nl

Van Gogh Museum [27]
Paulus Potterstraat 7
1071 CX Amsterdam
T +31 20 570 5200
E info@vangoghmuseum.nl
W www.vangoghmuseum.nl

Van Ravenstein [23]
Keizersgracht 359
1016 EJ Amsterdam
T +31 20 639 0067
W www.van-ravenstein.nl

Vivian Hann [25]
Haarlemmerdijk 102
1013 JG Amsterdam
T +31 6 2204 9465

W139 [27]
Warmoesstraat 139
1012 JB Amsterdam
T +31 20 622 9434
E info@w139.nl
W www.w139.nl

Walem [21]
Keizersgracht 449
1017 DK Amsterdam

T +31 20 625 3544
E walem@diningcity.com

Westergasfabriek [27]
Haarlemmerweg 8–10
1014 BE Amsterdam
T +31 20 586 0710
E info@westergasfabriek.nl
W www.westergasfabriek.nl

Winston [11]
Warmoesstraat 129
1012 JA Amsterdam
T +31 20 623 1380
E winston@winston.nl
W www.winston.nl

Wynand Fockink [21]
Pijlsteeg 31
1012 HH Amsterdam
T +31 20 639 2695
E info@wynand-fockink.nl
W www.wynand-fockink.nl

ANTWERP

Ann Demeulemeester [39]
38 Verlatstraat
Antwerp 2000
T +32 3 216 0133

Den Artist Brasserie [34]
45 Museumstraat
Antwerp 2000
T +32 3 238 0995

**Augustinus
Muziekcentrum** [41]
81 Kammenstraat
Antwerp 2000
T +32 3 202 4669
E info@amuz.be
W www.amuz.be

Bar Tabac [37]
43 Waalse Kaai
Antwerp 2000
T +32 3 238 1937
W www.bartabac.be

Bassin [34]
1 Tavernierkaai
Antwerp 2000
T +32 3 225 3637
W www.bassin.be

Berlin [41]
1–3 Kleine Markt
Antwerp 2000
T +32 3 227 1101

Brasserie National [43]
32 Nationalestraat
Antwerp 2000
T +32 3 227 5656
E info@nationalantwerp.be
W www.nationalantwerp.be

Burie [38]
3 Korte Gasthuisstraat
Antwerp 2000
T +32 3 232 3688
E info@chobel.be
W www.chobel.be

Café Beveren [35]
2 Vlasmarkt
Antwerp 2000
T +32 3 231 2225
E info@cafebeveren.com
W www.cafebeveren.com

Centraal Station [43]
Koningin Astridplein

Antwerp 2000
W www.b-rail.be

Charles Rogier XI [33]
11 Karel Rogierstraat
Antwerp 2000
T +32 3 475 299 989
e charlesrogierxi@skynet.be
W www.charlesrogierxi.be

Copyright Bookshop [43]
28a Nationalestraat
Antwerp 2000
T +32 3 232 9416
E info@copyrightbookshop.be
W www.modenatie.com

Désiré de Lille [37]
14–18 Schrijnwerkersstraat
Antwerp 2000
T +32 3 232 6226
E info@desiredelille.be
W www.desiredelille.be

Designcenter de Winkelhaak [43]
26 Lange Winkelhaakstraat
Antwerp 2060
T +32 3 727 1030
E info@winkelhaak.be
W www.winkelhaak.be

Diamantmuseum [43]
19–23 Koningin Astridplein
Antwerp 2018
T +32 3 202 4890
E info@diamant.provant.be
W www.diamantmuseum.be

Dôme [35]
2 Grote Hondstraat
Antwerp 2018
T +32 3 239 9003
W www.domeweb.be

Dôme sur Mer [35]
1 Arendstraat
Antwerp 2018
T +32 3 281 7433

L'Entrepot du Congo [37]
42 Vlaamse Kaai
Antwerp 2000
T +32 3 238 9232

Fish & Chips [41]
36–38 Kammenstraat
Antwerp 2000
T +32 3 227 0824
E info@fishandchips.be
W www.fishandchips.be

Flamant [39]
12–14 Lange Gasthuisstraat
Antwerp 2000
T +32 3 226 7760
E flamant.antwerpen@flamant.com
W www.flamant.com

Galalith [39]
42 Zirkstraat
Antwerp 2000
T +32 3 231 4751

Goossens [38]
31 Korte Gasthuisstraat
Antwerp 2000
T +32 3 226 0791

Grand Café Horta [43]
2 Hopland
Antwerp
T +32 3 232 2815
E info@grandcafehorta.be
W www.grandcafehorta.be

Hippodroom [34]
10 Leopold de Waelplaats
Antwerp 2000
T +32 3 248 5252
E resto@hippodroom.be
W www.hippodroom.be

Hotel 't Sandt [35]
13–19 Zand
Antwerp 2000
T +32 3 232 9390
E info@hotel-sandt.be
W www.hotel-sandt.be

Huis A Boon [38]
2–4 Lombardenvest
Antwerp 2000
T +32 3 232 3387

Justitiepaleis [43]
20 Bolivarplaats
Antwerp 2000
T +32 3 257 8011

King Kong [37]
58 Volkstraat
Antwerp 2000
T +32 3 216 3777
W www.kingkong.be

Kledingzaak [41]
28 Oever
Antwerp 2000
T +32 3 225 5221

De Kleine Zavel [35]
2 Stoofstraat
Antwerp 2000
T +32 3 231 9691

**Koninklijk Museum voor
Schone Kunsten** [43]
2 Leopold de Waelplaats
Antwerp 2000
T +32 3 238 7809
W www.kmska.be

Louis [39]
2 Lombardenstraat
Antwerp 2000
T +32 3 232 9872

Lux [34]
13 Adriaan Brouwerstraat
Antwerp 2000
T +32 3 233 3030
E info@luxantwerp.com
W www.luxantwerp.com

ModeMuseum [43]
28 Nationalestraat
Antwerp 2000
T +32 3 470 2770
E info@momu.be
W www.momu.be

ModeNatie [43]
28 Nationalstraat
Antwerp 2000
T +32 3 226 1447
E info@modenatie.be
W www.modenatie.com

Het Modepaleis [41]
16 Nationalestraat
Antwerp 2000
T +32 3 470 2510
E info@driesvannoten.be
W www.driesvannoten.be

**Museum van Hedendaagse
Kunst Antwerpen** [43]
32 Leuvenstraat
Antwerp 2000

T +32 3 260 9999
E info@muhka.be
W www.muhka.be

**Onze-Lieve-
Vrouwekathedraal** [43]
21 Groenplaats
Antwerp 2000
T +32 3 213 9951
E info@dekathedraal.be
W www.dekathedraal.be

Philip's Biscuits [38]
11 Korte Gasthuisstraat
Antwerp 2000
T +32 3 231 2660

Het Pomphuis [34]
7 Siberiastraat
Antwerp 2030
T +32 3 770 8625
E info@hetpomphuis.be
W www.hetpomphuis.be

Prêt à Partir [41]
110 Nationalestraat
Antwerp 2000
T +32 3 225 0577
W www.pretapartir.be

**Provinciaal Museum
voor Fotografie** [43]
47 Waalse Kaai
Antwerp 2000
T +32 3 242 9300
E info@fotografie.provant.be
W www.fotomuseum.be

Restaurant Bernardin [34]
17 Sint-Jacobsstraat
Antwerp 2000
T +32 3 213 0700
W www.restaurantbernardin.be

Rubenshuis [43]
9–11 Wapper
Antwerp 2000
T +32 3 201 1555
E info.rubenshuis@stad.antwerpen.be
W http://museum.antwerpen.be/
rubenshuis

Slapen Enzo [33]
20 Karel Rogierstraat
Antwerp 2000
T +32 3 216 2785
E info@slapenenzo.be
W www.slapenenzo.be

Soep & Soup [41]
89 Kammenstraat
Antwerp 2000
T +32 3 707 2805

De Vagant [37]
25 Reyndersstraat
Antwerp 2000
T +32 3 233 1538
E info@devagant.be
W www.devagant.be

Véronique Branquinho [41]
73 Nationalestraat
Antwerp 2000
T +32 3 233 6616
E info@veroniquebranquinho.be
W www.veroniquebranquinho.com

Verso [39]
11 Lange Gasthuisstraat
Antwerp 2000
T +32 3 226 9292
E info@verso.be
W www.verso.be

Violetta & Vera Pepa [41]
24 Nationalestraat
Antwerp 2000
T +32 3 238 0021
E info@pepa.be
W www.pepa.be

Walter [38]
10 Sint-Antoniusstraat
Antwerp 2000
T +32 3 213 2644
E walterstore@skynet.be
W www.waltervanbeirendonck.com

De Witte Lelie [32]
16–18 Keizerstraat
Antwerp 2000
T +32 3 226 1966
E hotel@dewittelelie.be
W www.dewittelelie.be

Zoo Antwerpen [43]
26 Koningin Astridplein
Antwerp 2018
T +32 3 202 4540
W www.zooantwerpen.be

ATHENS

48 The Restaurant [54]
48 Armatolon & Klefton
Ambelokipi 11471 Athens
T +30 210 641 1082
E 48_ilta@otenet.gr
W www.48therestaurant.com

Aristera Dexia [52]
140 Pireos & 3 Andronikou
Rouf, Athens
T +30 210 342 2380/2606
E info@aristeradexia.gr
W www.aristeradexia.gr

Aristokratikon [64]
9 Karagiorgi Servias
Syntagma 10563 Athens
T +30 210 322 0546
W www.aristokratikon.com

Astir Palace Resort [51]
40 Apollonos
Vouliagmeni 16671 Athens
T +30 210 890 2000
E reservation@astir.gr
W www.astir-palace.com

Athens Arena [57]
166 Pireos
11854 Athens
T +30 210 942 5754
E info@athenspantheon.com
W www.athenspantheon.com

Athinais [63]
34–36 Kastorias
Votanikos 10447 Athens
T +30 210 348 0000
E athinais@athinais.com.gr
W www.athinais.com.gr

Balthazar [57]
27 Veranzerou
Ambelokipi, Athens
T +30 210 644 1215
E info@balthazar.gr
W www.balthazar.gr

Balux [57]
58 Leof Posidonos
Glyfada 16674 Athens
T +30 210 894 1620
E escape@balux-septem.com
W www.balux-septem.com

Benaki Museum [63]
1 Koumbari & Vassilissis Sofias
Kolonaki 10674 Athens
T 30 210 367 1000
E benaki@benaki.gr
W www.benaki.gr

Café Avyssinia [57]
7 Kinetou, Avyssinia Square
Monastiraki 10555 Athens
T +30 210 321 4047
E info@avissinia.gr
W www.avissinia.gr

Eleftheroudakis [59]
17 Panepistimiou
10564 Athens
T +30 210 325 8440
E elebooks@books.gr
W www.books.gr

Fanourakis [59]
23 Patriarchou Ioakim
Kolonaki 10675 Athens
T +30 210 721 1762
E fanourakis@altecnet.gr
W www.fanourakis.gr

Frame [57]
1 Dinokratous, Plateia Dexameni
Kolonaki 10675 Athens
T +30 210 721 4368

Gaia Centre [63]
100 Othonos
Kifissia 14562 Athens
T +30 210 801 5870
E info@gnhm.gr
W www.gnhm.gr

Galaxy Bar [57]
Athens Hilton
46 Vassilissis Sofias
Kolonaki 11528 Athens
T +30 210 728 1000
W www.hilton.co.uk/athens

**Gefsis Me Onomasia
Proelefsis** [54]
317 Kifissias
Kifissia, Athens
T +30 210 800 1402

**Goulandris Museum
of Cycladic Art** [64]
4 Neofytou Douka
Kolonaki 10674 Athens
T +30 210 722 8321
E info@cycladic-m.gr
W www.cycladic-m.gr

**Goulandris Museum
of Natural History** [64]
13 Levidou
Kifissia 14562 Athens
T +30 210 801 5870
E info@gnhm.gr
W www.gnhm.gr

Hadzilias [59]
21 Voulis
Syntagma, Athens
T +30 210 321 9591

Half Note Jazz Club [57]
17 Trivonianou
Mets 11636 Athens
T +30 210 921 3310
W www.halfnote.gr

Hotel Grande Bretagne [49]
Syntagma Square
Syntagma 10563 Athens
T +30 210 333 0000

E info@grandebretagne.gr
W www.grandebretagne.gr

Ideal [54]
46 Panepistimiou
Omonia 10678 Athens
T +30 210 330 3000

**Ilias Lalaounis Jewelry
Museum** [59]
12 Karyatidon & Kallisperi
11742 Athens
T +30 210 922 1044
E info@lalaounis-jewelrymuseum.gr
W www.lalaounis-jewelrymuseum.gr

Island [57]
27th km Leof Athinon-Souniou
Varkiza 16672 Athens
T +30 210 892 5000
E sales@island-central.gr
W www.island-central.gr

Ithaki [53]
28 Apollonos
Vouliagmeni 16671 Athens
T +30 210 896 3747

Jimmy & the Fish [54]
46 Alexandrou Koumoundourou
Piraeus, Athens
T +30 210 412 4417
E info@jimmyandthefish.gr
W www.jimmyandthefish.gr

Kalogirou [59]
4 Patriarchou Ioakim
Kolonaki 10674 Athens
T +30 210 335 6401
E info@lemonis.gr
W www.lemonis.gr

Kombologadiko [60]
9 Amerikis
Kolonaki 10672 Athens
T +30 210 700 0500
E info@kombologadiko.gr
W www.kombologadiko.gr

Krisa Gi [52]
23 Agiou Konstantinou
Maroussi, Athens
T +30 210 8056666

Liana Vourakis [61]
42 Pindarou
Kolonaki 10673 Athens
T +30 210 361 9441

Life Gallery Athens [48]
103 Thiseos
Ekali 14565 Athens
T +30 210 622 0400
E info-lifegallery@bluegr.com
W www.bluegr.com

Martinos [60]
50 Pandrossou
Plaka 10555 Athens
T +30 210 321 3110
E martinof@otenet.gr
W www.martinosart.gr

Mastiha Shop [61]
6 Panepistimiou & Kriezotou
Syntagma 10671 Athens
T +30 210 363 2750
E info@matihashop.com
W www.mastihashop.com

Mihalarias Art [64]
260 Kifissias & Diligianni
Kifissia 14562 Athens
T +30 210 623 4320

E art@mihalarias.gr
W www.mihalarias.gr

National Gardens [64]
Irodou Attikou
Syntagma 10563 Athens

Odeon of Herodes Atticus [63]
Dionisou Areopagitou
Athens
T +30 210 323 2771

Old Athens [61]
1–3 Argiropoulou & Levidou
Kifissia, Athens
T +30 210 801 7023

Papadakis Restaurant [53]
15 Fokilidou
Kolonaki, Athens
T +30 210 360 8621

Planet Earth [60]
7 Ploutarchou
Kolonaki 10675 Athens
T +30 210 729 3690
E kkhats@otenet.gr
Workshop:
17 Dorileou
11521 Athens
T +30 210 645 5821

Prytaneion [57]
37 Kolokotroni, Kefalari Square
Kifissia 14562 Athens
T +30 210 808 9160
E info@prytaneion.gr
W www.prytaneion.gr

Semiramis Hotel [50]
48 Harilaou Trikoupi
Kifissia 14562 Athens
T +30 210 628 4400
E info@semiramisathens.com
W www.semiramisathens.com

**Spathario Museum
of Shadow Theatre** [64]
Vassilissis Sofias & D. Ralli
Kastalias Square
Maroussi 15124 Athens
T +30 210 612 7245
E info@karagiozismuseum.gr
W www.karagiozismuseum.gr

Spondi [53]
5 Pyrronos, Varnavas Square
Pangrati 11636 Athens
T +30 210 752 0658
E spondi@relaischateaux.com
W www.spondi.gr

Ta Kioupia [55]
2 Olympionikon & Dexamenis
Politia Square
Kifissia 14563 Athens
T +30 210 620 0005

To Ouzadiko [52]
25–29 Karneadou
Kolonaki, Athens
T +30 210 729 5484

Varoulko [55]
80 Pireos
Keramicos 10435 Athens
T +30 210 522 8400
E info@varoulko.gr
W www.varoulko.gr

BARCELONA

Antonio Miró [86]
Carrer del Consell de Cent, 349

08007 Barcelona
T +34 93 487 06 70

Bad Habits [85]
Carrer de València, 261
08007 Barcelona
T +34 93 487 22 59

La Balsa [81]
Carrer Infanta Isabel, 4
08022 Barcelona
T +34 93 211 50 48

Bar Bodega Teo [83]
Carrer d'Ataulf, 18
Barcelona
T +34 93 315 11 59

Borneo [82]
Carrer del Rec, 49
08003 Barcelona
T +34 93 268 23 89

Botafumeiro [78]
Carrer Gran de Gràcia, 81
08012 Barcelona
T +34 93 218 42 30

Cacao Sampaka [85]
Carrer del Consell de Cent, 292
08007 Barcelona
T +34 93 272 08 33
E bc1@cacaosampaka.com
W www.cacaosampaka.com

Cafè Salambó [83]
Carrer de Torrijos, 51
08012 Barcelona
T +34 93 218 69 66
E cafesalambo@telefonica.net
W www.cafesalambo.com

Casa Almirall [81]
Carrer de Joaquín Costa, 33
08001 Barcelona
T +34 93 318 99 17
E casalmirall@telefonica.net

Casa Batlló [88]
Passeig de Gràcia, 43
08007 Barcelona
T +34 93 488 06 66
E infovisites@casabatllo.es
W www.casabatllo.es

Casa Camper [75]
Carrer d'Elisabets, 11
08001 Barcelona
T +34 93 342 62 80
E barcelona@casacamper.com
W www.casacamper.com

Casa Leopoldo [78]
Carrer Sant Rafael, 24
08001 Barcelona
T +34 93 441 30 14
W www.casaleopoldo.com

Cata 1.81 [82]
Carrer de València, 181
08011 Barcelona
T +34 93 323 68 18
E cata181@hotmail.com
W www.cata181.com

La Central [86]
Carrer d'Elisabets, 6
08001 Barcelona
T +34 93 317 02 93
E informacio@lacentral.com
W www.lacentral.com

Cinc Sentits [77]
Carrer d'Aribau, 58

08011 Barcelona
T +34 93 323 94 90
E info@cincsentits.com
W www.cincsentits.com

Comerç 24 [79]
Carrer del Comerç, 24
08003 Barcelona
T +34 93 319 21 02
E info@comerc24.com
W www.comerc24.com

Comité [85]
Carrer del Notariat, 8
08001 Barcelona
T +34 93 317 68 813

E&A Gispert [85]
Carrer dels Sombrerers, 23
08003 Barcelona
T +34 93 319 75 35
E info@casagispert.com
W www.casagispert.com

Escribà [81]
Rambla de les Flors, 83
08002 Barcelona
T +34 93 301 60 27
E rambla@escriba.es
W www.escriba.es

Església Santa Maria del Mar [90]
Plaça de Santa Maria, 1
08003 Barcelona
T +34 93 310 23 90

Fernández [78]
Passeig de Gràcia, 116
08008 Barcelona
T +34 93 238 48 46
E fernandez@fernandezbcn.com
W www.fernandezbcn.com

FoodBall [77]
Carrer d'Elisabets, 9
08001 Barcelona
T +34 93 270 13 63
W www.camper.com

Fundació Antoni Tàpies [89]
Carrer d'Aragó, 255
08007 Barcelona
T +34 93 487 03 15
W www.fundaciotapies.org

Fundació Joan Miró [88]
Avinguda de Miramar
Parc de Montjuïc
08038 Barcelona
T +34 93 443 94 70
E fjmiro@bcn.fjmiro.es
W www.bcn.fjmiro.es

Gimlet [82]
Carrer del Rec, 24
08003 Barcelona
T +34 93 310 10 27

Gotham [87]
Carrer de Cervantes, 7
08002 Barcelona
T +34 93 412 46 47
E gotham@gotham-bcn.com
W www.gotham-bcn.com

Gran Hotel la Florida [70]
Carretera de Vallvidrera al
Tibidabo, 83–89
08035 Barcelona
T +34 93 259 30 00
E info@hotellaflorida.biz
W www.hotellaflorida.com

Granja Dulcinea [81]
Carrer de Petritxol, 2
08001 Barcelona
T +34 93 302 68 24

Herboristeria del Rei [86]
Carrer del Vidre, 1
08002 Barcelona
T +34 93 318 05 12
W www.herboristeriadelrei.com

Hipòtesi [85]
Rambla de Catalunya, 105
08008 Barcelona
T +34 93 215 02 98
E hipotesi@sct.ictnet.es

Hotel Banys Orientals [73]
Carrer de l'Argentería, 37
08003 Barcelona
T +34 93 268 84 60
E reservas@hotelbanysorientals.com
W www.hotelbanysorientals.com

Hotel Neri [71]
Carrer de Sant Sever, 5
08002 Barcelona
T +34 93 304 06 55
E info@hotelneri.com
W www.hotelneri.com

Hotel Omm [74]
Carrer del Rosselló, 265
08008 Barcelona
T +34 93 445 40 00
E reservas@hotelomm.es
W www.hotelomm.es

Iguapop Gallery & Shop [87]
Carrer del Comerç, 15
08003 Barcelona
T +34 93 319 68 13
E info@iguapop.net
W www.iguapop.net

Lobby [85]
Carrer de la Ribera, 5
08003 Barcelona
T +34 93 319 38 55
E lobby@lobby-bcn.com
W www.lobby-bcn.com

La Maseria de la Boqueria [90]
La Rambla, 91
08002 Barcelona

Mau Mau [83]
Carrer Fontrodona, 33
08004 Barcelona
T +34 93 441 80 15
E info@maumaunderground.com
W www.maumaunderground.com

Mercat de Santa Caterina [88]
Avinguda de Francesc Cambó
Barcelona

**Mercat de la Boqueria
Sant Josep** [90]
La Rambla, 85–89
08002 Barcelona

Orígens 99.9% [87]
Carrer de la Vidrieria, 6–8
08003 Barcelona
T +34 93 310 75 31
E origen99@origen99.com
W www.origen99.com

La Paloma [81]
Carrer del Tigre, 27
08001 Barcelona
T +34 93 301 68 97
E lapaloma@lapaloma-bcn.com

W www.lapaloma-bcn.com

Parc Güell [89]
Carrer d'Olot
08024 Barcelona

Park Hotel [72]
Avinguda Marquès de l'Argentera, 11
08003 Barcelona
T +34 93 319 60 00
E info@parkhotelbarcelona.com
W www.parkhotelbarcelona.com

Passadís del Pep [79]
Plaça de Palau, 2
08003 Barcelona
T +34 93 310 10 21
E restaurant@passadis.com
W www.passadis.com

Pavelló Barcelona [90]
Avinguda del Marquès de Comillas
08038 Barcelona
T +34 93 423 40 16
E pavello@miesbcn.com
W www.miesbcn.com

La Pedrera at Night [81]
Passeig de Gràcia, 92
08008 Barcelona
T +34 93 484 59 00

Pinotxo [90]
La Boqueria, 66
08002 Barcelona
T +34 93 317 17 31

Pitín Bar [82]
Passeig del Born, 34
08003 Barcelona
T +34 93 319 50 87
E pitinbar@mx2.redestb.es

Plastic Bar [82]
Passeig del Born, 19
08003 Barcelona

Els Quatre Gats [81]
Carrer de Montsió, 3 bis
08002 Barcelona
T +34 93 302 41 40
W www.4gats.com

Quimet i Quimet [79]
Carrer del Poeta Cabanyes, 25
08004 Barcelona
T +34 93 442 31 42

El Racó d'en Freixa [77]
Carrer de Sant Elíes, 22
08006 Barcelona
T +34 93 209 75 59
W www.elracodenfreixa.com

Romesco [77]
Carrer de Sant Pau, 28
08001 Barcelona
T +34 93 318 93 81

Sita Murt [85]
Carrer d'Avinyó, 18
08002 Barcelona
T +34 93 301 00 06
W www.sitamurt.com

So_Da [85]
Carrer d'Avinyó, 24
08002 Barcelona
T +34 93 412 27 76

Tèxtil Café [82]
Museu de Tèxtil i Indumentària
Carrer de Montcada, 12
08003 Barcelona

T +34 93 268 25 98
E info@textilcafe.com
W www.textilcafe.com

La Venta [77]
Plaça del Doctor Andreu
08035 Barcelona
T +34 93 212 64 55

Vila Viniteca [85]
Carrer dels Agullers, 7
08003 Barcelona
T +34 93 268 32 27
E info@vilaviniteca.es
W www.vilaviniteca.es

La Vinya del Senyor [82]
Plaça de Santa Maria, 5
08003 Barcelona
T +34 93 310 33 79

El Xampanyet [77]
Carrer de Montcada, 22
08003 Barcelona
T +34 93 319 70 03

[Z]INK [85]
Carrer d'Avinyó, 14
08002 Barcelona
T +34 93 342 62 88

BERLIN

Adidas Originals Berlin [109]
Münzstraße 13–15
10178 Berlin
T +49 30 2759 4381
E berlin.store@adidas.de
W www.adidas.com/de

Berlinomat [109]
Frankfurter Allee 89
10247 Berlin
T +49 30 4208 1445
E info@berlinomat.com
W www.berlinomat.com

Breathe [107]
Rochstraße 17
10178 Berlin
T +49 30 4424 2577
E welcome@breathe-cosmetics.com
W www.breathe-cosmetics.com

Brot und Rosen [101]
Am Friedrichshain 6
10407 Berlin
T +49 30 423 1916

Café Adler [101]
Friedrichstraße 206
10969 Berlin
T +49 30 251 8965

Café am Neuen See [105]
Lichtensteinallee 2
10787 Berlin
T +49 30 254 4930

Café Einstein [103]
Kurfürstenstraße 58
10785 Berlin
T +49 30 261 5096
E contact@cafeeinstein.com
W www.cafeeinstein.com

Café Schönbrunn [105]
Am Friedrichshain 8
10407 Berlin
T +49 30 4202 819

Chocolaterie Estrellas [108]
Akazienstraße 21
10823 Berlin

T +49 30 7895 6646

Claudia Skoda [108]
Alte Schönhauser Straße 35
10789 Berlin
T +49 30 280 7211
E contact@claudiaskoda.com
W www.claudiaskoda.com

Dachgarten [102]
Reichstag, Platz der Republik 1
11011 Berlin
T +49 30 2262 9933

Dorint am Gendarmenmarkt [98]
Charlottenstraße 50–52
10117 Berlin
T +49 30 203 750
E h5342@accor.com
W www.dorint.com

Engelbecken [103]
Witzlebenstraße 31
14057 Berlin
T +49 30 615 2810
W www.engelbecken.de

Facil [101]
Potsdamer Straße 3
10785 Berlin
T +49 30 5900 51234
W www.facil-berlin.de

Felsenkeller [105]
Akazienstraße 2
10823 Berlin
T +49 30 781 3447

Fiona Bennett [107]
Große Hamburger Straße 25
10115 Berlin
T +49 30 2809 6330
E info@fionabennett.com
W www.fionabennett.com

Hamburger Bahnhof [111]
Invalidenstraße 50–51
10557 Berlin
T +49 30 3978 3411
E hbf@smb.spk-berlin.de
W www.hamburgerbahnhof.de

Hotel Adlon Kempinski [96]
Unter den Linden 77
10117 Berlin
T +49 30 22 610
E adlon@kempinski.com
W www.hotel-adlon.de

Hotel Brandenburger Hof [99]
Eislebener Straße 14
10789 Berlin
T +49 30 214 050
E info@brandenburger-hof.com
W www.brandenburger-hof.com

Hut Up [107]
Oranienburger Straße 32
10117 Berlin
T +49 30 2838 6105
E shop@hutup.de
W www.hutup.de

Die Imaginäre Manufaktur [109]
Oranienstraße 26
10999 Berlin
T +49 30 2850 30121
W www.blindenanstalt.de

Jules Verne [102]
Schlüterstraße 61
10625 Berlin
T +49 30 3180 9410
E info@jules-verne-berlin.de

W www.jules-verne-berlin.de

KaDeWe [107]
Tauentzienstraße 21–24
10789 Berlin
T +49 30 21210
E info@kadewe.de
W www.kadewe.de

Kumpelnest 3000 [105]
Lützowstraße 23
10785 Berlin
T +49 30 261 6918
W www.kumpelnest3000.com

Kunst-Werke Berlin [111]
Auguststraße 69
10117 Berlin
T +49 30 243 4590
E info@kw-berlin.de
W www.kw-berlin.de

Little Red Riding Hood [107]
Quartier 206/1
Friedrichstraße 71
10117 Berlin
T +49 30 2045 5619
E shop@littleredridinghood.de
W www.littleredridinghood.de

Lubitsch [101]
Bleibtreustraße 47
10623 Berlin
T +49 30 882 3756

Lutter & Wegner [102]
Schlüterstraße 55
10629 Berlin
T +49 30 881 3440
E lutterundwegner@gmx.de
W www.restaurantlutterundwegner.de

Mauerpark [111]
Eberswalder Straße & Gleimstraße
Berlin

Newton Bar [104]
Charlottenstraße 56
10117 Berlin
T +49 30 2029 5421
E info@newton-bar.de
W www.newton-bar.de

Nix [108]
Oranienburger Straße 32
10117 Berlin
T +49 30 281 8044
W www.nix.de

Noesa [107]
Behrenstraße 29
10117 Berlin
E contact@noesa.com
W http://noesa.com

Ottenthal [101]
Kantstraße 153
10623 Berlin
T +49 30 313 3162
E restaurant@ottenthal.com
W www.ottenthal.de

Paris Bar [101]
Kantstraße 152
10623 Berlin
T +49 30 313 8052
W www.parisbar.de

Pasternak [105]
Knaackstraße 22–24
10405 Berlin
T +49 30 441 3399
E info@restaurant-pasternak.de
W www.restaurant-pasternak.de

Pfefferberg [111]
Fehrbelliner Straße 92
10119 Berlin
T +49 30 4438 3485
E public@pfefferberg.de
W www.pfefferberg.de

Pratergarten/Hecht Club [104]
Kastanienallee 7–9
10435 Berlin
T +49 30 448 5688
W www.pratergarten.de

Pro QM [107]
Almstadtstraße 48
10119 Berlin
T +49 30 2472 8520
E info@pro-qm.de
W www.pro-qm.de

Q! [97]
Knesebeckstraße 67
10623 Berlin
T +49 30 810 0660
E q-berlin@loock-hotels.com
W www.loock-hotels.com/hotelq

Sale e Tabacchi [102]
Kochstraße 18
10969 Berlin
T +49 30 252 1155
E saleetabacchi@aol.com
W www.gourmetguide.com/
saleetabacchi

Sammlung Hoffmann [111]
Sophie-Gips-Höfe, Sophienstraße 21
10178 Berlin
T +49 30 2849 9121
E sammlung@sophie-gips.de
W www.sophie-gips.de

Storch [101]
Wartburgstraße 54
10823 Berlin
T +49 30 784 2059
E storch@sehrgut.de
W www.storch-berlin.de

Tacheles [111]
Oranienburger Straße 54–56a
10117 Berlin
T +49 30 282 6185
E office@tacheles.de
W www.tacheles.de

Tiergarten [111]
Straße des 17 Juni 1
10785 Berlin

Topographie des Terrors [111]
Niederkirchnerstraße 8
10963 Berlin
T +49 30 2548 6703
E info@topographie.de
W www.topographie.de

Trippen [107]
Rosenthaler Straße 40/41
10178 Berlin
T +49 30 2839 1337
E info@trippen.com
W www.trippen-shoes.com

Würgeengel [104]
Dresdener Straße 122
10997 Berlin
T +49 30 615 5560

BRUSSELS

À la Bécasse [121]
11 rue de Tabora
Brussels 1000

T +32 2 511 0006

Annemie Verbeke [123]
64 rue Antoine Dansaert
Brussels 1000
T +32 2 511 2171
W www.annemieverbeke.be

L'Archiduc [123]
6 rue Antoine Dansaert
Brussels 1000
T +32 2 512 0652
E info@archiduc.net
W www.archiduc.net

Atomium [128]
Square de l'Atomium
Brussels 1020
T +32 2 475 4777
E info@atomium.be
W www.atomium.be

Aux Vieux Bruxelles [119]
35 rue Saint-Boniface
Brussels 1050
T +32 2 503 3111
E info@auvieuxbruxelles.be
W www.auvieuxbruxelles.com

Belga Queen [119]
32 rue du Fossé-aux-Loups
Brussels 1000
T +32 2 217 2187
E brussels@belgaqueen.be
W www.belgaqueen.be

Belgo Belge [119]
20 rue de la Paix
Brussels 1050
T +32 2 511 1121
E info@belgobelge.be
W www.belgobelge.be

Bonsoir Clara [123]
22–26 rue Antoine Dansaert
Brussels 1000
T +32 2 502 0990

Bozar (Palais des Beaux-Arts) [128]
23 rue Ravenstein
Brussels 1000
T +32 2 507 8444
W www.bozar.be

Café Belga [127]
place Eugène Flagey Plein
Brussels 1050
T +32 2 640 3508
W www.cafebelga.be

Centre Belge de la Bande Dessinée [127]
20 rue des Sables
Brussels 1000
T +32 2 219 1980
E visit@cbbd.be
W www.comicscentre.net

Chambres en Ville [116]
19 rue de Londres
Brussels 1050
T +32 2 512 9290
E ph.guilmin@belgacom.net

Christa Reniers [123]
29 rue Antoine Dansaert
Brussels 1000
T +32 2 510 0660
E info@christareniers.com
W www.christareniers.com

Christophe Coppens [124]
2 rue Léon Lepage

Brussels 1000
T +32 2 512 7797
Atelier:
23 place du Nouveau Marché
aux Grains
Brussels 1000
T +32 2 538 0813
E info@christophecoppens.com
W www.christophecoppens.com

Le Cirio [121]
18–20 rue de la Bourse
Brussels 1000
T +32 2 512 1395

Comme Chez Soi [119]
23 place Rouppe
Brussels 1000
T +32 2 512 2921
E info@commechezsoi.be
W www.commechezsoi.be

Comptoir Florian [119]
17 rue Saint-Boniface
Brussels 1050
T +32 2 513 9103

Cospaia [119]
1 Capitaine Crespel
Brussels 1050
T +32 2 513 0303
E info@cospaia.be
W www.cospaia.be

Dandoy [127]
31 rue au Beurre
Brussels
T +32 2 511 0326
W www.biscuiteriedandoy.be

Delvaux [124]
27 boulevard de Waterloo
Brussels 1000
T +32 2 513 0502
31 Gallerie de la Reine
Brussels 1000
T +32 2 512 7198
E info@delvaux.com
W www.delvaux.com

Design Flanders [123]
19 Kanselarijstraat
Brussels 1000
T +32 2 227 6060
E info@designflanders.be
W www.designflanders.be

Emery & Cie [125]
27 rue de l'Hôpital
Brussels 1000
T +32 2 513 5892
E brussels@emeryetcie.com
W www.emeryetcie.com

Flagey [127]
place Sainte-Croix
Brussels 1050
T +32 2 641 1020
E info@flagey.be
W www.flagey.be

Goupil le Fol [121]
22 rue de la Violette
Brussels 1000
T +32 2 511 1396

Le Greenwich [121]
7 rue des Chartreux
Brussels 1000
T +32 2 511 4167

L'Idiot du Village [119]
19 rue Notre-Seigneur
Brussels 1000

T +32 2 502 5582

L'Image de Nostre Dame [121]
8 rue du Marché aux Herbes
Brussels 1000
T +32 2 219 4249

Jean Paul Knott [123]
20 boulevard Barthelemy
Brussels 1000
T +32 2 514 1835
E contact@jeanpaulknott.com
W www.jeanpaulknott.com

La Manufacture [119]
12 rue Notre Dame du Sommeil
Brussels 1000
T +32 2 502 2525
W www.manufacture.be

Marie [127]
40 rue Alphonse de Witte
Brussels 1050
T +32 2 644 3031

Marolles Flea Market [119]
place du Jeu de Balle
Brussels 1000
T +32 2 648 8746

Martin Margiela [123]
40 rue Léon Lepage
Brussels 1000
T +32 2 223 7520
W www.maisonmartinmargiela.com

Modo Bruxelles [123]
38 rue Léon Lepage
Brussels 1000
T +32 2 502 5264
E info@modobruxellae.be
W www.modobruxellae.be

Monty [117]
101 boulevard Brand Whitlock
Brussels 1200
T +32 2 734 5636
E info@monty-hotel.be
W www.monty-hotel.be

Musée David et Alice van Buuren [128]
41 avenue Léo Errara
Brussels 1180
T +32 2 343 4851
E info@museumvanbuuren.be
W www.museumvanbuuren.com

Musée Horta [127]
25 rue Américaine
Brussels 1060
T +32 2 543 0490
E info@hortamuseum.be
W www.hortamuseum.be

Musée des Instruments de Musique [127]
2 rue Montagne-de-la-Cour
Brussels 1000
T +32 2 545 0130
W www.mim.fgov.be

Musées Royaux des Beaux-Arts [128]
3 rue de la Régence
Brussels 1000
T +32 2 508 3211
W www.kmskb.be

Nicolas Woit [123]
80 rue Antoine Dansaert
Brussels 1000
T +32 2 503 4832
E nicolaswoit@yahoo.fr

W www.nicolaswoit.com

Olivier Strelli [125]
72 avenue Louise
Brussels 1000
T +32 2 512 5607
44 rue Antoine Dansaert
Brussels 1000
T +32 2 512 0942
E olivier@strelli.be
W www.strelli.be

Pierre Marcolini [125]
39 place du Grand Sablon
Brussels 1000
T +32 2 514 1206
E info@marcolini.be
W www.marcolini.be

La Quincaillerie [119]
45 rue du Page
Brussels 1050
T +32 2 533 9833
E info@quincaillerie.be
W www.quincaillerie.be

Restaurant Vincent [119]
8–10 rue des Dominicains
Brussels 1000
T +32 2 511 2607
E info@restaurantvincent.com
W www.restaurantvincent.be

Le Roi des Belges [121]
35–37 rue Jules van Praet
Brussels 1000
T +32 2 503 4300

Royal Windsor Hotel Grand Place [117]
5 rue Duquesnoy
Brussels 1000
T +32 2 505 5555
E resa.royalwindsor@
warkwickhotels.com
W www.royalwindsorbrussels.com

Shampoo & Conditioner [123]
18 rue des Chartreux
Brussels 1000
T +32 2 511 0777
E shampooconditioner_av@yahoo.fr

Stijl [123]
74 rue Antoine Dansaert
Brussels 1000
T +32 2 512 0313

't Kelderke [127]
15 Grand Place
Brussels 1000
T +32 2 513 7344

Toone [121]
21 petite rue des Bouchers
Brussels 1000
T +32 2 513 5486

L'Ultime Atome [119]
14 rue Saint-Boniface
Brussels 1050
T +32 2 511 1367

Wittamer [121]
6 place du Grand Sablon
Brussels 1000
T +32 2 546 1110
E wittamer@wittamer.com
W www.wittamer.com

Y-Dress? [124]
102 rue Antoine Dansaert
Brussels 1000
T +32 2 502 6981

E aleks@ydress.com
W www.ydress.com

Zebra [121]
33 place Saint-Géry
Brussels 1000
T +32 2 511 0901

DUBLIN

Aqua [139]
1 West Pier
Howth, Co. Dublin
T +353 1 832 0690
E dine@aqua.ie
W www.aqua.ie

Avoca Café [143]
11–13 Suffolk Street
Dublin 2
T +353 1 672 6019
E info@avoca.ie
W www.avoca.ie

Bang Café [140]
11 Merrion Row
Dublin 2
T +353 1 676 0898
W www.bangrestaurant.com

Bewley's [144]
78/79 Grafton Street
Dublin 2
T +353 1 672 7720
E info@bewleysgraftonstreet.com
W www.bewleyscafe.com

Brown Thomas [147]
88–95 Grafton Street
Dublin 2
T +353 1 605 6666
W www.brownthomas.com

Cavistons Food Emporium [140]
58/59 Glasthule Road
Sandycove, Co. Dublin
T +353 1 280 9245
E infocavistons.com
W www.cavistons.ie

Chapter One [139]
18/19 Parnell Square
Dublin 1
T +353 1 873 2266
E info@chapteronerestaurant.com
W www.chapteronerestaurant.com

Chica Day/Chica Night [147]
25 and 3–4 Westbury Mall,
Clarendon Street
Dublin 2
T +353 1 671 9836/633 4441

The Clarence [134]
6–8 Wellington Quay
Dublin 2
T +353 1 407 0800
E reservations@theclarence.ie
W www.theclarence.ie

Costume [147]
10 Castle Market
Dublin 2
T +353 1 679 4188

Cross Gallery [147]
59 Francis Street
Dublin 8
T +353 1 473 8978
E info@crossgallery.ie
W www.crossgallery.ie

Davy Byrne's [145]
21 Duke Street

Dublin 2
T +353 1 677 5217
W www.davybyrnes.com

Dolls [147]
32 Westbury Mall, Clarendon Street
Dublin 2
T +353 1 672 9004

Dublin Writers Museum [149]
18 Parnell Square
Dublin 1
T +353 1 872 2077
W www.writersmuseum.com

L'Ecrivain [140]
109a Lower Baggot Street
Dublin 2
T +353 1 661 1919
E enquiries@lecrivain.com
W www.lecrivain.com

Eden [139]
Meeting House Square
Temple Bar, Dublin 2
T +353 1 670 5372
E eden@edenrestaurant.ie
W www.edenrestaurant.ie

Ely Wine Bar [139]
22 Ely Place
Dublin 2
T +353 1 676 8986
E elywine@eircom.net
W www.elywinebar.ie

Fallon & Byrne [139]
11–17 Exchequer Street
Dublin 2
T +353 1 472 1010
W www.fallonandbyrne.com

Farmleigh House [149]
Phoenix Park, Farmleigh
Castleknock, Dublin 15
T +353 1 815 5900
E farmleighinfo@opw.ie
W www.farmleigh.ie

Finnegans [143]
2 Sorrento Road
Dalkey, Co. Dublin
T +353 1 285 8505

The Globe Bar & Café [144]
11 South Great Georges Street
Dublin 2
T +353 1 671 1220
E info@globe.ie
W www.globe.ie

Grafton House [136]
26–27 South Great Georges Street
Dublin 2
T +353 1 679 2041
E booking@graftonguesthouse.com
W www.graftonguesthouse.com

Gruel [143]
68a Dame Street
Dublin 2
T +353 1 670 7119

Guinness Storehouse [148]
St James's Gate
Dublin 8
T +353 1 408 4800
E guinness-storehouse@
guinness.com
W www.guinness-storehouse.com

Irish Museum of Modern Art [148]
Military Road
Kilmainham, Dublin 8

T +353 1 612 9900
E info@imma.ie
W www.imma.ie

Jenny Vander [147]
50 Drury Street
Dublin 2
T +353 1 677 0406

Kehoe's [143]
9 South Anne Street
Dublin 2
T +353 1 677 8312

Liffey Voyage [149]
Bachelors Walk
Dublin
T +353 1 473 4082
E info@liffeyvoyage.ie
W www.liffeyvoyage.ie

Locks [139]
1 Windsor Terrace
Portobello, Dublin 8
T +353 1 454 3391

The Long Hall [143]
51 South Great Georges Street
Dublin 2
T +353 1 475 1590

National Botanic Gardens [148]
Glasnevin
Dublin 9
T +353 1 804 0300
W www.botanicgardens.ie

**No 29 Lower Fitzwilliam
Street** [149]
29 Lower Fitzwilliam Street
Dublin 2
T +353 1 702 6165

Number 31 [135]
31 Leeson Close, Lower Leeson Street
Dublin 2
T +353 1 676 5011
E info@number31.ie
W www.number31.ie

Odessa Club [145]
13 Dame Court
Dublin 2
T +353 1 670 3080
E info@odessaclub.ie
W www.odessaclub.ie

Pembroke Townhouse [137]
90 Pembroke Road
Ballsbridge, Dublin 4
T +353 1 660 0277
E info@pembroketownhouse.ie
W www.pembroketownhouse.ie

Peploe's [139]
16 St Stephen's Green
Dublin 2
T +353 1 676 3144

**The Porterhouse Brewing
Company** [143]
16–18 Parliament Street
Temple Bar, Dublin 2
T +353 1 679 8847
W www.porterhousebrewco.com

Queen of Tarts [144]
4 Cork Hill, Dame Street
Dublin 2
T +353 1 670 7499

**Restaurant Patrick
Guilbauds** [140]
Merrion Hotel, 21 Upper Merrion Street

Dublin 2
T +353 1 676 4192
E reservations@
restaurantpatrickguilbaud.ie
W www.restaurantpatrickguilbaud.ie

Ron Blacks [145]
37 Dawson Street
Dublin 2
T +353 1 672 8231
E info@ronblacks.ie
W www.ronblacks.ie

Smock [147]
Unit 5, 20–22 Essex Street West
Dublin 8
T +353 1 613 9000

Temple Bar Food Market [149]
Meeting House Square
Temple Bar, Dublin 2
T +353 1 677 2255
E info@templebar.ie
W www.templebar.ie

Trocadero Restaurant [139]
3 St Andrew Street
Dublin 2
T +353 1 677 5545
W www.trocadero.ie

Tulle [147]
28 Market Arcade
South Great Georges Street
Dublin 2
T +353 1 679 9115

The Winding Stair [147]
40 Lower Ormond Quay
Dublin 1
T +353 1 872 7320

ISTANBUL

360 İstanbul [164]
İstiklal Caddesi 309/32
Beyoğlu 80600 Istanbul
T +90 212 251 1042
E 360istanbul@360istanbul.com
W www.360istanbul.com

A La Turca [166]
Faikpaşa Yokuşu 4
Çukurcuma 34433 Istanbul
T +90 212 245 2933

Abdulla + Hamam [167]
Halıcılar Çarşısı Caddesi 53
Kapalıçarşı 34440 Istanbul
T +90 212 522 9078
E info@abdulla.com
W www.abdulla.com

A'jia [154]
Kanlıca-Çubuklu Caddesi 27
Kanlıca 34805 Istanbul
T +90 216 413 9300
E info@ajiahotel.com
W www.ajiahotel.com

Anemas Zindanları [172]
Dervişzade Caddesi
Ayvansaray, Istanbul

Aşşk Café [163]
Muallim Naci Caddesi 64/b
Kuruçeşme 34345 Istanbul
T +90 212 265 4734
W www.asskcafe.com

Autoban [166]
Tatar Bey Sokak 1/1
Galata 34420 Istanbul
T +90 212 243 8642

E info@autoban212.com
W www.autoban212.com

Aya Andrea [171]
Mumhane Caddesi 103
Karaköy 34425 Istanbul

Aya İlya [171]
Karanlık Fırın Sokak 6/a
Karaköy 34425 Istanbul

Aya Panteleymon [171]
Hoca Tahsin Sokak 19
Karaköy 34425 Istanbul

Ayasofya Pansiyonları/
Konuk Evi [172]
Soğukçeşme Sokak
Sultanahmet 34400 Istanbul
T +90 212 513 3660
E info@ayasofyapensions.com
W www. ayasofyapensions.com

Balıkçı Sabahattin [158]
Seyit Hasan Kuyu Sokak 50
Sultanahmet 34122 Istanbul
T +90 212 458 1824

Beylerbeyi Sarayı [171]
Abdullahağa Caddesi
Beylerbeyi 34676 Istanbul
T +90 216 321 9320

Bis Wear [168]
Hayriye Sokak 20/3
Çukurcuma 34433 Istanbul
T +90 212 244 7735
E info@biswear.com.tr
W www.biswear.com.tr

Boğaziçi Borsa Restaurant [160]
Lütfi Kırdar Kongre Sarayı
Harbiye 34367 Istanbul
T +90 212 232 4201
E info@borsarestaurants.com
W www.borsarestaurants.com

Bulgar Kilisesi (Sveti Stefan) [171]
Mürsel Paşa Caddesi 87
Balat 34087 Istanbul
T +90 212 248 0921

Buz Teşvikiye [165]
Abdi İpekçi Caddesi 42/2
Nişantaşı 34367 Istanbul
T +90 212 291 0066

Cağaloğlu Hamamı [171]
Kazım İsmail Gürkan Caddesi 34
Cağaloğlu 34110 Istanbul
T +90 212 522 2424
E info@cagaloglühamami.com.tr
W www.cagaloglühamami.com.tr

Çemberlitaş Hamamı [172]
Vezirhanı Caddesi 8
Çemberlitaş 34440 Istanbul
T +90 212 522 7974
E contact@cemberlitashamami.com.tr
W www.cemberlitashamami.com.tr

Cezayir [163]
Hayriye Caddesi 16
Beyoğlu 34425 Istanbul
T +90 212 245 9980
E cezayir@cezayir-istanbul.com
W www.cezayir-istanbul.com

Cuppa [163]
Yeni Yuva Sokak 26
Beyoğlu 34425 Istanbul
T +90 212 249 5723
E cuppa@cuppajuice.com
W www.cuppajuice.com

Derishow [166]
Yeşilçimen Sokak 17
Fulya 34353 Istanbul
T +90 212 259 7255
W www.derishow.com.tr

Erguvan [159]
Radisson SAS Bosphorus Hotel
Çırağan Caddesi 46
Ortaköy 34349 Istanbul
T +90 212 327 6093
E erguvan@istanbulyi.com
W www.istanbulyi.com

Feriye Lokantası [160]
Çırağan Caddesi 40
Ortaköy 34347 Istanbul
T +90 212 227 2216
E feriye@feriye.com
W www.feriye.com

Galata Kulesi [172]
Galata Kulesi Sokak
Galata 34420 Istanbul
T +90 212 293 8180
E info@galatatower.net
W www.galatatower.net

Galata Mevlevihanesi [171]
Galip Dede Caddesi 15
Tünel 34430 Istanbul
T +90 212 245 4141
E info@galatamevlevi.com
W www.galatamevlevi.com

Gönül Paksoy [168]
Atiye Sokak 1/3
Teşvikiye 34365 Istanbul
T +90 212 236 0209
Atiye Sokak 6/a
Teşvikiye 34365 Istanbul
T +90 212 261 9081

Haydarpaşa Tren İstasyonu [171]
Istasyon Caddesi
Raimpaşa 34714 Istanbul
T +90 216 348 8020

Hotel Daphnis [155]
Sadrazam Ali Paşa Caddesi 26
Fener 34220 Istanbul
T +90 212 531 4858
E info@hoteldaphnis.com
W www.hoteldaphnis.com

Hünkar [160]
Mim Kemal Öke Caddesi 21
Nişantaşı 34360 Istanbul
T +90 212 225 4665

İstanbul Arkeoloji Müzeleri [172]
Osman Hamdi Bey Yokuşu
Sultanahmet 34122 Istanbul
T +90 212 520 7740

İstanbul Modern [172]
Meclis-i Mebusan Caddesi
Karaköy 34425 Istanbul
T +90 212 334 7300
E info@istanbulmodern.org
W www.istanbulmodern.org

Kalsedon Maden İşletmeleri [172]
Ayasofya Caferiye Sokak 2
Sultanahmet 34122 Istanbul
T +90 212 513 4570
E info@kalsedon.com.tr
W www.kalsedon.com.tr

Kantin [159]
Akkavak Sokak 16/2
Nişantaşı 34365 Istanbul
T +90 212 219 3114

Kanyon [168]
Büyükdere Caddesi 185
Levent 34394 Istanbul
T +90 212 353 5300
E bilgi@kanyon.com.tr
W www.kanyon.com.tr

Kıyı [161]
Kefeliköy Caddesi 126
Tarabya 80880 Istanbul
T +90 212 262 0002
E info@kiyi.com.tr
W www.kiyi.com.tr

Lale Plak [168]
Galip Dede Caddesi 1
Tünel 34420 Istanbul
T +90 212 293 7739

Leb-i Derya [163]
Kumbaracı Yokuşu 115/7
Beyoğlu 34433 Istanbul
T +90 212 293 4989
E info@lebiderya.com
W www.lebiderya.com

Loft [160]
Lütfi Kırdar Kongre Sarayı
Harbiye 34367 Istanbul
T +90 212 219 6384
E info@loftrestbar.com
W www.loftrestbar.com

Lucca [163]
Cevdet Paşa Caddesi 51/b
Bebek 34342 Istanbul
T +90 212 257 1255
E contact@lucastyle.com
W www.luccastyle.com

Mangerie [158]
Cevdet Paşa Caddesi 69
Bebek 34342 Istanbul
T +90 212 263 5199

Mine Kerse [167]
Faikpaşa Yokuşu 1/a
Çukurcuma 34425 Istanbul
T +90 212 243 0047

Müze de Changa [159]
Sakıp Sabancı Caddesi 22
Emirgan, Istanbul
T +90 212 323 0901
W www.changa-istanbul.com

NuPera + NuTeras [163]
Meşrutiyet Caddesi 149
Tepebaşı 34430 Istanbul
T +90 212 245 6070
E nuteras@istanbulyi.com
W www.istanbulyi.com

Orient Bar [165]
Pera Palas Hotel
Meşrutiyet Caddesi 98–100
Tepebaşı 34430 Istanbul
T +90 212 251 4560
W www.perapalas.com

Les Ottomans [156]
Muallim Naci Caddesi 168
Kuruçeşme 34345 Istanbul
T +90 212 287 1024
E info@lesottomans.com
W www.lesottomans.com

Pandeli [159]
Mısır Çarşısı 1
Eminönü 34116 Istanbul
T +90 212 522 5534

Paşabahçe [167]
Teşvikiye Caddesi 117

Teşvikiye 34365 Istanbul
T +90 212 233 50 05
W www.pasabahce.com.tr

Patisserie Markiz [163]
İstiklal Caddesi 360
Beyoğlu 34430 Istanbul
T +90 212 251 7581
E info@markiz.com.tr
W www.markiz.com

Pera Müzesi [171]
Meşrutiyet Caddesi 141
Tepebaşı 34443 Istanbul
T +90 212 334 9900
E info@peramuzesi.org.tr
W www.pm.org.tr

Pied de Poule [168]
Faikpaşa Yokuşu 19/1
Çukurcuma 34425 Istanbul
T +90 212 245 8116

Pierre Loti Café [163]
Gümüşsuyu Balmumcu Sokak 1
Eyüp 34050 Istanbul
T +90 212 581 2696

Santral İstanbul [172]
Kazım Karabekir Caddesi 1
Eyüp Istanbul
T +90 212 311 5000
E info@santralistanbul.org
W www.santralistanbul.com

Sarnıç Restaurant [172]
Soğukçeşme Sokak
Sultanahmet 34122 Istanbul
T +90 212 513 3660

Sofa Art & Antiques [168]
Nuruosmaniye Caddesi 85
Cağaloğlu 34440 Istanbul
T +90 212 520 2850
E kasif@kashifsofa.com
W www.kashifsofa.com

The Sofa Hotel [157]
Teşvikiye Caddesi 123
Nişantaşı 34367 Istanbul
T +90 212 368 1818
E info@thesofahotel.com
W www.thesofahotel.com

Süleymaniye Camii [171]
Prof. Sıddık Sami Onar Caddesi
Süleymaniye, Istanbul

Sunset Grill & Bar [160]
Yol Sokak 1
Ulus 34340 Istanbul
T +90 212 287 0357

Türk ve İslam Eserleri
Müzesi [172]
Atmeydanı Sokağı 46
Sultanahmet 34122 Istanbul
T +90 212 518 1805
W www.tiem.org

Tuus [161]
Teşvikiye Caddesi 123
Nişantaşı 34367 Istanbul
T +90 212 224 8181

Ulus 29 [158]
Ahmet Adnan Saygun Caddesi
Ulus 34340 Istanbul
T +90 212 358 2929
E ulus29@club29.com
W www.club29.com

Ümit Ünal [168]
Ensiz Sokak 3

Asmalı Mescit Mahallesi
Tünel 34430 Istanbul
T +90 212 245 7886
E umitunal@umitunal.com
W www.umitunal.com

Vefa Bozacısı [165]
Katip Çelebi Caddesi 104/1
Vefa 34470 Istanbul
T +90 212 519 4922
E vefa@vefa.com.tr
W www.vefa.com.tr

Vogue [164]
Suleyman Seba Caddesi
BJK Plaza 92, 13th Floor
Beşiktaş 34357 Istanbul
T +90 212 227 2545

Yakup 2 [164]
Asmalı Mescit Sokak 35–37
Tünel 34430 Istanbul
T +90 212 249 2925

Yuşa Tepesi [171]
Yuşa Tepesi Yolu
Ortaçeşme Istanbul

Zeynep Erol [168]
Atiye Sokak 8/3
Nişantaşı 80200 Istanbul
T +90 212 236 4668
W www.zeyneperol.net

LISBON

A Casa do Bacalhau [183]
Rua do Grilo, 54
1900–706 Lisbon
T +351 21 862 0000
E acasadobacalhau@netcabo.pt
W www.acasadobacalhau.restaunet.pt

A Ginjinha [184]
Largo de São Domingos, 8
Lisbon

A Outra Face da Lua [190]
Rua da Assunção, 22
Lisbon
T +351 21 886 3430
E baixa@aoutrafacedalua.com
W www.aoutrafacedalua.com

A Travessa [183]
Convento das Bernardas, 12
1200–638 Lisbon
T +351 21 394 0800
E a.travessa@netcabo.pt
W www.atravessa.com

Agência 117 [186]
Rua do Norte, 117
Bairro Alto, Lisbon
T +351 21 346 1270

Alcântara Café [185]
Rua Maria Luisa Holstein, 15
Alcântara 1300–388 Lisbon
T +351 21 363 7176
W www.alcantaracafe.com

Alma Lusa [189]
Rua de São Bento, 363
1250–220 Lisbon
T +351 21 388 4094

Alves/Gonçalves [189]
Rua Serpa Pinto, 15b
Chiado 1200–443 Lisbon
T +351 21 346 0690
W www.alvesgoncalves.com

Ana Salazar [189]
Rua do Carmo, 87
1200 Lisbon
T +351 21 347 2289
W www.anasalazar.pt

Antiga Confeitaria de Belém [193]
Rua de Belém, 84–92
Belém 1300–085 Lisbon
T +351 21 363 7423
E pasteisdebelem@pasteisdebelem.pt
W www.pasteisdebelem.pt

Bairro Alto Hotel [179]
Praça Luís de Camões, 8
Bairro Alto 1200–243 Lisbon
T +351 21 340 8288
E reservations@bairroaltohotel.com
W www.bairroaltohotel.com

Bar Terraço [193]
Centro Cultural de Belém
Praça do Império
Belém 1400 Lisbon
T +351 21 301 0623

Bica do Sapato [183]
Av. Infante D. Henrique, Armazém B
Santa Apolónia 1900 Lisbon
T +351 21 881 0320
W www.bicadosapato.com

Café A Brasileira [186]
Rua Garrett, 120
Chiado, Lisbon
T +351 21 8346 9541

Café Martinho da Arcada [186]
Praça do Comércio, 3
Baixa, Lisbon
T +351 21 886 6213

Café Nicola [186]
Praça Dom Pedro IV, 24
Rossio, Lisbon
T +351 21 346 0579

Casa da Comida [183]
Travessa das Amoreiras
Lisbon
T +351 21 388 5376
E r.alcantara@casadacomida.pt
W www.casadacomida.pt

Casa do Alentejo [184]
Rua das Portas de Santo Antão, 58
Baixa 1150–268 Lisbon
T +351 21 346 9231

Casa do Leão [193]
Castelo de São Jorge
Alfama, Lisbon
T +351 21 887 5962

Castelo de São Jorge [193]
Largo do Chão da Feria
Alfama 1100–129 Lisbon
T +351 21 880 0620
E castelodesaojorge@egeac.pt
W www.castelosaojorge.egeac.pt

Caza das Vellas Loreto [189]
Rua do Loreto, 53
Bairro Alto, Lisbon

Centro Cultural de Belém [193]
Praça do Império
Belém 1499–003 Lisbon
T +351 21 361 2400
E ccb@ccb.pt
W www.ccb.pt

Centro de Arte Moderna [193]
Rua Dr Nicolau de Bettencourt

1050–078 Lisbon
T +351 21 782 3474
E camjap@gulbenkian.pt
W www.camjap.gulbenkian.org

Cervejaria Trindade [185]
Rua Nova da Trindade, 20
1300–330 Lisbon
T +351 21 342 3506
E trindade@cervejariatrindade.pt
W www.cervejariatrindade.pt

Clube de Fado [185]
Rua de São João da Praça, 94
Alfama 1100–521 Lisbon
T +351 21 888 2694
E info@clube-de-fado.com
W www.clube-de-fado.com

Confeitaria Nacional [191]
Praça da Figueira, 18b
Rossio 1100–241 Lisbon
T +351 21 342 4470
E info@confeitarianacional.com
W www.confeitarianacional.com

Conserveira de Lisboa [190]
Rua dos Bacalhoeiros, 34
Baixa, Lisbon
T +351 21 887 1058

Cutipol [190]
Rua do Alecrim, 113–115
T +351 21 322 5075
E loja.lisboa@cutipol.pt
W www.cutipol.pt

Delidelux [183]
Av. Infante D. Henrique, Armazém B
Santa Apolónia 1900–264 Lisbon
T +351 21 886 2070
E geral@delidelux.pt
W www.delidelux.pt

Espaço Lisboa [185]
Rua da Cozinha Económica, 16
1300–149 Lisbon
T +351 21 361 0212

Estufa Real [193]
Jardim Botânico da Ajuda
Calçada do Galvão
1400 Lisbon
T +351 21 361 9400
E geral@estufareal.mail.pt
W www.estufareal.pt

Fábrica Sant'Anna [191]
Rua do Alecrim, 95
Chiado 1200–015 Lisbon
T +351 21 342 2537
Factory:
Calçada da Boa-Hora 96
1300–096 Lisbon
T +351 21 363 82 92
W www.fabrica-santanna.com

Fátima Lopes [190]
Rua da Atalaia, 36
Bairro Alto 1200–041 Lisbon
T +351 21 324 0546
E info@fatima-lopes.com
W www.fatima-lopes.com

Galeto [186]
Avenida da República, 14
Saldanha, Lisbon
T +351 21 354 4444

Happy Days [186]
Rua do Norte, 60
Bairro Alto, Lisbon
T +351 21 342 1015

Jardim Botânico da Ajuda [193]
Calçada da Ajuda
Ajuda 1300–011 Lisbon
T +351 21 362 2503
E botanicoajudi@isa.utl.pt
W www.jardimbotanicodaajuda.com

Luvaria Ulisses [189]
Rua do Carmo, 87a
1200–093 Lisbon
T +351 21 342 0295
E luvariaulisses@sapo.pt
W www.luvariaulisses.com

Lux Frágil [183]
Av. Infante D. Henrique, Armazém A
Santa Apolónia 1950–376 Lisbon
T +351 21 882 0890
E lux@luxfragil.com
W www.luxfragil.com

Mahjong [186]
Rua da Atalaia, 3–5
Bairro Alto 1200 Lisbon
T +351 21 342 1039

Margarida Pimentel Jewelry [193]
Centro Cultural de Belém
Praça do Império
Belém 1400 Lisbon
W www.margaridapimentel.com

Mosteiro dos Jerónimos [193]
Praça do Império
Belém 1400–206 Lisbon
T +351 21 362 0034
E mosteirojeronimos@
mosteirojeronimos.pt
W www.mosteirojeronimos.pt

Mousse [189]
Rua das Flores, 41–43
1200–193 Lisbon
T +351 21 342 0781
E mousse@mousse.com.pt
W www.mousse.com.pt

Museu Calouste Gulbenkian [193]
Avenida de Berna, 45a
São Sebastião 1067–001 Lisbon
T +351 21 782 3000
W www.museu.gulbenkian.pt

Museu da Marioneta [183]
Convento das Bernardas
Rua da Esperança, 146
1200–660 Lisbon
T +351 21 394 2810
E museudamarioneta@egeac.pt
W www.museudamarioneta.egeac.pt

Museu-Escola de Artes Decorativas Portuguesas [193]
Largo das Portas do Sol, 2
Alfama 1100–411 Lisbon
T +351 21 888 1991
E museu@fress.pt
W www.fress.pt

Museu Nacional do Azulejo [193]
Rua da Madre de Deus, 4
1900–312 Lisbon
T +351 21 810 0340
E mnazulejo@ipmuseus.pt
W www.mnazulejo-ipmuseus.pt

Museu National dos Coches [193]
Praça Afonso de Albuquerque
1300–044 Lisbon
T +351 21 361 0850
E mncoches@ipmuseus.pt
W www.museudoscoches-ipmuseus.pt

Nininha Guímarães dos Santos [189]
Rua de São Julião, 7
1100–524 Lisbon
T +351 21 8 877 525
E nininha007@sapo.pt

Origens Bio [183]
Alameda dos Oceanos
1990–039 Lisbon
T +351 21 894 61 66
E restaurante@origensbio.pt
W www.origensbio.pt

Padrão dos Descobrimentos [193]
Avenida de Brasília
1400–038 Lisbon
T +351 21 3 031 950
E padraodosdescobrimentos@egeac.pt
W www.padraodosdescobrimentos.egeac.pt

Pap' Açorda [183]
Rua da Atalaia, 57–59
Bairro Alto, Lisbon
T +351 21 346 4811

Pasteleria Versailles [186]
Avenida da República, 15a
Saldanha, Lisbon

Pavilhão Chines [186]
Rua Dom Pedro V, 89–91
Príncipe Real, Lisbon
T +351 21 342 4729

Portas Largas [185]
Rua da Atalaia, 103–105
Bairro Alto, Lisbon
T +351 21 346 6379

Restaurante Eleven [183]
Rua Marquês de Fronteira
Jardim Amália Rodrigues
1070 Lisbon
T +351 21 386 2211
E 11@restauranteeleven.com
W www.restauranteeleven.com

Sneakers Delight [186]
Rua do Norte, 30–32
Bairro Alto, Lisbon
T +351 21 347 9976
E sneakers@sneakersdelight.pt
W www.sneakersdelight.pt

Solar do Castelo [180]
Rua das Cozinhas, 2
1100–181 Lisbon
T +351 21 880 6050
E heritage.hotels@heritage.pt
W www.heritage.pt

Solar do Vinho do Porto [184]
Rua de São Pedro de Alcântara, 45
Bairro Alto 1250–237 Lisbon
T +351 21 347 5707

Solar dos Mouros [178]
Rua do Milagre de Santo António, 6
Alfama 1100–351 Lisbon
T +351 21 885 4940
E reservation@solardosmouros.com
W www.solardosmouros.com

Tavares [183]
Rua da Misericórdia, 35
Bairro Alto 1200–270 Lisbon
T +351 21 342 1112

Terreiro do Paço [183]
Praça do Comércio
1100–148 Lisbon
T +351 21 031 2850

E terreirodopaco@quintadaslagrimas.pt
W www.terreiropaco.com

Torre de Belém [193]
Mosteiro dos Jerónimos
Praça do Império
1400–206 Lisbon
T +351 21 362 00 34
E torrebelem@mosteirojeronimos.pt
W www.mosteirojeronimos.pt

ViniPortugal [183]
Praça do Comércio
1147–010 Lisbon
T +351 21 342 0690
W www.viniportugal.pt

Vista Alegre [191]
Largo do Chiado, 20–23
1200 Lisbon
T +351 21 346 1401
W www.vistaalegre.pt

York House [181]
Rua das Janelas Verdes, 32
1200–691 Lisbon
T +351 21 396 2435
E reservations@yorkhouselisboa.com
W www.yorkhouselisboa.com

LONDON

Anglesea Arms [209]
15 Selwood Terrace
London SW7 3QG
T +44 20 7373 7960

Annie's [214]
12 Camden Passage
London N1 8ED
T +44 20 7359 0796

Antoni & Alison [214]
43 Rosebery Avenue
London EC1R 4SH
T +44 20 7833 2141
E info@antoniandalison.co.uk
W www.antoniandalison.co.uk

Aquaint [213]
38 Monmouth Street
London WC2 9EP
T +44 20 7240 9677
W www.aquaintboutique.com

Bam-Bou [205]
1 Percy Street
London W1T 1DB
T +44 20 7323 9130
W www.bam-bou.co.uk

Blue Bar [210]
The Berkeley Hotel
Wilton Place
London SW1X 7RL
T +44 20 7201 1680
E info@the-berkeley.co.uk
W www.the-berkeley.co.uk

Bluu Bar [210]
1 Hoxton Square
London N1 6NU
T +44 20 7613 2793
E hoxton@bluu.co.uk
W www.bluu.co.uk

Browns + Browns Focus [214]
Browns: 24–27 South Molton Street
London W1K 5RD
Browns Focus: 38–39 South Molton Street
London W1K 5RN
T +44 20 7514 0016

E southmoltonstreet@brownsfashion.com
W www.brownsfashion.com

Cath Kidston [214]
8 Clarendon Cross
London W11 4AP
T +44 20 7221 4000
W www.cathkidston.co.uk

Chelsea Physic Garden [219]
66 Royal Hospital Road
London SW3 4HS
T +44 20 7352 5646
E enquiries@chelseaphysicgarden.co.uk
W www.chelseaphysicgarden.co.uk

Christ Church Spitalfields [219]
Commercial Street
London E1 6QE
T +44 20 7247 7202
E admin@christchurchspitalfields.org.uk
W www.christchurchspitalfields.org.uk

Cinnamon Club [205]
30–32 Great Smith Street
London SW1P 3BU
T +44 20 7222 2555
E info@cinnamonclub.com
W www.cinnamonclub.com

Coco de Mer [213]
23 Monmouth Street
London WC2H 9DD
T +44 20 7836 8882
E sales@coco-de-mer.co.uk
W www.coco-de-mer.co.uk

The Crown [209]
116 Cloudesley Road
London N1 0EB
T +44 20 7837 7107
E crown.islington@fullers.co.uk

Daunt Books [213]
83 Marylebone High Street
London W1U 4QW
T +44 20 7224 2295
E marylebone@dauntbooks.co.uk
W www.dauntbooks.co.uk

Dennis Severs' House [219]
18 Folgate Street
London E1 6BX
T +44 20 7247 4013
E info@dennissevershouse.co.uk
W www.dennissevershouse.co.uk

The Draper's Arms [209]
44 Barnsbury Street
London N1 1ER
T +44 20 7619 0348

The Duke of Cambridge [209]
30 St Peters Street
London N1 8JT
T +44 20 7359 3066
E duke@dukeorganic.co.uk
W www.sloeberry.co.uk

Dunhill [217]
48 Jermyn Street
London SW1Y 6DL
T +44 20 7290 8600
E customer.services@dunhill.com
W http://store.dunhill.com

The Eagle [207]
159 Farringdon Road
London EC1R 3AL
T +44 20 7837 1353

Egg [213]
37 Kinnerton Street
London SW1X 8ES
T +44 20 7235 9315
E egg@eggtrading.com

Electricity Showrooms [210]
39a Hoxton Square
London N1 6NU
T +44 20 7739 6934

Eleven Cadogan Gardens [203]
11 Cadogan Gardens
London SW3 2RJ
T +44 20 7730 7000
E letterbox@number-eleven.co.uk
W www.number-eleven.co.uk

Eley Kishimoto [217]
27 Greek Street
London W1D 5DF
E info@eleykishimoto.com
W www.eleykishimoto.com

Elk in the Woods [214]
39 Camden Passage
London N1 8EA
T +44 20 7226 3535

Fino [205]
33 Charlotte Street
London W1T 1RR
T +44 20 7813 8010

Fish Shop on St John Street [206]
360–362 St John Street
London EC1V 4NR
T +44 20 7837 1199
E info@thefishshop.net
W www.thefishshop.net

Floris [217]
89 Jermyn Street
London SW1Y 6JH
T +44 845 702 3239
E fragrance@florislondon.com
W www.florislondon.com

Frederick's [214]
106 Camden Passage
London N1 8EG
T +44 20 7359 2888
E eat@fredericks.co.uk
W www.fredericks.co.uk

The French House [210]
49 Dean Street
London W1D 5BG
T +44 20 7437 2477

Gordon's Wine Bar [209]
47 Villiers Street
London WC2N 6NE
T +44 20 7930 1408
W www.gordonswinebar.com

Great Eastern Dining Rooms [210]
54–56 Great Eastern Street
London EC2A 3QR
T +44 20 7613 4545
E greateastern@rickerrestaurants.com
W www.greateasterndining.co.uk

The Guinea [205]
30 Bruton Place
London W1J 6NL
T +44 20 7409 1728

Harvie & Hudson [217]
96–97 Jermyn Street
London SW1Y 6JE
T +44 20 7839 3578
E info@harvieandhudson.com

W www.harvieandhudson.com

The Havelock Tavern [205]
57 Masbro Road
London W14 0LS
T +44 20 7603 5374
E info@thehavelocktavern.co.uk
W www.thehavelocktavern.co.uk

Hayward Gallery [220]
Belvedere Road, South Bank Centre
London SE1 8XZ
T +44 20 7921 0813
E hginfo@hayward.org.uk
W www.hayward.org.uk

Hazlitt's [199]
6 Frith Street, Soho Square
London W1D 3JA
T +44 20 7434 1771
E reservations@hazlitts.co.uk
W www.hazlittshotel.com

Her House [213]
26 Drysdale Street
London N1 6LS
T +44 20 7729 2760
E morag@herhouse.uk.com
W www.herhouse.uk.com

Hoxton Square Bar & Kitchen [210]
2–4 Hoxton Square
London N1 6NU
T +44 20 7613 0709

Inn the Park [209]
St James's Park
London SW1A 2BJ
T +44 20 7451 9999
E info@innthepark.com
W www.innthepark.com

J. Sheekey [207]
28–32 St Martin's Court
London WC2N 4AL
T +44 20 7240 2565
W www.j-sheekey.co.uk

James Smith & Sons Umbrellas [214]
53 New Oxford Street
London WC1A 1BL
T +44 20 7836 4731
W www.james-smith.co.uk

Knightsbridge Hotel [201]
10 Beaufort Gardens
London SW3 1PT
T +44 20 7584 6300
E knightsbridge@firmdale.com
W www.knightsbridgehotel.com

Koh Samui [213]
65–67 Monmouth Street
London WC2H 9DG
T +44 20 7240 4280

Liquid [210]
8 Pitfield Street
London N1 6HA
T +44 20 7729 0082

London Review Bookshop [214]
14 Bury Place
London WC1A 2JL
T +44 20 7269 9030
E books@lrbshop.co.uk
W www.lrbshop.co.uk

Maggie Jones [205]
6 Old Court Place
London W8 4PL
T +44 20 7937 6462

Magma [213]
8 Earlham Street
London WC2H 9RY
T +44 20 7240 8498
E enquiries@magmabooks.com
W www.magmabooks.com

The Main House [202]
6 Colville Road
London W11 2BP
T +44 20 7221 9691
E caroline@themainhouse.co.uk
W www.themainhouse.co.uk

The Mall [214]
359 Islington High Street
London N1 0PD
T +44 20 7351 5353
E info@themallantiques.co.uk
W www.themallantiques.co.uk

Manolo Blahník [213]
49–51 Old Church Street
London SW3 5BS
T +44 20 7352 8622

Matthew Williamson [213]
28 Bruton Street
London W1J 6QH
T +44 20 7629 6200
E info@matthewwilliamson.com
W www.matthewwilliamson.co.uk

Medicine Bar [210]
89 Great Eastern Street
London EC2A 3HX
T +44 20 7739 5173
E medicine@medicinebar.net
W www.medicinebar.net

Miller Harris [214]
14 Needham Road
London W11 2RP
T +44 20 7221 1545
E info@millerharris.com
W www.millerharris.com

Monmouth Coffee Co. [213]
27 Monmouth Street
London WC2H 9EU
T +44 20 7379 3516
E beans@monmouthcoffee.co.uk
W www.monmouthcoffee.co.uk

Mount Street Gardens [220]
South Audley Street
London W1K 2TH

Neal's Yard Dairy [213]
17 Shorts Gardens
London WC2H 9UP
T +44 20 7240 5700
E coventgarden@nealsyarddairy.co.uk
W www.nealsyarddairy.co.uk

Neal's Yard Remedies [213]
15 Neal's Yard
London WC2H 9DH
T +44 20 7379 7222
E cgarden@nealsyardremedies.com
W www.nealsyardremedies.com

Oki-Ni [217]
25 Savile Row
London W1S 2ES
T +44 20 7494 1716
E enquiries@oki-ni.com
W www.oki-ni.com

Passione [205]
10 Charlotte Street
London W1T 2IT
T +44 20 7636 2833
W www.passione.co.uk

People's Palace [220]
Royal Festival Hall, South Bank Centre
London SE1 8XX
T +44 20 7928 9999

Pied à Terre [205]
34 Charlotte Street
London W1T 2NH
T +44 20 7636 1178
E info@pied-a-terre.co.uk
W www.pied-a-terre.co.uk

Poetry Café [209]
22 Betterton Street
London WC2H 9BX
T +44 20 7420 9880
E poetrycafe@poetrysociety.org.uk
W www.poetrysociety.org.uk

The Portrait Restaurant [209]
The National Portrait Gallery
St Martin's Place
London WC2H 0HE
T +44 20 7312 2490
W www.npg.org.uk

Rasa Samudra [205]
5 Charlotte Street
London W1T 1RE
T +44 20 7637 0222
E info@rasarestaurants.com
W www.rasarestaurants.com

Rasoi Vineet Bhatia [206]
10 Lincoln Street
London SW3 2TS
T +44 20 7225 1881
W www.vineetbhatia.com

Roka [205]
37 Charlotte Street
London W1T 1RR
T +44 20 7580 6464
E info@rokarestaurant.com
W www.rokarestaurant.com

Rokit [214]
42 Shelton Street
London WC2 9HZ
T +44 20 7836 6547
E info@rokit.co.uk
W www.rokit.co.uk

The Rookery [200]
Peter's Lane, Cowcross Street
London EC1M 6DS
T +44 20 7336 0931
E reservations@rookery.co.uk
W www.rookery.co.uk

Royal Festival Hall [220]
Belvedere Road, South Bank Centre
London SE1 8XX
T +44 870 380 4300
W www.rfh.org.uk

St Etheldreda [219]
14 Ely Place
London EC1N 6RY
T +44 20 7405 1061
W www.stetheldreda.com

St John [205]
26 St John Street
London EC1M 4AY
T +44 20 7251 0848
W www.stjohnrestaurant.co.uk

St Stephen Walbrook [219]
39 Walbrook
London EC4N 8BN
T +44 20 7606 3998
W www.ststephenwalbrook.net

Shakespeare's Globe [220]
21 New Globe Walk
London SE1 9DT
T +44 20 7902 1400
E info@shakespearesglobe.com
W www.shakespeares-globe.org

Sir John Soane's Museum [219]
13 Lincoln's Inn Fields
London WC2A 3BP
T +44 20 7405 2107
W www.soane.org

Solange Azagury-Partridge [213]
187 Westbourne Grove
London W11 2SB
T +44 20 7792 0197
E info@solange.info
W www.solangeazagurypartridge.com

Tadema Gallery [214]
10 Charlton Place
London N1 8AJ
T +44 20 7359 1055
E info@tademagallery.com
W www.tademagallery.com

Tate Modern [220]
Bankside
London SE1 9TG
T +44 20 7887 8000
E visiting.modern@tate.org.uk
W www.tate.org.uk/modern

Tom Aikens [206]
43 Elystan Street
London SW3 3NT
T +44 20 7584 2003
E info@tomaikens.co.uk
W www.tomaikens.co.uk

Trailer Happiness [209]
177 Portobello Road
London W11 2DY
T +44 20 7727 2700
E bookings@trailerh.com
W www.trailerh.com

Turnbull & Asser [217]
71–72 Jermyn Street
London SW1Y 6PF
T +44 20 7808 3000
W www.turnbullandasser.co.uk

Victoria & Albert Museum [220]
Cromwell Road
London SW7 2RL
T +44 20 7942 2000
E vanda@vam.ac.uk
W www.vam.ac.uk

Windsor Castle [210]
114 Campden Hill Road
London W8 7AR
T +44 20 7243 9551

The Wolseley [207]
160 Piccadilly
London W1J 9EB
T +44 20 7499 6996
W www.thewolseley.com

Ye Olde Mitre Tavern [209]
1 Ely Court
London EC1N 6SJ
T +44 20 7405 4751

The Zetter [198]
86–88 Clerkenwell Road
London EC1M 5RJ
T +44 20 7324 4444
E info@thezetter.com
W www.thezetter.com

PARIS

Les Ambassadeurs [234]
Hôtel de Crillon
10, place de la Concorde
75008 Paris
T +33 1 44 71 16 16
E restaurants@crillon.com
W www.crillon.com

L'Ambroisie [235]
9, place des Vosges
75004 Paris
T +33 1 42 78 51 45

L'Ami Jean [233]
27, rue Malar
75007 Paris
T +33 1 47 05 86 89

A-poc [241]
47, rue des Francs-Bourgeois
75004 Paris
T +33 1 44 54 07 05
E a-poc@issey-europe.com
W www.isseymiyake.com

L'Arpège [233]
84, rue de Varenne
75007 Paris
T +33 1 47 05 09 06
E arpege@alain-passard.com
W www.alain-passard.com

L'Astrance [233]
4, rue Beethoven
75016 Paris
T +33 1 40 50 84 40

L'Avant-Goût [233]
26, rue Bobillot
75013 Paris
T +33 1 53 80 24 00

Azzedine Alaïa Hotel [229]
5, rue de Moussy
75004 Paris
T +33 1 44 78 92 00
E info@3rooms5ruedemoussy.com

Bar du Plaza Athénée [237]
25, avenue Montaigne
75008 Paris
T +33 1 53 67 65 00
W www.plaza-athenee-paris.com

Le Baratin [234]
3, rue Jouye-Rouve
75020 Paris
T +33 1 43 49 39 70

Le Café Marly [238]
93, rue de Rivoli
75001 Paris
T +33 1 49 26 06 60

Caves Miard [237]
9, rue des Quatre-Vents
75006 Paris
T +33 1 43 54 99 30

Les Caves Pétrissans [237]
30 bis, avenue Niel
75017 Paris
T +33 1 42 27 52 03

Centre Pompidou [244]
place Georges Pompidou
75004 Paris
T +33 1 44 78 12 33
W www.centrepompidou.fr

Charvet [241]
28, place Vendôme

75001 Paris
T +33 1 42 60 30 70

Chez Jean [233]
8, rue St-Lazare
75009 Paris
T +33 1 48 78 62 73

Christian Louboutin [241]
19, rue Jean-Jacques Rousseau
75001 Paris
T +33 1 42 36 05 31
W www.christianlouboutin.fr

Colette [241]
213, rue St-Honoré
75001 Paris
T +33 1 55 35 33 90
E contact@colette.fr
W www.colette.fr

Créations Cherif [246]
13, avenue Daumesnil
75012 Paris
T +33 1 43 40 01 00
E info@creations-cherif.com
W www.creations-cherif.com

Cyrille Varet [246]
67, avenue Daumesnil
75012 Paris
T +33 1 44 75 88 88
E mail@cyrillevaret.com
W www.cyrillevaret.com

De la Ville Café [237]
34, boulevard Bonne-Nouvelle
75010 Paris
T +33 1 48 24 48 09

Dominique Kieffer [242]
8, rue Hérold
75001 Paris
T +33 1 42 21 32 44
E info@dkieffer.com
W www.dominiquekieffer.com

**Editions de Parfums
Frédéric Malle** [241]
37, rue de Grenelle
75007 Paris
T +33 1 42 22 77 22
W www.editionsdeparfums.com

La Famille [233]
41, rue des Trois-Frères
75018 Paris
T +33 1 45 52 11 12

Fish/La Boissonnerie [237]
69, rue de Seine
75006 Paris
T +33 1 43 54 34 69

Fondation Cartier [245]
261, boulevard Raspail
75014 Paris
T +33 1 42 18 56 50
W www.fondation.cartier.fr

**Fondation Pierre Bergé,
Yves Saint Laurent** [246]
5, avenue Marceau
75116 Paris
T +33 1 44 31 64 00
W www.fondation-pb-ysl.net

Georges [244]
Centre Pompidou, 6th floor
place Georges Pompidou
75004 Paris
T +33 1 44 78 47 99

L'Hôtel [231]
13, rue des Beaux Arts
75006 Paris
T +33 1 44 41 99 00
E reservation@l-hotel.com
W www.l-hotel.com

Hôtel Bourg Tibourg [226]
19, rue du Bourg-Tibourg
75004 Paris
T +33 1 42 78 47 39
W www.hotelbourgtibourg.com

L'Hôtel de Sers [230]
41, avenue Pierre 1er de Serbie
75008 Paris
T +33 1 53 23 75 75
E resa@hoteldesers.com
W www.hoteldesers.com

Hôtel Thérèse [227]
5-7, rue Thérèse
75001 Paris
T +33 1 42 96 10 01
E info@hoteltherese.com
W www.hoteltherese.com

Institut du Monde Arabe [244]
1, rue des Fossés-St-Bernard
75005 Paris
T +33 1 40 51 38 38
E rap@imarabe.org
W www.imarabe.org

Iunx [241]
48-50, rue de l'Université
75007 Paris
T +33 1 45 44 50 14

Jamin Puech [241]
68, rue Vieille du Temple
75003 Paris
T +33 1 48 87 84 87
W www.jamin-puech.com

Juvenile's [237]
47, rue de Richelieu
75001 Paris
T +33 1 42 97 46 49

Lagerfeld Gallery [246]
40, rue de Seine
75006 Paris
T +33 1 55 42 75 50

Librairie Gourmande [242]
4, rue Dante
75005 Paris
T +33 1 43 54 37 27
W www.librairie-gourmande.fr

Lucien Pellat-Finet [242]
1, rue Montalembert
75007 Paris
T +33 1 42 22 22 77
E info@lucienpellat-finet.com
W www.lucienpellat-finet.com

Maison Fey [246]
15, avenue Daumesnil
75012 Paris
T +33 1 43 41 22 22
E contact@maisonfey.com
W www.maisonfey.com

La Maison des Trois Thés [238]
33, rue Gracieuse
75005 Paris
T +33 1 43 36 93 84

Malhia [246]
19, avenue Daumesnil
75012 Paris
T +33 1 53 44 76 76

Marie Lavande [246]
83, avenue Daumesnil
75012 Paris
T +33 1 44 67 78 78
W www.marie-lavande.com

La Mosquée de Paris [238]
39, rue St-Hilaire
75005 Paris
T +33 1 43 31 38 20
E contact@lamosqueedeparis.com
W www.la-mosquee.com

Murano Urban Resort [228]
Murano Urban Resort Bar [237]
13, boulevard du Temple
75003 Paris
T +33 1 42 71 20 00
E paris@muranoresort.com
W www.muranoresort.com

Musée Gustave Moreau [246]
14, rue de La Rochefoucauld
75009 Paris
T +33 1 48 74 38 50
E info@musee-moreau.fr
W www.musee-moreau.fr

Musée Nissim de Camondo [245]
63, rue de Monceau
75008 Paris
T +33 1 53 89 06 40
W www.ucad.fr

Musée Rodin [246]
Hôtel Biron
79, rue de Varenne
75007 Paris
T +33 1 44 18 61 10
E penseur@musee-rodin.fr
W www.musee-rodin.fr

Palais de Tokyo [245]
13, avenue du Président Wilson
75016 Paris
T +33 1 47 23 54 01
E info@palaisdetokyo.com
W www.palaisdetokyo.com

La Palette [237]
43, rue de Seine
75006 Paris
T +33 1 43 26 68 15

Les Papilles [242]
30, rue Gay-Lussac
75005 Paris
T +33 1 43 25 20 79

Parc André Citroën [246]
quai André-Citroën
75015 Paris

Pierre Gagnaire [233]
Hôtel Balzac
6, rue Balzac
75008 Paris
T +33 1 58 36 12 50
E info@pierregagnaire.com
W www.pierre-gagnaire.com

Pierre Hermé [242]
72, rue Bonaparte
75006 Paris
T +33 1 43 54 47 77
E info@pierreherme.com
W www.pierreherme.com

Le Pré Catalan [233]
route de Suresnes
Bois de Boulogne
75016 Paris
T +33 1 44 14 41 14

Sadaharu Aoki [241]
56, boulevard de Port Royal
75005 Paris
T   +33 1 45 35 36 80
E   paris@sadaharuaoki.com
W   www.sadaharuaoki.com

Spoon, Food & Wine [235]
14, rue de Marignan
75008 Paris
T   +33 1 40 76 34 56
W   www.spoon.tm.fr

La Table du Joël Robuchon [234]
16, avenue Bugeaud
75016 Paris
T   +33 1 56 28 16 16

Vanessa Bruno [242]
25, rue St-Sulpice
75006 Paris
T   +33 1 43 54 41 04
12, rue de Castiglione
75001 Paris
T   +33 1 42 61 44 60
W   www.vanessabruno.com

Le Verre Volé [238]
67, rue de Lancry
75010 Paris
T   +33 1 48 03 17 34

Vertical [246]
63, avenue Daumesnil
75012 Paris
T   +33 1 43 40 26 26
E   courrier@vertical.net
W   http://lanore.club.fr

Via [246]
29–35, avenue Daumesnil
75012 Paris
T   +33 1 46 28 11 11
E   via@mobilier.com
W   www.via.asso.fr

Le Viaduc Café [246]
43, avenue Daumesnil
75012 Paris
T   +33 1 44 74 70 70
E   infos@viaduc-cafe.fr
W   www.viaduc-cafe.fr

Le Villaret [235]
13, rue Ternaux
75011 Paris
T   +33 1 43 57 89 76

Ze Kitchen Galerie [233]
4, rue des Grands Augustins
75006 Paris
T   +33 1 44 32 00 32
E   contact@zkg.fr
W   www.zekitchengalerie.fr

ROME

Agata e Romeo [261]
Via Carlo Alberto 45
00185 Rome
T   +39 06 44 66 115
E   ristorante@agataeromeo.it
W   www.agataeromeo.it

Aleph Hotel [256]
Angelo Lounge Bar [263]
Via di San Basilio 15
00187 Rome
T   +39 06 42 29 01
E   reservation@aleph.boscolo.com
W   www.boscolohotels.com

L'Altro di Mastai [259]
Via Giraud 53

00186 Rome
T   +39 06 68 30 1296
E   restaurant@laltromastai.it
W   www.laltromastai.it

Antico Arco [259]
Piazzale Aurelio 7
00152 Rome
T   +39 06 58 15 274

Arancia Blu [259]
Via dei Latini 55/65
00185 Rome
T   +39 06 44 54 105
W   www.aranciabluroma.com

**Auditorium Parco
della Musica** [271]
Viale Pietro de Coubertin 30
00196 Rome
T   +39 06 80 24 1281
E   info@musicaperroma.it
W   www.musicaperroma.it

Baba [260]
Via Casale di Tor di Quinto 1
00191 Rome
T   +39 06 33 30 745
E   info@babaristorante.it
W   www.babaristorante.it

Bar della Pace [263]
Via della Pace 3/7
00186 Rome
T   +39 06 68 61 216

Bar Taruga [264]
Piazza Mattei 8
00186 Rome

Basilica di San Clemente [270]
Via Labicana 95
00184 Rome
T   +39 06 77 40 021

Baullà [267]
Via dei Baullari 37
00186 Rome
T   +39 06 68 67 670

Bomba Abbigliamento [267]
Via dell'Oca 39
00186 Rome
T   +39 06 32 03 020

Bulgari [269]
Via dei Condotti 10
00187 Rome
T   +39 06 69 62 61
W   www.bulgari.com

Bush [264]
Via Galvani 46
00153 Rome
T   +39 06 57 28 8691

Caffè Farnese [265]
Piazza Farnese 106/107
00186 Rome
T   +39 06 68 80 2125

Il Caffè di Sant'Eustachio [263]
Piazza di Sant'Eustachio 82
00186 Rome
T   +39 06 68 80 20 48
E   info@santeustachioilcaffe.it
W   www.santeustachioilcaffe.it

Casa Bleve [263]
Via del Teatro Valle 48–49
00186 Rome
T   +39 06 68 65 970
E   info@casableve.it
W   www.casableve.it

Casa Howard [252]
Via Capo le Case 18
Via Sistina 149
00186 Rome
T   +39 06 69 92 4555
E   info@casahoward.it
W   www.casahoward.com

Centrale Montemartini [272]
Via Ostiense 106
00154 Rome
T   +39 06 82 05 9127
W   www.centralemontemartini.org

Colline Emiliane [260]
Via degli Avignonesi 22
00187 Rome
T   +39 06 48 17 538

C.U.C.I.N.A. [267]
Via Mario de' Fiori 65
00187 Rome
T   +39 06 67 91 275
W   www.cucinastore.com

Cul de Sac [259]
Piazza di Pasquino 73
00186 Rome
T   +39 06 68 80 1094

Diego Percossi Papi [269]
Via di Sant'Eustachio 16
00186 Rome
T   +39 06 68 80 1466

L'Enoteca Antica [265]
Via della Croce 76b
00187 Rome
T   +39 06 67 90 896

Enoteca Ferrara [259]
Piazza Trilussa 41
00153 Rome
T   +39 06 58 33 3920
W   www.enotecaferrara.it

Fabio Salini [267]
Via di Monserrato 18
00186 Rome
T   +39 06 68 30 11 72
W   www.fabiosalini.it

Ferrazza [265]
Via dei Volsci 59
00185 Rome
T   +39 06 49 05 06

Galleria Borghese [272]
Piazzale del Museo Borghese 5
00197 Rome
T   +39 06 32 810
W   www.galleriaborghese.it

Galleria Doria Pamphilj [272]
Piazza del Collegio Romano 2
00186 Rome
T   +39 06 67 97 323
E   arti.rm@doriapamphilj.it
W   www.doriapamphilj.it

Galleria Pino Casagrande [272]
Via degli Ausoni 7a
00185 Rome
T   +39 06 44 63 480

Le Gallinelle [269]
Via del Boschetto 76
00184 Rome
T   +39 06 48 81 01
W   www.legallinelle.it

Giggetto [260]
Via del Portico d'Ottavia 21a–22
00186 Rome

T   +39 06 68 61 105
W   www.giggettoalportico.com

Il Goccetto [264]
Via dei Banchi Vecchi 14
00186 Rome
T   +39 06 68 64 268

Hosteria del Pesce [260]
Via di Monserrato 32
00186 Rome
T   +39 06 68 65 617

Hotel Art [254]
Via Margutta 56
00187 Rome
T   +39 06 32 87 11
E   info@hotelart.it
W   www.hotelart.it

Joia Music Restaurant [264]
Via Galvani 20
00100 Rome
T   +39 06 57 40 802
E   info@joiacafe.it
W   www.joiacafe.it

The Keats–Shelley House [271]
Piazza di Spagna 26
00187 Rome
T   +39 06 67 84 235
E   info@keats-shelley-house.org
W   www.keats-shelley-house.org

Ketumbar [264]
Via Galvani 24
00153 Rome
T   +39 06 57 30 5338
W   www.ketumbar.it

Laura Urbinati [267]
Via dei Banchi Vecchi 50a
00186 Rome
T   +39 06 68 13 6478
W   www.lauraurbinati.com

Lavori Artigianali Femminili [267]
Via Capo le Case 6
00187 Rome
T   +39 06 67 92 992

Letico [264]
Via Galvani 64
00153 Rome
T   +39 06 57 25 0539

La Libreria del Viaggiatore [267]
Via del Pellegrino 78
00186 Rome
T   +39 06 68 80 1048

Macro [270]
Via Reggio Emilia 54
00198 Rome
T   +39 06 67 10 70400
E   macro@comune.roma.it
W   www.macro.roma.museum

Magazzini Associati [267]
Corso del Rinascimento 7
00186 Rome
T   +39 06 68 13 5179

Museo de Chirico [271]
Piazza di Spagna 31
00187 Rome
T   +39 06 67 96 546
E   fondazionedechirico@tiscali.it
W   www.fondazionedechirico.it

Orto Botanico [271]
Largo Cristina di Svezia 24
00165 Rome
T   +39 06 68 32 300

Osteria della Frezza [261]
Via della Frezza 16
00100 Rome
T +39 06 32 26 273
W www.gusto.it

**Palazzetto at the International
Wine Academy** [253]
Vicolo del Bottino 8
00187 Rome
T +39 06 69 90 878
E info@wineacademyroma.com
W www.wineacademyroma.com

Palazzo Altemps [272]
Piazza Sant'Apollinare 44
00186 Rome
T +39 06 68 97 091

Pantheon [272]
Piazza della Rotonda
00186 Rome
T +39 06 68 30 0230

Relais Banchi Vecchi [255]
Via dei Banchi Vecchi 115
00187 Rome
T +39 06 32 11 783
W www.banchivecchi115.com

Riccioli Café [263]
Via delle Coppelle 13
00186 Rome
T +39 06 68 21 0313
W www.ricciolicafe.com

Ripa Hotel [257]
Via degli Orti di Trastevere 3
00153 Rome
T +39 06 58 611
E info@ripahotel.com
W www.ripahotel.com

Roscioli [259]
Via dei Giubbonari 21–22a
00186 Rome
T +39 06 68 75 287

La Rosetta [259]
Via della Rosetta 8
00186 Rome
T +39 06 68 61 002
E info@larosetta.com
W www.larosetta.com

San Luigi dei Francesi [270]
Piazza di San Luigi dei Francesi 5
00186 Rome

Sant'Ivo alla Sapienza [272]
Corso del Rinascimento 40
00186 Rome

Santa Sabina [272]
Piazza Pietro d'Illiria
00153 Rome
T +39 06 57 43 573

Santo Stefano Rotondo [272]
Via di Santo Stefano Rotondo 7
00184 Rome
T +39 06 48 19 333

Scala Quattordici [267]
Via della Scala 13
00153 Rome
T +39 06 58 83 580

Sisters [268]
Via dei Banchi Vecchi 143
00186 Rome
T +39 06 68 78 497
E info@sistersinart.it
W www.sistersinart.it

Sora Lella [259]
Via di Ponte Quattro Capi 16
00186 Rome
T +39 06 68 61 601
E soralella@soralella.com
W www.soralella.com

TAD [268]
Via del Babuino 155a
00187 Rome
T +39 06 32 69 5122
E roma@taditaly.com
W www.taditaly.com

Tram Tram [259]
Via dei Reti 44–46
00185 Rome
T +39 06 49 04 16

Trattoria [260]
Via del Pozzo delle Cornacchie 25
00186 Rome
T +39 06 68 30 1427
E info@ristorantetrattoria.it
W www.ristorantetrattoria.it

Uno e Bino [260]
Via degli Equi 58
00185 Rome
T +39 06 44 60 702

Villa Farnesina [271]
Via della Lungara 230
00165 Rome
T +39 06 68 02 7267
E farnesina@lincei.it
W www.lincei.it

La Vineria Reggio [263]
Piazza Campo de' Fiori 15
00186 Rome
T +39 06 68 80 3268

Volpetti [268]
Via Marmorata 47
00153 Rome
T +39 06 57 42 352
Via Alessandro Volta 8
00153 Rome
T +39 06 57 44 305
E info@volpetti.com
W www.volpetti.com

ROTTERDAM

De Beurs [283]
Kruiskade 55
3012 EE Rotterdam
T +31 10 240 90 94

Blits [280]
Boompjes 701
3011 XZ Rotterdam
T +31 10 282 90 51
E info@blits-rotterdam.nl
W www.blits-rotterdam.nl

Catwalk [283]
Weena Zuid 33
3012 NH Rotterdam

Centrum Beeldende Kunst [288]
Witte de Withstraat 50
3012 BR Rotterdam
T +31 10 413 54 98
E tent@cbk.rotterdam.nl
W www.tentplaza.nl

Club Rotterdam [283]
Wilhelminakade 699
3072 AP Rotterdam
T +31 10 290 84 42
E info@club-rotterdam.com
W www.club-rotterdam.com

Dudok [283]
Meent 88
3011 EH Rotterdam
T +31 10 433 31 02
E rotterdam@dudok.nl
W www.dudok.nl

Euromast [287]
Parkhaven 20
3016 GM Rotterdam
T +31 10 436 48 11
E info@euromast.nl
W www.euromast.nl

Hotel Bazar [281]
Witte de Withstraat 16
3012 BP Rotterdam
T +31 10 206 51 51
E guests@hotelbazar.nl
W www.bazarrotterdam.nl

Hotel New York [278]
Koninginnenhoofd 1
3072 AD Rotterdam
T +31 10 439 05 00
E info@hotelnewyork.nl
W www.hotelnewyork.nl

De Kijk-Kubus [287]
Overblaak 70
3011 MH Rotterdam
T +31 10 414 22 85
E kijkkubus@planet.nl
W www.kubuswoning.nl

De Kunsthal [288]
Museumpark, Westzeedijk 341
3015 AA Rotterdam
T +31 10 440 03 00
E communicatie@kunsthal.nl
W www.kunsthal.nl

Marlies Dekkers [285]
Witte de Withstraat 2
3012 BP Rotterdam
T +31 10 280 9184
W www.marliesdekkers.nl

**Museum Boijmans van
Beuningen** [287]
Museumpark 18–20
3015 CX Rotterdam
T +31 10 441 94 00
W www.boijmans.rotterdam.nl

**Nederlands
Architectuurinstituut** [288]
Museumpark 25
3015 CB Rotterdam
T +31 10 440 12 00
E info@nai.nl
W www.nai.nl

Nederlands Fotomuseum [288]
Wilhelminakade 332
3001 KJ Rotterdam
T +31 10 203 04 05
E info@nederlandsfotomuseum.nl
W www.nederlandsfotomuseum.nl

NieuweOntwerpers [284]
William Boothlaan 13a
3012 VH Rotterdam
T +31 10 212 41 50
E info@nieuwontwerpers.nl
W www.nieuwontwerpers.nl

Nighttown [283]
West-Kruiskade 26–28
3014 AS Rotterdam
T +31 10 436 12 10
E info@nighttown.nl
W www.nighttown.nl

Off_Corso [283]
Kruiskade 22
3012 EH Rotterdam
T +31 10 280 73 59
E off-corso@off-corso.nl
W www.off-corso.nl

Proef [281]
Mariniersweg 259
3011 NM Rotterdam
T +31 10 280 72 97
E info@proefrotterdam.nl
W www.proefrotterdam.nl

Restaurant de Engel [280]
Eendrachtsweg 19
3012 LB Rotterdam
T +31 10 414 62 83
E info@engelgroep.com
W www.engel.nl

Stroom Rotterdam [279]
Lloydstraat 1
3024 EA Rotterdam
T +31 10 221 40 60
E info@stroomrotterdam.nl
W www.stroomrotterdam.nl

Thalia Lounge [283]
Kruiskade 31
3012 EE Rotterdam
T +31 10 214 25 47
E info@thaliarotterdam.nl
W www.thaliarotterdam.nl

Van Dijk [285]
Van Oldenbarneveltstraat 105
3012 GS Rotterdam
T +31 10 411 26 44

Van Oosterom [284]
Van Vollenhovenstraat 15
3016 BE Rotterdam
T +31 10 241 00 24
E info@voosterom.nl
W www.voosterom.nl

Wijn of Water [283]
Loods Celebes 101
3024 WH Rotterdam
T +31 10 477 84 54
E info@wijnofwater.nl
W www.wijnofwater.nl

**Witte de With Center for
Contemporary Art** [288]
Witte de Withstraat 50
3012 BR Rotterdam
T +31 10 411 01 44
E info@wdw.nl
W www.wdw.nl

Zer010 [285]
Oude Binnenweg 122
3012 JG Rotterdam
T +31 10 270 97 95
E info@zer010.nl
W www.zer010.nl

Zin [283]
Lijnbaan 40–42
3012 EP Rotterdam
T +31 10 281 09 10
W www.zinrotterdam.nl

VIENNA

3mpc [309]
Pressgasse 25
A-1040 Vienna
T +43 1 586 48 72
E contact3mpc@hotmail.com
W www.3mpc.net

Altstadt Vienna [296]
Kirchengasse 41
A-1070 Vienna
T +43 1 522 66 66
E hotel@altstadt.at
W www.altstadt.at

Architekturzentrum Wien [309]
Museumsplatz 1
A-1070 Vienna
T +43 1 522 31 15
E office@azw.at
W www.azw.at

Bio-Kosmetika & Wein [305]
Stiftgasse 19/1
A-1070 Vienna
T +43 1 890 26 49
E info@bio-kosmetika.com
W www.bio-kosmetika.com

Café Amacord [299]
Rechte Wienzeile 15
A-1040 Vienna
T +43 1 587 47 09
E café.amacord@aon.at

Café Central [302]
Herrengasse 14
A-1010 Vienna
T +43 1 533 37 64 24
E cafe.central@palaisevents.at
W www.ferstel.at

Café Konditorei Gerstner [303]
Kärntner Straße 13–15
A-1010 Vienna
T +43 1 512 49 63
E konditorei@gerstner.at
W www.gerstner.at

Café Korb [302]
Brandstätte 9
A-1010 Vienna
T +43 1 533 72 15

Café Sperl [302]
Gumpendorferstraße 11
A-1060 Vienna
T +43 1 586 41 58
E melange@cafesperl.at
W www.cafesperl.at

Çombinat [306]
Museumsplatz 1
A-1070 Vienna
T +43 699 1200 8920
E info@combinat.at
W www.combinat.at

Dogan & Acer [309]
Naschmarkt 358
A-1040 Vienna
T +43 1 586 47 15

Europa [303]
Zollergasse 8
A-1070 Vienna
T +43 1 526 33 83
W www.hinterzimmer.at

Gatto Möbel [306]
Kettenbrückengasse 14
Vienna
T +43 699 1150 5665
E ga.tto@gmx.at
W www.gatto-moebel.at

Glacis Beisl [301]
Breitegasse 4
A-1070 Vienna
T +43 1 526 56 60
E mail@glacisbeisl.at
W www.glacisbeisl.at

Gradwohl [309]
Naschmarkt 239
A-1040 Vienna
T +43 1 586 01 56
E office@gradwohl.info
W www.biovollwert-gradwohl.at

Grüne Erde [305]
Mariahilfer Straße 11
A-1060 Vienna
T +43 1 403 48 10
E office@grueneerde.at
W www.grueneerde.at

Hansen [299]
Wipplinger Straße 34
A-1010 Vienna
T +43 1 532 05 42
E restaurant@hansen.co.at
W www.hansen.co.at

Hollmann Beletage [294]
Köllnerhofgasse 6
A-1010 Vienna
T +43 1 961 19 60
E hotel@hollmann-beletage.at
W www.hollmann-beletage.at

Hotel Rathaus Wine & Design [295]
Lange Gasse 13
A-1080 Vienna
T +43 1 400 11 22
E office@hotel-rathaus-wien.at
W www.hotel-rathaus-wien.at

Huth Gastwirtschaft [300]
Schellinggasse 5
A-1010 Vienna
T +43 1 513 56 44
E info@zum-huth.at
W www.zum-huth.at

Immervoll [299]
Weihburggasse 17
A-1010 Vienna
T +43 1 513 52 88

J. & L. Lobmeyr [305]
Kärntner Straße 26
A-1010 Vienna
T +43 1 512 05 08
E office@lobmeyr.at
W www.lobmeyr.at

Julius Meinl am Graben [300]
Am Graben 19
A-1010 Vienna
T +43 1 532 33 34 6000
E restaurant@meinlamgraben.at
W www.meinlamgraben.at

Kaffee Rösterei Alt Wien [305]
Schleifmühlgasse 23
A-1040 Vienna
T +43 1 505 08 00
E office@altwien.at
W www.altwien.at

Kantine [299]
Museumsplatz 1
A-1070 Vienna
T +43 1 523 82 39

Loos American Bar [303]
Kärntner Durchgang 10
A-1010 Vienna
T +43 1 512 32 83
E office@loosbar.at
W www.loosbar.at

Lutz Die Bar [303]
Mariahilfer Straße 3
A-1060 Vienna
T +43 1 585 36 46

E bar@lutz-bar.at
W www.lutz-bar.at

Das Möbel Café [303]
Burggasse 10
A-1070 Vienna
T +43 1 524 94 97
E an@dasmoebel.at
W www.dasmoebel.at

Mühlbauer [307]
Seilergasse 5
A-1010 Vienna
T +43 1 513 70 70
E office@muehlbauer.at
W www.muehlbauer.at

Museum of Applied Arts [309]
Stubenring 5
A-1010 Vienna
T +43 1 711 36 0
E office@mak.at
W www.mak.at

Naschmarkt [309]
Linke Wienzeile & Rechte Wienzeile
A-1040 Vienna

Naturkost St Josef [300]
Zollergasse 26
A-1070 Vienna
T +43 1 526 68 18
E st.josef.natur@aon.at

Österreicher im MAK [299]
Stubenring 5
A-1010 Vienna
T +43 1 714 01 21
E reservierung@
oesterreicherimmak.at
W www.mak.at

**Österreichisches
Theatermuseum** [309]
Lobkowitzplatz 2
A-1010 Vienna
T +43 1 525 24 610
E info@theatermuseum.at
W www.theatermuseum.at

Palmenhaus [301]
Burggarten
A-1010 Vienna
T +43 1 533 10 33
E office@palmenhaus.at
W www.palmenhaus.at

La Petite Boutique [305]
Lindengasse 25
Vienna
T +43 1 923 94 23
E office@sandragilles.com
W www.sandragilles.com

Pregenzer Fashion Store [305]
Schleifmühlgasse 4
A-1040 Vienna
T +43 1 586 57 58
E office@pregenzer.com
W www.pregenzer.com

R. Horn's Wien [306]
Bräunerstraße 7
A-1010 Vienna
T +43 1 513 82 94
E rhorns@rhorns.com
W www.rhorns.com

Renate Asenbaum [307]
Tuchlauben 12
A-1010 Vienna
T +43 1 532 89 29

Schella Kann [307]
Singerstraße 14
A-1010 Vienna
T +43 1 513 22 87
E office@schellakann.at
W www.schellakann.com

Secession [309]
Friedrichstraße 12
A-1010 Vienna
T +43 1 587 53 07
E office@secession.at
W www.secession.at

Sektcomptoir Szigeti [303]
Schleifmühlgasse 19
A-1040 Vienna
T +43 664 432 5388
E office@sektcomptoir.at
W www.sektcomptoir.at

Sigmund Freud Museum [309]
Berggasse 19
A-1090 Vienna
T +43 1 319 15 96
E office@freud-museum.at
W www.freud-museum.at

Stefan Pagacs Weinhandel [305]
Stallburggasse 2/37
A-1010 Vienna
T +43 1 967 01 98
E weinhandel-pagacs@chello.at

Steirereck im Stadtpark [301]
Am Heumarkt 2a
A-1030 Vienna
T +43 1 713 31 68
E wien@steirereck.at
W http://steirereck.at

Das Studio [305]
Kirchengasse 17
A-1070 Vienna
T +43 676 453 2266
E olymp@das-studio.at
W www.das-studio.at

Theater an der Wien [309]
Linke Wienzeile 6
A-1060 Vienna
T +43 1 588 30 660
E oper@theater-wien.at
W www.theater-wien.at

Das Triest [297]
Wiedner Hauptstraße 12
A-1040 Vienna
T +43 1 589 18 0
E office@dastriest.at
W www.dastriest.at

**Wagner:Werk
Museum Postsparkasse** [309]
Georg Coch-Platz 2
A-1018 Vienna
T +43 1 534 53 33 088
E museum@ottowagner.com
W www.ottowagner.com

Werkprunk [305]
Kirchengasse 7/11
A-1070 Vienna
T +43 1 990 64 32
E art@werkprunk.com
W www.werkprunk.com

Zum Schwarzen Kameel [299]
Bognergasse 5
A-1010 Vienna
T +43 1 533 81 25
E info@kameel.at
W www.kameel.at

best of

SLEEP

Classic Hotels
Canal House Hotel, Amsterdam
Casa Howard, Rome
Charles Rogier XI, Antwerp
Eleven Cadogan Gardens, London
L'Hôtel, Paris
Hotel Adlon Kempinski, Berlin
Hotel Grande Bretagne, Athens
Seven One Seven, Amsterdam
De Witte Lelie, Antwerp
York House, Lisbon

Stylish Hotels
A'jia, Istanbul
Aleph Hotel, Rome
Astir Palace Resort, Athens
Bairro Alto Hotel, Lisbon
Chambres en Ville, Brussels
The College Hotel, Amsterdam
Dorint am Gendarmenmarkt, Berlin
The Dylan, Amsterdam

Gran Hotel la Florida, Barcelona
Hôtel Bourg Tibourg, Paris
Hotel Neri, Barcelona
Hôtel Thérèse, Paris
Knightsbridge Hotel, London
Les Ottomans, Istanbul
Palazzetto at the International Wine Academy, Rome
Royal Windsor Hotel Grand Place, Brussels
Solar do Castelo, Lisbon

'Design' and Modern Hotels
The Clarence, Dublin
Hollmann Beletage, Vienna
Hotel Art, Rome
Hotel Banys Orientals, Barcelona
Hotel Brandenburger Hof, Berlin
L'Hôtel de Sers, Paris
Hotel Omm, Barcelona
Life Gallery Athens, Athens
The Lute Suites, Amsterdam
Monty, Brussels
Murano Urban Resort, Paris
Q!, Berlin
Ripa Hotel, Rome
Semiramis Hotel, Athens
Slapen Enzo, Antwerp
The Sofa Hotel, Istanbul
Solar dos Mouros, Lisbon
Stroom Rotterdam, Rotterdam
Das Triest, Vienna
The Zetter, London

Funky Hotels
Casa Camper, Barcelona
Grafton House, Dublin
Hotel New York, Rotterdam
Hotel Rathaus Wine & Design, Vienna
The Rookery, London
Winston, Amsterdam

Home away from Home
Altstadt Vienna, Vienna
Azzedine Alaïa Hotel, Paris
Hazlitt's, London
Hotel Daphnis, Istanbul
The Main House, London
Number 31, Dublin
Pembroke Townhouse, Dublin
Relais Banchi Vecchi, Rome

EAT

Classy, Classic Restaurants
Alcântara Café, Lisbon
L'Ambroisie, Paris
L'Altro di Mastai, Rome
L'Arpège, Paris
Les Ambassadeurs, Paris
Boğaziçi Borsa Restaurant, Istanbul
Chapter One, Dublin
Comme Chez Soi, Brussels
Dôme, Antwerp
L'Ecrivain, Dublin
The Guinea, London
Ideal, Athens
Julius Meinl am Graben, Vienna
Locks, Dublin
Lutter & Wegner, Berlin
Le Pré Catalan, Paris
Restaurant Bernardin, Antwerp
Restaurant de Engel, Rotterdam
Restaurant Patrick Guilbauds, Dublin
Spondi, Athens
Steirereck im Stadtpark, Vienna
La Table du Joël Robuchon, Paris
Terreiro do Paço, Lisbon
Tom Aikens, London
Tuus, Istanbul
Ulus 29, Istanbul
Zum Schwarzen Kameel, Vienna

Seafood Restaurants
Aqua, Dublin
Balıkçı Sabahattin, Istanbul
Botafumeíro, Barcelona
Cavistons Food Emporium, Dublin
Fish Shop on St John Street, London
Hosteria del Pesce, Rome
Ithaki, Athens
J. Sheekey, London
Jimmy & the Fish, Athens
Kıyı, Istanbul
La Rosetta, Rome
Varoulko, Athens

Progressive Cuisine
Arancia Blu, Rome
Aristera Dexia, Athens
L'Astrance, Paris
Cinnamon Club, London
Comerç 24, Barcelona
Eden, Dublin
FoodBall, Barcelona
Loft, Istanbul
Papadakis Restaurant, Athens
Pierre Gagnaire, Paris
Pygma-Lion, Amsterdam
El Racó d'en Freixa, Barcelona
Spoon, Food & Wine, Paris
Ze Kitchen Galerie, Paris

Local Flavour
Agata e Romeo, Rome
Baba, Rome
Café Amacord, Vienna
Casa do Alentejo, Lisbon
Casa Leopoldo, Barcelona
Chez Jean, Paris
The Eagle, London
Engelbecken, Berlin
La Famille, Paris
Gefsis Me Onomasia Proelefsis, Athens
Giggetto, Rome
Glacis Beisl, Vienna
The Havelock Tavern, London
Hünkar, Istanbul

Krisa Gi, Athens
Pandeli, Istanbul
Pap' Açorda, Lisbon
Quimet i Quimet,
  Barcelona
Romesco, Barcelona
Roscioli, Rome
St John, London
Storch, Berlin
Ta Kioupia, Athens
Tavares, Lisbon
To Ouzadiko, Athens
Trocadero Restaurant,
  Dublin
Uno e Bino, Rome
Le Villaret, Paris
El Xampanyet, Barcelona
Yakup 2, Istanbul

Modern Restaurants
48 The Restaurant, Athens
Altmann, Amsterdam
Blits, Rotterdam
Cospaia, Brussels
Fernández, Barcelona
Huth Gastwirtschaft,
  Vienna
Restaurante Eleven,
  Lisbon
Trattoria, Rome

Chocolate, Cakes and Pastries
Burie, Antwerp
Cacao Sampaka,
  Barcelona
Café Konditorei Gerstner,
  Vienna
Chocolaterie Estrellas,
  Berlin
Escribà, Barcelona
Granja Dulcinea,
  Barcelona
Les Papilles, Paris
Patisserie Markiz, Istanbul
Pierre Hermé, Paris
Pierre Marcolini, Brussels
Pompadour, Amsterdam
Puccini Bomboni,
  Amsterdam
Queen of Tarts, Dublin

Sadaharu Aoki, Paris
De Taart van m'n Tante,
  Amsterdam

DRINK

Traditional Cafés and Brasseries
Den Artist Brasserie,
  Antwerp
Café A Brasileira, Lisbon
Café Adler, Berlin
Café Avyssinia, Athens
Café Central, Vienna
Café de Jaren, Amsterdam
Café Einstein, Berlin
Café Korb, Vienna
Le Café Marly, Paris
Café Martinho da Arcada,
  Lisbon
Café Nicola, Lisbon
Café Sperl, Vienna
Il Caffè di Sant'Eustachio,
  Rome
La Palette, Paris
Palmenhaus, Vienna
Paris Bar, Berlin
Pasteleria Versailles,
  Lisbon
Els Quatre Gats, Barcelona
Sale e Tabacchi, Berlin
Restaurant Vincent,
  Brussels
The Wolseley, London

Traditional Bars and Pubs
A Ginjinha, Lisbon
À la Bécasse, Brussels
Anglesea Arms, London
Bar Tabac, Antwerp
Casa Almirall, Barcelona
Cervejaria Trindade,
  Lisbon
Le Cirio, Brussels
Felsenkeller, Berlin
Finnegans, Dublin
The French House, London
In 't Aepjen, Amsterdam
Kehoe's, Dublin
The Long Hall, Dublin

Loos American Bar,
  Vienna
Orient Bar, Istanbul
Pavilhão Chines, Lisbon
Toone, Brussels
De Vagant, Antwerp
Vefa Bozacısı, Istanbul
Windsor Castle, London
Wynand Fockink,
  Amsterdam
Ye Olde Mitre Tavern,
  London

Modern and Design Bars and Cafés
Bar Taruga, Rome
Blue Bar, London
Dudok, Rotterdam
Murano Urban Resort Bar,
  Paris
Newton Bar, Berlin
Walem, Amsterdam

Wine Bars and Shops
Le Baratin, Paris
Casa Bleve, Rome
Cata 1.81, Barcelona
Caves Miard, Paris
Les Caves Pétrissans,
  Paris
Cul de Sac, Rome
Ely Wine Bar, Dublin
L'Enoteca Antica, Rome
Enoteca Ferrara, Rome
Ferrazza, Rome
Fish/La Boissonnerie,
  Paris
Juvenile's, Paris
Peploe's, Dublin
Sektcomptoir Szigeti,
  Vienna
Solar do Vinho do Porto,
  Lisbon
Stefan Pagacs Weinhandel,
  Vienna
Le Verre Volé, Paris
Vila Viniteca, Barcelona
La Vineria Reggio, Rome
La Vinya del Senyor,
  Barcelona

SHOP

Boutiques
Alves/Gonçalves, Lisbon
Bad Habits, Barcelona
Baullà, Rome
Berlinomat, Berlin
Browns + Browns Focus,
  London
Çombinat, Vienna
Comité, Barcelona
Costume, Dublin
Derishow, Istanbul
Dolls, Dublin
Egg, London
Hipòtesi, Barcelona
Koh Samui, London
Little Red Riding Hood,
  Berlin
Louis, Antwerp
NieuweOntwerpers,
  Rotterdam
Nix, Berlin
Oki-Ni, London
Sisters, Rome
Smock, Dublin
Tulle, Dublin
Van Dijk, Rotterdam
Van Ravenstein,
  Amsterdam
Verso, Antwerp

Fashion Designers, Labels, Haute Couture
Ana Salazar, Lisbon
Ann Demeulemeester,
  Antwerp
Antonio Miró, Barcelona
A-poc [Issey Miyake], Paris
Claudia Skoda, Berlin
Eley Kishimoto, London
Fátima Lopes, Lisbon
Le Gallinelle, Rome
Lucien Pellat-Finet, Paris
Mart Visser Haute
  Couture, Amsterdam
Matthew Williamson,
  London
Het Modepaleis (Dries van
  Noten), Antwerp
Olivier Strelli, Brussels

Schella Kann, Vienna
Ümit Ünal, Istanbul
Vanessa Bruno, Paris
Walter, Antwerp

Design and Housewares
A La Turca, Istanbul
Alma Lusa, Lisbon
Autoban, Istanbul
Cath Kidston, London
C.U.C.I.N.A., Rome
Cutipol, Lisbon
Design Flanders, Brussels
Droog @ Home,
    Amsterdam
Emery & Cie, Brussels
Fábrica Sant'Anna, Lisbon
Gotham, Barcelona
Her House, London
Die Imaginäre Manufaktur,
    Berlin
J. & L. Lobmeyr, Vienna
Magazzini Associati, Rome
Paşabahçe, Istanbul
Pol's Potten, Amsterdam
Vivian Hann, Amsterdam

Jewelry
Diego Percossi Papi, Rome
Fabio Salini, Rome
Fanourakis, Athens
Galalith, Antwerp
Ilias Lalaounis Jewelry
    Museum, Athens
Nininha Guímarães dos
    Santos, Lisbon
Renate Asenbaum, Vienna
Solange Azagury-
    Partridge, London
Werkprunk, Vienna
Zeynep Erol, Istanbul

Bookshops
La Central, Barcelona
Daunt Books, London
Eleftheroudakis, Athens
JOOT, Amsterdam
Librairie Gourmande,
    Paris
La Libreria del Viaggiatore,

Rome
The Winding Stair, Dublin

Leathergoods
Delvaux, Brussels
Hester van Eeghen,
    Amsterdam
Huis A Boon, Antwerp
Jamin Puech, Paris
Luvaria Ulisses, Lisbon
Mine Kerse, Istanbul
R. Horn's Wien, Vienna

Shoes
Adidas Originals Berlin,
    Berlin
Christian Louboutin, Paris
Kalogirou, Athens
Manolo Blahník, London
Old Athens, Athens
Paul Warmer, Amsterdam
Trippen, Berlin

Perfume, Cosmetics, Health
Abdulla + Hamam,
    Istanbul
Breathe, Berlin
Editions de Parfums
    Frédéric Malle, Paris
Grüne Erde, Vienna
Herboristeria del Rei,
    Barcelona
Iunx, Paris
Mastiha Shop, Athens
Miller Harris, London
Neal's Yard Remedies,
    London
Noesa, Berlin

Food
Confeitaria Nacional,
    Lisbon
Conserveira de Lisboa,
    Lisbon
E&A Gispert, Barcelona
Fallon & Byrne, Dublin
Kaffee Rösterei Alt Wien,
    Vienna
Neal's Yard Dairy, London
Orígens 99.9%, Barcelona

Volpetti, Rome

Menswear
Charvet, Paris
Dunhill, London
Turnbull & Asser, London

Milliners
Cristophe Coppens,
    Brussels
Fiona Bennett, Berlin
Hut Up, Berlin
Mühlbauer, Vienna
Planet Earth, Athens

'Concept' Stores
Colette, Paris
Lobby, Barcelona
Mousse, Lisbon
TAD, Rome
Zer010, Rotterdam

Series concept and editor: Lucas Dietrich
Jacket and book design: Grade Design Consultants
Original design and map concept: The Senate
Maps: Peter Bull

Research and texts by [Amsterdam] Siân Tichař
[Antwerp] Simon Richmond [Athens] Julia Klimi,
Ioanna Kopsiafti [Barcelona] Cristina Redondo,
Phyllis Richardson [Berlin] Nils Peters, Siân Tichař
[Brussels] Simon Richmond [Dublin] Lizzie Gore-
Grimes [Istanbul] Damla Kürklü, Zeynep Yener
[Lisbon] Simon Richmond [London] Phyllis
Richardson [Paris] Sébastien Demorand, Phyllis
Richardson [Rome] Sara Manuelli [Rotterdam] Siân
Tichař [Vienna] Tamara Thiessen

Specially commissioned photography by
[Amsterdam] Will Falize, Anthony Webb [Antwerp]
Anne and Philippe Croquet-Zouridakis [Athens]
Julia Klimi [Barcelona] Natalia Cedrés, Lucas
Fernández, Ingrid Rasmussen, Anthony Webb
[Berlin] Robert Lyons [Brussels] Anne and Philippe
Croquet-Zouridakis [Dublin] Peter Matthews
[Istanbul] Bahadir Tanriöver [Lisbon] Lydia Evans
[London] Ingrid Rasmussen, Anthony Webb,
Francesca Yorke [Paris] Angela Moore, Ingrid
Rasmussen, Anthony Webb [Rome] Angela Moore
[Rotterdam] Will Falize [Vienna] Tamara Thiessen

First published in 2007 in paperback in the United
States of America by Thames & Hudson Inc.,
500 Fifth Avenue, New York, New York 10110

thamesandhudsonusa.com

Library of Congress Catalog Card Number
2007900797

ISBN 978-0-500-21020-8

Printed in China by C & C Offset Printing Co Ltd